The Political Philosophy of the European City

Political Theory for Today

Series Editor: Richard Avramenko, University of Wisconsin, Madison

Political Theory for Today seeks to bring the history of political thought out of the jargon-filled world of the academy into the everyday world of social and political life. The series brings the wisdom of texts and the tradition of political philosophy to bear on salient issues of our time, especially issues pertaining to human freedom and responsibility, the relationship between individuals and the state, the moral implications of public policy, health and human flourishing, public and private virtues, and more. Great thinkers of the past have thought deeply about the human condition and their situations—books in *Political Theory for Today* build on that insight.

Titles Published
The Political Philosophy of the European City: From Polis, through City-State, to Megalopolis by Ferenc Hörcher
John Locke and the Uncivilized Society: Resistance and Individualism in America Today, by Scott Robinson
Welcoming the Other: Student, Stranger, and Divine edited by N. Susan Laehn and Thomas R. Laehn
Cosmopolitanism and its Discontents: Rethinking Politics in the Age of Brexit and Trump, edited by Lee Ward
Eric Voegelin's Asian Political Thought edited by Lee Trepanier
The Spartan Drama of Plato's Laws by Eli Friedland
Idolizing the Idea: A Critical History of Modern Philosophy by Wayne Cristaudo
Eric Voegelin Today: Voegelin's Political Thought in the 21st Century, edited by Scott Robinson, Lee Trepanier, David Whitney
Walk Away: When the Political Left Turns Right, edited by Lee Trepanier and Grant Havers
Plato's Mythoi: The Political Soul's Drama Beyond by Donald H. Roy
Democracy and Its Enemies: The American Struggle for the Enlightenment, by Paul N. Goldstene
Tradition v. Rationalism: Voegelin, Oakeshott, Hayek, and Others, edited by Gene Callahan and Lee Trepanier
Aristocratic Souls in Democratic Times edited by Richard Avramenko and Ethan Alexander-Davey

The Political Philosophy of the European City

From Polis, through City-State, to Megalopolis?

Ferenc Hörcher

LEXINGTON BOOKS
Lanham • Boulder • New York • London

Published by Lexington Books
An imprint of The Rowman & Littlefield Publishing Group, Inc.
4501 Forbes Boulevard, Suite 200, Lanham, Maryland 20706
www.rowman.com

6 Tinworth Street, London SE11 5AL, United Kingdom

Copyright © 2021 Ferenc Hörcher

All rights reserved. No part of this book may be reproduced in any form or by any electronic or mechanical means, including information storage and retrieval systems, without written permission from the publisher, except by a reviewer who may quote passages in a review.

British Library Cataloguing in Publication Information Available

Library of Congress Cataloging-in-Publication Data

Names: Horkay Hörcher, Ferenc, author.
Title: The political philosophy of the European city: from polis, through city-state, to megalopolis? / Ferenc Hörcher.
Description: Lanham, Maryland: Lexington Books, 2021. |
  Series: Political theory for today | Includes bibliographical references and index. |
  Summary: "The Political Philosophy of the European City offers a wide-ranging panorama of urban political culture in Europe. Its historical scope ranges from the ancient polis through Italian city-states to the ideal of 'small is beautiful' in the 20th century. As a political theory, it offers an analysis of conservative, urban republicanism" —Provided by publisher.
Identifiers: LCCN 2021014941 (print) | LCCN 2021014942 (ebook) |
  ISBN 9781793610829 (cloth) | ISBN 9781793610836 (epub) |
  ISBN 9781793610843 (pbk)
Subjects: LCSH: City-states—Europe—History. | Cities and towns—Europe—History. | Municipal government—Europe—History. | Political science—Europe—History. | Political culture—Europe—History.
Classification: LCC JC352 .H67 2021 (print) | LCC JC352 (ebook) | DDC 940—dc23

Contents

Preface and Acknowledgments — vii

Introduction: The Intellectual History of the City — 1

1 From the "Reason of the City" to the "Practical Wisdom of the City" — 13

2 The City of the Italian Renaissance and the German City — 71

3 The City of Ancient Greece and Christian Europe — 125

4 From the Megalopolis to the City of Human Scale — 177

Conclusion: The City as a Work of Art — 229

Bibliography — 257

Name Index — 273

Subject Index — 279

About the Author — 289

Preface and Acknowledgments

I started to work on this book within the institutional framework of the Institute of Philosophy of the Hungarian Academy of Sciences years ago, and finished it at the Research Institute of Politics and Government of the University of Public Service in January, 2021. It is a follow up of my earlier book, *A Political Philosophy of Conservatism. Prudence, Moderation and Tradition* (Bloomsbury Academic, 2020). I am grateful to the following colleagues for discussions about the main themes of it: Mario Ascheri, Miklós Bakk, Sándor Bene, Cesare Cuttica, Gabriella Erdélyi, James Hankins, Frank Judo, Imre Körmendy, Jaroslav Miller, Alexander Nehamas, István Németh, Walter Nicgorski, Kálmán Pócza, Adam Potkay, David Reeve, Dániel Schmal, Ádám Smrcz, the late Sir Roger Scruton, Katalin Szende, Bernát Török, Iwona Tylek, Árpád Tóth, Kálmán Tóth, Péter András Varga, Domonkos Wettstein, Jan Waszink and so many others. I am especially grateful to Professor Maurizio Viroli for his support and help. Special thanks are due to Stephen Patrick for revising the English of the text and Andrea Robotka, who took care of the typescript, notes, and bibliography. As always, the greatest debt I owe to my wife, Dr. Ildikó Marosi, justice of the Constitutional Court of Hungary, for all that she gave me during the years. I dedicate this volume to the memory of my grandparents on my father's side, burghers of Buda, the royal seat of Hungary.

January 2021

Introduction
The Intellectual History of the City

To assert that Europe is basically a network of cities is not a brave claim. After all, almost all of Europe's finest achievements—from the university to the printing press, from the guild to the stock exchange and the insurance company—are closely linked to the groups of cooperating, competing, and conflicting citizens inhabiting its thriving urban centers. The urban dweller—the "burgher"—is a creative force precisely because of his inclination to live and work together with others, under the balanced rule of a singular leader, the leadership of an urban elite representing the whole, or the assembly of the citizens in a lot of cases. The citizenry of the European city are ready to take great risks to take good care of the common good(s) of the city. Cities have almost never been truly self-sustaining economic and political units, and the legal forms employed to regulate the coexistence of cities with the state, market, and countryside have taken different forms. In every major epoch of European history, however, cities and citizens have taken responsibility for their own fortunes and negotiated with external powers in order to gain or preserve the liberty to mind their own business among themselves. Similarly, certain typical character traits of cities can be identified which are relevant for a general theory of politics, no matter what scale it is applied on. The basic idea of this book is to collect the wisdom generated in the European city on the political philosophy of the European city.

Two approaches will be taken in this work. While ultimately aiming toward a reconstruction of the conceptual order of the changing phenomenon of the European city, it will at the same time develop a political philosophy informed by a historical way of understanding—even if it has no pretensions to being a work of primary historical research into the urban past. Nevertheless, its methodology is indebted to the history of political thought by Collingwood and the so-called Cambridge school. Behind a historically minded investigation of political thought lies an assumption that the practices and institutions and the physical infrastructure, interpersonal links, and mindsets of this urban citizenry were in a dynamic state of constant change and transformation. It is for this reason that one cannot provide a definitive description of the political mentality of the urban dweller. The theory which will be worked out here, will not therefore, address directly the problem of the metropolis in the modern and late-modern sense, as this ground has been adequately covered among others by Baudelaire, Simmel, and Certeau. Neither is it a late romantic or Marxist criticism of the bourgeois value-system. Nor is it simply the idealization of a political community, as represented in the works of Arendt, Tönnies, or Gierke. On the contrary: it tries to reconstruct the golden ages of the European city, but not for its own historical sake, but rather for its relevance for the here and now. Nor is the aim to plunge into a séance of Rousseauist nostalgia, with the fake historical exclamation "Back to Nature!" There will be no attempt to construct a metanarrative and argue for utopian alternatives as the marvelous Lewis Mumford did. Instead, what will be offered here is simple: a suggestion that the political practice of the European city has accumulated a large dose of practical knowledge about politics, and the task is not to formalize it, in other words to set down the rules one can draw from this knowledge, but rather to make it available for the general reader and through her acquaintance with this tradition to let her become an active contributor of its reformation herself.

This book was originally planned and intended as a dialogue. When I was constructing the plan with my intended co-author, Dr. Iwona Tylek, who teaches the history of political doctrines at Jagiellonian University in Kraków, we agreed that the dialogue form would be particularly appropriate for this venture for several reasons. We thought that when reading about politics, the genre of the dialogue is more exciting than that of the monologue. If realized, it would have made it possible for us to approach the set of problems we were confronted with from two different angles, which promised better results than working from a single perspective. We also believed that the different ways of thinking we represent and embody would be fruitful for our specific subject. Although both of us adored Aristotle, we apparently did so for different reasons. As we realized, while she seems to have approached Aristotle's practical philosophy from a more Stoic point of view, my own approach was closer to a practical-realistic position. Also, she believes in philosophy as a free intercourse and exchange of ideas of the great minds of its history, while I myself believe in the contextual understanding of the great minds, and therefore lean toward a more intensive interpretive work, which includes the interpretation of the actions of these civic theorists as active citizens, and, what is more, understanding their thoughts themselves as perforrmative actions.

As mentioned, this approach is greatly influenced by the chapter on historical logic in *Collingwood's Autobiography*. According to Collingwood, to understand a thinker requires an awareness of the question he was trying to answer with the particular statement we are examining. Collingwood calls this the logic of question and answer. The example he cites is directly relevant for us. He claims that Plato's *Republic* and Hobbes's *Leviathan* cannot be directly compared as their subjects were radically different (i.e., the Greek polis and the early modern "absolutist state"). To construct a meaningful dialogue between them (and others) an interpretation needs to be—as we would put it today—proactive. In light of this demand he gives the following definition of the history of political theory: it "is not the history of different answers to one and the same question, but the history of a problem more or less constantly changing, whose solution was changing with it."[1]

If we accept this historicist approach to the history of urban political thought, how, then, can I claim to be able to build "a" political philosophy of the city? After all, the political thought of and about cities must have changed just as radically as other philosophies, and therefore its different phases (the ancient Greek and Roman, medieval, early modern, and modern forms of it) can hardly be compatible with each other. Also, at a certain point Collingwood claims that when we approach past thinkers, we cannot do it with two separate sets of questions, one philosophical, the other historical. There is, he claims, only one set of questions which can be put: the historical set. Yet this does not make Collingwood some kind of weird antiquarian, who thinks that to approach the problems of the past, we need to do it by reminding ourselves that the past "is dead and gone, and in no sense at all living in the present."[2]

Collingwood himself reminds us that the past can be explained by reading its signs (Collingwood calls them *traces*) which need to be present here and now, otherwise we could have no access to it. As soon as we find traces of the past still existing in the present, the two states, past and present, can be connected to each other. The interpreter of the past (not only the professional historian but also, for example, the author of the present historically oriented enquiry into political thinking) must be one whose "business is to reveal the less obvious features hidden from a careless eye in the present situation."[3] So I will always have in my mind the present situation, but my discussion will be historically tuned. Its success will largely depend on how these two temporal dimensions can be connected, which in turn depends on the author's historical sense—the ability to analyse past events and thoughts in order to address present concerns. If the reader is ready to travel this road, he or she, too, needs to sharpen his or her own sense of the historical.

One further potential source of error in this historical-analytical approach can also be excluded with the help of Collingwood. In a truly Aristotelian fashion, he warns us that human action is only in a very limited sense rule-bound. "There is a kind of action which is not determined according to rule, and where the process is directly from knowledge of the situation to an action appropriate to that situation."[4] This sort of action is crucial in politics, as we know from Aristotle's discussions of *phronesis*, or practical knowledge. A large part of what this book discusses belongs to this realm of human activity. When reconstructing the political thought which is characteristic of the builders, inhabitants, and operators of the European city in different epochs of its history, I will not operate like an urban or legal historian, whose primary source is the written legal material available from a given historical context. My aim is to try to make sense of the rather loosely defined political culture of different historical sorts of urban milieu, and then use that material in a brave but cautious way to address some of the political challenges we are confronting here and now. For this reason, once again, I have to stress that this research into the past will not be pursued according to the historian's strict professional standards. Instead, historical awareness is to a large extent only an acknowledgment that politics is the art of the moment.

In framing a political philosophy of the city I will, therefore, pay special attention to the historical dimension of the ever-changing phenomenon of the city, in order to become sensitive to its context, and thus avoid utopian suggestions, and to keep the discourse grounded. Its aim is not to construct a complex theoretical paradigm on the basis of the historical phenomenon of the city, but to try to offer—often neglected—insights into the deepest meanings of the practical wisdom of an ever-changing political environment. Yet it also aims, through these minute details, to reveal the quintessence of this unparalleled phenomenon, the European city.

"URBS" AND "CIVITAS"

"Civitas and *Urbs*, either of which we translate by the word city, were not synonymous words among the ancients. Civitas was the religious and political association of families and tribes; Urbs was the place of assembly, the dwelling-place, and, above all, the sanctuary of this association."[5] These are the words of the eminent nineteenth-century historian and archaeologist, Numa Denis Fustel de Coulanges, in his monograph on the ancient city published in 1864. The distinction is clear-cut: while the physical environment of the city, the "hardware" in contemporary terms, is the *urbs*, the *civitas* is the human dimension within that physical environment, or in present-day terms, its software. Fustel de Coulanges used the two categories as technical terms. It is instructive to consider two further quotations of his careful use of these expressions. The first one is about Troy, and its inhabitants who survived that the material part perished: "The urbs of the Trojans, the material part of Troy, has perished, but not the Trojan civitas; thanks to Æneas, the sacred fire is not extinguished, and the gods have still a worship."[6] In other words, although the architectural environment of the city might be destroyed, its essence, the spirit of its people can survive, as long as the god(s) of the city is/are still worshipped. The opposite point is made about the cities occupied by Rome: "Their city (urbs) might remain standing, but the state (civitas) had perished."[7] This is imagined in a way which parallels the mind-body dualism of the human being in Cartesian metaphysics. According to Descartes, these two parts of the human being have different natures: while the mind is a thinking, non-extended thing, the body is an extended, non-thinking thing. Descartes claims that due to these differences the one should be seen as conceptually different and separated from the other. This separation, however, makes it difficult to conceptualize their cooperation. In the case of the *urbs–civitas* distinction, the relationship between the two is also rather interesting; as we have seen in the cases mentioned by Fustel de Coulanges, each of them can survive without the other.

Of course, the distinction itself is not Fustel de Coulanges's own invention. It was already known in the seventh century, in the definition of the city provided by Isidore of Seville, who Montalembert called "the last scholar of the ancient world."[8] This is Isidore's definition: "A city (civitas) is a number of men joined by a social bond. It takes its name from the citizens who dwell in it. As an *urbs*, it is only a walled structure, but inhabitants, not building stones, are referred to as a *city*."[9] As one can see, in the classical tradition the human element is all-encompassing and the physical surroundings are of secondary importance. Yet in Isidore's thinking there is no absolute separation between the "cities of stone" and the "cities of people." The separation is much more absolute in the St. Augustine's *City of God*. Even in the earthly city, characterized by a "lust for domination," "Augustine was concerned with the city as community (*civitas*) rather than physical environment (*urbs*)."[10]

If we wish to look further back into the historical past, Aristotle is an obvious reference point. It was he who first tried to distinguish the concept of the community of people in a polis from the place where they live: "a state . . . is a community of families and aggregations of families in well-being, for the sake of a perfect and self-sufficing life. Such a community can only be established among those who live in the same place and intermarry."[11] As can be seen from the quote above, for Aristotle it was a necessary condition of a polis that its people live "in the same place." The relevance of *urbs*, then, is due to the fact that in ordinary circumstances, a continuity of the place is crucial for the survival of a city: "if the Roman *cives* formed the political community of the city (civitas) in the city (urbs), it was the Greek city (polis), as a spatial entity, which formed the body politic of its citizens (polités)."[12]

Given this relevance of the spatial dimension in Aristotle's thinking, the most important notion of a polis was for him, too, the community (*koinonia*).

The lesson to be drawn from this historical etymological overview is that there are two basic components of the city, the community of people who gather in it, and the physical environment which they inhabit. Apparently, of the two, the first has precedence, even if the community of people, as we shall see, is also, to a large extent, dependent on and therefore largely determined by the physical attributes of the both the natural and man-made environment.

THE CITIZEN OF GENEVA AND HIS TWO CONCEPTS OF CITIZENS' LIBERTY

The conceptual distinction between the two concepts of the city was also drawn in a famous French text. Rousseau, in a footnote to *Du Contrat Social* (1762), also complained that: "The real meaning of this word (*Cité*) has been almost wholly lost in modern times; most people mistake a town (*ville*) for a city (*cité*), and a townsman (*bourgeois*) for a citizen (*citoyen*). They do not know that houses make a town, but citizens a city."[13] Rousseau attributed his own specific meaning to the distinction. In fact, he was responding to Delamare's *Traité de la police* (1705–1738). According to Daniel Gordon, Delamare's "pseudo-Aristotelian conception of a state as a collection of towns differed from the traditional French view of the polity as a collection of corporate groups."[14] Yet Delamare's real intention was not to return to the classic notion of the city. Rather, he was concerned with reinterpreting the function of policing the state. It was Delamare's understanding of the state as a collection of non-independent towns, which depended on an administrative oversight, that was heavily criticized by Rousseau, "the citizen of Geneva." He suggested in a republican spirit that a non-independent town is not a city.

It is worth recalling that Rousseau was in the minority within the French Enlightenment. Although the entry for *Cité* written by Diderot for the third volume of the *Encyclopaedia* (1753) tried to preserve as much as possible of the original understanding of the term, he himself had to admit that by his day the word's original significance had changed: "The word *city* formerly referred to a state, a nation with all its dependencies, a specific republic. That meaning no longer applies today except to certain German cities and Swiss cantons."[15] He was certainly aware of the fact that the political meaning of the word refers to a "corporate body or moral being," whose main *raison d'etre* was "reasons of security, internal and external safety, and all the other advantages of life."[16] While Diderot seems to apply and accept the term *civitas* instead of city, or to give its modern equivalent the state, instead of the term *city* when referring to a body politic, Rousseau seems to have remained loyal to his native town of Geneva.

Geneva, the town of Calvin, was a model town of the early modern experiment in reorganizing the relationship between spiritual and the secular power within urban administration. While Calvin did not succeed in fully taking over the civil government of the town, the principles of Reformed theology served as the main ideology of the Republic of Geneva.[17] Citizenship was subordinate to theological premises. Yet by the eighteenth century the town had grown into a financial center of European influence, which was run by that time by a very narrow patrician class, which was in constant conflict with the urban bourgeoisie.

Rousseau, the son of a watchmaker, seems to have indeed been a son of Geneva: his whole life and oeuvre can be explained as an effort to redefine his position toward and within the city's internal political struggle. His efforts might not look too successful in this respect, however. He was forced to leave the city as a young man, and only returned there for a short while as a middle-aged man in 1754. During that short stay, he returned to the Calvinist church of Geneva, without which he could not have regained his citizenship of the city. Yet his efforts to find his way back as a member of the citizen body ended in failure. Even his offer to publish the *Second Discourse* with the Dedication in and by Geneva had to be withdrawn. His lifelong quest to belong to this urban community did inspire a great and original work of philosophy, however.

Politically, Rousseau always occupied a very well-defined position in the internal political conflicts of eighteenth-century Geneva. He supported the struggle of the bourgeoisie against the patrician elite of the country, who were gradually taking over the government of the city. His work in political philosophy served to underpin that position and reinforced it with powerful arguments. The relevance of Rousseau's work for a political philosophy of the European city can be found in the famous *Dedication to the Republic of Geneva*, which served as an introduction to his *Second Discourse*.[18] Before looking at it, however, it is instructive to recall an important point of Rousseau's whole intellectual attitude. While as a rebellious youngster he fled from Geneva, as well as disowning his religion, and converting to Catholicism, it was not long before he realized that he was on the wrong track. His *First Discourse* (1750) was intended as a moral criticism of the luxury and corruption of the cultured Parisian salons and their Enlightened spiritual nihilism, in favor of a more austere moral stance. His famous *Letter to M. D'Alembert on Spectacles* (1758) was another example of such cultural criticism, expressing his moral objections to the introduction of a theater suggested by the *Encyclopedia* entry by D'Alembert. These two famous samples of Rousseau's criticism of the manners of commercial society and of metropolitan high culture show his changing attitude toward both French enlightened circles and the way of life of the patrician elite of his hometown. His *Dedication to the Republic of Geneva* can be interpreted in light of this gradual disillusionment on Rousseau's part, which led to his ambition to return to Geneva, and once again become a member of the body politic of this provincial city.

Rousseau addressed the General Council in the *Dedication*, which was the widest assembly of the citizens of Geneva, instead of the governing body, that was in the hands of a few elite patrician families. This was a sign that Rousseau could only accept as sovereign the whole body politic of the city, subsumed in the institution of the General Council. Yet he took one more step in the text beyond taking this critical stance: he was ready to propose an idealizing, or even blatantly utopian alternative to the traditional operation of the body politic of Geneva. His famous *Second Discourse, Discourse on the Origin of Inequality* (1755) was published in the next year. In the Dedication of this work Rousseau explains his understanding of the workings of the body politic of his native city.[19] When explaining one's relationship to his city, he distinguished between a "love of the citizens" and a love "of its soil," a distinction parallel with the *civitas/urbs* duality. He regarded the size of Geneva to be optimal, attributing to it the advantages of a face-to-face society. In this, he seems to have remained faithful to the philosopher referred to in the motto of this work: Aristotle. Yet Rousseau was, no doubt, also a *philosophe* in the French sense of the word, and he could not fully identify with the traditional role of the citizens of Geneva. Instead of simply demanding that they preserve the mores or *moeurs* of the forefathers of the city, which was the usual strategy of the urban citizenry in the early modern context, the *Dedication* in fact presents an ideal city, a theoretical construct by Rousseau. His indirect, but rather radical criticism of the status quo goes much further. Instead of accepting the traditional language of urban politics, which usually relied on ancient wisdom and a demand to return to the ideals of the founding documents of the city, he had the courage to present his own ideal scenario. To be more precise, his rhetoric includes both references to the specific Genevan manners, the republican spirit of the city, and a daring philosophical vision that he claims was guided by reason, in a typical Enlightened manner. These two levels of his text represent two different concepts of civil liberty.

The first level, the traditionalist, or conservative republican discourse is based on past glory. It also stresses that observing the customs of the ancestors is all important in the city. Rousseau referred, for example, to "the pleasant custom of seeing and knowing one another,"[20] and claimed that he would not like to live "in a republic of recent institution," for such a State might run "the risk of overthrow and destruction almost as soon as it came into being."[21] In his view it takes long time to get "accustomed by degrees to breathe the health-giving air of liberty." This latter expression is, of course, a reformulation of the medieval dictum: *Stadtluft macht frei*.[22] He warned of "dangerous innovations," and ascertained that "it is above all the great antiquity of the laws which makes them sacred and venerable." He held views which were almost Burkean in their traditionalism: "States, by accustoming themselves to neglect their ancient customs (*amciens usages*) under the pretext of improvement, often introduce greater evils."[23] He explicitly recommended the long-time maintenance (*conserve*) of sovereignty, as the aim of politics, and he wishes that a Republic should "last for ever."[24]

Yet there is a second level of the text. The aforementioned conservative dictum in the rhetoric of the *Dedication*, which—I claim—belongs to the traditional understanding of civil liberty was counterbalanced by another one which was rather critical about the present circumstances, and offered an alternative to it. As the recent literature on Rousseau and Geneva points out, the *Dedication* presents as an alternative "an outline of Rousseau's theory of the ideal democratic state."[25] Although the monographer claims that "Rousseau defended the *Règlement* of 1738," in fact he went much further than that with his philosophical apparatus. He defended the exclusive right, and indeed the sovereignty of the General Council to draft the laws, leaving to the magistrates only the duty to apply and execute them: "I should have thought a country, in which the right of legislation was vested in all the citizens," adding as a precaution against the tyranny of the majority that the right "to propose new laws . . . should belong exclusively to the magistrate."[26] Interestingly, although the idea of the rights of a community or corporate body came from the medieval tradition (see Gierke's recollections of the idea of *Genossenschaft*[27]), Rousseau went much further in a communitarian direction when he introduced his concept of general will, for example, in his *Discourse on Political Economy*: "The body politic, therefore, is also a corporate being possessed of a will; and this general will, which tends always to the preservation and welfare of the whole and of every part, and is the source of the laws, constitutes for all the members of the State . . . the rule of what is just or unjust."[28] He went even further: his wishful thinking painted an ideal urban landscape of virtue and harmony. When he described the upright manners of the magistrates of Geneva (posing the poetic question: "who can find, throughout the universe, a more upright, more enlightened and more honourable body than your magistracy"), he claimed one could be forgiven for suspecting irony and caricature. Surprisingly, however, he made further overstatements about the citizenry: "let equity, moderation, and firmness of resolution continue to regulate all your proceedings, and to exhibit you to the whole universe as the example of a valiant and modest people, jealous equally of their honour and of their liberty."[29] These are extraordinary demands, characteristic of Rousseau's unrealistic mindset. His aim was more than just to turn the clock back: he wanted to ameliorate human nature and remodel the power relations of the city. At the end of the century, the French revolutionaries took these extraordinary political demands of Rousseau literally, which required the citizenry to achieve a life of virtue in the service of the patria, as witnessed by the *Declaration of the Rights of Man and of the Citizen* (1789). They straightforwardly executed the punishment he only advised theoretically in connection with those who "dared to condemn the principles established in this work": "I would pursue him criminally as a traitor to the fatherland."[30] It is at this point that Rousseau's traditionalist defense of Calvinist bourgeois and ancient Roman heroic virtues morphed into the language of revolutionary violence, establishing the new republican ethos of the French Republic.

There are two steps in the process whereby Rousseau's second concept of political liberty—his ideal picture of the virtuous citizenry—transferred from the local community to the national level. First, he himself had to move away from Geneva, a very clear indication that the city's elite was not up to applying his radical political advice. This is even more significant if we keep in mind that Rousseau did all he could to incite the ordinary citizens against their magistrates, and he had his allies in this political conspiracy. This happened after he realized that his intention to integrate into the citizen body was unrealistic, and that he would never succeed in achieving that aim in his life. Rousseau certainly did not strike the right tone in addressing the citizenry of Geneva, and this was because he demanded too much from them. As a Genevese bourgeois wrote to him, "You are feared, you are too free, and one is afraid that we might want to be as free as you."[31] A further problem was that he did not take into account the religious sensitivity of the burghers. His religious views were considered unorthodox, and even his supporters required him to make a religious confession anew. Although for some time he did not feel ready to do so, eventually, in a letter, he was ready to claim that: "I am Christian, and sincerely Christian, according to the doctrine of the Gospel."[32]

All in all, as a result of political manipulation on the part of the magistracy, the urban citizenry of Geneva did not receive him back into its corporate body. Apparently, the French nation was more grateful to him—at least posthumously. His views inspired some of the revolutionaries, and the revolution was ready to canonize him: his remains were ceremoniously transferred to the Panthéon, to express the debt of the nation to its greatest philosopher. The refusal of the urban citizenry of Geneva to accept him and the glorification of him by the revolution proves that his main message had nothing to do with the conservative republican idea of liberty, and had more to do with a modern and potentially revolutionary concept of the liberty of the *citoyen* of the state. This distinction proved to be the deepest divide in the republican tradition. This demarcation line detached the traditional (ancient-medieval-early modern) urban concept of citizen liberty from the new (modern) one of the liberty of the state's citizens. Yet, as we shall see, an undercurrent of the older tradition survived, in the intellectual milieu of modernist "statism," and one of the indirect aims of this book is to show that it remains highly topical even today.

NOTES

1. For reasons of availability I quote from the republished version of the chapter in: R. G. Collingwood, "The Historical Logic of Question and Answer," in *The History of Ideas. An Introduction to Method*, ed. Preston King (London and Canberra: Croom Helm; Totowa, NJ Barnes and Noble Books, 1983), 135–152, 143.
2. Ibid., 149.
3. Ibid., 150.
4. R. G. Collingwood, "An Autobiography," in R. G. Collingwood, *An Autobiography and Other Writings: With Essays on Collingwood's life and Work*, ed. Teresa Smith (Oxford: Oxford University Press, 2013), 1–174, 108.
5. Numa Denis Fustel de Coulanges, *The Ancient City. A Study on the Religion, Laws, and Institutions of Greece and Rome*, with a new foreword by Arnaldo Momigliano and S. C. Humphreys (Baltimore and London: The Johns Hopkins University Press, 1980), 110.
6. Ibid., 120.
7. Ibid., 324.
8. "(L)e dernier savant du monde ancien, as well as the first Christian encyclopedist". Ernest Brehaut, *An Encyclopedist of the Dark Ages: Isidore of Seville* (New York: Columbia University, 1912), 7.
9. Chiara Frugoni, ed., *A Distant City: Images of Urban Experience in the Medieval World*, trans. William McCuaig (Princeton, NJ: Princeton, 1991), 3.
10. Philip F. Sheldrake, "A Spiritual City? Place, Memory, and City Making," in *Architecture, Ethics, and the Personhood of Place*, ed. Gregory Caicco (Hanover and London: University Press of New England, 2007), 50–68, 54.
11. Aristotle, *Politics*, 3.9. 1280b32-35.
12. Joan-Anton Sánchez de Juan, "Civitas et Urbs. The Idea of the City and the Historical Imagination of Urban Governance in Spain, 19th–20th Centuries" (PhD diss., Department of History and Civilization, European University Institute, Florence, 2001), 18.
13. Jean-Jacques Rousseau, "The Social Contract," in Rousseau, *The Social Contract and Discourses*, trans. and intr. G.D.H. Cole (London: Everyman, 1993), 180–341, n.192.
14. Daniel Gordon, *Citizens without Sovereignty. Equality and Sociability in French Thought, 1670-1789* (Princeton: Princeton University Press, 1994), 21.
15. Denis Diderot, "Cité," in Diderot, *Political Writings*, trans. and ed. John Hope Mason and Robert Wokler (Cambridge: Cambridge University Press, 1992), 12–14, 13.
16. Ibid., 12.

17. To be sure, Geneva could not be recognized as a sovereign state in the early modern international scene, as it was under "the joint protection of Berne, Zürich, and France." See footnote of Rousseau, *The Social Contract*, 349, n.181(1).

18. I use the following edition of the work: Jean-Jacques Rousseau, "Dedication to the Republic of Geneva," in *Rousseau, A Discourse on a Subject Proposed by the Academy of Dijon: What Is the Origin of Inequality among Men, and Is It Authorized by Natural Law*, in *The Social Contract and Discourses*, trans. G.D.H. Cole, rev. and augmented by J. H. Brumfitt and John C. Hall, updated by P. D. Jimack (London: Everyman, 1993), 31–42.

19. Rousseau, *Dedication*, 33.
20. Ibid.
21. Ibid.
22. Ibid., 34.
23. Ibid., 35.
24. Ibid., 37.
25. Helena Rosenblatt, *Rousseau and Geneva* (Cambridge: Cambridge University Press, 1997), 159.
26. Rousseau, *Dedication*, 35.
27. John D. Lewis, *The Genossenschaft—Theory of Otto von Gierke; A Study in Political Thought* (Madison: University of Wisconsin, 1935).
28. Jean-Jacques Rousseau, "A Discourse on Political Economy," in *Rousseau, The Social Contract*, 127–168, 132. A classic description of Rousseau's invention, the general will is this one: "As long as several men in assembly regard themselves as a single body, they have only a single will which is concerned with their common preservation and general well-being." Chapter IV of *The Social Contract*, 274.
29. Rousseau, *Dedication*, 38.
30. Rousseau's letter to Marcet de Mézières, 24 July 1762, quoted by Rosenblatt, *Geneva*, 275.
31. Quoted by Rosenblatt, *Geneva*, 273, from a letter by Paul Moultou, a pastor in Geneva from 1755.
32. *Lettre à Christophe de Beaumont*, quoted by Rosenblatt, *Geneva*, 275, n.44.

Chapter 1

From the "Reason of the City" to the "Practical Wisdom of the City"

The title of the introduction refers to Viroli's famous claim that there was an unfortunate turn in European history from the concept of politics to that of the reason of state.[1] Viroli does not hide his republican sympathies and the normative dimension of his narrative is nothing less than a history of a loss.[2] The earlier ideology of the concept of politics—a community of burghers who were ready and able to manage their own affairs on their own, both in antiquity and in the high Middle Ages—gave way to the absolute and sovereign power of the newly born centralized state (which Hobbes dubbed the Leviathan), which was the theoretical background of the concept of the reason of state. Beside the changing concept of agency or the subject of politics the problem with the latter ideology is that it abandons the rich, value-laden concept of practical wisdom (*prudentia, phronesis*) for a sort of secretive cunning, the modern concept of prudence, informed by Machiavellian immoral *virtù*. The introduction will show that this book seeks to reconstruct a parallel story: the birth and rise and decline of the European city. While it will take a special interest in the early modern period, which saw the rise of the nation-state, it will also reconstruct the grand narrative of the city from ancient Athens to our contemporary small and medium-sized cities. However, the overtone of this narrative promises to be somewhat different: while Viroli seems to tell a simple story of loss, the present work hopes to present the European city not only as an item of the nostalgic past, but also as the promise of the future. That is why we claim that this story runs from the reason of the city (as opposed to the reason of the state) to the specific wisdom of the city (as opposed to the general notion of political wisdom).

THE CITY AS EXPERIENCE I: THE *FLANEUR* IN NINETEENTH-CENTURY PARIS AND THE *VOYEUR* IN NEW YORK

To illustrate the role played by the architectural environment in the citizens' life, we will leave the confines of academic prose, usually associated with an objective-seeming external standpoint, in order to also make use of first-person singular narratives, to present an internal standpoint. We borrow this distinction between external and internal standpoint from H. L. A. Hart, the British legal philosopher, who employed it in his work *The Concept of Law*.[3] Hart claimed that to fully explain the actual operation of the law an external description of how norms can change human behavior is not enough. To fully understand and explain it, one has to enter the mind of the citizen who is ready to follow the instructions of the law. In the same way, conceptualizing the city is not a simple matter of describing an objective phenomenon. Instead, what need to be reconstructed are the attitudes of citizens to their respective cities. After all, as we have seen, an important component of what we call the city in the sense of a certain kind of community does not amount to much more than the common experience of its inhabitants. This attitude is not easily conveyed by a conceptual analysis. It is easier to present it in practical activity, as its rationale is usually not abstract, but practical. In order to provide an insight into the relationship between city and inhabitant, object and subject, I will make an effort to reconstruct my own reflective and non-reflective relationship to my own urban surroundings. To be able to do so, I will rely on two earlier attempts. I will rely first of all on the concept of the *flaneur*, a creation, real or imagined, of nineteenth-century Parisian literature and figurative art. A theoretician of interest here is Michel de Certeau, a twentieth-century French Jesuit writer and social scientist. I will use these original accounts of people's perception of their architectural environment in a city to help to make explicit my own lived experiences of a Central European city, Budapest.[4]

Flânerie is "the activity of strolling and looking which is carried out by the *flaneur*."[5] Its best known eulogist in nineteenth-century Paris was Baudelaire, who "gave a poetic vision of the public places and spaces of Paris."[6] The most important element of this poetic vision is a subjective viewpoint, representative of the post-romantic brand of poetry of Baudelaire. The subject who expresses his impressions as he happens to find himself in the streets and arcades of metropolitan Paris, reporting on what he sees walking by, partly as physical (architectural) environment, and partly as a direct experience of being lost in the midst of a crowd of human beings. As Baudelaire put it in his essay *The Painter of Modern Life*, for the *flaneur*, "for the perfect idler, for the passionate observer, it becomes an immense source of enjoyment to establish his dwelling in the throng, in the ebb and flow, the bustle, the fleeting and the infinite."[7] The flaneur is one of the moving mob, but he also distances himself from the others. His strolling enables him to gain a first-hand experience of the city as a three-dimensional object, but also one that is enlivened by that very mob. Strolling along the streets he hunts for the aesthetically relevant, and he transforms it at once by lending it an artistic form in real time. He establishes "a connection between the intuited fluidity of things in the environment of the city and the physical negotiation of the space and other bodies carried out by the poet during his walks in the crowds."[8] Importantly, the poet remains alone in the midst of the crowd, which gives him the chance to remain an "impartial spectator,"[9] yet he comes into contact with the flow of people as well as with the physical environment, by way of experiencing it aesthetically, that is both sensually and in order to make sense of it. While the poet lost in the crowd is incognito, he is able to catch sight of everything: he is the perfect observer—the detective. Or to change the metaphor, he is the perfect art critic, a member of the audience in the theater, at this moment watching a spectacle on the stage of a magnificent setting, Paris, in a moment of high drama, reporting on his experiences once again in real time.

While Baudelaire, as (re)presented in his essays and poetry, is the most important embodiment of the *flaneur*, the figure itself is not his invention. A whole body of literature in French deals with this phenomenon.[10] This makes the question of his historical existence pertinent. In fact, most probably, the phenomenon only existed on the pages of that very literature, as the figure is more complex than its historical alter ego might have been. In other words, it expresses more the subconscious of French culture than its actual character traits, more its wishful thinking and desires than its actual deeds.

A further point to be taken into account in our investigation of the *flaneur* is that a substantial body of secondary literature has accumulated on the subject. Of that secondary literature the most important author so far was an admirer of French culture and critic of bourgeois values, a German of Jewish origin, Walter Benjamin. Benjamin's family had some French background, his father having spent some of his life in Paris as a banker, which made the child feel at home in French culture. His *Passagen-Werk* (1982)[11] is a posthumously edited and published collection of Benjamin's notes for a projected opus magnum, consisting mainly of quotes from the French literature of the age, fictional and non-fictional, about urban life in Paris, and in particular concerning the way of life of the *flaneur* in the arcades of Paris, the covered passageways which were one of its architectural innovations, together with some reflections on them by the author. The twist given to the idea of the flaneur by Benjamin makes him all the more mysterious. This is partly due to Benjamin's special way of thinking, oscillating between his original Jewish mysticism and Marxist social criticism, the trend of his day. Benjamin had a close relationship with Adorno, one of the pillars of the Frankfurt School, who tried to influence him to give the work a more radical Marxist political edge. However, Benjamin's attitude as a thinker was much less fervent and much too reflective for him to be able to push his project in that direction too far and too fast. He was fully saturated by French culture, and yet his German Jewish identity made it possible, indeed unavoidable, for him to distance himself from the phenomenon of the *flaneur*. His position was the sympathetic observer of these observers of Paris street life, and he described his object of study with such exceptional empathy that it is hard not to suspect that to a certain extent he identified himself with the *flaneur*, instead of remaining a stranger, who pins down his experimental object with scholarly detachment and an unbiased curiosity. Benjamin's ways of reconfiguring the figure of the *flaneur* make him a symbolic representative of the individual lost in the modern metropolis, who manages, however, to preserve some traces of the poetic and the intellectual in himself, and who has a psychoanalytical relevance, as a counterpoint to the law-abiding and unimaginative bourgeois of the era of Napoleon III. In urban history, this period saw the total reconstruction of the structure of Paris by Baron Haussmann, which increasingly fostered feelings of nostalgia for a bygone way of life, even becoming the spirit of a whole generation.

Benjamin's project of reconstructing that spirit is all the more fascinating, as he used it as an occasion to experiment with his own way of writing, a very characteristic style of note-taking (it should be noted that the work remained unfinished). The collection, inspired chiefly by both the intellectual presence and the textual heritage of Charles Baudelaire, was meant to function like a collage, building up an ever-larger whole from very small, often borrowed, particles. Besides being reminiscent of the artistic genre of the collage, this style has also been compared to a palimpsest. This term, originally Greek, taken over by the Romans, designates a text written typically on parchment, which covered earlier layers of writings in order to reuse the material which served as its medium. Palimpsests were quite frequent in ancient literature, including some parts of the Bible which have been preserved in this manner. Benjamin's work has the air of a palimpsest about it because he worked on the Arcades Project for a long time between 1927 and 1940, constantly writing and rewriting the material he collected for it. This makes the actual identity and meaning of the text less than obvious.

A further mysterious aspect of Benjamin's work on a Paris which had disappeared by the time he was writing was the fate of its author. Benjamin was not part of the academic establishment of his age, but in fact lived on the periphery of Berlin's thriving intellectual life. This made him a fervent observer and critic of the culture of his age, although this criticism was full of sensitivity due to his wounded spirit and perplexing refinement. The fact that the project remained unfinished, that its author either committed suicide or was killed on the Spanish-French border during his escape from the Nazi takeover, and that the manuscript was preserved by Bataille, in those days working as an archivist of the Bibliothèque Nationale, who hid it in the library where it was later discovered—all these serve to make the text the more enigmatic.

The *flaneur*, evoked by Benjamin, was the detective of social life, who, by keeping an eye on others, tried to solve the enigma of interpersonal relationships. "The figure of the *flaneur* prefigures that of the detective . . . It suits him perfectly to see his indolence presented as a façade behind which he hides the sustained attention of an observer, never letting his eyes off the unsuspecting criminal."[12] He strives to see everything in the city, always keeping an eye out. His profession is nothing less than *"connoisseurship"* and *"scopophilia."*[13] It is also important to note, however, that his work is the discovery of the secrets of a whole city, an always changing, camouflaging built environment. His observation of others is "a spatial practice of specific sites: the interior and exterior public spaces of the city. These include parks, sidewalks, squares, and shopping arcades or malls."[14] The city is a location where one can comfortably watch others, somewhat in the manner of a nature reserve, or rather a jungle of human beings. What is all the more paradoxical is that this city is the dwelling place of both the hunter and the hunted beings. The hunting of the *flaneur* is linked to public spaces, and to unidentified members of the crowd, rather than to individuals, and intimate, personal spaces. The city is a true wilderness, where anything can happen. The *flaneur* usually hunts by night, which makes the chase even more exciting. Flânerie could not be conceived of in a small town or in a face-to-face society. This is a sign which proves that it is a paradigmatically modern activity, connected to the urbanized environment of the metropolitan city. The *flaneur* enters the stage at "a moment when the city is more than urbs but is also orbs, that is, it becomes a cosmopolis, where the world (read European empire) is every place co-present."[15] In this space, human relations become distorted: "Ties based on long-established, people-centred social relations were displaced by brief interactions based on commodity price-competition."[16] The female variant of the *flaneur*, or perhaps of the dandy, the elegant, yuppie version of it, is the bourgeois wife, who spends much of her free time shopping in the fashionable shops and department stores of the arcades. An even more negative equivalent of the *flaneur* could be the prostitute, who commodifies her own body and innocence to sell it to respectable husbands or well-to-do bachelors. Benjamin writes about this process of dehumanization in a language which deploys Marxist critical vocabulary: "Fundamentally, the identification with a piece of merchandize is an identification with its exchange value. The *flaneur* is the virtuoso of this identification. He takes even the concept of venality out for a walk. Even when the department store is his last hangout . . . the sandwich man his last incarnation."[17] *Flânerie*, in this narrative, is proof of the alienation which arises in the oversized city, a typical phenomenon of the industrialized European capital of the nineteenth century. It exemplifies the deadlock of urban developments, in its original form, a moment when the burgher is lost in his own milieu, the oversized *urbs*.

What crucial aspects of *flânerie* are worth applying in our own investigation? For example, the ability to look at the familiar cityscape with a neutral eye, as if it were unknown, in order to make sense of it. The *flaneur* was able to do this, and we should learn this from him, looking at the European city with fresh eyes. More than that, what is needed is not simply detachment from the familiar, and a suitable balance in judging it, but also an appreciation of aesthetics. We should also take from the *flaneur* an interest in human nature, as it manifests itself in the city dwellers of the European city: their ordinary habitat, their dwelling place. Finally, the *flaneur* can teach us lessons of moral seriousness to be constantly vigilant about our surroundings, architectural and human. We can learn from him a refined technique of building a mental map more detailed than the one we have as a result of smart phones and tablets, which are in danger of taking over moral responsibility from us. He is also exemplary in that his interest is always toned aesthetically, and his aesthetic interest is intentional in the sense that his attention is always directed toward the other, human phenomena. Finally, we can learn from him to have a dynamic, historically informed, but also critical perception of our cities. There is, of course, no Archimedean point from which the city will be seen in its totality, yet by strolling in it, or flowing in it, we can obtain a processed, dynamic view of the whole.

At this point one can also pay tribute to the eccentric views of another famous stroller, Michel de Certeau, a French Jesuit author, as revealed in his work on *Walking in the City*.[18] In this work he finds there an Archimedean point, from where New York City as a whole can be grasped: "To see Manhattan from the 107th floor of the World Trade Center."[19] Certainly, Certeau could not have been aware of the tragic fate of the building, but it was already an iconic building at the time he wrote these lines. The top of the skyscraper provided a vantage point which ordinary people do not often see it from and which therefore captures people's imagination. No wonder, that in Wim Wender's cult film *Wings of Desire*, angels live on the top of the high buildings of contemporary Berlin, where they are with us, but at the same time above us. "To be lifted to the summit of the World Trade Center is to be carried away by the city's hold. (. . .) Above those waters Icarus can ignore the tricks of Daedalus, in his shifting and endless labyrinths. His altitude transforms him into a voyeur."[20] Certeau also adds one further dimension to this account: the sense that from such a distance the city becomes readable.

The high position of his body "changes an enchanting world into a text. It allows him to read it; to become a solar Eye."[21]

Certeau's endeavor connects this modern, Wenders-like scene with art history. This desire to see the whole was already present in medieval and early modern paintings. There too, the divine element of this panoramic view of the urban vista is emphasized: "The panorama transformed the spectator into a celestial eye. It created gods."[22] Yet Certeau makes great efforts to counterbalance this angelic dehumanization, which stands in opposition to the dehumanization described by Benjamin. His authorial interest is in the walkers down below, their minute activities, their antlike bustle, which is in fact parallel with the movement of writing, even if the latter follows the whisper of angels. This writing will preserve aspects of strolling: "The paths taken by strollers consist of a series of turnings and returnings that can be likened to 'turns of phrase' or 'stylistic devices.'"[23] This will be important for us: the physical space of the built environment frames the text, the style of which is determined by the ways of life and thought of the inhabitants, who perambulate the streets of the city, like the scribbles leaving traces between the lines of the exercise book of pupils. These childhood experiences were crucial for Certeau, too. His psychanalysis goes back to the unconscious differentiation of the child between himself and his mother's body. He compares this early life experience to the recognition of the physical difference between our home place and ourselves. Certeau suggests "To employ space, therefore, is to repeat the joyous and silent experience of childhood: it is, in the site, *to be other* and *to pass to the other*."[24] In other words: we, the *flaneur*-like walkers of the city—and this is a symbolic analogue—experience the chaotic world around us, along the lines we have learned as a child. "Childhood, which determined the practices of space . . . creates in the panned city a 'metaphorical' city or a city in movement."[25]

THE CITY AS EXPERIENCE II: CHILDHOOD MEMORIES FROM COMMUNIST BUDAPEST

In what follows, I will try to reconstruct my own childhood memories of my family's locality in Budapest, Hungary, in Central Europe. This will serve as a case study, inspired by Benjamin's and de Certeau's projects, to trace how the kind of attachment one has to one's dwelling place actually grows within ourselves. This should be seen partly as a form of self-analysis, to draw to the surface what lies deep and hidden, in order to establish an internal view of this relationship, and partly as a retrospection with the aim of delineating the contours of the past, in order to use it as a factual example to make generalizations about the present. To make proper sense of the narrative below, it is especially important to remember that it took place in the midst of what political historians call the Kádár regime. János Kádár was the first secretary of the communist party, who led a campaign of revenge against the participants of the 1956 revolution, including death and imprisonment sentences, as well as maintaining punishment measures for decades against the youth who had supported the revolution, like my parents.[26]

My family on my father's side was burghers of Buda, the western side of the capital on the map, a hilly, green, fairy-tale quarter. I still have a strong attachment to this part of the city. I was born in Buda in 1964, just eight years after 1956, and lived in one area of Buda for the first few years of my life, staying in the near vicinity of Buda for the remainder of my childhood—all three of the flats my parents owned during their marriage were within a few kilometer radius, and all were council-owned properties. When I was eighteen, I left my home town for one year to attend university in Szeged, 200 kilometers from the capital in 1982. As my fiancée remained in Budapest, I managed to return to the capital. My wedding took place when I was only twenty-two, when we were both fourth-year university students. We moved from my wife's family's flat in Buda to Pest, on the other side of the Danube, our parents helping us to find our first flat on a housing estate. The news of obtaining this flat took me by surprise during my year as a visiting graduate in Oxford in 1987–1988, not long before the political transition in Central and Eastern Europe. As soon as we could afford it, however, we returned to Buda, once again with the help of our parents, and have lived there ever since. We acquired a privately owned flat in between the flats of our parents. My identity as a city dweller is that of a Buda burgher, father, and husband of a middle class family, a typical inhabitant of the second district of the Hungarian capital. All four of our nuclear family (me, my wife, my son, and my daughter) pursue intellectual professions, and three of us still live in Buda. Even my daughter would like to return to Buda, with her husband, as soon as they can afford it, an intention we also support. In what follows, let me try to identify some of the memories, which define my identity as a burgher of Buda. What follows offers an internal viewpoint narrative about Buda, a narrative of my lived experience in my hometown under Communist rule.

The Castle Hill district is approached from Central Buda through the *Bécsi Kapu* (Vienna Gate). It was here that the route to Buda from Vienna (appr. 220 kilometers) reached the inner city of Buda, built on top of the hill in parallel with the Danube. From an early age we lived in a nearby area called *Országút* (Highway). I used to walk up the hill and passed through the arch of the gate each day on my way to my office in the former, historical building of the Hungarian Academy on *Országház* (House of the Diet) street for years. The building itself was part of a historical complex, part of it having housed earlier a convent of nuns, and including a finely decorated festivity hall where some of the meetings of the lower house of the Diet actually convened in the late eighteenth and early nineteenth centuries. A part of the building complex later served the *Helytartótanács* (*Statthalterrat*, council of governor-general), and it was claimed that there were prison cells in the basement of this building, where I had my office as director of the Institute of Philosophy of the Hungarian Academy of Sciences.

Rebuilt in 1936, the city gate is a memento for present-day tourists of the traditional way of entering a walled city like Buda. Visitors have to climb a rather steep slope before entering the gate, which was originally called the *Porta Sabbati* (Saturday Gate). In my childhood, it was also through this gate that we walked to the Matthias Church (*Mátyás-templom, Church of our Lady*), a neo-Gothic church, with my family on the first day of Christmas, and on Easter Saturdays. In its original form the Church was used by the burghers of Buda as early as the eleventh century and it has also served as the coronation church of Hungary. It was a quarter of an hour's walk from my family's flat in a bourgeois multi-family residential house built by Count Mailáth in the early twentieth century, where I was brought up with my brother in the 1970s and 1980s, in a part of central Buda historically called *Országút* (Highway). When we walked up the steep slope on *Ostrom* street (the name of the street translates as Siege street) my father told stories of the Ottomans' attack of Buda some 350 years earlier. My family on my father's side regards itself as belonging to the originally German-speaking middle class population of ancient Buda, which is Roman Catholic on my father's line. It was quite natural for us to attend Matthias Church for the procession after the Easter Saturday mass even if we did not belong to that particular parish. One has to add also, that my mother's side of the family was Lutheran, and they, too had a pretty little chapel, opposite the Vienna Gate. We had to pass it on our way to the Cathedral, but we never thought that this was the place where the obsequy of my mother would be arranged decades later. At Easter time the weather was usually cool and quite windy, and we had a long wait until darkness finally fell, and the huge and heavy gates of the cathedral opened, to let the procession leave the church. We heard the voices of the choir and the respectable sound of the organ, and a short time later we caught sight of the long queue of young altar boys and girls with candles in their hands illuminating their faces. They were followed by the relics of the church, in the hands of elderly priests and young ordinands who themselves were singing loudly, competing to be heard with the low-pitched ringing of the bells of the tower and their own high-pitched hand bells. These in turn were followed by the crowded congregation of believers, also with candles in their hands, and joining in the singing of the Easter songs. I always liked this holiday, which was crowned by the Easter dinner which we ate after the evening mass in our best suits, from very nice porcelain plates with a silver or silver-plated dinner-service.

Let me recall two further childhood memories of the Castle Hill. One of them has to do with the National Gallery, which moved to the Royal Palace, the most prestigious building in Buda, in my youth, in 1975, as a representative collection of the history of fine arts in Hungary. A creative fine arts workshop was held for children in a room near the dome of the National Gallery, led by two leading artists of the age. I remember the dark afternoons when I walked to the Gallery, and how after the class we walked down to the bridgehead of Chain Bridge, the first stone bridge over the Danube, built in the mid-nineteenth century, with a friend and a girlfriend of mine, whose mother was a family acquaintance. As we descended, the whole city seemed to be under our feet, with small spots of light sparkling along the streets of the city, some of them coming from the "eyes" of small vehicles, slowly flowing in neat lines, inaudible to us and thus appearing like those in a miniature city of a model railway. The other memory connected with the Castle Hill comes from the year during which I spent as junior research fellow in the newly founded *Collegium Budapest, Institute for Advanced Study*, opposite the Cathedral. It was just after the fall of the Berlin Wall, and the location of the international research institute was the reconstructed old town hall of Buda Castle. The research institute was opened here in order to allow an internationally selected group of researchers feel at home in Budapest, which had supposedly been liberated from its Communist overlords.

My memories, then, are connected with some of the most important public buildings, either religious or secular, of the Castle Hill area of Buda, within its historical walls, including the temporary building of the lower house of the Diet, the Roman Catholic Matthias Church and the small chapel of the Lutheran Church, the Royal Palace, which was never put into use by the Habsburg dynasty, the royal family of the country with whom the nation made an uneasy settlement, and the old town hall. Yet my special attachment to Buda can be better explained by my historical fantasies in relation to a row of houses, to be precise of four private houses on *Bécsi kapu tér* (Vienna Gate Square, formerly called Saturday Market place), which I saw each day for several years on my walk to my office, in the summer heat or in winter snow, at the Institute of Philosophy of the Hungarian Academy of Sciences.

Entering the Castle through the Vienna Gate, one is greeted by the sight of the pleasant little evangelical church I mentioned. Passing to the right of this church leads to four historical buildings. Although the present buildings are not exactly the medieval originals, they look and smell historical. It was very easy for me to imagine how, in the heyday of the city, heavy horse carriages passed into the courtyards of the houses and how the servants helped to unload their cargo. I always regarded these houses as my imaginative entry into the historical life of this district. I was thus happy to discover that local history describes all of these historical sites. We know, for example, that no 5. *Bécsi kapu tér* (Square of Vienna Gate) was owned in the first half of the fifteenth century by János Bátai, landowner and member of the council of Buda, and later by his widow. The present form of the house owes a great deal to János Pál Lobner, who was a blacksmith in the eighteenth century. The next house, no. 6. belonged to the court knight László Töttös, who sold it to the chapter of *Fehérvár* in 1392. After the Turks left Buda, the house was owned first by a tailor and later by a butcher. It was destroyed in the great fire of Buda, but later, in the eighteenth century, it was owned by the deputy judge of Buda, Antal Szeth. The next house was owned in the fifteenth century by a weaver, Konrad Gündelwein, and later by his family. In the late eighteenth century, the house was bought by József Grigely, a priest of the Piarist order, philosopher, teacher of Greek and Latin. In the early twentieth century it was bought by Baron Lajos Hatvany, founder of the legendary literary journal, *Nyugat* (the West), who was a critic and a generous sponsor of literature. The house hosted such famous Hungarian authors as Sándor Márai and Géza Ottlik, as well as Thomas Mann, whom they both admired; all of whom will figure later in this volume. Finally, the house on the corner was owned in 1418 by a sworn member of Buda council, by the name of Benedek Bátor. After the Turkish occupation a master builder bought the plot and built a new house on the ruins of the old one. The house was demolished in the great fire of 1723. In the nineteenth century we know of a tailor and a doctor among its owners. It was bought by Count Móric Esterházy, a member of parliament, who had served briefly as prime minister, in 1929. He was taken to the concentration camp at Malthausen by the Gestapo, because of his support of the efforts of Prime Minister Kállay to leave the German alliance. Although he survived, he was also interned by the Russian occupying forces who sent him to the village of *Hort*, where he worked as a gravedigger.

The stories of these four houses of Vienna Gates Square (*Bécsi kapu tér*) trace, in a concentrated line of episodes and with a symbolic overtone, the history of the place. Owners or tenants of the buildings on these sites belonged variously to the aristocracy, the patrician families of Buda, or to the social stratum of artisans. Knowing the micro-level history of these places, including the personal histories of owners and inhabitants of the houses, can help us reconstruct the way of life of the *civitas* with the help of the surviving remnants of the historic *urbs*. Seemingly, and often in unexpected ways, houses can keep the memory of their owners and inhabitants alive. Consider the decorations of the façade of house no. 7., with reliefs of Virgil, Cicero, Socrates, and Livius, as well as Quintilian and Seneca in the center. Around them the symbols of music, poetry, grammar, and alchemy help to reconstruct the culturally refined *Weltanschauung* of the owner of the house, who belonged to the specific *Bildungsbürgertum* of Buda. In the very center of the façade decoration, we find Pallas Athene, surrounded by painting, sculpture, history, and geography. This frontage can clearly tell us much about the self-perception of the owner, a pious priest. It is also able to color our reconstruction of the historical narrative of a highly educated burgher community, which has disappeared, but whose ideals are well worth reconsidering.

THE CITY AS SUBJECT MATTER OF HISTORY WRITING: SIEGES OF BUDA

Besides such recollections of subjective experiences of how local attachments are born as those narrated above, one can also dig into the urban past through the channel of professional historical narratives. The factual historical information they can provide is essential when writing a political philosophy of the city. Yet one has to be careful: historical narratives are themselves rhetorical exercises, which fact renders them open to question. This is also true of the historical accounts of Buda, the authors of which could not avoid choosing certain historical value, and the particular historical investigation of these choices is also loaded with the partisan alliances of their authors. Still, after delving into the micro historical mosaics, a broader consideration of grand narrative also promises to bear fruit for our investigation. I will turn to it now by looking at the professional historical accounts of Buda, biased or unbiased, paying special attention to the city's political crisis situations, which were quite frequent in that narrative.

Although not the capital of Hungary from its very beginning, and with some interruptions even later, Buda was, for most of the late medieval period, the Royal seat of the Hungarian Kingdom and acknowledged as the capital city of the country. It took some time to take on this central role. Medieval documents refer to the city as *sedes, solium,* and *thronus,* all very prestigious terms for a settlement, but not yet that of the legally first city of the country.[27] Originally built on what came to be called Castle Hill in the second half of the thirteenth century, it belonged to the second wave of city foundations which spread across Europe. Its birth was to a large extent due to the Mongol Tatar invasion in 1241–1242, when the invaders crossed the frozen Danube from Pest, which was unwalled and therefore an easy target for the Barbarian troops, who destroyed the earlier settlement of *Óbuda,* originally built on the ruins of an ancient Roman military camp, *Aquincum.* The reigning king, King Béla IV of Hungary was forced to flee to the Adriatic coast from the Tatars and subsequently decided that the cities of his realm needed real stone walls to defend them from brutal foreign attacks of this kind. In particular, he ordered the German settlers of Pest who had survived the Tatar invasion to cross to the other side of the Danube, and move up the hill, around which were built heavy stone walls. Béla IV later recalled the measures he took thus: "we have taken care to apply our hands efficaciously to the reform, repair, consolidation and strengthening of our kingdom and among those castles (*castra*) consistent with the defence of the realm we have had built a certain *castrum* on the Mount of Pest filled it with a great multitude of persons."[28] This is how Buda was established, and it received a royal charter from the king, by extending the rights and privileges of the inhabitants of Pest to also include the citizens of Buda. This is a "form of settlement transference involving persons, right and even nomenclature."[29] Elemér Mályusz claims that some of the leading burghers of Pest were "actively involved as contractors in the commercial enterprise of founding the new town[30] (*Siedlungsverlegung*)." This is relevant for the following two reasons. First, because it will be crucial from the point of view of our own understanding of urban development that some cities were founded and therefore closely controlled by rulers while others were from the very beginning the enterprises of burghers. Apparently, there is a third type where these two types of impulse for founding a city, from above or from below, came together and supported each other. Second, it is relevant because the German model of urban development was characteristic in the Central European area generally, and in the Hungarian Kingdom in particular. Buda, too, was a German city, or at least a German-speaking city for several centuries, for most of its history.

The fact that the original founding generations of Buda were mostly German had a major impact on the history of the city. It defined both the specific urban texture and the way it was governed. Second, it caused internal ethnic conflicts from an early date, and these ethnic enmities played a major role in the specific Hungarian constitutional setting, which was characterized by major constitutional handicaps for cities. Burghers had to suffer a kind of feudal discrimination in the Hungarian Kingdom because of their supposed opposition to the national political elites of the country, and in particular, of the national nobility.

As regards its urban texture, Buda was at least partially a planned settlement. This can be seen from the structure of its street-network on top of the Castle Hill, including the way streets follow the direction of the walls, and how plots for individual properties were positioned along the streets. In other words, the city's well-ordered internal structure expressed the will of the founder as mediated by the plans of the town designer. Furthermore, the walls that surrounded the city strictly determined its territory. The walls were required to house the functions of the court and of the central government. In fact, according to historians, the city was dominated by the palace and the institutions of royal government. Besides this royal architecture, there had to be space for private homes and such important public facilities as the market, several churches (in fact three), as well as church organizations, including monasteries and cloisters of different orders. The high number of public buildings explains why the number of the new settlement's permanent civic inhabitants remained rather low by European standards during the Middle Ages (it had not more than 15,000 inhabitants).[31]

The cohabitation of burghers and the court was also to have a number of further consequences for the urban development of Buda. First of all, the original charter of King Béla IV allowed the populous of Buda (originally Pest) to elect their magistrates: "They /the citizens/ may elect a mayor of the town, whomever they want and once elected they shall present him to us, and he should judge all their secular affairs."[32] The same privilege was confirmed by king Ladislas IV in 1276: "We further grant to them /the citizens/ that they shall not be forced to accept any judge appointed by us, but they shall have as headman whomever they wish by free election... and the headman should annually resign his office into the hands of the citizens."[33]

As for the governing bodies and functions of the city, although the council is not mentioned in any of these founding documents, we know of a *Rat* or council, consisting of twelve members, headed by a judge (*Richter*) or headman (*villicus*) as early as 1268. The community originally elected them directly. However, a disadvantage of the residential town became apparent, when the ruler, Béla IV, was taking decisions in his own hands, by appointing his own representative, who held the title of rector, as headman of the council. Historians have ascertained that only a few influential families held the privilege of supplying a rector, who often also had a royal function, as officer of the royal mint. What is more, in this period the patrician families of the council members were often connected to each other or the rectors: for example, "a half of council places were in the 1330s held by relatives of the rectors Johannes and Nicholas."[34] This means that royal patronage determined who could belong to a small circle of the elite of the town, who had a monopoly on the major political roles, and who would determine the present and the future of the city.

By the middle of the fourteenth century, self-government was once again in the ascendant. By this time a very detailed division of labor had emerged among the members of the magistracy. The judge (called in Latin language documents the *iudex*) and the councilors (*iurati*) had to take an oath to serve the community in fidelity. They appointed a notary (*Stadtschreiber*) who was in charge of the city's chancellery. There were subordinate magistrates for the suburbs. Another official, responsible for the city's finances (*Geldrichter*), was chosen by the judge from among the members of the council, and the holder of this position later served as a deputy judge. Besides sitting as a court of law, the council ran the city's practical affairs. As for the most important resource, tax collection, the community was served by an advisory board of twenty-four citizens, who were appointees of the council.[35]

This rather refined medieval city government structure proves that Buda was well advanced in its institutional development. The burghers of the city learned through their own mistakes that paying attention to organization is crucial for the smooth running of a city. They even collected these institutional arrangements into a book of laws, generally called the Buda Law Code. This was a collection of local customs together with generally accepted principles taken over from other contemporary or earlier German *Stadtrechtsbuch*s. This collection of the "regulation of the crafts" and "civic rituals," contains ordinances such as one that the judge should be "a German of pure descent" and another that "ten of the city councillors should be German."[36] It was no doubt in reference to these ethnic proportions and consequent legal provisions that the nineteenth-century Hungarian writer and statesman, who drew up the law on national minorities in 1868, Baron József Eötvös, who himself came from a German-speaking family, writes in one of his novels that medieval Hungarian cities were "alien, representing a separate element outside the collective nation. They stood like German islands in the midst of a Hungarian sea. They had their own foreign language and customs, and, as the Buda *Stadtrecht* confirms, their own foreign laws too."[37] It is because of the intrusions into city life by the king and his court, together with an opposite force, the nobility's resistance toward this alien element, that a recent historian, Martyn Rady claims in his reconstruction of medieval Buda: "Buda was thus never free to develop the autonomy and legal and jurisdictional independence which were characteristics of urban government elsewhere in Central Europe."[38] This seems to be an obvious, although perhaps somewhat overstated evaluation: no doubt, Buda was in the shadow of the royal court, and its competences were confined from the very beginning by both royal prerogative and the customary law of the (noble) nation. However, it was also the first city of the country. The former fact meant that it was destined to lag behind some of its German competitors. The latter fact made it an urban center, which had an unparalleled prestige among the other cities of the Kingdom. Putting together these two features, Buda was a leading regional urban center before the Turkish occupation in the middle of the sixteenth century. It is also true, however, as far as I can see, that the whole network of urban centers in the Kingdom of Hungary was underrated by the political elites of the country. This customary treatment of the towns exacerbated the devastating effects of the Turkish occupation, which in turn long delayed urban modernization when other parts of Europe had already embarked on it.

However, late medieval Buda, as an urban paradigm, also had a forward-looking aspect. In the fifteenth century a very detailed and sensitive system of *paritas* was worked out in its system of local government to regulate the representation of ethnic nationalities and the guilds. The background of the advent of this refined system of government was a sharp conflict between two groups of burghers lasting several decades; this time both of them were of German ethnic background.[39] The old-style, landed burgher elite, which was ready to enter into intermarriage with the Hungarian nobility had new rivals: the cloth-merchants from Nuremberg, who occupied some of the council positions in Buda from the 1370s onward. A third group was that of the so-called middle burghers, consisting of well-to-do artisans, who also demanded representation on the council. For some time, King Sigismund attempted to defuse the conflict of representation by returning to the original scheme, ridding the reformed council of the upwardly mobile new forces, and filling the position of the judge with his own candidate. However, this time the earlier power tactics did not work so easily: from that time on artisans were present on the council, which led to a new situation, in which Hungarians were represented in a higher proportion (three to four members out of the twelve) in the leadership, even if the Lawbook of Buda (*Ofner Stadtrecht*) still preserved the custom that only two Hungarians could be elected to the council, and leadership is to the preserve of a German burgher, with four German grandparents. Yet leadership for the moment remained in the hands of cloth-merchants from Nuremberg. In 1436, the Hungarian patricians, including royal administrators, lawyers, merchants, and people of noble origin, along with some of the rich artisans, decided to take control into their hands. Their struggle was led by György Budai, a scribe, who had worked earlier both on the council of the city and in the fiscal administration of the king, and who, by that time, was vice president of the appellate court of the royal-free cities, known as the tavernical bench (*tárnokszék*). In retaliation to the moves of the Hungarian burghers, and in contradiction with the Lawbook of Buda, the Germans elected their own judge, and killed the leader of the Hungarians (a certain John, the Goldsmith—*János ötvös*). When the people found his corpse, a popular uprising broke out and the urban poor attacked the houses of the rich, even those of rich Hungarians. To cool their passions, King Albert the Magnanimous was compelled to intervene, and he promulgated a new regulation of how to elect the city council. This proved to be a decision of epochal importance, forcing a compromise between the German elite and the strengthened Hungarian urban patrician group. From then on, a new judge was elected on a year-by-year basis, alternating between a German and a Hungarian, in a systematic manner. Membership of the council was decided on a parity basis between the two nationalities. A new assembly, called the Council of One Hundred, and also divided equally between the two nationalities, was established. Its members served as electors, electing the new council. The city council, when stepping down, elected the hundred men's council, with the rule that half of them had to be German, and other half Hungarian. It was also prescribed that the guilds and the groupings of artisans also had to take their part in this assembly. This system of precise proportionate representation proved to be durable. The negotiation and consolidation of the conflict, by a settlement based on mutual allowances also served as a precedent for other cities, and the Lawbook of Buda was applied by other urban centers (including, for example, *Kolozsvár/ Cluj*), which affirms its legitimacy. In other words, cities were able to learn from the dictates of political reality, including the acceptance of enforced negotiations. This potential, however, was not realized on the national level for long, leading to the exclusion of urban elites from the affairs of the state, which represented a real loss for the nation, but was in accordance with the realities of power, which dictated that the two greatest forces, the court and the Diet, solve the matters of state, for the most part excluding the burghers of cities from their affairs.

The burghers, however, had their own ways to make themselves known and honored. The burghers of Buda played a significant role in the constitutionally regulated political rituals and celebrations in their city. This illustrates the peculiar relationship between court and the *civitas* of Buda, which also functioned as a capital city. New kings had to lead a procession in full royal attire in the streets of Buda, to promulgate their new function in the capital city of Hungary. Furthermore, before their burial, kings had to be laid out for a kind of wake in the Church of Our Lady, in Buda. The burghers of Buda also served as gatekeepers at the basilica in *Székesfehérvár*, deciding whom to allow to enter the church when coronation services or other exceptional state occasions were held. These constitutionally significant functions of the burghers of Buda illustrate the influence exercised by this civic body in late medieval Hungary.

It can be concluded, then, that Buda, although a royal seat, was both a vibrant *civitas* and an important *urbs*, in the original senses of these terms at the end of the medieval period. Within the territory surrounded by its walls, and also outside of it, it had a well-developed urban architectural assembly, worthy of a community of burghers with a wide-ranging network of commercial and industrial contacts inside and outside the kingdom. Strolling through its streets, even today, after most of its buildings were bombed out in the two world wars, one can sense the essentially medieval character of the settlement. Even more importantly, though, the burghers of Buda, after much competition and rivalry, and sometimes after intense struggles between antagonistic ethnic, religious, and professional groups, were able to consolidate a certain level of self-governance by establishing the procedures for electing the leadership of their urban community. Learning from the fierce tensions and great losses resulting from acts of internal violence, they were compelled to accept royal regulation. The burghers of Buda, as a corporate entity, operated a political system on the basis of paritas, which was exemplary for other urban communities in the kingdom, and even outside of it.

This system made it possible for all affected groups (except, of course, the Jews and the urban poor, who were still excluded) to take part in the political affairs of the city.

This vibrant and lively community was seriously damaged (both in terms of the architectural infrastructure and human capital), first by the rivalry of the two kings (Habsburg and of Hungarian nationality, respectively) after the death of the legitimate ruler, King Louis II, at the Battle of *Mohács* (1526). The tactical military operations of both the contenders proved to be fatal for Buda: at various times they both besieged and defended Buda against each other. This internal division of the nation led to the fatal Turkish occupation of Buda in 1541, which allowed the Ottoman invader to remain in the central parts of the kingdom for one and a half century, until the siege of Buda in 1686.

With the loss of the capital city, both as a *civitas* and as an *urbs*, the kingdom lost much of its power, and the urban development in most of the territories of the kingdom came to a halt. As we shall see, this delay in urbanization proved fatal for Hungarian society and politics for centuries, and its effects can be felt up to the present day. This fatal backsliding is a grim reminder of the political relevance of a lively urban life based on local autonomy, so characteristic of European modernity and post-modernity, even after the peace treaty of Westphalia brought the age of the autonomous city-state to a close in the region. In this respect, this Central European story of medieval urban success (the completion of plans to build a defendable capital city, and the gradual, pieacemeal development of a refined system of self-government) and descent (due to internal schism and external invasion) conveys a message that remains relevant on a European level: without the active political involvement of the *civitas* (in other words a certain level of urban self-government) taking part in the management of the common good, European politics has less chance of surviving in an uncertain twenty-first century. The aim of the present volume is to show that if the state does not view cities as its partners, but simply exploits them, Europe cannot preserve its civilized political face. This is a lesson we have drawn from the historical narrative of the medieval administrative and commercial center of Buda, with its two phases of flourishing and decline.

THE CITY IN FICTION: GÉZA OTTLIK AND SÁNDOR MÁRAI

So far, we have taken two approaches to the past of the city: a subjective account of the author's early urban experiences of his hometown, Buda, followed by a summary of the historical narratives of professional historians about the thriving medieval period of the city and the subsequent disaster of the Turkish occupation. Arguably, there is a third form, besides a subjective and a historical account, of tracing the past histories of cities, through fictional writings. I will deal with two specific forms of fiction: novel writing and drama. Authors in both these genres can and must rely on historical facts, but they are also allowed to have the artistic freedom to apply those historical facts to achieve artistic effects.

Except for a few earlier works, the novel as an artform was born in eighteenth-century Britain, and served to present the life and thought of the middle classes.[40] The authors of classic European and American novels often wrote about the modern city of the nineteenth and twentieth centuries—whether it be Stendhal, Balzac, Flaubert, or Proust on Paris or Tolstoy and Dostoyevsky on Saint Petersburg or Moscow. As we shall see, when writing the modern histories of cities, writers need to return to the historical roots of these places. Drama, including modern scripts of theatric performance, is another genre which allows writers to present the struggles and conflict of urban life. The example we shall examine is exceptional in that it deals not only with a few members of a medieval urban community, but also aims to portray the life of the urban community as a whole.

The first example we will consider is once again an account of Buda. The last novel by Géza Ottlik, a twentieth-century Hungarian writer, bears the stark title: *Buda*.[41] In this unusual, posthumously published valedictory work Géza Ottlik, a typical representative of what might be labelled as bourgeois culture, and a key author of late twentieth-century Hungarian literature, celebrated the city of his birthplace in his own, very special way. At the beginning of the story, for example, he borrows the stylistic register of the history writer: "Buda, where we so miraculously found ourselves again, is that part of the Hungarian capital that lies on the right bank of the River Danube. An ancient settlement, it was already a town in the Bronze Age. Having survived a succession of occupants, Celts, Romans, Huns, Goths, Lombards and Avars, it will no doubt survive us Magyars too, forever young because always torn down. The First District: the Castle, Krisztinatown, and Tabán. The Second District: Watertown, and the Highway."[42] Is this really the language of fiction, or is it rather a human geographical, historical narrative, attempting to describe a locality in four dimensions, including the temporal, from a perspective far above the ordinary human being's spectrum? Clearly, this neutral, "academic" terminology is a stylistic device, which serves its own artistic purpose. For us, however, it is very useful. First, because in this description Ottlik, too, differentiates between *urbs* and *civitas*. Naturally, a description is better at dealing with physical objects, than with the fleeting, fluid ideas and emotions of human beings. On the other hand, an artistically formed narrative is a superb way of recreating longer sequences from the life of an individual or for that matter, of a community, in its complexity and variety, including internal conflicts and betrayals, as well as moments of dedicated loyalty, unbreakable heroism, and a rather surprising ritual: celebrating defeat—themes which play a major role in Ottlik's novel. In other words, while descriptions of physical reality cover the spatial aspects of the city, narration is able to recall the intellectual and emotional life of the people.

Ottlik worked on this unfinished text in the last decades of his life, in the final phase of the forty-five-year-long historical interval of communism in Hungary in the second half of the twentieth century. He allows a great deal of historical material to creep into his story, often in the form of childhood memories of his heroes. The hardware of the city, the *urbs,* plays a major role in the life of his protagonists. Take for example the huge canvas painted by the main protagonist, B.B., entitled Dawn (*Hajnal*), which was inspired by the light of the sun in the courtyard of the huge mansion house where the main hero and narrator of the novel was brought up. The writer is even more interested, of course, in the life of the *civitas,* the community of the "burghers" of Buda—although he never identifies his topic in as direct a fashion as Sándor Márai did in his drama of the burghers of *Kassa.*

Ottlik and Márai represent two different, but connected phases of "bourgeois literature" (*bürgerliche Literatur*) in Hungary. The term itself has a resonance in Continental, and particularly in German-speaking Central European cultures, where the problem of the bourgeois had a significance which was historical, social, and sometimes even political. Although the *bourgeois-citoyen* distinction employs a French terminological coupling, this foreign borrowing by the philosopher Hegel reveals a certain inferiority complex on the part of German-speaking cultures. The fact is, that politically, this region lagged behind, for example, British parliamentary developments, while culturally the French hegemony in the Age of Enlightenment inflicted a lasting wound on the self-confidence of the peoples of the region.

Even if German urban centers had enjoyed unparalleled success in the medieval period and played a major role in the international city alliances of the late medieval and early modern period, including such networks as the Hanseatic League, the political involvement of the middle classes, represented by the abstract term *citoyen,* would not be possible in the modern period for long. This was partly due to the fragmented nature of the territory of the Holy Roman Empire, and partly caused by the absolutist forms of governance that prevailed there. Although Johann Wolfgang von Goethe, the great icon of bourgeois literature, played a major political role in Weimar, this role was still within a feudally governed principality, and was far from something that could be labeled simply as civic responsibility for one's community, as was the case in more fortunate urban communities in Britain or France. While Goethe remained attached to the hierarchical court culture of Weimar, his friend, Schiller, was much influenced by the political slogans of the American and French freedom fighters, and fought his own war of liberty in his youth. His rebellious way of life approached more closely the ideology of the modern middle classes, as he earned his living to a large extent from his own work.

The works of both Goethe and Schiller could usually be found on the shelves of the private libraries of the middle classes in nineteenth- and early twentieth-century Central Europe, in the newly united Germany, Austria, and in Hungary, the junior member of the Austro-Hungarian Dual Monarchy. This is because culture, or as the Germans preferred to call it, *Bildung,* played a major role in the self-perception of members of this social stratum.[43] The *Bildungsbürger* was neither simply a bourgeois—in other words not necessarily a private investor, nor a capitalist entrepreneur in the economic sense of these terms—nor purely a citizen, in the sense of being a politically active participant of his or her community. While the *Bildungsbürgers* were typically well off, they were distinguished by a certain well-mannered behavior and style. The idea went back to the Renaissance humanist idea of education, as presented, for example, in Baldassare Castiglione's *The Book of the Courtier* (1528). According to the ideology of the middle classes, education did not mean only developing lexical knowledge, but was more concerned with developing style, taste, refinement, and posture, all of which were attributes of the particular form of self-presentation which set apart gentlemen and true ladies from the rest.[44]

Though the burghers were easily distinguishable from the higher classes, the nobility and the aristocracy, by their financial and economic power as well as by their specific ways of life, at the same time they tried to imitate the aristocracy as far as their manners were concerned, at least in Continental Europe. This is because culture was mainly associated with high culture, with the culture of the social and political elite. In the mid-seventeenth century, Molière wrote *The Bourgeois Gentleman* (*Le Bourgeois gentilhomme,* first performed in 1670), a caricature of the pretentious middle classes. His depiction of middle class aspirations continued to ring true in nineteenth- and early twentieth-century Central Europe. Hungary, with its longstanding ruling noble elite and underprivileged and underrepresented bourgeoisie was a case in point. To link this story back to our own story, I remember my grandmother, who was born before WWI, saying to me and my brother, when we were naughty: *úri gyerek ilyet nem csinál.* (A child of noble birth would not behave like that.) Certainly, in Hungary, the birth of the middle classes in modernity can be viewed as a result of the sinking of the lower nobility, first becoming members of what was called the gentry (called *dzsentri* in Hungarian), and later frequently ending up as either members of the civil service or of the professional classes. This process was not unproblematic, and it hindered the middle classes in Hungary from playing as decisive a role as their more fortunate contemporaries in Western societies. The bourgeoisie is a topic of much debate for both historical scholarship and public discussion in Germany and Central Europe, chiefly because of its misfortunes, and this discussion focuses on the historical responsibility of this class, in particular on its responsibility for Hitler's rise to power, and in general for the support enjoyed by totalitarian regimes in the region.[45] As we have seen, Ottlik claimed that the self-perception of the bourgeoisie does not allow the burgher to serve a totalitarian power, but, as is usually the case, there can be a distance here between ideology and reality. In connection with Ottlik, the question of moral corruption or political collaboration can be raised in connection with the fact that in 1985, at the end of the Communist era, he finally won the Kossuth Prize, a prestigious annual cultural award, and more generally, in view of his friendship with a key member of the political leadership and influential cultural ideologist of the communist party, György Aczél.

What are the major findings of these historical investigations and the key issues of the debates of urban history? One of them is how to properly identify the middle classes. A further point of interest is the decline of the traditional middle classes of the turn of the century, most of whom had a family background with a respectable heritage. Urban historians of Hungary are keen to distinguish a so-called historical Christian middle class, which crystallized from the lower gentry and noble spectrums of society. They tend to distinguish them first from the upwardly mobile new urban strata, members of whom were ethnically either German or Jewish, and for whom life in the cities was the only way to social success, and second from the earlier burgher communities of Hungarian cities, who were also mostly German speaking, and who established a certain way of life, and wanted to preserve it against the tide of history, threatened as they were by industrialization and new forms of globalizing capitalist venture.[46]

It is in this context that one should read the novel by Ottlik on Buda. The western side of the Danube was historically associated with what were called, in the interwar period, the Christian middle classes.[47] Ottlik was proud to belong to this group. *Buda*, the novel, was conceived, in the final decades of Communist rule, as a summary in hindsight of the best elements of the ideology of the Buda burghers, without its anti-semitic overtones, which were often attributed to the Christian middle class due to their anti-semitic subculture, which led to the Hungarian state's catastrophic involvement in the deportation of more than half a million Hungarian Jews—themselves Hungarian citizens—to the death camps of Nazi Germany.[48] Ottlik's own "ideology" was detached from that which was typical of his class, because Ottlik's conception of Bourgeois Hungary was not based on ethnic grounds, but was instead a cultural construct—*Bildungsbürgerlichkeit*. In another, shorter, work he identifies his ideal as "the other Hungary."⁴⁹ This other Hungary was united by a sepcific urban culture, and saturated by urban values.

This ideal homeland is demonstrated in the posthumously published *Buda*, written during the final decades of the Communist regime. One of the key notions of the ideology of Buda's historical middle classes that Ottlik presents is its culturally tuned opposition to all kinds of totalitarian regimes, including right-wing totalitarianism, in the form of the Nazi ideology, and left-wing totalitarianism, as experienced under the Soviet occupation. An emblematic presentation of this opposition can be found in an episode in a collection of short pieces by Ottlik, where he recalls a conversation he had with an editor of a newspaper during WWII. The editor asked him to keep on working for them, while Ottlik excused himself that his writings are inadequate for powerfully criticizing the Germans' and their supporters' military ambitions, as they are never connected to recent news. The editor claimed that those writings serve as *Wunderwaffe* (magic weapons) against the Nazis. The writer added that his objections to Nazism are not political, but "first: aesthetic, because it is hideous, second: what is connected to it: moral-ethical. And third: simply police-like: its disgusting crimes run against the legal system of our civilisation for two thousand years." To which the editor simply replies: "for four thousand."⁵⁰ As is clear from this episode, in Ottlik's prose the sense of civil, which is synonymous with German *bürgerlich* or French *bourgeois*, is the opposite of military, called in political terms oppressive or tyrannical.

It is also noteworthy that all forms of totalitarian rule and military activity can bring him, or his narrator in a bad mood. He returns to a scene in Buda, during the siege of Budapest in 1944–1945, where he seemed to oppose both foreign powers, both the earlier invaders, the Germans, and the liberators, the Russians.

> In the winter of '44–'45, during the siege of Buda I had to shovel the snow daily from the flat tin roof over my room. I was kidded a lot about this because someone noticed from down below that when I realized, up on the roof, that there were bullets zinging in a delicate pattern around my head, German ones from the west and Russian ones from the east, I sternly shook my shovel at both warring parties: "Hold your fire, you animals! And you too, you savages!"⁵¹

As the siege was destroying his city, he regarded both the German defenders and the Russian invaders as his enemies.⁵²

Yet, in spite of this characteristically civil attitude, Ottlik's attitude to combat is not straightforward. Although he seems to be peace-loving, his prose chimes with Hungarian historical memory, which records a number of heroic battles, albeit lost ones, in order to commemorate them. His take on this exercise of communal memory is that it is through these recollections are supposed to enable Hungarians to save their national integrity and identity in difficult political situations, against foreign invaders. Perhaps the most obvious example of such a lost battle is *Mohács*, which also plays an important role in another novel by Ottlik. In his posthumous novel, *Buda*, the revolution of 1956 (once again a lost battle, to be sure) has a similar function. This time, however, it is presented as the concrete experience of the highest peak of happiness:

> On the 23rd of October 1956 we were no longer in Monostor but right in the middle of the city. If you weren't there from the beginning to the end, then no amount of poetic imagination, revolutionary ardour, or even genius suffices to make you comprehend what happened on that day. I could not have imagined beforehand the nature of this happiness, the happiness of walking the streets of Budapest that day—for I had not known, hadn't the least notion, that such happiness could exist. It could not exist until you experienced it yourself, coming and going on those streets, on those cobblestones; it wasn't something that you could make up, either before or afterward.[53]

This description is remarkable, because of the heights of happiness associated with the revolution, and also because this revolution is closely associated with, indeed emerges together with this new experience of the city, in which one needs to stroll up and down to feel that happiness ("coming and going on those streets"). Ottlik relies here on a communal experience of the *civitas*, which was also closely attached to the urban environment, the *urbs*, as embodied by its cobblestones..

That Ottlik's interest, as a writer, is indeed in cities both as a community of its citizens and as a built environment of human life, is proven by the fact that beside *Buda* he wrote another novel "about" a city. His magnum opus is *School at the frontier*, about his childhood experiences in the military school of the minor frontier city of *Kőszeg*. Once again, the reader should be aware of the importance of the fact that this city is presented through the eyes of a child—which, as I tried to show, is an exceptionally sensitive perspective on the city.

Ottlik perceives Kőszeg, a small city close to Austria, quite differently from the experience of Buda, the capital city, described from the perspective of both the child and the adult (and even from the perspective of an old man). The name of the frontier city is not actually mentioned directly in the novel, and only mentioned once indirectly, but one can easily identify it. Two points can aid this identification. In the first one, Medve, a friend of the narrator, Bébé, both of them about ten years old, undergoes surgery, and has to stay in the special hospital room of the school for several days. It is there that he hears from old Mrs. Majvald about 1532, "of the Turkish siege of the little town." Now 1532 is the year of the famous siege of Kőszeg by the Turks, when a few hundred defenders (most of them the burghers of the city, and the peasants from the nearby villages) saved the city (more properly the castle, which was within the walls of the city) from capture by 300,000 trained Turkish soldiers. This is how this attack and defense is described in another episode, presenting the city as a role model of military heroism:

> In older times the small town had had a powerful little fort, and six years after the total defeat at Mohacs it was still holding back the Turks, and had finally repulsed them. Throughout a whole summer month two thousand men had defended it against impossible odds with preposterous courage and wise strategy because by then they already knew whom they had to deal with. The fortress and its defenders—citizens, burghers, peasants, soldiers—had withstood eighteen fierce attacks; the exhausted besiegers gave up after that and departed for ever.[54]

The paradoxical element of the defense is also crucial: that, being a frontier city on the Western side of the country, it was actually defending the border from an enemy attacking from the invaded homeland the neighboring country, Austria, from inside the kingdom, and had they not defended their city, the enemy could have left the country, to besiege Vienna. This is why the legend held that the defense was indeed paradoxical:

> There wouldn't have been any sense in it, had the defenders not realized that they possessed, besides the conquered fatherland, two other countries; the first one much smaller and the second much larger; so they set about defending them both: their own little home town and also the great continent to which they belonged and where shaved craniums weren't part and parcel of the common heritage.[55]

What Ottlik presents here is a three-layered model of political loyalty: the city represents the most intimate circle of belonging, the next step is one's homeland, the country, while Europe is the broadest basis of loyalty, the source of a common Christian cultural heritage. All three layers have specific functions in serving the citizen's sense of identity, and all can demand the citizens' loyalty, and oblige them in their own particular ways. This multi-layered account of human attachment to political and cultural communities will turn out to be crucial in the discussions below, and makes Ottlik's vantage point quite relevant four present purposes.

Let us once more return to an important notion: Ottlik's perception of belonging to the social stratum of the middle classes. As we have already seen, he had a very pronounced notion of civility, a term, which keeps returning in his novels. This term can be traced back through its French equivalent to the Latin term *civilis*, which means "relating to a society, pertaining to public life, relating to the civic order, befitting a citizen," and to the Latin term of *civis*, which means "townsman."[56] Once again, as we have seen, in Ottlik's private, fictional vocabulary, "civil" denotes the opposite of "military." It is therefore crucial to ask whether his perception of Kőszeg was as a military barracks, or if he also saw the civil side of the city, independently of the "siege mentality" he so aptly, and so emphatically, described in connection with its historical past. It is no accident that the young boys are so engaged with the military struggles of their country—they were brought up in that mentality at the military school. Yet when they have a chance to enter the civil city, they also appreciate its homeliness, its comfortable *Gemütlichkeit*, and their memories of their earliest childhood. These are recollections of the civil face of the city, in direct contrast with its fortress image, its *Burgstadt* identity. The description plays on Proust: his recollections and his vision of bourgeois identity. An afternoon visit by the boys to a distant relative of Medve in Kőszeg is recounted thus: "The gate of the ancient house, carpets, rooms, civilian world. The table set for tea: ham, sliced-up hard-boiled eggs, tea. Tea. Cream cakes, hardboiled eggs tasting of ham. Marble cake. Tea."[57] This is a whole conversation piece, in the style of eighteenth-century British, or later nineteenth-century painters of Paris: "I'd remembered in detail practically all the furnishings, the windows, the curtains, the furniture, the pictures, the cutlery. The conversation, and every moment of our visit there. We played mah-jong."[58] These small details of bourgeois life gain importance in opposition to the reality of the ordinary days of the military school. Yet a further level of interpretation can also be proposed. Published in 1959, this was nothing less than a protest against the brutality of communist rule, which was directing a full-scale attack against the bourgeois values of the Christian middle classes, including their particular local, national, and European attachments, in favor of the international unification of the proletariat. Ottlik's work was read by his audience in Communist Hungary as a secret rebellion against all totalitarian regimes—including Communist Hungary. This reception of his work is crucial, I suggest, even if it is tainted by his notorious collaboration with Aczél. The important thing is that in his narratives he remained loyal to the traditional Hungarian desire for independence—a notion which was present both in the mentality of the elite, of the petty nobility, and also in that of the middle classes (including Germans and Jews), and the petty bourgeoisie and the artisans, as well as in the national loyalty of the peasant community.

After introducing Ottlik as a representative of the *bürgerliche Literatur* of Hungary, let us turn now to Sándor Márai, another twentieth-century Hungarian language writer, much better known in the English-speaking world than Ottlik, and in fact most probably a master of Ottlik. Márai's is one of the most important voices of the surviving old, traditionally German-speaking burgher communities of upper Hungary, today's Slovakia, a part of which became fully Hungarian in spirit of their own accord in the second half of the nineteenth century, especially after the Settlement of 1867. His self-perception connects him in many ways to the ideal of the cultured burgher represented by Thomas Mann in the context of German urban culture. As we shall see at the end of the introduction, Mann himself is a player in our story as a dominant voice in the twentieth century of the European City as an intellectual to describe the world view of the middle classes. Márai represents the Central European pillar of this edifice. It is all the more precious, as in Central Europe this tradition was much less fully preserved, and his own case demonstrates how Hungarian nationalism became a determining factor in the self-perception of the burgher class of German cultural origin. Yet apparently Márai and the people he claimed to represent managed to live with this dual identity of being a burgher of German descent, loyal to Hungary and its culture, while also preserving their citizenship of Europe. This is how city, country, and continent were built upon each other in their mental landscape. The monument he builds for his hometown, *Kassa*, is characteristic of the general nature of the European City in this Central European context for this very reason.

Márai's hometown was Kassa (*Kosice*), a historical town in Upper Hungary, present-day Slovakia. As historians keep emphasizing, Kassa used to be one of the most important royal-free cities of the Kingdom of Hungary, under tavernical control, and even among them it was second to Buda.[59] Yet at some point its modern development was broken, and since then it has never been as dynamic as many of its rivals, and by the early twentieth century it had become a holdout of an earlier form of urban life.

The mentality of this holdout was one of the wellsprings of the literature of Sándor Márai,[60] one of the best known Hungarian writers of the interwar period. Márai was born into a leading burgher family of Kassa. As his monographer describes it, it was "a family belonging to the German (Saxon) bourgeoisie of what was Upper Hungary until 1920."[61] He left his hometown at a relatively young age, to make his name first in Budapest, and later in the cultural centers of contemporary Europe, first in Germany, later in Paris. He made a career in journalism in Germany then became acquainted with figures of the avantgarde elite in Paris, but came back to Hungary, to make his name as a writer of novels in his chosen first language, Hungarian. The image he built in his works was that of the bourgeois writer of Hungary, where the stress is on the adjective "bourgeois" (*polgári* in Hungarian, *bürgerlich* in German). This stamp is based on his autobiographic novel, *The Confessions of a Burgher* (*Egy polgár vallomásai*, 1934–1935).[62] In this opus magnum he recalls his memories of the town and his family's life in it, and gives an account of his own youthful rebellion against it and describes his later return to the value-system attached to the burghers and to his family, in particular.

As one of his interpreters claims: "The description of the life of the German bourgeoisie of Kassa is transformed by the narrator into an impressive vision of the social stability of Central Europe before the Great War" (of 1918).[63] This stability is claimed to come from the common culture of a middle class across the region and more generally, across Europe, which shared the same values, and guaranteed stability for the whole society.

The success of the story and of the image of the burgher provided in it encouraged the writer to take further steps in this direction. Márai's *The Burghers of Kassa* (*A kassai polgárok*, 1942) was his most successful play. The play, dedicated to the memory of his father, presents the medieval *urbs* and *civitas* of Kassa as it must have looked at the dawn of modernity. In 1941 he published another work, entitled *Kassai Őrjárat* (*Patrol in Kassa*), which is partly a continuation of his earlier *Napnyugati őrjárat* (*Patrol in the West*[64]), and partly a marvelous defense of the ancien régime of his hometown at the moment of the Nazi attack in WWII. His role in this respect resembles that of Thomas Mann, a writer who was a major role model for Márai. Márai, like Thomas Mann, relied on the traditional wisdom of the European burgher in opposition to both the Nazi and the Communist totalitarian political experiment. But while Mann started out as a conservative, and arrived at a mainstream liberal position by his middle age, Márai started out as an avantgarde rebel, and turned into something of a cultural conservative by the time his art fully developed.

In what follows, I would like to shed some light on the vision Márai presents of the burghers of Kassa, which brings to mind the title of Rodin's famous group statue, *The Burghers of Calais*. The heroes of the Burgher elite of Calais, who would sacrifice themselves for their town, are represented by the 1889 statue of Rodin not in the classical style, in antique robes, but more as common folk, with whom the onlookers should feel sympathy. Another work of art which might throw light on Márai's effort is T. S. Eliot's poetic drama, *Murder in the Cathedral*, first performed in 1935. It presents the murder of Archbishop Thomas Becket in Canterbury Cathedral in 1170. Ritual murder also crops up in Márai's drama, together with the presence of the community (*communitas*)—in Eliot's case it is the chorus, in Márai's case the great council of the city, who represent the whole community on the stage. The historical episode which is dramatized by Márai is the attack on Kassa by the Palatine Amade (in the drama he is referred to by the name of *Ómodé*) and his troops in 1311. This was launched in accordance with a decision of the king, who donated the city to the Palatine as a way to placate his opponent. The city does not accept the decision, however, and after a crucial debate in the town hall, they decide to defend themselves against the intruder.

Márai presents the crucial debate on stage, where the chief judge, the rector, the twelve members of the senate, the fifty members of the *Communitas*, the elected community, the *Fürmender* (something like the demagogue), the captain of the Quarter and the *Czeigwart* (prison guard) are also present. The process of decision-making which he presents on the stage is made easier by the determination of the main protagonist, Master John (*János Mester*), a stone mason, who is brave enough to say no to the king's order, because it endangers the legally secured independence of the city. As he argues: "Kassa should defend its law. It should defend its houses, children, women, professions. As long as there is a chance for a deal, defend it with words. But if the law is disregarded, it should defend itself in another way."[65] This means that it should defend itself with arms against injustice, no matter who the intruder is. Márai is careful to put the struggle of the city in a European context. Here is the argument of the Fürmender: "Wherever you look around in the world, the burgher demands and gets more rights. Here at home and in foreign countries too. Buda, Szeben, Brassó, Lubló and Lőcse are already free cities. The cities of the Rhine are already in an alliance. The Hansa is also alive, led by Lübeck. In Lombard, the city is the castle of the burgher. He has rights and power."[66]

Master John is an artisan, a stone mason, but he is presented as someone close to becoming an artist. A member of the external council, he is also member of the *Communitas*. By embodying these two identities (as a representative citizen of the city and as an artisan) he connects the political realm of the *civitas* (the community) with its physical context (the built environment). When John models a statue in his own workshop, he is an artisan. When he joins the leaders of the city to debate and make decisions, he is an active citizen of the city, in fact one of its earthly leaders. Márai makes this duality between the two dimensions of the city and its citizens very explicit at the beginning of the play, in a discussion between Master John and Albertus, a (somewhat anachronistic) writer. Master John defines the *city* as follows: "The city is stone and order. House and law. Cellar, chamber, and gravestone (. . .). The city is bastion and law. This is a deep order." His definition is answered by the writer in the following way: "The city is emotion and passion. Courtesy and doubt. Enthusiasm and greed. It is of stone, a lot of stone, and you are master of that. But it consists of men, too, a lot of men, locked up. And I am the master of how to deal with men."[67] It seems here that Márai is modeling Albertus as a self-representation, a self-portrait of the author within this wide urban panorama.

Márai, the author, deliberately puts the story on stage in a somewhat anachronistic fashion, while preserving many of the historical facts and details. His characters have a modern soul, they are buffeted by strong passions, and struggle with the fallible traits of their own individual characters. Throughout the drama, though, one feels Márai's admiration for the community as a whole, presented as a corporate body, moving together whenever there is a need to do so. Márai had such admiration for the communal whole because

Kassa, his hometown, played such a major role in Márai's self-perception, and also in his understanding of European culture and society. As he saw it, modern high culture is the offspring of medieval artisanship, while the *Bildungsbürger* is the descendant of the medieval burgher.

Certainly, this disproportionate emphasis on an idealized past of Kassa might be an effect of the author's leaving the city so young, and never returning to it (except as a visitor) in his whole life. This hometown-centric understanding of artists, and of European culture in general, is crucial for us. Local attachment can counterbalance both exaggerated forms of nationalism and an uprooted form of cosmopolitanism. Though himself a rebel against the rigid order of bourgeois society, Márai, the cosmopolitan writer, returns to the values developed in this specific way of life and system of interpersonal relationships in his fiction as well as in his diary. In his works based on cultural history, Márai abandons the earlier modernist, avantgarde agenda, even if he himself had been an early participant in that very development as a young journalist and artist in Berlin. He returns home in his art works.

Márai makes a significant allusion in his drama. One of his protagonists, the burgher Jacob, a goldsmith, also had a house in Verona, which hosted Dante when Cangrande della Scala, prince of Verona and Vicenza, invited the poet to Verona. In fact, burgher Jacob explicitly refers to Dante's *De Monarchia*, thus revealing that the brave fight of the burghers of Kassa against the intruders, and even against the unjust decision of the king (who, by the way, after their victory accepted the terms and conditions of the freedom of the city the burghers demanded) was based on firm political philosophical foundations, even if these foundations were more tradition-based than modern liberal ideology would otherwise presuppose.

An important part of this urban tradition is its Christian component. While in most histories of the early modern city the city is presented as engaged in fighting the Church for control over the citizen body and its resources, Márai returns to the religious foundations of urban life in the medieval cities of Europe. When he presents the council hall his description emphasizes that behind the stage we overlook the main square of the city, with the Saint Michael Chapel and the old Elizabeth Church.[68] In other words, the operations of the city council and the *communitas* take place under a divine guardianship. It is, therefore, all the more dramatic when the burghers see their cathedral in flames. The *Fürmender* gives voice to their metaphysical horror: "The city's burning and the church is burning. (Everyone kneels down.) Merciful God, who judges over the living and the dead, look down on us, and judge us. We are puppets in your hands and sinners. Mother of God, you see our sins. Forgive the living and the dead."[69] This horror stems from the fact that the burning church is a meaningful sign, nothing less than a message of God. This episode is meant to reveal the metaphysical foundation of the urban *Communitas* in the medieval city: the community is held together by the divine will. This is not simply true of the cities of the Christian Middle Ages, it is also true of those of classical antiquity and even of the early modern, post-Reformation European towns. In all of these towns individuals who turn against the community, or who simply disregard their duty to the city, should expect the punishment of God. On the other hand, when Master John ritually murders the palatine to prevent his take-over of the city, and in so doing defends the autonomy of the city, the citizen body offers him their full support, and the royal investigation was forced to conclude that sentencing him would be interpreted as a declaration of war against the whole urban community. Márai's drama of medieval Kassa is a powerful illustration of the strength of the metaphysical or spiritual bonds which can keep the physical body of a European city together, giving it the potential to act as a corporate body.

THE CITY IN TRAVELOGS: MÁRTON SZEPSI CSOMBOR

If an important source of the power of the medieval city was the cohesion provided by its metaphysical foundation, the role Protestantism played in the shift in the character of the early modern European city cannot be neglected. Certainly, the most influential account of the impact of Protestantism on the European city is to be found in Max Weber's work on Protestant ethics. Yet his account is arguably greatly influenced by further developments, including classical German idealism, Nietzsche, and the politics of his own time. Although I will deal with Weber later, for the present purposes it is perhaps enough to look at early modern urban reality with the help of a contemporary, in order to get closer to the actual mentality of the time. In what follows, I will try to decipher some relevant ideas of a Hungarian travel journal from the early seventeenth century.

Márton Szepsi Csombor, a would-be teacher in the city of Kassa, published an account of his travel experiences from 1616–1618, including the one-and-a-half-year period of study in Danzig, shortly after he arrived home. His travelog was published in the first half of 1620. It belongs to the contemporary genre of *ars apodemica*, which is defined as a "comprehensive descriptions of cities, countries, polities and peoples based on autopsy," that is to say on direct experience.[70] This genre was to become vital in an age of global discoveries, but even within Europe it played a crucial role, as an *ancilla* of the new science based on Cartesian-Baconean foundations. Travel literature, which was claimed to be "more prominent in the recently reformed countries"[71] is a source of new knowledge and also a form of self-education, both for its author and, in a different way, also for its readers. Crucial figures of the culture of the age, including Montaigne and Descartes, were connected to this genre: "From Montaigne in the 1580s to Descartes in the 1630s, the impact of travel and travel literature was directly related to epistemological questions concerning all kinds of scientific pursuit."[72] They are connected to the genre partly by their accounts of their own travel experiences, but also because they represent characteristic positions within the new field of epistemology.

Travel literature became a typical genre of the new ways to learn, in other words to collect experience through direct contact with the world. For urban explorers the booming or potentially developing cities of Europe served as operating theaters. They had a specific professional literature to rely on. Theodor Zwinger's *Methodus Apodemica,* for example, "was itself conceived as an aid to an ambitious encyclopaedic project, the Theatrum umanae vitae."[73] Regarding this author, we learn that

> (w)ith the *Methodus Apodemica* (1577) of the Basle philosopher and physician Theodor Zwinger travelling becomes an ars of great heuristic and formative value. Indeed, Zwinger's book provides a modern method of analysis that predates the Scientific Revolution of the Seventeenth Century. For the first time, the city is studied as political space. The city is the center of ethical, political, and civic values and the main arena of the human experience in history.[74]

Philosophers themselves took a keen interest in the genre. "Francis Bacon's endorsement of travel for the sake of the universal light of knowledge, in his posthumous scientific utopia New Atlantis (. . .) identifies well the strategic place that travel literature had come to occupy in the culture of early seventeenth-century Europe."[75] Interestingly, the classics of the period, including Turler, Zwinger, and Pyrckmair, were produced by a small circle of scholars, some of whom studied at the University of Padua, and who were associated with publishing centers like Basel.[76]

A painter who illustrates the relevance of knowledge of cities in the early modern age is, of course, Vermeer, whose love of maps mirrors the general interest of the age in geography and spatial orientation in general. It is worth recalling his pair of scientists.[77] The geographer is an expert on the earth, the astronomer an expert on the heavens. By putting these two figures side by side, Vermeer stresses the connection between the two professions, both of which are engaged in the description of privately experienced data, of the land and of the sky, respectively. Vermeer also gives very important hints of the knowledge of cities, learning from the geographer, but also taking a step beyond him, which is made possible by the specific methodology of art. In his *The view of Delft* he manages to represent the whole city in one single picture, transcending the limitations of a two-dimensional canvas to reconstruct a three-dimensional object. Historians revealed the fact that his representation of the city is not always strictly mimetic, as he replaces certain motives, and creates his own, specific composition, in order to reflect the essence of the city, instead of its "surface" representation. In his *The Allegory of Painting*, as in a number of further paintings, he presents a map of Holland, together with small vedutas framing the map of the country, thus making a comparison between the sort of depiction a map can provide of a city (a perpendicular view from above) and that of a painting (offering a side view, with the horizon somewhere in the middle of the pictorial space).[78] As Svetlana Alpers emphasizes, Vermeer's art is an outstanding example of the early modern Dutch effort to render a faithful description of the world in order to tackle the challenges it presents, specifically those facing the celebrities of its art market, which flourished especially in the booming cities of its divided territory.

It is obvious that travelers were dependent on the knowledge of the cartographer. As a traveler, Márton Szepsi Csombor would have consulted, or was aware at least of the maps and atlases of Mercator, Honter, Münster, and Braun-Hogenberg.[79] It is also important, however, to see from the opposite perspective: geographers were themselves dependent on travelers, or became travelers themselves. Both of these aspects prove the significance of the connection between the activities of both "professional" travelers and professional geographers. The key here, I would argue, is the term *decriptio*: both of them strived to put what they saw down on paper: the landscape, and more particularly, the human settlements they visited. As we have seen, Svetlana Alpers, the influential monographer of a specific understanding of Golden Age Dutch painting, also dealt specifically with Vermeer. Considering Vermeer's *The Art of Painting*, she posed the question: "If this map is presented like a painting, to what notion of painting does it correspond?" and she goes on to answer her own question: "Vermeer suggests an answer to this question in the form of the word *Descriptio* prominently written on the upper border of the map just where it extends to the right of the chandelier over the easel."[80] She explains the use of the term *descriptio* thus: "This was one of the most common terms used to designate the mapping enterprise. Mapmakers or publishers were referred to as 'world describers' and their maps or atlases as the world described."[81] According to its theoretician, then, early modern travel literature is not simply a "discovery of the world" (Jacob Burckhardt), but "the discovery of how to describe the world."[82]

It is perhaps not so surprising that *descriptio* is a term which returns in the title of Szepsi Csombor's work. It is entitled "A brief account (le irása) of the various things (külömb külömb féle dolgoknak) seen and heard," where the Hungarian term *leiras* means *descriptio*, while the direct visual and audio experience reminds us of the observations of the natural scientist and of the direct sensual enjoyment of the art connoisseur. In this respect, the travelog serves as the research notes and diaries of the researcher, keeping track of the experiments, and the notes of the art critic, preparing a critical account of the artist's work.[83] This second parallel of the travelog with the critical reception of a work of art is reinforced by a further point of the title: by the reference to the "delight" and "benefit" of the reader, both of which terms come from the terms *dulce et utile* in Horace's *Ars Poetica*. Csombor, too, relies on "the legitimation of autopsy," the direct sensual enjoyment of works of art.[84] According to Stagl, Szepsi Csombor's approach to description is indeed rooted in the *ars apodemica*, and while he does not seem to be aware of Zwinger, he draws on Turler and Pyrckmair, early theoreticians of the genre. As he sees it, though, the direct influence comes "from the rules laid down for 'descriptio singularis' by his master Keckermann."[85]

An illustrative example can be found in his travelog, the *Europica varietas*: "So much for the general description (derék le irása) of Poland; I will now proceed to the road by which I went, and as it is revealed will set before the reader (az Oluasonak szeme eleiben vetem) the towns, villages and castles through which I passed, together with the things to be seen in them (bennek látot) and events which happened there."[86] The concept of general description is paired here with the category of the *descriptio singularis*. Szepsi Csombor describes his own methodology as to "set before the reader" (just like a painter would do) "things to be seen" in "towns, villages and castles." He even makes the distinction between describing stable, unmoving things, such as architectural ensembles, and dramatic changes (i.e., the description of events). This conceptual distinction (between the description of stable and changing things) can be interpreted to refer to the *civitas* and *urbs* dimension of cities. That Szepsi aimed at offering his readers a real picture of the world, just like the scientist or the painter does, is quite easy to understand. He seeks not only to present a true reflection, but also tries to color his description, to enliven it. The liveliness of the description comes from the text's literary qualities; the notes he takes are able to express the writer's first reactions to the visual experiences. In this respect, he approaches the writer of fiction, and his Latin didactic poems show that he even harbored ambitions of becoming a humanist poet.

Szepsi Csombor never misses an occasion to express his delight about the aesthetic qualities of buildings or other man-made urban details. Take for example the following quote:

> Vinnheim is a costly, fine (drága szép) town, which has strong stone walls, wide, spacious streets, fine and shining (szép fényes) buildings, large churches, and at this end a fine (szép) fountain; On the top stands a big iron statue of a German, armed, and gilded all over; . . . a wonder to behold (czudara melto).[87]

At one point he defines his task on his journey as "to foster, increase and delight my slender intellect (vékony elmémet . . . éltetni, öregbiteni, gyönyörködtetni) with the sight and hearing of the marvels of Nature in the countryside and the works of men in the towns."[88] This comparison between observing nature and observing man-made towns recalls the medieval concept of reading the book of nature. Szepsi Csombor is not far from identifying his constant and diligent work of observation with a form of town-reading: what he provides in his description is a recording, criticism, and interpretation of the sights he encounters, mostly of architectural, urban phenomena. No doubt this is why the literary historian regards this travelog as being equivalent to the descriptions (*ekphrasis*) of art historians: "the first and for a long time only Hungarian language description of some of the outstanding products of European architecture."[89]

The three-dimensional placement of the major public buildings within the internal, wall-defended space of European cities, is, indeed, readable for a traveler in two senses of the word. First, in the sense that it presents easily identifiable objects: church, council house, castle, marketplace, hospital, school, and so on. But the readability also means that these objects operate like signs: they tell us a lot about the general features of the specific community of the inhabitants as well as of the local political traditions and the social composition of the particular city. Even the traditional types of regime in a given settlement can sometimes be read from the spatial political geography. Consider the description by Szepsi Csombor of Emden.[90] Not much is shared with the reader but it provides a very succinct account of the politico-economical and even religious features of the city. The interesting thing about it is, of course, that Emden was the city where the political philosopher Johannes Althusius took the lead, both in the city's secular and ecclesiastic power. He succeeded in calming down the passions that had been enflamed there after an episode of civil unrest at the turn of the sixteenth century, and, capitalizing on the Spanish-Dutch war, he turned the city into a booming commercial center.

The method of "reading" the spatial allocations of a city made it possible, also, to use the travelog in an exercise of comparative urban studies. The space occupied by a city, and the form it took, rendered its power relations easily recognizable. These data can be studied with a comparative method, a legitimate exercise as European-wide competition between cities had already emerged by this time. Szepsi Csombor, coming from a thriving Hungarian-German city of the Upper Hungarian region, itself in a somewhat disadvantageous part of Europe, of course, used his hometown as the standard to which he could compare other cities, for example in a spatial sense. It is instructive the way in which he conducts this comparative exercise in his recollection of his memories of Paris, which was already an exceptionally powerful center of Europe, when the king, Louis XIII took over from his mother Marie de Medici, who had ruled the country as regent when the king was still a minor. The author seems to be aware of the delicate political situation within the royal family, as one can see in the text describing the gate erected by the young king, to commemorate his assassinated father, "Henricus IV," and his mother—whom he exiled in 1617. In other words, he uses a description of an architectural element to allude to the internal politics of the royal family.

As well as drawing attention to the indirect political commentary encoded in his architectural descriptions, let us now consider an example of their comparative aspect. This is how Szepsi Csombor compares the architectural hardware of the French Royal court in Paris, the Louvre to his hometown, Kassa, spatially: "This court is all of dressed stone and it occupies as much space as half of the walled town of Kassa; it . . . is being enlarged by thirty fathoms in length."[91] The point he is making is the shocking difference in scale, even if it is somewhat exaggerated, between the French royal city and a Central European city.

Elsewhere he makes another spatial comparison, this time between an arsenal of Paris and the whole castle of Szatmár: "one armoury alone occupies as much space as the whole castle of Szatmár with all its wall."[92] It is well known that the French absolutist state always made every effort to express with its public architecture the grandeur and glory of the (king of the) state. Szepsi Csombor's spatial comparisons simply decode these spatial messages in the natural language of the descriptions of the travel journal. From the perspective of a general theory of the European city, the example of Paris, and its description by Szepsi Csombor is telling. It proves that an early modern city's fate has been always greatly determined by its connections with the court. Royal seats, such as Paris or Buda, had a privileged position compared to all other kinds of cities. The narrative's function is to reveal this major factor in a city's fate. Szepsi Csombor records, for example, the Latin text of an inscription which refers to the king in two different functions, as the ruler of a whole country, or as the lord of a city: "Henri III, Most Christian King of France and Navarre, born for the common good . . . by which he has merited the title of creator anew of the city (*urbis restitutor*) no less than that of father of the country (*pater patriae*)."[93]

The Protestant Szepsi Csombor is surprisingly ready to admire the greatness of the capital of a Catholic country, where not long earlier during the St Bartholomew's Day massacre of 1572, scores of Protestants were killed.[94] However, his confessional priorities are, of course, with Protestant urban centers. Take the example of Amsterdam and Danzig. But before that let me add one more word about another Catholic Royal seat, Krakkó (as Kraków is called in Hungarian), capital of the Polish kings. Szepsi Csombor is generous with his praise of the buildings. He is more critical of the morals of the people of the city, and one has the suspicion, that this impression of his must have been colored by a prejudice against Catholics on his part. He writes, for example, "I do not believe that the life of lechery enjoyed greater freedom in Sodom and Gomorrah than in Krakkó," adding that "The university (Schola) is not a house of moral practice," and, one suspects, somewhat exaggerating: "They kill one another freely in the market-place."[95] In other words, to an attentive observer the *urbs* aspect does not necessarily harmonize with the *civitas* aspect: the external surface does not chime with the internal essence of the city.

If the author is so critical about the *civitas* of Kraków, how does he paint the life of Protestant urban centers, such as Danzig and Amsterdam? Danzig held a special place in Szepsi Csombor's affections, as he spent most of his time abroad here, studying at the famous school of the city for one and a half years. His description of the public buildings of the city is quite reserved and modest. He describes the architecture of "the metropolis of Prussia" in the following simple words: "It has gained its fame and reputation . . .by its surprising buildings and its wealth."[96] He calls it the "principal emporium (place for buying and selling goods that are brought by sea)" and "the mistress of the whole country."[97] This stress on commerce rather than beauty is not a criticism on his part, although references to wealth keep recurring in the long description of the city. He seems to pay tribute to its urban prosperity, even if he is somewhat critical of the manners of the inhabitants. Unlike any cities of the Hungarian Kingdom, Danzig is "a great power on the sea, and the fishermen there make large profits,"[98] an insight which is quite remarkable from someone from the mainland.

From the point of view of deciphering urban ideology, it is valuable that the author frequently records the inscriptions on the buildings. For example, on a gateway he reads: "These three things are most desirable of all for the state (*Civitati*): Peace (*Pax*), Concord (*Concordia*) and Freedom (*Libertas*)."[99] This is, of course, a reference to three concepts which played a truly crucial role in early modern urban ideology. Another inscription was recorded by the author at a well-appointed garden: "Our fathers laid in store for us, and we for our posterity."[100] This is, once again, a crucial quote, for it shows the historical dimension of the urban community, underscoring the conservative element of the urban ideology. A link connects the generations of a *civitas*, just like in families, which bestows responsibility on the shoulders of the present generation, saving the family treasures for the next generation.

Danzig, as these inscriptions and Szepsi Csombor's description of its internal and external character traits prove, taught the author some important lessons. Another city which taught Szepsi Csombor much was Amsterdam, although he was not uncritical of it. He regards that city as "the greatest emporium in the world except for Lisibona, Venice, Quinzai and Anverpia."[101] Emporium, as we have seen from his description of Danzig, means commercial center for Szepsi Csombor, and he seems to attribute a crucial value to it, as a sign of the significance of the settlement in the emerging European commercial network, as he finds it in the early seventeenth century. The adjectives he most frequently applies to the urban environment in Amsterdam are handsome and clean. He specifically refers to its cultural and educational institutions, the "fine schools and famous book-printers." Among the public buildings, as he calls them, he lists "churches, the Arsenal, the council House, the hospitals and the *Zuchthaus*."[102] He provides a more detailed description of two churches, and records the inscription above the door of the Council House, which translates as: "Hear the other side too," a quotation from Seneca.[103] This inscription illustrates that the Council house also serves as the local forum of jurisdiction. Yet he seems to be shocked by another function of the council: that they erected a *Zuchthaus* for those "depraved boyes" who are causing public outcry. They are brought here, in order that "their evil ways may in time be curbed."[104] He feels horrified when he reads above the gate the following inscription in Latin as part of a carved emblem: "It is the function of virtue (*virtutis*) to tame those things of which all men are afraid."[105] The level of detail of his description of the workings of the *domus disciplinaris* reflects the author's sense of horror at its actual operation. Szepsi Csombor does not hide the shock he feels about the disciplinary mechanisms of the early modern city, a topic which has been famously analyzed by Foucault. Szepsi Csombor finds it—with good reason—an inhumane practice, but beside the inhumanity of the practice he seems to be struck also by the efficiency with which the public interest has been served by the council. The same is true, *mutatis mutandis*, of the commercial (and imperial) expeditions of the Dutch around the globe, which he mentions only in passing, and somewhat tentatively: "This town is famous for its many exploits, but in particular for three voyages."[106] His own attitude toward the local inhabitants and their practices is a mixture of appreciation for northern Protestant efficiency and shock at the shameless use of power and knowledge in the interests of the urban community and of its wealthy entrepreneurs. Coming from a more peripheral region of Europe, Szepsi Csombor's travel account reconstructs the author's emotionally charged impressions of his first-hand experiences of a rising capitalist commercial order, with the attendant brutality and concept of pure cost efficiency. He admires the wealth and the communal wisdom of the cities, while keeping a critical distance from some of the practices he witnessed. His description is proof that the genre of the travelog could be utilized to investigate the urban phenomenon from a comparative perspective, considering both the past of a city and its prospects for the future.

THE VISUAL REPRESENTATION OF
THE *CIVITAS*: REMBRANDT

If the travelog is a literary genre which is suited to representing first-hand observations of the urban reality of early modern Europe, with the author's reflections on these experiences, another genre, or rather art form, can do this even more successfully, as far as the visual aspects are concerned. This medium is fine art, and in particular, oil painting, which had become fashionable in early modern Holland. One of its greatest and best known masters was Rembrandt. An important part of his oeuvre was group portraits of the members' local communities, especially of guilds he painted for wealthy groups of clients. If one painting by Rembrandt expresses Dutch perceptions of the urban community in this period, it is his famous composition entitled *The Night Watch*.[107]

The painting was commissioned by the *Kloveniersdoelen* Civic Guard of Amsterdam, the oldest guard to use a special type of musket, the *arquebus*, to defend the peace of the city. They ordered the huge canvas for the great hall of their newly built building. This *schutterij* (civic guard) was the oldest of the three civic guards of Amsterdam, and dated back to the Middle Ages. Its primary function was to defend the city from external attack. These volunteer armed bodies of civic guards "were basically a volunteer force that sought to protect their towns and cities, showing a civic devotion to the place where many of them were born and raised."[108] In 1580, on the orders of William of Orange, this Amsterdam guild was reorganized to enable it to participate in the patriotic war against the Spanish known as the Eighty Years War. The rearranged guards were led by officers from the elite of the city: "The officers of the militia companies were usually closely related to members of the city government."[109] In fact it is known that the leader of this group, Captain Banning Cocq, "captain of one of six subdivisions of the Amsterdam Militia Company of Musketeers in 1642," "was elected burgomaster of Amsterdam, a position he held on and off until his death in 1655."[110]

By the end of the long war, this civic guard had more or less served its purpose, yet they preserved their company as a social grouping. The elegant building served as both a place of public gathering and also as a reception hall. It was here that the city welcomed Marie de Medici in 1638, the former regent of France, mentioned in connection with the travel journal of Szepsi Csombor above.

Rembrandt's huge painting records a moment before the group draws up in military formation to start its parade around the city. The large format of the canvas allows the artist to present the details of the firearms of the group, including the ways they were prepared for the actual watch. One of them is shown at the moment of firing his gun. There is no sign of fear or worry on the faces of the group, however. The leaders are represented in very elegant costumes, which is proof of their high social standing, and this suggests that this is more of a celebration than an actual military operation. As the title of a recent exhibition in Washington, "Civic Pride" underlines, Rembrandt's painting was meant to pay tribute to the public spirit and pride of the local patricians.[111]

In spite of its representative function, the scene is evidence that the city took seriously its duty of defending the citizen body from external threat. The sheer number of firearms in the picture suggests that the city spent a lot of money on defense. As we have seen, Szepsi Csombor noted that the arsenal was one of the main public buildings of the town. That self-defense was a key to the ideology of the city is proven by the fact that in the eighteenth century Rembrandt's huge canvas was cut to size in order fit it into the hall of the Council House where it was going to be exhibited, in order to send the required ideological message to those who enter the hall. The particular attention paid to details by the painter is connected with the aim of the painting, which was—besides expressing "power, glory, individual expression, action and prominence"[112]—to show "the traditions and rights" of the guard, as a corporate identity.[113] It reminded the viewers "of their duties and roles" and it was meant to "inspire future generations to also serve the community."[114]

In a series of writings Maartin Prak explained the specific nature of the urban citizenry of Dutch cities of the Golden Age. As we shall see below, his explanations owed something to those of Johan Huizinga, as far as the interpretation of the character and self-perception of the bourgeoisie of the age was concerned. Prak attributes a special relevance and social function to the civil militia in the Dutch context in the early modern period. Basically, they claimed to be, and were generally regarded as "representatives of the citizen community," or as the "embodiment of the community."[115] This social standing was mirrored by the fact that they were "commonly known as the *burgers*, a word that in Dutch denotes citizens as well as members of the middle class."[116]

In Leiden, for example, a dual system of neighborhood communities was in place: one of the functions of official wards was "in the registration of aliens and the creation of tax registers," while the "gebuurten, which consisted of no more than a block of houses most of the time, mainly served purposes of sociability."[117] In all of these variants, the local civil bodies had the mandate, besides keeping order in the streets, to keep a vigilant eye on whether everyone was complying with the rules of local governance. Most of the time, when citizens had complaints about the way power was exercised in early modern Dutch cities, you will find the militia among those grumbling and putting forward programs of reform, which usually meant nothing more than a return to the original constitution of the community. In other words, as corporate embodiments of their communities, the civil militia groups were expected to be actively involved in public debates about the proper procedure for governing their city, and to put it back on track when it became corrupted.

THE BOURGEOIS WAY OF LIFE AS CULTURE: JOHAN HUIZINGA

While Prak's work is crucial in recent discussions of local self-governance in early modern Dutch cities, he has a constant point of reference: the work of Johan Huizinga. In his account of seventeenth-century Dutch culture, Johan Huizinga established a discourse on the role of civil society in early modern Dutch life.[118] As he saw it, the Dutch tend to cling, in a conservative manner, to two old forms of socializing and culture, namely to the institutions of the shooting union and bodies known as chambers of rhetoric. Huizinga reconstructed these two typical forms of public life, where different strata of society could meet and enjoy themselves, the upwardly mobile patricians alongside the well-to-do burghers, which preserved a certain homogeneity of culture, divided in other countries, where aristocrats had a special access to culture, while others were left out of its enjoyment, for example, in France. Spiritual life in Holland only showed traces of such aristocratic features, while everyday culture preserved a predominantly bourgeois tone. The shooting company played a significant role in the preservation of bourgeois character of Dutch culture.

Johan Huizinga is the classic historian, making sense of twentieth-century Dutch identity while referring to seventeenth-century Dutch culture. His *Dutch Civilisation in the Seventeenth Century* was published in 1941. While it was certainly a courageous political statement against the military aggression of Hitler's Germany, this does not detract from its relevance and interest for our topic. The work has a more general meaning, which resonated in the imagination of generations of Dutch readers, who read the text as a classic statement of Dutch identity. As Maarten Prak, a later interpreter of that same Dutch bourgeois identity puts it: "Johan Huizinga remains Holland's most famous historian" and his work "remains the single most famous text on this particular episode in Dutch history."[119] The special relevance of this book is that it focuses on a single element of Dutch life, its bourgeois character. Prak does not disagree with this characterization, but proposes a different understanding of the term. For Huizinga, "'bourgeois' was first and foremost a lifestyle, and most likely the lifestyle that he had experienced first-hand himself, as a member of the Dutch upper middle class."[120] This bourgeois way of life was contrasted with the picture of the aristocracy he presented in his famous opus magnum, *The Autumn of the Middle Ages*. Prak's own alternative interpretation "associates 'bourgeois' with civil society and its institutions, and especially urban citizenship."[121]

It is worth taking a closer look at both of these interpretations of the bourgeois character of Dutch life, in order to show the continuity between them, rather than their differences. Huizinga uses the evidence of geography to deduce the very early historical development of small towns all over the territory of the would-be Netherlands. Because of the fragmented nature of the land, due to the rivers and channels which dismembered it, each locality had to rely on its own resources, which led to their circumscribed, but very resolute autonomy. This natural factor transformed the territory into a network of smaller and larger cities by the end of the Middle Ages, connecting them with each other, but not allowing centralized powers to emerge and gain control of larger territories. The cities were dominated by merchants, who formed an exceptionally large proportion of society, and these cities were distributed all over the country uniformly. Huizinga does not attribute specific importance to either the spiritual movement of the Reformation, or the economic innovation called capitalism, which other narratives gave great weight to. According to Huizinga, neither of these historical phenomena was able to make major transformations to Dutch society. Instead, he reconstructs the golden age of Dutch society, when it regained its independence from Spain, as being a founded upon conservative set of arrangements, which had grown organically from the medieval roots of town life.

Accepting that merchants were unusually prevalent in Dutch society, Huizinga's main line of enquiry was into the specific way of life that he pursued. One of the key characteristics of merchant life in Dutch cities was that the highest, patrician level of this society supplied the personnel for the magistracies of the cities. The takeover of local governance by this stratum—while still preserving its place in commercial, economic life—was a gradual process. Due to this slow historical growth, the merchant class was able to develop the skills necessary to run whole cities in cooperation, and with the necessary efficiency. Their success led to the birth of a new type of local leadership, which became known as regents in the early modern Dutch context, or *vroescip ende rycheit* (urban magistrates and the elite). Huizinga's description of a typical member of this urban leadership stresses that he (they were almost exclusively males) had a relatively high standard of erudition, partly gained in the chambers of rhetoric, partly in the schools of the *devotio moderna*. In other words, they were an elite based on economic wealth, but also on cultural achievements and social prestige. Young members of the prestigious bourgeois families tended to study for a law degree in Leiden, before embarking on a grand tour to France or Italy. When they arrived back home, they could be proud of their education and European experience, and built nice houses in the new districts of the towns, commissioned and collected paintings, defended and sponsored poetry, and supported the Church and science. In other words, this stratum became a real urban aristocracy of the middle classes, which consumed and invigorated public culture, while defending its own, and its groups' corporate longstanding traditions and interests.

As noted previously, collecting paintings, was a typical pastime of the Dutch urban middle class elite, and Huizinga's description of Rembrandt is worth mentioning in this regard. While the historian criticizes the high-flying ambitions of the painter, his ideal of baroque monumentality, he praises the painter when he paints as representative of his people and his country. Holland can be understood through Rembrandt, claims Huizinga, when he paints the sober orderliness of its daily life. Simplicity, modesty, self-restraint, together with an exceptional sensibility and warmth: these are the values of the painter as well as of the way of thinking of the bourgeois middle classes who governed the cities.

While Huizinga's account of the Golden Age is based on his understanding of the bourgeois character of early modern Holland as a cultural phenomenon, Maarten Prak is more interested in the political dimension of the way of life of the Dutch bourgeoisie. While he, too, starts out from the fragmented territories of the cities, of which the country consisted, in his book *The Dutch Republic of the Seventeenth Century* he keeps emphasizing the advantages of urban autonomy, self-governance, and a custom of communication which created forums for public debate within and among the cities.[122] "The Republic was a league of cities and provinces, each of which derived its identity from its political independence," he claims, but also adds that "(t)he Republic, lacking both an adequate central government and a well-oiled bureaucracy, could, however, boast reasonably efficient local authorities. The proximity of these local authorities to those they ruled meant that people usually had faith in the government," while such "faith was often lacking in other countries."[123]

In the following section I will argue, albeit necessarily in condensed form, that the Dutch bourgeois is to be understood both as he was described by Prak, as an active civic agent, blessed with the political virtues of prudence, justice, and courage, in the service of his city, even when he is currently ruling it, and as presented by Huizinga—a cultured, fully developed personality, whose industry, discipline, civility, self-restraint, and other civil virtues all played a major role in the birth of a Golden Age in the Dutch cities and provinces. In other words, the analyses developed by Huizinga and Prak of the Dutch burgher are not opposites of each other, but rather two complementary sides of the bourgeois character. If the bourgeois elite of early modern Holland had something to teach Europe, it is this duality of the bourgeois character, composed of civic (political and military) as well as civil (economic and moral) virtues. The practical political philosophy of the European city, which may be regarded as the ideal type of urban republicanism, required both of these dimensions of the character of the bourgeois.

THE TRADITION OF THE GERMAN BÜRGER: THOMAS MANN AND MAX WEBER

If Prak was able to convincingly argue that the fragmented nature of the administrative structure of the country actually served to nurture a lively and effective form of urban republicanism, the same can surely be said of the medieval German lands, which were not united in a centralized state until the end of the second third of the nineteenth century. Until then, the remnants of the Holy Roman Empire served as a hotbed of city autonomies, which fostered a culture of urban citizenry, and a rather specific *Weltanschauung*, which drove that corporate body, as well as offering to each of its members a personal identity and strategy of life. In the final section of this first chapter, I would like to present two late examples of German *Bürgerlichkeit*: that of the writer Thomas Mann, and that of the eminent social scientist, Max Weber. As I see them, the two belonged to a very similar social milieu, and their work in fiction and in social science was an expression of a specific package of traditional erudition, which formed the middle class mentality of the German Bürger from the medieval to the modern era.

The most obvious heir of the *Bürger* tradition in German culture is Thomas Mann. This is because he did not hide his traditional identity. On the contrary, he built his professional success on this very identity. His first great success, the *Buddenbrooks* (1901), a multi-generational novel of a north German merchant family, living in the same Lübeck where Mann was brought up, represented this genre of *bürgerliche* literature. In a later recollection of the process of writing this first novel, Mann confessed: "In having rendered a picture of Hanseatic life in the nineteenth century. . . . I not only had traced the history of my own family but had rendered an aspect of the psychological history of the German bourgeoisie in general."[124] This essay, which claimed to recall his hometown's specific intellectual life (in the German original *geistige Lebensform*), connected the medieval forerunners of the urban middle classes and their later descendants. Interestingly, his claim was not only that his family's history represented the German bourgeoisie in general, but also that it embodied a European ideal type, the European burgher.

Another important element of Mann's story is that it connects this long family history with a decline of the values of this social type. In this respect, Mann's novel was typical of the decline literature of the early twentieth century, and showed that even if a burgher mentality was still alive in him, he viewed the prospects of his kind rather pessimistically. Mann also pointed out the fact that in times of crisis the individual tends to trace back his inheritance, his own tradition, in order to strengthen his identity. "We search in books," I wrote at the time, "(for) the oldest spiritual traditions of the hard-pressed self." In 1926 he looked back at his first novel as an effort to identify himself. He claimed that it was in fact in this book that he found his real self: "I am a townsman, a burgher, a child and great-grandchild of German middle class culture."[125]

If he was indeed a burgher, his novel can be seen as a "town chronicle."[126] While psychology claims that to become adult one needs to distance oneself from one's father, Mann tried to find his real self by retracing his connections to his father. To do so he needed to recreate him. He drew up a detailed catalog of the values appreciated by his father. This catalog is rather instructive, for it coincides on a number of points with the catalog of values in Max Weber's famous description of what he called Protestant ethic. The values attributed to his father by Mann included "(h)is dignity and good sense, his ambition and industry, his personal and intellectual distinction, his social talents and his humour, the affability which he used to practice toward the common folk." There is no need to comment on this, the typical marks of the bourgeoisie, as painted by Huizinga. Elsewhere he describes his father as: "A man dedicated to self-control and to success, who had early achieved prestige and honors in the world," and finally: "Our father endowed us with 'the serious conduct of life' (*des Lebens ernstes Führen*) the ethical note that so strikingly coincides with the bourgeois temper. For the ethical bent, in contrast to the p3urely aesthetic impulse . . . the ethical bent is really the bourgeois spirit applied to life (*Lebensbürgerlichkeit*)."[127] Seriousness and an ethical bent: these notions become crucial for Mann in hose days, in 1926, when Germany was torn apart by right- and left-wing radicals, and when Hitler was preparing to take over the political leadership of the country. It is clear that Mann presents an ideal type of the burgher in his novels, and delineated this in his essay as an alternative to the uncivilized brutality of the totalitarianisms of the twentieth century. While as a young man he considered himself a conservative, in his Lübeck essay Mann claims that the German bourgeois is politically (and not simply socially) in the middle, and that he represents the real, the spiritual Germany: "Germanism itself means . . . the bourgeois spirit itself, *Bürgerlichkeit* on the grandest scale (. . .) it means the refusal to be carried away."[128] The argument that he put forward to explain this concept of Germanism, *Bürgerlichkeit* and finding a happy medium is roughly this: the Holy Roman Empire was a territory and an institutional arrangement where cities played a major role. City dwellers thus played an exceptionally important role in the history of these lands, and their success was partly due to their work ethic and cooperative nature, which were the fruits of the kind of virtues that Mann attributed to his father. A logical and historical connection is thus made between Germanism, bourgeoisie, and finding the middle way. This is encapsulated in these affirmative questions posed by Mann: "Is not the German nature itself the mean, the middle, the mediator; is not the German the man in the middle par exellence? Germanism is the mean, and the mean is the bourgeois spirit, the spirit of the middle class." In order to dispel any lingering doubts, he gave Aristotelian answers to his own rhetorical questions, asserting that Germanism is "against all extremists of the Right and Left."[129] Finding the middle can "mediate (the) position of the German burgher spirit, and not the bourgeoisie as a middle class in economic terms."[130] He sought the Via Media not so much in economic terms, but as a product of history, as embodied by the everyday culture of the bourgeoisie.

If Thomas Mann represented the ideal type of the German bourgeois spirit, that of the man of culture, of the artist, in full swing, just before the very breakdown and fall of German culture, Max Weber represents another type, that of the scholar. More than ten years older than Mann, Weber represented the great generation of late nineteenth-century German bourgeois science, and in particular of social science, which had its heyday before World War I. Weber, generally considered to be the founding father of the discipline of sociology, published a long, unfinished essay which is directly relevant to the present venture. Long enough to be published as a book, *Die Stadt* (The City) was most probably written in 1913 (or possibly in 1914) but was only published in 1920–1921, at first as a series of articles, and was included posthumously in his opus magnum, *Economy and Society*.[131]

According to Weber, the European city as an ideal type can be characterized by a set of character traits.[132] While a number of its elements are also present in other cultures, the specific mixture of these elements is characteristic only of the European city. In keeping with the specific professional interests of Weber, the social scientist, he identified the economic, military, administrative, and political functions of the city. It was obvious to him that the city is "a market settlement."[133] From this starting point a number of conclusions could be drawn. In order to defend its economic interests, "(t)he city must still be considered to be a partially autonomous association, a 'community' with special political and administrative arrangements."[134] To defend this autonomy a military function is required: "The city in the past, in Antiquity, and the Middle Ages, outside as well as within Europe, was also a special fortress or garrison. At present this property of the city has been entirely lost."[135] Like Huizinga, Weber, too, discusses the civil militia in his analysis, as the organ of urban self-defense. As he saw it, "(g)uard and garrison duty as the oldest specifically 'civic' obligations were attached to certain persons or pieces of land."[136] The important thing is that the privilege of being a citizen of a city was accompanied by certain duties, and participating in the defense of the territory was one of the most important of these. He referred to Maitland's description of the "military association of the city" thus: "The inhabitants of . . . the castle . . . (w)ere bound as citizens (burgess) to the performance of certain military duties such as building and repair of the walls, guard duty, defence service and, at turns, other military services such as communication and supply for the urban military noble."[137] The citizens performed these duties in smaller communities, but in the name of the whole—it is a crucial aspect of the city that it has its own, (Roman Law–based) corporate identity, of which individual citizens can become members, but which is institutionalized, in other words, made independent from the particular members. Relying on the historical findings of von Gierke, Weber claimed that the European city was a "joint association representing a community of city burghers."[138] This institutionalized (or as von Gierke puts it, corporate) form of existence was guaranteed by some sort of official legal documents (e.g., letters of privileges or immunities), which served as guarantees of the liberties of the citizens, but this derived only from their status of citizens, in other words to their membership in the corporate body of the city.

Taken together, Max Weber's reconstruction of the typical building blocks of the ideal type of the European city included: "1.) a fortification, 2.) a market, 3.) a court of its own and at least partially autonomous law, 4.) a related form of association, and 5.) at least partial autonomy and autocephaly, thus also an administration by authorities in the election of whom the burghers participated."[139] Looking at this list, it is clear that an element is missing: Weber did not include the religious element of the city as one of its defining character traits. One can certainly try to reflect on this telling lacuna, for example, by considering how much he strived for a secular image of the European city, or how far, on the contrary, his view of the city is by definition a Protestant one (in the sense of the concept included in his book on the Protestant ethic). The fact is that he left out this element from his definition, and we can only guess why, which it is better to avoid, in order not to slide into some sort of a fictitious narrative.

To be sure, the religious foundation of the European city is addressed directly and indirectly in the historical reconstruction of the main body of the text, including in a later subchapter entitled *The City and the Church*. The main point of this subchapter is that the nature of the city is to be distinguished from the nature of the church. The two historical entities are so far from each other, according to Weber, that he compares the role of church people in the city to that of the Jews of the city: "(o)utside the Jews, the priesthood was the only alien body within the city after the separation of State and Church, in the Investiture struggle."[140] Although this claim refers to a medieval controversy, it makes it explicit that Weber takes the post-separation city as his paradigm, in other words, he adopts a Protestant perspective. He makes a long list of causes of the conflicts "between ecclesiastical and especially monastic landlords and the cities."[141] This list includes the exemption of the church lands and properties from taxes, the fact that members of the Church were not obliged to take part in the defense of the city, and did not regard themselves as bound by the duties one of ordinary citizens. What is more, the walls of the cloister functioned to defend those inside from the intrusion of the city magistracy. Furthermore, the Church had its own legal system (Canon law), and city law did not apply to its members, while the courts of the church were still involved in the (spiritual) affairs of the citizens. Finally, the religious prohibitions on usury were rather detrimental to the new innovative spirit of the commerce and industry of the city, which came to be called capitalism.[142]

On the other hand, Weber also pointed out the material advantages of the presence of the church within the city wall, or of having a cloister nearby. As he pointed out, religiously motivated pilgrimages were a source of economic gain for city dwellers. Religious foundations also brought money to the city, and they provided some sort of social security, in the form of "asylums, charitable homes etc."[143] Weighing up the pros and contras, the relationship was not as agonistic as it is sometimes presented in narratives of the spread of the Reformation. Yet the fact remains that the Church was regarded, according to Weber, as "an inconvenient and unassimilable foreign body."[144]

A possible interpretation of Weber's way of presenting the relationship of City and Church is that he also wanted to distinguish between an outmoded medieval version of political theology and a modern one. His ideological construct of the Middle Ages included such elements as: "traditional law," "patriarchal ecclesiastical power," "Roman Catholicism," and "Feudalism." As opposed to this negative pole, he presented an ideal construction of the modern age, with "formal-rational law," the "bureaucratic state," the "emergence of Protestantism," and the "rise of capitalism."[145] This interpretation is useful for the thesis of his influential book on Protestant ethic is concerned. It is less applicable to his book on the City, however, where he seems to have been aware of a rather strong religious element in the birth and nature of the European city. We should not forget about a key component of cities, the self-consciousness of the European burgher. As we have seen, Weber thought that the key to this consciousness was a sense of confraternity: "More than anything else the fully developed ancient and medieval city was formed and interpreted as a fraternal association."[146] In this line Weber reveals a shared interest in early religiosity with Fustel de Coulanges (*The Ancient City*, 1864) and the early sociology of religion of Durkheim. Even more importantly, Weber is aligned here with von Gierke and Tönnies, and their analysis of Corporation and Community (*Genossenschaft* and *Gemeinschaft*).[147] These authors contrasted community with society, *Gemeinschaft* and *Gesellschaft*, and Weber, too, related to a differentiation between the natural basis of a political community built on human sociability and its legal, institutionalized form. Here he distinguished between the ancient and the medieval city. "Even in Antiquity the concept of the 'community' began to differentiate from that of the 'state.'"[148] This was a consequence of the transformation of the *poleis* into the Hellenistic and Roman empires. On the other hand, as Weber saw it, "the medieval city was a 'commune' from the beginning of its existence irrespective of the degree to which the legal concept of 'corporation' as such was brought to clear consciousness."[149] Weber emphasizes this point, elaborating the idea with a detailed analysis of a term he borrows from Latin, *conjuratio*. While cities were sometimes founded by a formal act or a legal process, more often it happened in revolutionary circumstances. In such conditions the basic symbolic act was conjuration, which is "taking joint oath," which created an "oath-bound fraternity" (*conjuratio*).[150] Besides the German example of Cologne, Weber points out that French and Italian cities were also homes of *conjuratio*. In Italy, the "conjuratio . . . as *campagne communis* (or under similar name) prepared the way for the political association of the later city."[151] The similarity is obvious to Weber's thinking, not only between this medieval oath-taking political community and its religious forerunners, but also between the urban phenomenon in general and its religious precursor, the religious fraternity of the religious orders. It is not difficult to see here the parallels in his thinking with von Gierke's notion of *Genossenschaft* and Tönnies's *Gemeinschaft*. Yet the term also has a military dimension, deriving from the ancient Latin terminology. The brotherhood of man is united to defend themselves as a body from external and, if necessary, internal enemies: "The initial aim of the oath-bound fraternity was the union of the locally resident land-owners for offensive and defensive purposes, for the peaceable settlement of internal disputes."[152] This military community, which was connected by an oath, soon established its own law. According to Weber, well versed in legal history, burgher law was "an estate law of the members of the oath-bound confederacy."[153] It was just such a law which helped them to defend their community against external legal disputes. The law, then, became crucial for this community. They regarded taking the oath as a foundational, almost constitutional moment, establishing the institution of the body of the burghers' community. "In most civic formations the citizens' assembly, in Italy called the '*parlámento*,' was the highest official, sovereign body of the community."[154] This body is established like the body of believers who build a church, or, within the church, particular religious orders. This community has a legal aspect as well as an aspect of conviction. This is the sense in which urban law resembled Canon law in Weber's interpretation of the burgher community.

This legal aspect of the quasi-religious foundation of the city (e.g., the role of articles of faith for Protestantism) is relevant to our story for two reasons. First, because it is through this legalistic approach that the revolutionary nature of the foundational moment can become a legitimate (though sometimes fictitious) moment establishing the city as a corporate body. Second, the major role attributed to law in this foundation of the burgher's body will also make law crucial for the internal life of the city: it permits the concept of the law ruling the city rather than powerful princes. This made it possible to refer to a common good, as well as to the city as an autonomous being, with its own interests and its own property.[155]

In order to have a transcendental basis for the "fraternal association" of the burgher community, a religious aspect of the city was also preserved: "There was usually a city-god or city-saint specifically available to the burghers."[156] Again similarly to religious communities, a hierarchy and a division of labor between certain communal functions within the community soon developed. Ancient examples were useful in this respect, leading to the establishment of the office of consuls, who were not appointed by the sovereign, but instead by "election by the sworn citizens' confederation,"[157] bringing an elective element into the political life of the city. These leaders were, however, supported by an elite community: "A *collegium* (association) of *sapientes* (sages) or *credenza* stood beside and rigidly controlled the consuls."[158] This element introduced the idea that the use of power requires constant oversight by a community of influential citizens, presaging later developments of the constitutional division of power, or checks and balances. Again, the ideological background of this development was in the surviving teachings of the ancients, in particular the Aristotelian and Ciceronian heritage of a mixed constitution, carefully distinguished between different levels of political powers, each with separate functions.

Besides these legalistic aspects of the burgher brotherhood, which led to the birth of city law and lawful procedures for acquiring power and controlling its use, a whole body of rules and other social norms were followed in cities which were never written down. In other words, besides the law, there were informal social requirements, including accepted usage, customs and habits, and local ways of doing things, which amounted to what came to be called a civilized, urbane way of behavior. This tight social control had a basis in the particular prehistory of the community. Its tradition could be written or oral, transmitted from generation to generation. This whole realm of the social enabled "the emergence of the patrician," an elite who took care of the *res publica*, of the common good of the *civitas*, the burgher community. They were entitled to do so because "as a rule only such persons participated in the council and discussed the common management of affairs who could spare the time from their economic activities."[159] On the other hand, the common people often organized themselves into what came to be called the *popolo* in Italy. The emergence of competing interest groups led to a sometimes rather unhealthy conflict between different levels of the city hierarchy. To be sure, however, the final word within the city was usually preserved for the "*parlámento*," "the highest official, sovereign body of the community."[160] While internal conflict could sometimes drive the development of a city (as in Florence), it could also lead to the decline of communal rule, when infighting paved the way for takeover of by powerful individual prince, who could play on the internal divisions of the city, and, by dividing the citizenry, keep hold of power (once again, the example is Florence). On the other hand, if the constitutional arrangement of the different levels of power was more fortunate, internal conflict could be avoided, leading to political stability and a flourishing communal life, as in Venice. But even there, being a member of an urban community was in many respects quite a demanding function, which had obvious advantages, but which also came with some fairly heavy responsibilities and duties to the community. This could only be legitimized by a powerful urban ideology, of the kind we are trying to reconstruct here. This ideology was made more effective by harking back to its ancient antecedents. In particular, the Italian civil narrative was continuous with its ancient Roman predecessors.

NOTES

1. Maurizio Viroli, *From Politics to Reason of State* (Cambridge: Cambridge University Press, 1992).

2. I received a new publication by Viroli from the author too late to be included in the manuscript. However, it is quite fascinating to see how he connects the urban architectural environment with the life of the citizenry, claiming that: "the good political community can only live and flourish in cities that speak to the soul of the citizens and inspire the love of order, of harmony, and of decorum that has always sustained, over the centuries, the love of political liberty." Maurizio Viroli, "The City as a Political Order and Urban Space," in *City, Civility and Capitalism* (Stockholm: Bokförlaget Stolpe, 2020), 9–19.

3. H. L. A. Hart, *The Concept of the Law*, 3rd ed., and intr. Leslie Green (Oxford: Oxford University Press, 2012), 56–58.

4. The reader should be aware of the fact that I use the term Central Europe, to cover that part of the continent where historically there was a German cultural infuence, including presentday Germany and Austria, together with those parts of the Austro-Hungarian Empire, which happened to fall beyond the Iron Curtain after WW I.

5. Keith Tester, "Introduction," in *The Flaneur*, ed. Keith Tester (London and New York: Routledge, 1994), 1–21, 1.

6. Ibid., 1.

7. Charles Baudelaire, *Selected Writings on Art and Artists*, trans. and ed. P.E. Charwet (Harmondsworth: Penguin, 1972), 399.

8. Tester, "Introduction," 5.

9. This is a notion attributed to Adam Smith. See his: Adam Smith, *The Theory of Moral Sentiments*, ed. D. D. Raphael and A. L. Macfie (Oxford: Oxford University Press, 1976), 129, 135.

10. For a good overview and summary of that literature, see: Priscilla Parkhurst Ferguson, "The Flaneur On and Off the Streets of Paris," in *The Flaneur*, ed. Tester, 22–42. For a more detailed account see her booklength study: *Paris as Revolution: Writing the 19th-Century City* (Berkeley: University of California Press, 1994).

11. Walter Benjamin, *Das Passagen-Werk. Gesammelte Schriften*, Vol. 5, ed. R. Tiedemann (Franfurt am Main: Suhrkamp Verlag, 1982). Translated into French as *Paris Capital du XIXe Siècle: Le Livre des passages*, trans. R. Lacoste, ed. R. Tiedemann (Paris: Ed. du CERF, 1989).

12. M 13a, 21, Benjamin, *Paris Capital*, 458, quoted in Rob Shields, "Fancy Footwork. Walter Benjamin's Notes on Flanerie," in *The Flaneur*, ed. Tester, 61–80, 63.

13. Ibid., 64.

14. Ibid., 65.

15. Ibid., 72.

16. Ibid., 74.

17. M 17a, 2, Benjamin, *Paris Capital*, 466.

18. Michel de Certeau, "Walking in the City," in *The Certeau Reader*, ed. Graham Ward (Oxford: Blackwell, 2000), 101–119.
19. Ibid., 101.
20. Ibid., 101–102.
21. Ibid., 102.
22. Ibid.
23. Ibid., 108.
24. Ibid., 116.
25. Ibid.
26. My mother was kicked out of the Budapest Technical University, because of her participation in the typesetting of the drafting of the university students' demands for their street demonstrations, while my father lost his job for being elected to be a member of the workers' council at his firm as a leading engineer. Ironically, they got acquainted with each other as a result of these measures. As a side effect of the punishment, as she explained to us when we were grown ups with my brother, for some years my mother was forced to cooperate with the secret agency of the communist party, giving oral and written confidential reports of her social environment, which she eventually managed to gain exemption from with reference to the jealousy of her suitor and later husband.
27. András Kubinyi, "Buda, Medieval Capital of Hungary," in *Medieval Buda in Context*, ed. Balázs Nagy, Martyn Rady, Katalin Szende and András Vadas (Leiden, Boston: Brill's Companions to European History, Brill, 2016), 366–85.
28. Dezső Csánki and Albert Gárdonyi, eds., *Monumenta diplomatica civitatis Budapest (Budapest történetének okleveles emlékei)* I. (1148–1301) (Budapest, 1936), 55.
29. Martyn Rady, *Medieval Buda: A Study of Municipal Government and Jurisdiction in the Kingdom of Hungary* (Boulder: East European Monographs, 1985), 5.
30. These are the words of M. Rady, referring to the historical explanation of Elemér Mályusz, in his "A mezővárosi fejlődés," in *Tanulmányok a parasztság történetéhez Magyarországon a 14. században*, ed. György Székely (Budapest: Akadémiai Kiadó, 1953), 142.
31. Martyn Rady, "The Government of Medieval Buda," in *Medieval Buda in Context*, ed. Balázs Nagy et al., (Leiden, Boston: Brill, 2016) 303–21, 304.
32. Elenchus fontium historiae urbanae III/2, ed. András Kubinyi (Budapest: Balassi Kiadó, 1997), 39–41 (no 34), quoted by Rady, *The Government*, 305.
33. Quoted by Rady, *Government*, 305, from EFHU 64–65, no 55. English language translation of the charter published in Ágnes Ságvári, *Budapest: the History of a Capital* (Budapest: Corvina, 1973), 78–9.
34. Rady, *Government*, 307.
35. Ibid., 310.
36. Ibid., 313.
37. József Eötvös, *Magyarország 1514-ben* (Pest: Hartleben, 1847), chap. 1, quoted in Rady, *Government*, 320.
38. Rady, *Government*, 321.
39. I will rely here on the work of András Kubinyi, "Buda, Pest, Óbuda és környékük 1686-ig," in Vera Bácskai, Gábor Gyáni and András Kubinyi, *Budapest*

története a kezdetektől 1945-ig (Budapest: Budapest Főváros Levéltára, 2000), 13–76, 38ff.

40. For a fruitful use of the analysis of novels to understand ways of thinking of and about the bourgeoisie, see Franco Moretti, *The Bourgeois. Between History and Literature* (London and New York: Verso, 2014).

41. Géza Ottlik, *Buda*, trans. John Bátki (Budapest. Corvina, 2004).

42. Ibid., 13.

43. Ferenc Hörcher, "Culture, Self-Formation and Community-Building," *Ethos: Kwartalnik Instytutu Jana Pawla II KUL* 28, no. 109 (2015): 64–83.

44. On the sociable aspects of self-presentation see the classical work by Erving Goffman, *The Presentation of Self in Everyday Life* (Edinburgh: Edinburgh University Press), 1956.

45. On the history of the Hungarian middle classes, see Balázs A. Szelényi, *The Failure of the Central European Bourgeoisie. New Perspectives on Hungarian History* (New York: Palgrave-MacMillan, 2006).

46. A key author and centre of the school of urban historians in Hungary was Vera Bácskai. Her representative statement on the older bourgeoisie is Vera Bácskai, "A régi polgárságról," in *Zsombékok. Középosztályok és iskoláztatás Magyarországon*, ed. György Kövér (Budapest: Századvég Politikai Iskola Alapítvány, 2006), 15–37. There is a debate in the scholarly literature about what is called dual society in the Hungarian part of the Dual Monarchy, authors like Gábor Gyáni and György Kövér questioning the historical validity of the claim that one can so easily distinguish the old bourgeoisie from the newcomers and the upwordly mobile new middle classes. See Gábor Gyáni, György Kövér and Tibor Valuch, eds., *Social History of Hungary from the Reform Era to the End of the Twentieth Century* (New York: East European Monographs, 2004). For a new generation of scholars, more accustomed to the English language discourse of urban history, see Szelényi, *The Failure*.

47. This classification tried to distinguish well-established members of the traditional bourgeoisie from the newly arrived, often Jewish members of the urban communities. See Szelényi's account of this duality: "there was (...) a duality to Hungary's middle class which also had an ethnic base. But this duality between the Gentleman Christian middle class—as it was called—and the liberal Jewish middle class did not represent a struggle between a backward, feudal force on the one hand and a progressive, modernizing one on the other. Both segments of Hungary's ethnically fragmented bourgeoisie were modern, but they were traveling on very different trajectories." Szelényi, *The Failure*, 157. In this respect see the volume by Sándor Márai, the title of which claimed that to live in Buda is a worldview. Sándor Márai, *Budán lakni világnézet*, ed. Tibor Mészáros and Noémi Saly (Budapest: Helikon, 2011).

48. See Randolph L. Braham and Scott Miller, eds., *The Nazis' Last Victims: The Holocaust in Hungary* (Detroit: Wayne State University Press, 1998); Randolph L. Braham, *The Politics of Genocide: The Holocaust in Hungary*, 1. (New York: Columbia University Press, 2016).

49. Géza Ottlik, "A másik Magyarország," in *A Valencia-rejtély. Hajónapló. Pályákon* (Budapest: Magvető, 1989), 72–92.

50. Géza Ottlik, "A régi Városi Színház lejtős folyosója," in *Próza* (Budapest: Magvető, 2005), 62–65, 64–65.
51. Ottlik, *Buda*, 173.
52. For a similar attitude, it is worth watching the famous opening scene of Andrzej Wajda's film Katyn (2007), where the Polish refugees find themselves on a bridge which is attacked from one side by the Germans, on the other side by the Russians.
53. Ottlik, *Buda*, 207.
54. Géza Ottlik, *School at the Frontier*, trans. Kathleen Szász (New York: A Helen and Kurt Wolff Book, Harcourt, Brace and World, Inc., 1966), 342.
55. Ibid., 343.
56. See the term "civil" in the Online Etymology Dictionary, at https://www.etymonline.com/search?q=civil.
57. Ottlik, *School*, 345–46. The original reads "ornate sugar bowl" instead of the term "marble cake."
58. Ibid., 346.
59. György Granasztói, *A városi élet keretei a feudális kori Magyarországon. Kassa társadalma a 16. század derekán* (Budapest: Korall, 2012), 17.
60. His original name was Márai Grosschmid Sándor Károly Henrik.
61. Mihály Szegedy-Maszák, "The Bourgeois as Artist. Sándor Márai (1900–1989)," *The New Hungarian Quarterly* 33, no. 125 (1992): 12–19, 12.
62. Szegedy-Maszák translates the title as *Confessions of a Man of the Middle Class*. He also refers to the fact that Márai must have been inspired by a conservative writer's, Cécile Tormay's *The Old House* (*A régi ház*, 1914).
63. Szegedy-Maszák, *The Bourgeois*, 13.
64. This title is itself a reference to the famous *Decline of the West* by Spengler (New York: Knopf, 1932), as well as to Huizinga's *The Autumn of the Middle Ages*, trans. Rodney J. Payton and Ulrich Mammitzsch. (Chicago: University of Chicago Press, 1996).
65. Sándor Márai, *A kassai polgárok (The Burghers of Kassa)* (Budapest: Helikon, 1942/2003), 120.
66. Márai, *The Burghers*, 110,
67. Ibid., 25.
68. Ibid., 102.
69. Ibid., 158.
70. Justin Stagl, *A History of Curiosity. The Theory of Travel, 1550–1800* (Amsterdam: Harwood Academic Publishers, 1995, 1997), 94.
71. Joan-Pau Rubiés, "Instructions for Travellers: Teaching the Eye to See," *History and Anthropology* 9, no. 2–3 (1996): 139–90, 150.
72. Ibid., 163.
73. Ibid., 147.
74. Felici Lucia, "Theodor Zwinger's Methodus Apodemica: An Observatory of the City as Political Space in the Late Sixteenth Century," *Cromohs* 14 (2009): abstract.
75. Joan-Pau Rubiés, "Travel Writing as a Genre: Facts, Fictions and the Invention of a Scientific Discourse in Early Modern Europe," *International Journal of Travel and Travel Writing* 5, no. 33 (2000): 5–33, 5.

76. Rubiés, *Instructions*, 150.
77. Jan Vermeer van Delft, *The Astronomer* (1668), *The Geographer* (c. 1668–1669). For his specific interest in cities see the further analysis of his *View of Delft* (c. 1660–1663), *The Little Street* (c. 1657–1661) as well, below.
78. Alpers explains the relationship between map and perspectival view: in his *Art of Painting* Vermeer recapitulated the map-to-painting sequence, for the small but carefully executed city views that border the map return his own *View of Delft* to its source. Vermeer puts the painted city view back into the mapping context from which it had emerged as if in acknowledgment of its nature. Svetlana Alpers, *The Art of Describing. Dutch Art in the Seventeenth Century* (Chicago: The University of Chicago Press, 1983), 122–24.
79. See: *Europica Varietas*, or A brief account of the various things seen and heard by Márton Szepsi Csombor in his journeying in Poland, Mazovia, Prussia, Denmark, Frizia, Holland, Zealand, Britannia, Gaul, Germany and the Czech lands, and on the seas of Prussia, Pomerania, Sweden, Norway, Frisia, Zealand and Britannia, which may serve not only to the delight of all Readers but also to their great benefit (Kassa: printed by János Festus, 1620), trans. and intr. Bernard Adams (Budapest: Corvina, 2014), 22, 35–36. See also: János Buza, "Szepsi Csombor Márton Nürnbergjének forrásai," *Gerundium, Egyetemtörténeti közlemények* 8, no. 1 (2017): 127–35, 129, n. 8, referring to Márton Szepsi Csombor, "Europica varietas," in *Szepsi Csombor Márton összes művei*, eds. Sándor Iván Kovács and Péter Kulcsár (Budapest: Akadémiai Kiadó, 1968), 52, 418, 419.
80. Alpers, *The Art of Describing,* 122.
81. Ibid., 124.
82. J. R. Hale, ed., *The travel journal of Antonio de Beatis. Germany, Switzerland, the Low Countries, France and Italy 1517–1518* (London: The Hakluyt Society, 1979), 56, quoted by Rubiés, *Instructions*. Among the traditions utilized in the travel literature from earlier times, Hale mentions the "civic eulogies of proud cities." (Ibid.)
83. A Hungarian scholar claims, that the work of Szepsi Csombor is the "first work of Hungarian descriptive statistics." Robert A. Horváth, "La France en 1618 vue par un statisticien hongrois, Marton Szepsi Csombor," in *Population* 2 (1985): 335–46, 335, quoted by Stagl, *A History of Curiosity*, 93.
84. Ibid., 93.
85. Ibid.
86. Szepsi Csombor, *Europica Varietas*, 27.
87. Ibid., 175.
88. Ibid., 18.
89. Sándor Iván Kovács, "Szepsi Csombor Márton," in *Szepsi Csombor Márton összes művei*, 53.
90. Szepsi Csombor, *Europica Varietas*, 85.
91. Ibid., 138.
92. Ibid., 139.
93. Ibid., 144.
94. This is how he describes that horrific event: "A very great *bloodletting for the true faith* occurred on these two bridges in 1572, because the craftsmen and

merchants had travelled in foreign countries and been enlightened by God, had maintained their religion in their own land, and preserved it to the death." Szepsi Csombor, *Europica Varietas*.

95. Szepsi Csombor, *Europica Varietas*, 194.
96. Ibid., 46.
97. Ibid.
98. Ibid., 66.
99. Ibid., 49.
100. Ibid., 62.
101. Ibid., 90.
102. Ibid., 91.
103. Ibid., 92.
104. Ibid.
105. Ibid., 94. I changed courage to virtue in the translation offered by the translator of the English language edition I use.
106. Ibid., 95.
107. The longer titles of the painting are *Militia Company of District II under the Command of Captain Frans Banninck Cocq* or *The Shooting Company of Frans Banning Cocq and Willem van Ruytenburch*.
108. Thomas B. Lenihan, *Rembrandt's The Nightwatch: Epitome of the Dutch Golden Age*, National Endowment for the Humanities Seminar: "The Dutch Republic and Britain: The Making of Modern Society and a European World Economy," Dr. Gerard M. Koot, The University of Massachusetts-Dartsmouth. Available at: https://www.academia.edu/7384530/Rembrandts_The_Nightwatch_Epitome_of_the_Dutch_Golden_Age, 3.
109. Jonathan I. Israel, *The Dutch Republic: Its Rise, Greatness, and Fall 1477–1806* (Oxford: Oxford University Press, 1995), 121.
110. Peter Greenaway, *Nightwatching: A View of Rembrandt's The Night Watch* (Amsterdam: Veenman Publishers, 2006), xiii.
111. *Civic Pride: Group Portraits from Amsterdam*, March 10, 2012–August 28, 2017, West Building, National Gallery, Washington.
112. Lenihan, *Rembrandt's The Nightwatch*.
113. Mariët Westermann, *A Worldly Art: The Dutch Republic, 1585–1718* (New Haven: Yale University Press, 1996), 149.
114. Lenihan, *Rembrandt's The Nightwatch*, 4.
115. Maarten Prak, "The Dutch Republic as a Bourgeois Society," *BMGN – Low Countries Historical Review* 125, no. 2–3 (2010): 107–39, 117.
116. Ibid.
117. Ibid., 118.
118. Johan Huizinga, *Dutch Civilisation in the Seventeenth Century* (1941).
119. Prak, *Bourgeois Society*, 107.
120. Ibid.
121. Ibid., 108.
122. Maarten Prak, *The Dutch Republic in the Seventeenth Century* (Cambridge: Cambridge University Press, 2005).

123. Ibid., 2–3.
124. Thomas Mann, *Lübeck as a Way of Life and Thought* (1926), xiii.
125. Ibid., xv.
126. Ibid.
127. Ibid., xvi.
128. Ibid., xxiii.
129. Ibid., xxii.
130. Ibid., xxiii.
131. About the birth of the text see: Wilfried Nippel, "Introductory Remarks: Max Weber's 'The City' Revisited," in *City States in Classical Antiquity and Medieval Italy*, eds. Anthony Molho, Kurt Raaflaub and Julia Emlen (Ann Arbor: The University of Michigan Press, 1991), 19–30.
132. He speaks about the Occidental city, but I interpret the term as referring to the European city as such. The difference between the two terms that the Occidental city is conceptualized as the opposite of the term of the Oriental City, while this is not true about the term of the European city, which is not contrasted with anything else, but understood on its own terms. In other words, while for Weber it was important that the specific mixture of these elements is only characteristic of the European city, this is not the case in the present venture, which does not contrast the European city with any other versions of it.
133. I rely on the following English translation of the text: Max Weber, *The City*, trans. and ed. Don Martindale and Gertrud Neuwirth (New York: The Free Press, etc., 1958/1966). The expression is used in the title of the first subchapter.
134. Ibid., 74.
135. Ibid., 75.
136. Ibid., 76.
137. Ibid., 78.
138. Ibid., 83.
139. Ibid., 81.
140. Ibid., 192.
141. Ibid.
142. For this claim see Max Weber, *Protestant Ethic and the Spirit of Capitalism* (1920), present day edition: trans. Stephen Kalberg (New York: Oxford University Press, 2010).
143. Weber, *The City*, 193.
144. Ibid., 194.
145. This interpretation is offered by Harold J. Berman and Charles J. Reid, Jr., "Max Weber as Legal Historian," in *Cambridge Companion to Weber*, ed. Stephen Turner (Cambridge: Cambridge University Press, 2000), 239. I think that the criticism offered in this analysis (which is more a critique of Max Weber the legal historian, and not so much of the urban historian or the researcher of Protestantism) is more valid on the point of Weber's misrepresentation of the traditional nature of European (urban) law, of constinuity and discontinuity, and on the fact-value dichotomy.
146. Weber, *The City*, 96.
147. See the analysis of Weber on *Gemeinde* in Nippel, *Introductory Remarks*, 25–27, where we read about "*die Gemeinde*, the commune, as a self-governing body,"

about "confraternity, *Verbrüderung*, the constitution of an association with a common cult" and "a terminology borrowed from the medieval materials: *Verbrüderung, Gemeinde, Genossenschaft, Zunft.*"

    148. Weber, *The City*, 99.
    149. Ibid., 99.
    150. Ibid., 108. Weber's example is Cologne's conjuratio of 1112.
    151. Ibid., 109.
    152. Ibid., 110.
    153. Ibid., 112.
    154. Ibid., 121.
    155. Ibid., 96: "In the Occident the city association owned and controlled property."
    156. Ibid.
    157. Ibid., 111.
    158. Ibid.
    159. Ibid., 121.
    160. Ibid.

Chapter 2

The City of the Italian Renaissance and the German City

This chapter addresses the two basic forms of the medieval and early modern European city, the Italian city-state and the German city. While the usual assumption is that they represent two isolated spheres of historical experience, the following narrative will attempt to combine them.

THE DEVELOPMENT FROM THE ITALIAN COMMUNE TO THE CITY-STATE

Italy served as the role model of early modern European urban life. It is therefore appropriate to start any tour of European urban phenomenon in Italy. The social custom of the grand tour, an obligation of any young gentleman's upbringing, led him straight to Italy, which was an acknowledgment of the pre-eminence of Italy and its culture, as the direct heir of ancient Rome. There are two obvious ways to analyze late medieval and early modern Italian city life and the transformation which took place there in the period between the twelfth and the sixteenth centuries. While both approaches are comparative, they still offer different aspects of the object described. One approach employs a temporal axis for the analysis, in which case the *explanandum* is the shift taking place from the medieval to the early modern form of township. The other perspective is synchronic, comparing Italian development to other European examples, such as the development of the great empires of France, Spain, or the Holy Roman Empire, or Republics like the Dutch Netherlands or Switzerland. There is also a further topic for such analysis: an internal comparison between the particular regimes of the different Italian city-states and kingdoms, such as Florence, Venice, Milan, or Rome. In what follows, we shall apply two of the above mentioned approaches, while leaving a comparison of the archetypical cases of Venice and Florence for chapter 3. But before anything else, let us start from Shakespeare's famous tragedy, *Romeo and Juliet*, an exciting example of urban conflict in trecento Verona, as retold in late Renaissance London.

The two families of the lovers, Romeo and Juliet, the Montagues and Capulets, represent two rival factions of the city of Verona. The fact that they were such desperate enemies of each other is a result of the opposition between rival interest groups in the thriving late medieval Italian city. Their hostility was due to the families competing to influence the decision-maker of the city, which was how they sought to realize their aims.

The cities of medieval Italy were characteristically different from other European urban centers. This was due to their economic strength, which in turn was amplified by their trading power. The animosity between the two clans can also be explained in terms of formalized social rivalry within the urban nobility, which was notably rare anywhere else in Europe, but quite frequent in the Italian context. Historical research has demonstrated that Italian cities succeeded in attracting important segments of the rural nobility. These cities, most of which had ancient Roman backgrounds, were keen to keep trading at a high level. This mercantile activity produced their economic growth, which led to a rise in the numbers of their inhabitants, and to a sharpening of the competition both between the cities and within the cities among rival factions to reap the benefits of this development. Merchants and nobles could easily commit themselves to take part in joint ventures of mercantile adventures: while merchants took responsibility for the business transactions, which could bring very high profits if successful, the nobles were happy to provide the guards to defend the ships or the inland convoys of merchant expeditions, and thus contribute to the common venture.

Although in Shakespeare's much-loved tragedy the lovers had to sacrifice their lives to remain together forever, the unintended consequence of this sacrifice led to a new social compact between the rival factions of the city. While Juliet's father admits that the young became "Poor sacrifices of our enmity," the Prince, who may have been modeled after Bartolomeo I della Scala, a member of the Scaliger family, who ruled the city of Verona from 1301, announces that "A glooming peace this morning with it brings."[1] In other words, Shakespeare's play is a vivid criticism of certain practices of medieval Italian cities, but it also reveals the resources by which these problems might be handled. The Prince gives the following final summary of the conclusions of the drama: "Capulet, Montague, / See what a scourge is laid upon your hate, / That heaven finds means to kill your joys with love, / And I, for winking at your discords too, / Have lost a brace of kinsmen. All are punished."[2] From the point of view of the play, this is reminiscent of the *deus ex machina* technique of ancient tragedy. The reference to discord in his summary, however, is also a telling one for our story: it helps to understand early modern Italian cities, whose ideology made every effort to counterbalance internal factions and schisms. Not only was *concordia* a key concept for Cicero, perhaps the most honored author of late Republican Rome, but Sallust, too, played a major role in establishing the concept of *concordia* at the heart of the European city. His famous *bon mot* was regarded as the central truth of a city's security in the European urban tradition, and in particular, in Italy: "By union the smallest states thrive, by discord the greatest are destroyed."[3] Shakespeare's classical play reminds us of this Roman wisdom, still present in the urban way of thinking in Italy, which is expressed in the ritual handshake between the two fathers: "O brother Montague, give me thy hand."[4]

After witnessing the consequences of internal struggle in the city, let us return to the two alternative approaches to analyzing Italian urban development. One recent interpretation of this development holds that the diachronic aspect should start out from the fact that with the breakup of the Frankish Empire, the north of the Italian peninsula was left without central control. This was followed by a later phase when "local counts, bishops and dukes" took over local power.[5] In particular, this historical narrative emphasizes the administrative organization of the Church, governed by bishops who took direct control of urban centers. It was against these external influences that town dwellers organized themselves: "They formed communes, sworn associations for the exercise of public authority."[6] This happened from the end of the eleventh century, and led to the spread of the commune system throughout the northern part of the peninsula.

Italian communes are characterized by very complex institutional arrangements, which often included the powers taken over by the bishops, including "the powers of jurisdiction, the levying of tools, and control over weights and coinage."[7] The aim of the establishment and running of these institutions were obvious: "These communes claimed independence and ruled as sovereign powers."[8] Certainly, this focus on independence was itself part and parcel of the ancient Roman discourse, not typical in other parts of Europe, where feudalism built up a hierarchical chain of dependences, in which towns were very rarely close to the top of the hierarchy. To summarize the specificity of the Italian case: "Influenced by old Roman models of government, they freed themselves from ecclesiastical and lordly control and exercised regalian rights themselves."[9] This is the distinguishing mark of the medieval Italian city-state, the commune.

However, just as the commune was not the first institutional arrangement of the Italian cities, neither did it turn out to be the final one. In fact, the form of self-government lasted for a relatively short time in a number of cities. While the shift from the Roman *civitas* to the medieval commune took place between c. 500–1100 CE, the transition from commune to *signoria* only lasted c. 1100–1300.[10] Explaining the process of change from self-government to *signoria*, another historian distinguishes two transformative events, the first of which he calls the *commercial revolution*, the second the *political revolution*. This is the thesis of a pioneering study entitled *Communes and Despots: The City State in Late-Medieval Italy*, which had a large impact on the scholarship of Italian humanism. As the author of this great work saw it, the development of the communes led to a kind of duality:

> Italy—and more especially now the North and the Centre—became indelibly identified, to contemporaries and for posterity, with two subversive, "antifeudal" forces, republicanism and capitalism: of liberty and civility, "political man," civic ethic, and "polis-mindedness" and "of commerce (*mercatura*), 'economic man,' business ethic, and the embourgeoisement of civil and political society."

It is this tension, and later the conflict between these two forces that was to bring first progress, later crisis, and eventually the "revolution from commune to *signoria*."[11] However, this shift from one form of political rule to another one did not interrupt the development of these cities. In fact, as Jones keeps emphasizing: "Most impressive in scale and effect was the advance of urbanization: the growing concentration, to an extent unequalled in antiquity or Middle Ages, of population, resources and, over much of Italy, power in cities and towns, boroughs and greater castella."[12] The development from the "consular government of the early communes" to "more autocratic forms of rule" took place "between the late twelfth century and the early fifteenth century."[13] It was competition, both internal and external, that drove this process. One can identify the phase when "the communes turned to an alternative form of government—the rule by the *podesta*."[14] This happened from 1170 onward. Later, "from roughly 1270 onward, the temporary *Podesta* transformed into the permanent *signoria*."[15] In this interpretation, the *signoria* was simply "the rule by an aristocratic leader."[16] One can further refine the conflict between political and economic interests. The *signoria* regime is in fact a compromise between the political leadership of the nobility and the "*popolani grasso*, the moneyed class" which "would sometimes support such strongmen in order to control the lower commoners and the guildsmen."[17] It is also important to note that the regime of the *signoria* did not necessarily mean autocratic rule by a single prince. Instead, *signoria* "could also mean the rule by the few."[18]

Especially important in this respect was the development of Florence and Venice. In certain ways the strongest of the city-states, these two became paradigmatic cases of the process of transmutations, which Italian cities were sometimes subjected to from without, and sometimes initiated themselves.

While both Venice and Florence "maintained a republican oligarchy," it is important to distinguish between their particular constitutional histories. Venice seems to be the more straightforward of the two cases. While "Venice managed to maintain republicanism by concentrating government in the hands of a fixed number of influential families," in Florence "(o)ligarchical government was sporadically alternated with popular and dictatorial regimes."[19] In both cases, what brought this result was "continual compromise," a term made famous by Hans Baron.[20] In the narratives of Italian urban history, the two cities are held up as paradigms of different paths to self-rule.

FLORENCE AND VENICE: TWO MODELS OF ITALIAN URBAN REPUBLICANISM

Florence and Venice were paradigmatic cases as early as the later Renaissance, by their own great thinkers. In what follows, we shall draw on a comparison of these two constitutional regimes by Francesco Guicciardini, one of the great masters of Florentine political thought. The idea of employing his work in this comparison comes from Rubinstein, who contributed a concise chapter entitled: *Florence and Venice: Guicciardini*, to *The Cambridge History of Political Thought, 1450–1700*.[21] Guicciardini is viewed by Rubinstein as a competitor of the most influential Florentine thinker, Niccolo Machiavelli. While there are important similarities between the ways of thinking of the two thinkers—for example, the way that they consider politics to be not a matter of abstract ideals, but of pragmatic matters, and also that they regard republics as the best constitutional regime for Florence—Rubinstein points out the crucial differences between their thinking. He relies basically on Guicciardini's *Dialogue on the Government of Florence*, which he claims Guicciardini began to compose before the conspiracy against those who wanted to "initiate a constitutional reform leading to a restoration of the republican constitution," and finished four years later.[22] In her introduction to the modern English language edition of the *Dialogue* Alison Brown also emphasizes that it "belongs to the period when Florentines were optimistic about a return to a more republican government."[23] This is of particular relevance given the fact that Florence had a rather hectic history during the lifetime of these thinkers, dominated by internal struggles between competing groups of its political elites, leading to constitutional regimes alternating within a short span of time. It is also important that Guicciardini, just like Machiavelli, was a practicing statesman, who had experience of both of the major regimes with which Florence experimented, the republic and a kind of covered monarchy.[24] Guicciardini, unlike Machiavelli, came from a well-established patrician background, and inherited a different perception of the city than his rival, even if both were basically in favor of the republic. Florence was, after all, famous by that time—the early sixteenth century—for its republican regime. Yet it was also famous for the intensity of the internal strife between rival groups and rival visions of the constitutional arrangements. Unlike Machiavelli, who did not have much political success with the prince, Guicciardini was able to preserve his political influence for a comparatively long period of time.[25] It was only after he lost his political impact, though, that he started to write the book which made him famous in Italy as well as on the continent: *History of Italy* (1561). Both Machiavelli and Guicciardini strove to explain the two major types of political regimes which Florence was experimenting with, and which were engaged in a life and death struggle with each other.

Venice, on the other hand, also had a republican tradition, but it was most famous for the longevity of its constitutional framework. In fact, an interesting technique of Guicciardini's to distinguish his own position from that of Machiavelli was to present the Venetian model as an ideal of republicanism in his *Dialogue*, because of its constitutional stability, and because of the elimination of internal discord, perhaps the most dangerous enemy of the healthy growth of a city republic. Guicciardini observed political phenomena from an aristocratic point of view and so for him a republic had different merits from those identified by Machiavelli in his *Discorsi*. Guicciardini's vision of politics did not deny the suitability of princely rule, and as we have seen, he had no problem serving in different offices in different Medici regimes, which were sharply opposed to the republican regime he himself had cherished earlier. This is understandable if we take into account his vision of politics. As a practicing man of action, he did not believe that his task in the *Dialogue* was to find the best possible constitutional regime in theory. In fact, he did not accept the traditional approach to constitutional issues, which since Aristotle had been based on a comparative analysis of the Aristotelian and later Polybian classifications of possible forms of government. He did not buy the famous story of the Florentines's love of liberty and equality, a choice of values established by Bruni, who was—as we saw—one of the first theoreticians of the Florentine republic. Guicciardini felt that a commitment to these values was a propaganda tool, in other words, representing these ideals as the fundamental values of the city served the special interests of those who made this claim, and who could thus claim to represent the interests "of the underprivileged."[26] Guicciardini himself preferred the values of the rule of law and justice, and favored regimes which supported these values, as he thought in these regimes can be found the "most consideration of the good of all, while at the same time social distinctions are respected."[27] His approach to politics, in other words, was not idealistic, in the sense of finding the best possible system, but pragmatic, one of watching and evaluating the effects (*effeti*) of a particular regime. His exemplary republic is not republican Rome, as for Machiavelli, and the Florentine republican tradition in general, but, as we have seen, Venice. In other words, instead of the values of liberty and equality he opts for stability and balance of power, together with the dominance of the middling rank, and of civil concord as the most important values, even of an aristocratic republican arrangement. Rubinstein cites an example, in a short discourse from as early as 1512, of Guicciardini searching for a balance between rival forces in the city, which must be preserved by "an elite of wise and experienced citizens," who can check "the ignorance of the multitude."[28] He attributes a moderating function to a senate in his preferred type of constitution, which is directly taken from the model of the Venetian senate. The idea of the constitutional balance itself comes from the tradition of the mixed constitution, a special feature of which is a strengthened upper middle class. The elite he has in mind, from which the senate would be recruited, is in danger of turning into an oligarchy, as it actually happened. In Guicciardini's mind, however, it would not be a closed group, but rather "a meritocracy of the wisest and the best citizens who, while not identical with the patricians, would be more likely be found in their ranks than in those of the people."[29]

Guicciardini's somewhat jaded views on the general public are evident in the maxims which were collected between 1512 and 1530 in his *Ricordi*. He compared the masses to "a mad animal which is crammed with a thousand errors and confusions, without taste, discernment, and stability."[30] Apparently, these qualities of taste, discernment, and stability can be found among the well-educated and socially refined elite, the patrician families of Florence.

As member of the Florentine historical elite, Guicciardini, when necessary, accommodated his politics to the demands of the moment, and "became a counsellor of Duke Alessandro de' Medici in 1530, and after his assassination in 1537, helped Cosimo I to succeed him as duke." There may be an explanation for this turn of events. Guicciardini had served the Medicis before, and, as a pragmatic politician, he was able to find his way back, if that was the most rational course of action available to him. After all, "those men conduct their affairs well in this world, who always keep before their eyes their own interests."[31] He could also excuse himself with the argument that liberty is not for its own sake, but for justice, and if "one could be certain that justice was observed under the rule of one or a few, 'there would be no reason to desire' that liberty."[32] For us, the most relevant motivation for his supporting the Medicis was that he thought the aristocrats would be able to keep order in Florence by checking, or to put it bluntly, manipulating the individual ruler. This interpretation of his support for the Medicis is reaffirmed by the fact that in his late writings he was ready to call tyrants by this name. The late Guicciardini's pessimism is obvious from his references to Tacitus, about the theme of "how to live and conduct" oneself prudently. Interestingly, he admitted that Tacitus gives advice to tyrants about how to found a tyranny.[33]

Guicciardini's support for the Medicis was not exceptional in the age among supporters of the republican government. In fact, the hectic days of Florence had come to an end by the 1530s, with the Medicis strengthening their rule over the city. Instead of the aristocrats keeping the balance, it was this family that came to dominate the life of the city. Guicciardini buried himself in his writing. He had to admit that his city was quite different from Venice. In Florence internal struggles decided the political developments, either leading to short-lived republican experiments or to the autocratic rule of the Medicis. In Venice the ideology of concord and balance was so strong that internal struggles could not emerge as openly as in Florence, and neither the many, nor the few, or the one could take the lead alone. Instead, they checked each other's power mutually, which resulted in a balanced oligarchic power—because, after all, the operations of the city were controlled by a small number of patrician families. This patrician domination was a recurring scenario in the European city, apparently quite in harmony with the Aristotelian theory, where the aristocratic *politeia* was regarded as the optimal state of affairs, while democracy was regarded as very unstable. The only uncertainty was the point at which an aristocracy turns into oligarchy, which is a distorted form, because it disregards the common good.

Florence remained the symbol of a free urban community, as it was there that the widest community of citizens could participate actively in the political life of the city, and for a while they were able to run it freely themselves. On the other hand, the example of Florence was a reminder, or in fact a warning, that a doctrinaire form of participatory democracy lead to instability, turning this "democratic" system of power into a revolutionary regime (as in Savonarola's period of influence). Venice, on the other hand, remained widely regarded as having a balanced constitution, where the balance was due to its adherence to a shared exercise of power, in a constitutional arrangement where it was guaranteed that the many (the great council), the few (the senate), and the one (the *doge*) would all have well-defined roles. All three levels of power were able and ready to keep an eye on the way the others exercised their own privileges. It is also crucial that the patrician element had a special, privileged function, since the upper middle class occupied a central position in the life of the city. According such priority to the aristocratic element was a pipedream for Guicciardini, and was never realized in Florence, Venice remaining an exception in Europe.

The European prestige of the constitution of Venice was based on this aristocratic dominance. It is a convincing example of the bourgeois arrangement of the European city, according centrality to the middling rank. It remained emblematic of the way politics should be balanced in an urban environment even at a time when more absolutist tendencies were being felt on the national or imperial level. As Guicciardini puts it in his *Dialogue*: "the most useful type of citizens a city can have is the mediocrity in the middle; they are the ones on whom the city should build its foundations, both against those who want to tyrannise and against the plebs who want to behave in a disorderly way."[34] On the other hand, Guicciardini also distinguished between aristocracy and real meritocracy, as his "preferred government is not a hereditary aristocracy limited to the optimates, as it might appear, but rather a meritocracy."[35] In this way an element of social mobility was built into his system—which was in fact lacking even from the Venetian system, which would eventually lead to its decline. Guicciardini warned his readers of the dangers of a strict "class" system: "the optimates must not be drawn always from the same lines and families, but from the whole body of the city." His view of the senate as the political instrument of the middling socio-political stratum differed from the actual political practice in Venice. He demanded that "a senate must be elected to deal with difficult matters, containing the flower of the prudent noble and rich men of the city," and that it should not consist only of the members of a few established families.[36] On the other hand, Florence remained a prime example of a city in which the value of liberty was all important, even if it caused both internal wrangling and external conflict. Although Florence was not yet a democracy, but most frequently an oligarchy, it was the most obvious example of a city whose citizens were always ready to fight for the city's autonomy. As a modern historian puts it, there was in Florence "something exhilarating about the celebration of the creative layman, as the citizen of a free republic," adding that this city, so proud of its republican regime, was remembered "for its aspirations as well as for its shortcomings."[37] The Florentine example remained a double-edged sword in political propaganda, as "under the Medici, it gradually succumbed to princely rule."[38]

THE END OF THE CITY-STATE

According to the usual narrative of the history of early modern European political thought, the sixteenth century saw "the demise of the autonomous city and its style of politics, for with the city-state went republicanism and federal experiment. All were crushed by the weight of princely absolutism, (. . .) which pointed imperiously toward the modern sovereign state."[39] In this subchapter, we consider if that narrative is entirely true, and whether cities may actually have employed varying strategies to tackle the issue, some of them with remarkable success. There are good reasons to join those who consider this narrative to be somewhat oversimplified and who suggest that the relationship between the emerging modern centralized state and the town was more complicated.[40] Drawing on the thought of MacKenney, we shall refer to three major phenomena of the early modern sphere of urban politics, including the "military defeat of the urban liberties," the growing importance of capital cities, and the "tangled and neglected story of the survival and continued vigour" of certain autonomous cities.[41] While the first two phenomena are in harmony with the traditional narrative, the third type of outcome shows that the city remained an important laboratory of a participatory model of conservative republican political practice on the continent well into the onset of modernity.

Let us start this story with the first point, the defeat of the city in its military contest with the centralized state. In one sense, this defeat is simply a question of numbers. Warfare in Europe in the sixteenth century was invariably decided by the number of soldiers on each side, particularly the number of infantry. With the development of gunpowder, walls needed to be strengthened and bastions built to enable cities to defend themselves against the cannons of the enemy. Fully independent cities "whose wealth depended on the careful calculations of merchants," "could not mobilise such forces, or pay for such walls."[42] It is therefore fair to say that the decline of the city-state by the end of the sixteenth century was caused by the changes in military technology and the lack of resources to sustain such forces. This is a historical effect of what is known as the "military revolution" in the historical literature. As a result of this disruption to the military balance of power, the independence of the cities was almost everywhere questioned by territorial states. The logic of strengthening centralized powers was irresistible, and this skewed the competition between the cities and the states. "Autonomous cities could either attempt to centralize a power of their own, or succumb to the central power of the prince."[43]

At the time of the birth of the new territorial state, a specific way of thinking—called the reason of state—became dominant in political struggles. This way of thinking did not forget about the cities as such, it only made them subservient to its own purposes. In order to sustain its military capabilities, the centralized state had to fuel economic activity in the country, an area where cities played key roles. Yet the interaction between state and the urban economy was not voluntary: the state decided the priorities and the city submitted to them. This kind of cooperation was even more pronounced in the case of capital cities. The latter had to serve special state functions. The specific form of social space surrounding the ruler was the court. These developed into luxurious architectural ensembles in centralized states, most often settled in or near to capital cities, with specific military, financial, and economic demands. These courts of the absolute rulers witnessed "the cult of the prince, the expansion of the court and the growth of bureaucracy."[44] The court served as the stage of the grand theaters of monarchy and centralized power, which had a major impact on urban life even in cities such as Florence which had earlier been so proud of their republican pedigree. The Medicis were able to generate a remarkable material culture in Florence, built on the coalescence of the court and the city, to support their own centralized rule over the territory. Luxury was proportionate to the available resources of a particular political entity. While principalities in Italy and the Holy Roman Empire spared no effort to keep their position in an accelerating competition of Baroque pomposity and grandeur, the huge, centralized powers of Spain and France dictated the tempo in court buildings and their attendant military apparatus. The ever-increasing tempo of this continental power contest stoked the economies of the states, which resulted in the strengthening of the bourgeoisie and the growing of urban economic centers.

As Foucault has pointed out, new techniques were needed to maintain order and stability in the growing centers of the territorial state, especially in capitals, which were not only centers of military and political power but also often functioned as centers of the national market as well as of knowledge production. Yet while capital cities were able to grow beyond what would have been reasonable, they did so not without new challenges connected to this concentration of infrastructure. In fact, the growth of the population, together with the introduction of new technologies, led to unprecedented phenomena, including the growth of poverty among the ever-growing number of urban poor, a poverty that was "as conspicuous as the profligate extravagance of the courtly elite."[45] Traditional urban ways of handling the problem, such as poor relief offered by guilds and confraternities, were unable to overcome this issue. Similarly, urban delinquency, prostitution, and offenses by and against juveniles were also rising. A further aspect of the challenge of oversized populations was the disastrous public hygiene, resulting in sweeping epidemics, often sapping the strength of the citizen bodies of major cities, and consequently serving as a kind of "natural selection" mechanism, viewed in popular mythologies as divine redemption for the moral corruption of the city. All these phenomena painted the underworld of European capitals in rather negative colors in the public's imagination, leading to the concept of the sinful city, as opposed to the natural innocence of the countryside. An internal conflict also typically arose between the court and its immediate environment, between the central stage of the kingdom and the rest of the society, playing the role of the audience, leading to lasting animosity like that between court and country in Britain. In summary, "neither Aristotle's face-to-face community, nor the self-contained vigour of the medieval commune could survive in a world in which the traditional patterns of economic, social and political life were dislocated and swollen out of recognition."[46] On the other hand, in spite of all these difficulties, there were means of survival even for those cities which found themselves within a central state dominated by an absolute monarch. While military defeat and economic and social integration under princely rule were undeniable phenomena, a third possibility also existed, a way of surviving in a centralized state not only economically but also while preserving the city's independence. In exceptional cases, some cities even succeeded in keeping their earlier legal form, that of the city-state. In other cases, cities formed federations, as in the case of Switzerland, or city elites camouflaged centralized rule, like in Venice and Amsterdam. The most important aspect was not the formal independence and autonomy of the city, but the advantageous conditions it provided for economic and financial investment, the major driving forces of the newly born capitalist economy which had to serve the political interests of the ruler, but which also guaranteed the survival of economically well-positioned cities. For this reason "the most vital political nuclei of the sixteenth and seventeenth centuries were still the towns," and with clever diplomacy and prudent management of financial and economic affairs, they even "fought off princely armies and retained their economic independence."[47] In Italy, where the birth of the centralized state was delayed by powerful local princes, the loss of republican rule was a fact of history. Both Florence and Siena had to give up their republican regimes. Other cities like Lucca managed to save their independence, however, and Braudel called the period between 1557 and 1627 "the age of the Genoese."[48]

Venice is surely the outstanding counter-example of the early modern domination of the court of the territorial state. As MacKenney puts it: "if we seek a tale of survival, of economic adaptation and continuing political independence, we must turn to Venice."[49] Venice represented continuity, keeping the tradition of a self-governing community alive, from the Renaissance republic to the birth of modern republicanism at the end of the eighteenth century. We have already dealt with the "myth of Venice," a cult of the city's balanced mixed constitution, in which *Doge*, senate, and the Great Council each had its specific function. But it may be true that the long-lasting success and the stability of Venice were instead more due to a "careful regulation of material conditions."[50] As MacKenney explains, Venice was able to behave like a centralized state in the following senses: it acquired territory, invading cities on the main land of the Italian peninsula, obtaining a sizable territory, and a population not less than 1.6 million; the city of Venice acted as a quasi-capital of this territory, with an expanding population itself, balancing high death tolls from plague and other epidemic with a steady influx of immigrants. It had an exceptionally efficient infrastructure of logistics for feeding and taking care of this population, including poor relief provided by Catholic institutions. Surprisingly, the closed circle of the oligarchy, which governed the city and which led an opulent life, was also helpful in preserving the economy's dynamics. Venice itself consumed luxury products on a large scale, but its merchants (described so famously by Shakespeare in *Othello* or in *The Merchant of Venice*) also traded all over Europe at shockingly high rates of profit. Its military sea power is evinced by the victory of its navy of 200 ships against the Turks in the Battle of Lepanto in 1571. It is also an important point that although Venice can be characterized as a "collective absolutism," it behaved less absolutistically than the princes of other newly born states, because its commerce required the smooth operation of its court system: "as Shakespeare recognised in The Merchant of Venice, the unbending rigour of the courts of justice was essential to commercial prosperity, and commercial prosperity preserved the city as an independent republic."[51]

In several important ways, Venice embodied a republican experiment, which proved successful for centuries, representing an alternative to the ever-growing absolutism of the new territorial states of the continent. As we illustrated with the example of Guicciardini, Florentine republicans always looked to Venice for inspiration, but later the whole of Europe looked with admiration on the Venetian myth, including both the Swiss and the Dutch, the other two nations where republicanism had a promising future, pouring out from cities over the whole land, by a confederation of cities or of provinces dominated by cities. Perhaps the most famous summary of this myth was Gasparo Contarini's *The Government and Commonwealth of Venice* (1543), probably a direct reply to the wishful thinking of Thomas More in his *Utopia* (1516), to demonstrate that Venice in fact came quite close to its ideals. While Pocock's magisterial account of the Republican tradition has Florence in its subtitle ("Florentine Political Thought and the Atlantic Republican Tradition"), Venice deserves much more of the historian's admiration. This admiration is due to the rather pragmatic approach to life, including internal policing and external diplomacy that made the difference. This late Venice avoided daring experiments, and instead relied on a pervasive ideology, which tended to idealize the past in order to keep its best practices intact in the present. Pocock admits that Venetian politics had a conservative tendency, because "Venetian history proceeds through pragmatic reflection on past experience."[52] Yet he was referring to Venetian conservatism more in connection with the Florentine statesman, Francesco Guicciardini, rather than with Contarini's views of the good practices of Venetian politics. It is still worth recalling how he understands Contarini's model in his *De Magistratibus et Republica venetorum*.

As with Guicciardini, Pocock takes the author's social background as his point of departure in his analysis of Contarini's way of thinking—the Venetian author was both an aristocrat and a churchman. He also describes the political background to the writing of the book: his author wrote it "at an uncertain time during the twenties and thirties of the sixteenth century."[53]

Pocock's key point seems to be Contarini's emphasis on Venetian virtue as the key to the success of the city. This direct connection between the virtue of a city's citizenry and its political success is of course in line with what is called "virtue politics" in James Hankins's magnificent book on Italian Renaissance political thought.[54] Yet Pocock himself points out a crucial contradiction in this moralistic explanation—that Venice employed mercenaries in its wars, which means that its citizens remained unarmed, even though fighting for your city when it was attacked by the enemy was the prerequisite of a virtuous republican attitude. Contarini explains this practice of Venice as necessary for the careful avoidance of internal faction, which might lead to "ciuile warres and dissentions within the City."[55] It is one thing to explain the lack of military virtue in Venice, though, and quite another to explain the survival of republican virtues at all. According to Pocock, Contarini depicts virtue "as inherent in the Venetian aristocracy as a whole."[56] Yet the most important factor of the book seems to be, according to Pocock, the affirmation of what was called "the myth of Venice," and the conscious avoidance of a clear explanation of the mechanisms which nurtured virtue in the bosom of its aristocracy. Instead of providing a metanarrative explaining the city's "ideology," Contarini's work becomes a key building block of this very ideology, when it affirms the virtues, claimed to be persistent in the city's elite, which would lead to the most perfect constitution that was ever made or imagined: "I dare affirme, that in the discourses of those great Philosophers, which fashioned and forged commonwealths according to the desires of the mind, there is not any to be founde so well fayned and framed."[57] The critical edge of this claim was understood to be aimed at Platonist political constructivism. One should also keep in mind that More's work was read as an alternative to Machiavelli's famous *Prince* (1532). Like More, Contarini himself also made use of philosophical politics, specifically those of the mixed constitution, but less in their Polybian form, and closer to "the main lines of Christian Aristotelian politics."[58] Interestingly, the churchman adds to his explanation of success—beside divine council and aristocratic virtue—the undisturbed workings of the mind, in other words, Aristotelian rationality. It is rationality which has to rule, but to achieve that rational rule laws were also needed. After all "mankind through the inuention of lawes seemeth to have attained this point, that the office of gouerning assemblings of men should be giuen to the mind and reason onely."[59] Pocock frames this concise assertion in a way reminiscent of Aristotle's famous assurance of a rule of law: "The *mito di Venezia* consists in the assertion that Venice possesses a set of regulations for decision-making which ensure the complete rationality of every decision and the complete virtue of every decision-maker."[60] In other words, the key to the long-term survival of virtue in the city was a constitutional architecture, which will take care of the survival of that very virtue for generations to come. Pocock compares this "artificial angel" of the Venetian constitution to Hobbes's *Leviathan* constructed as an "artificial man." Through this artificial mechanism Venice contrived a perfect system, balanced, harmonious, and almost perfect. Pocock then refers to the views that "Venetian mixed government had been idealized by equation . . . with Plato's Laws," which seems to be surprising, if we earlier pointed out that Contarini went rather in the direction of Aristotelian rationality.[61] Pocock's thinking owes a debt to Gilbert, who attributes this idea of connecting the perfection of Venetian institutional arrangements to Plato's *Laws* to Francesco Barbaro and his circle. The Greek scholar, George of Trebizond, who was brought from Crete to Venice by Barbaro, wrote to the latter: "your ancestors who have founded your republic have certainly taken from Plato's *Laws* everything that makes the life of a republic long and happy." This comparison must have sounded quite flattering, and Barbaro did not pass up the opportunity to put it in print: "He asked him to write an introduction to his translation of Plato's *Laws* in which he should point out the similarity between Plato's theories and Venice's political practice." George of Trebizond was happy to do so, and although Barbaro died too early to compensate him for his kind words, the *Doge* was grateful for his service, and "George of Trebizond was appointed to the chair of humanities and rhetoric in the School of San Marco."[62]

It is interesting that Pocock's interpretation of Contarini emphasizes his affirmation of the myth of Venice, a Platonic story, in spite of all the Aristotelian sympathies of the author, which does not allow him to take into account the inherently instable nature of politics, and the risks of history: all those realistic details, which made Guicciardini (and even more Machiavelli, before him) more significant as political thinkers than their Christian predecessors. In fact, Pocock seems to lose sight of the conservative element in Contarini's story by the end of his narrative, while continuing to emphasize the conservative element of Guicciardini's way of thinking. Pocock's references to the conservative element in Guicciardini's *Dialogue* are unconcealed, as in this quote: "The argument is clearly pragmatic and loaded in favour of conservatism."[63] The conservatism attributed to Guicciardini is based on a different understanding of politics. The value proposed here is not participation and liberty for its own sake: "the purpose of *libertà* is not to ensure the participation of everyone at all levels of government, but to ensure the conservation of the rule of law and the common good (the verb *conservare* is used twice in the same sentence)."[64] This second meaning of the term *liberty* points directly to the Venetian example, or in other words to a state of affairs "in which laws, not men, are supreme."[65] Such laws can stem the corruption of men in Venice because of the constitutional arrangement of a mixed constitution, consisting of "a

Consiglio Grande, a Consiglio de' Pregati, a Collegio, and a Doge," ensuring that "the four members balance or check another."[66] One may suspect that the formulations used by Pocock anachronistically reflect the American constitutional debates, but for us the important thing is that he refers to the general perception of the secret of the longevity of Venice as a city-state, according to which moral corruption was delayed by this balanced constitutional arrangement, which helped to conserve "the rule of law and the common good." It is in connection with this formulation of Pocock that we can assert that the survival of a flourishing urban community in the early modern context—even under the jurisdiction of a centralized state—did indeed depend on this balance of its different political organs, that is to say, on a division of labor between its different parts. This constitutional mechanism allowed everyone to play a part in the smooth operation of the city, checking each other's work, excluding the possibility of moral corruption, without turning it into a participatory rule of the many, from which both the classics and most modern thinkers protected political communities. As we shall see, the cities which were able to survive the birth of the modern state often had very elaborate urban constitutions, partly written, but partly based on local customs and unwritten rules. These rules were based on certain recurring values, among which *concordia*, a cooperation approaching harmony—the sort of balance that external witnesses found in the Venetian regime—was crucial. The Aristotelian-Ciceronian views of a mixed constitution remained crucial in the surviving forms of urban self-rule, differentiating between different functions of running a city, and distributing power to the one, the few, and the many, in accordance with the specific functions they performed in the political machinery of the city.

THE AFTERLIFE OF THE ITALIAN CITY-STATE

This chapter started out from a reconstruction of the political thinking of the late medieval and Renaissance Italian city-state and arrived at some sort of a generalization as to its nature. Before we move on in the second part of the chapter to the urban life of the German lands and Central Europe and consider some further examples of typical early modern urban politics, let us examine two interesting cases of the later Italian historiography of the Italian city-state: the examples of Carlo Cattaneo and Marino Berengo.[67] The first of the two created a characteristic discourse and forged a specific historical imaginary during the political struggles of Italian unification, while the second one showed that even the memory of the city-states could serve as a counterbalance to both the Fascist and the Communist totalitarian temptations facing the territorial state. While these two influential historians did not have much in common, both of them illustrate the truth that the city-state left behind an intellectual legacy that for long captured the imagination of the Italian intellectual-political elites.

Carlo Cattaneo (1801–1868) was not a simple scholar. As well as being an intellectual and a philosopher, he was also a political activist and a revolutionary.[68] Norberto Bobbio, who published a volume of essays on Cattaneo, divided his career into three different phases. Before 1848 his primary interest was in culture. This was followed by a period of political engagement after the insurrection, and a third phase lasting from 1859 until 1869.[69] He played a significant role in politics even at the time of the Carbonari movement in Lombardy in his youth. His kairotic moment was the five days of the revolution of Milan in May 1848, when he actually served as the head of the uprising. These days, traditionally referred to as *Cinque Giornate*, had a major impact on his way of thinking. He became convinced that the real source of power lay in "the people of the cities," who, "without any science of war, (were) stronger than the armies of its monarchs."[70] Although he remained a supporter of the *Risorgimento*, he distanced himself from Mazzini, becoming more and more interested in federalism and the history of Italian cities. He even acquired the name: "the father of Italian federalism."[71] This topic remained crucial for him, as illustrated by his 1858 essay: "The City as an Ideal Principle in Italian histories." That Cattaneo should be fascinated, in the 1850s, by the life and history of the Italian cities is all the more remarkable considering that by the nineteenth century, which saw the birth of the nation-state, "this image of a Europe of free cities and city-states had lost its lustre."[72] This political shift from city to nation went hand-in-hand with a reorientation in political thought which can be traced back at least to Bodin and Hobbes, on a European spectrum. Yet not only did cities and their networks not disappear, they also kept their political relevance. It was for this reason that scholars such as Charles Tilly and Stein Rokkan write, of "the entanglements of European cities and states."[73] This entanglement gained extra complexity, when historians such as Mommsen and Fustel de Coulanges strove to recall the ancient city, as the predecessor of the medieval and early modern European city. In particular they showed how Rome transformed the Greek tradition and made it applicable to the new circumstances prevailing in a new environment. The example of Rome served, among others, to show the relevance of a supranational entity. However, Cattaneo also kept insisting on a subnational level of political organization: on the political relevance of quasi-autonomous cities. The two together served to counterbalance the romantic notion of the nation. He attributed the principle of confederation to Rome, while ascribing the values of liberty, experiment, and truth to the cities.[74] An admirer of the products of British industry, he was a modernist, but did not view cities as the heirs of the Spartan tradition of moral austerity, but rather as sources of culture and commerce, as Athens was conceived of in comparison with Sparta. His openness to global developments and attachment to the idea of local stewardship is well expressed in the notion of *incivilimento*, or the civilizing process, which was "tempered by a fascination of an almost Braudelian kind of slower pace of placed and culturally particular thoughts."[75] His priority was Milan, or more broadly speaking, Lombardy, but his place of exile, the Swiss canton of Ticino, and in particular, the city of Lugano, was also close to his heart. However, his revolutionary Milanese experience of 1848 convinced him of the relevance of the citizens' militia, a republican Machiavellian echo in his thought. It is this experience that led him to his ideal of the self-ruling community. Like Rousseau in Geneva, he favored the sovereignty of the citizen body, as opposed to an oligarchical elite rule. Yet this approach to municipal administration pushed him toward a radical democratic position, one which struck a discordant note in his own day, when the Milan insurrection of 1848 was taken over by moderates with aristocratic backgrounds, a tendency which led him once again to suspect the threat of "fatal hegemonies."[76]

Importantly, Martin Thom has pointed out traces of the teachings of the Scottish Enlightenment, especially of its stadial approach to history, in Cattaneo's work. In particular, Cattaneo drew inspiration from Adam Smith to understand Italy's history in terms not of negation—a failed unification—but in terms of its specificity. Cattaneo's early historical narrative explained why there was a difference between the cities of the North (of the Hanseatic League) and those of Italy: in the latter, the *città* and the *contado* (the surrounding rural area) were united. This meant that the municipal unit was both a mercantile center and the home of "intelligent" agriculture. "Out of such a city a region would emerge, as Lombardy[77] had issued from Milan." Obviously this was, for him, the proper scale of political unification, so different from the nation-state, which lacked historical legitimacy. Of course, critics of Cattaneo rightly pointed out that this is the product of ideologically driven overinterpretation of historical data. On the other hand, as a normative suggestion, Cattaneo's historically based political regionalism, born of the organic interaction of city and countryside and influenced by his anglophile bent, has an appeal even today, in a period of heated debate about the future of Europe. He painted his somewhat artificial composition of the evergreen Italian *veduta* with vivid brushstrokes, recalling the Roman heritage of "laws, families, municipalities, roads, bridges, aqueducts, dikes, irrigation ditches, temples resplendent in marble, colonnades, villas, delightful artworks and fountains, theatres, public libraries, (and) great schools, where a Virgil might study,"[78] based on a careful balance of unity (meaning the unifying urbane effect of the Roman empire) and particularity (meaning the traditional local marks on the architectural design). Cattaneo thus revealed that there can be both a lower and a higher level of the political community, beyond the national unit.

If Cattaneo succeeded, with the help of a detailed investigation of the past of the Italian city-states, in showing an alternative to the singular focus on the national level of political organization, while in the midst of the intense national transformation of politics known as the *Risorgimento*, the twentieth century, the time of totalitarian experiments, also witnessed similar efforts. A notable example of urban studies in the age of totalitarianism was that of Marino Berengo (1928–2000), who researched the *Risorgimento*—the era of Cattaneo himself. Berengo started his studies at the prestigious *Scuola Normale Superiore di Pisa*, but had to give them up due to his lung disease. Finally, he received his degree in philology from the University of Florence, interestingly, with a thesis on the history of Florence's eternal enemy, Venice, in the late eighteenth century. His whole career was mostly devoted to Italian urban history, with a special emphasis on the history of Venice, as well as publishing an important work on Lucca, and crowning his professional career with a general history of the European city, *L'Europa delle città*, 1999.[79] This overview or grand narrative benefited from the rise of urban history, with a special focus on social history, in the last decades of the twentieth century. Berengo did not seem to have been satisfied with the mainly social focus of earlier research, and regarded the city as a basically political organization, applying a definition which described a city by its citizens' self-identification as citizens, in other words by a minimal requirement of self-awareness of what citizenship meant. Having started his career as an archivist in Italy's State Archive he was able to go back to the study of archival sources in his research into the late medieval and early modern city, from approximately the twelfth to the eighteenth centuries. This Ranke-like methodology helped him to investigate the internal and external power struggles of cities, together with the rising self-awareness of citizen bodies, both in small towns like Lucca and in the greater ones such as Milan and Venice. His major achievement, however, was to deal with Italian internal affairs from a perspective which allowed him to see the big picture of European urban development. While Cattaneo's chief influence was Gian Dominico Romagnosi, an economist, jurist, and philosopher, Berengo's masters were Gino Luzzato, himself an economic historian, and Delio Cantimori, a historian and politician. Both of them were believers in the leftist totalitarian temptation, although the latter converted from Fascism in his youth to Communism. Berengo followed their example, himself becoming an advocate of Communism, as the local representative of the party in Venice.[80] His leftist personal political allegiances led him to openly support the student movements of 1968 in Milan, even though he condemned all forms of violence—both on the left and on the right. Apparently, this political partisanship did not distort his scholarly output. As

Molho phrases it: "In his work, he studiously kept his distance both from the orthodoxies of many Italian Marxist historians, and from the often neo-positivist convictions of historical demographers."[81] This is not a denial of the political nature of the urban enterprise, as Europe knows it. On the contrary, it is only a refusal to commit the error of anachronism, or become bound by a teleological philosophy of history, so characteristic of Marxist interpretations.

In his historical research, Berengo insisted on reading European urban life as a genuine republican political phenomenon, disregarding Marxist presuppositions or other leftist clichés.[82] For him, the life of a city was fundamentally a political issue: "as soon as we enter a city, to breathe its air and distinguish its forms of life, the first question that we address is political and institutional."[83] While Italian Marxist historians were generally interested in the life of the countryside, beyond the city, in order to show how the rural area was exploited and suppressed by the oligarchic rule of the city, Berengo had no such intentions. Instead, he presented the city as the locus where one could directly experience free life. In this respect, he may have been inspired by Sismondi, the early nineteenth-century Swiss political economist. Molho detects ideas of a classical liberal culture in this, influenced also by Adam Smith and already present in the age of Cattaneo himself. Yet there is an obvious contradiction here, between Berengo's historical reconstructions of the Italian city and his own political values. The distance between the two can be reduced, however, by identifying an element of social criticism in Sismondi's thought, and noting that the internal struggles of the cities also had a social dimension. What may be telling is the care which Berengo took to maintain this distance between his own political engagement and his historical methodology, although this did not prevent him from using his research into the urban past of the country as an ideal for his own age.

This effort to showcase the Italian city-state as an ideal for his own age, even if by doing so they swim against the tide, connects Cattaneo's and Berengo's research into this heritage. It is finally worth considering a celebratory speech by James Amelang, given in the *Ateneo Veneto di Scienze, Lettere ed Arti* in Venice, in the presence of Berengo, and later published in the *Rivista Storica Italiana*.[84] This text points out that Berengo's primary interest in the European city is concerned with "urban politics," besides reconstructing urban society, and with the relationships between the Church and the city. It also points out that, in addition to discussing the major urban territories of "England, France, the Low Countries, the Empire, and the Iberian and Italian peninsulas," Berengo does not forget about the continent's peripheries, including Eastern Europe and Scandinavia, to round out the portrait of comparative urban history. Berengo, with his primary interest in politics and its institutional framework, was characteristic of the deep change that Charles Tilly proposed had taken place in urban studies, including turning away from exclusively prioritizing social (and economic) history.[85] This new historiography suited him, because it privileged "particularities and the diversity of individual and collective trajectories." Yet all these detailed discussions of urban particularities, which eventually led Berengo to a transnational narrative, were centered around his own personal experiences of Venice, the paradigmatic European city in Berengo's grand narrative.

If Venice is the paradigm, then the most important feature of Berengo's European city is that it is walkable. Berengo's observer and narrator of the European city is a stroller, someone who experiences the city as a pedestrian and a passer-by. This is a perspective often neglected by urban planners, but one that the present study underlines. It is a point of view which helps one to identify with the local inhabitants, both the citizens and those city dwellers who do not yet have citizen rights. In a traditional European city, everything is traditionally seen from the perspective of the pedestrians.

This perspective also allows one to include all the members of the community in the affairs of the city. Venice is exemplary in this respect as well. It is not only a collection of nice vedute, but also a dynamic human community, a body politic. In this respect Berengo's Venice-based story is not simply about the European city, but also about civic Europe, because "the best this Europe can offer the rest of the world is precisely its *cultura civica e repubblicana*."[86] Like Cattaneo, Berengo distinguishes the urban republican political arrangement from the form of the territorial state, which does not respect the political identity of the city. In the preface to his long book on the city, Berengo claims, in connection with the late medieval, early modern city: "In this long span of time, urban space had been the privileged field of public coexistence—if we can define it that way—at times more loose and open, at times more compressed; since then the regional and national states—whatever their political regime—have no longer recognized in the cities their poles of animation and identity."[87] Amelang rightly points out that Berengo's historical excavation is not conducted for its own sake, but serves to present an ideal political community, based on the myth of Venice. Quoting the words of Giorgio Chittolini, Berengo reminds us of something valuable in the European tradition, "that with the decline of those forms of urban life something important has been lost."[88] This reminder seems to be the everlasting message of the Italian city-state, something which we, as inheritors of this urban culture, associate with those remarkable urban political communities in Italy.

URBAN SELF-GOVERNMENT IN THE HOLY ROMAN EMPIRE

The Venetian example had a European currency: only very few cities succeeded in surviving so long, even among the successful Italian urban communities as city-states, while preserving their full independence and sovereignty. Most of them had to learn how to run their own business within the new—or for that matter, within the traditional—political hierarchy of the supra-urban level of the territorial state.

A specific political context existed, however, in the Holy Roman Empire in the early modern period. The rich and powerful cities there did not necessarily enjoy full autonomy in the era before the Treaty of Westphalia, and in many cases even after it, but they did have a certain constitutional role in the Empire, and beyond that they cultivated negotiating strategies with higher powers, which helped them to preserve a degree of self-rule and room for economic maneuver. In contrast to the Italian city-states, the cities of the Holy Roman Empire did not lose their vitality and political role as the Italian ones did, although there too, there is a traditional narrative of decline and sclerosis. It is therefore well-worth taking a closer look at the development of the German cities in the pre-modern and early modern periods. Our general claim will be that the citizens' careful management of their own lives, as well as of common affairs (*res publica*) resulted in rather surprising results of long-term urban prosperity, due to the newly developed techniques of urban capitalism, which led to the establishment of common institutions of education, cultural consumption, and social care. We shall argue that the German city represents a distinct paradigm within the larger category of the European city. Central-European, and more specifically Hungarian urban history is a chapter within that greater narrative.[89]

Scholars of German urban history traditionally draw a sharp contrast between the ideal world of the Middle Ages and the less-than-perfect early modern period. The medieval period there also witnessed an institutionalized communal life (*Gemeinde* or *universitas civium*)[90] based on the *coniuratio* of the city dwellers, which allowed exceptional freedom both for individual citizens and public ventures, and which resulted in the special status of the German City within the constitutional arrangement of the Holy Roman Empire. As the story goes, after the Reformation, "the urban societies and especially the imperial cities lost their ability to transform and 'modernize' their social and political structures."[91] They "underwent a steady decline in the early modern period."[92] The cities had an all-too-powerful competitor, the territorial state, against which they had no means to defend their own positions. In this context, the famous "dominant conservative mentality of the citizens" is of special interest, but only in a negative sense as an inability to adapt.[93] However, the new trend of urban history writing rehabilitates the imperial cities (just as it has a much higher opinion of the whole functioning of the Empire), while distinguishing it from both the medieval city and the early modern territorial state and the court. While the earlier historiographical pattern talked about continuity between the Middle

Ages and the early modern period, and therefore decline, the new narrative emphasized transformation and a preservation of dynamics. The earlier discourse focused on the institution of the council, in its relationship to the communality (*Gemeinde*), as embodying the autocratic (*herrschaftlich*) and corporative (*genossenschaftlich*) principles.[94] In this paradigm, the debate was about which of the two principles was more influential, one camp arguing for the autocratic nature of this form of governance, while the other one stressed community and civic consensus (*konsensgestützte Herrschaft*).[95] While the imperial cities in the south and the west, for example, Cologne, were able to pursue corporate decision-making (*Zunftverfassung*), from the late 1400s the communal aspect declined, and the oligarchic and hierarchic aspects gained prevalence, with a short interval of "civic participation" and "communal ideas and institutions in the Reformation."[96] The imperial cities were seen as conserving autocratic constitutions, and only external powers, and particularly the modern state could modernize those institutions. There are, however, those who challenge these interpretations, including Peter Blickle with his theory of *Kummunalismus*, and Ernst Pritz and Robert Giel who also emphasize the role of "civic assemblies, commissions or corporations, in urban politics."[97] This view is reinforced by studies which have analyzed communal symbolism and rituals, as well as the approach, inspired by Habermas and Luhmann, which employs the framework of *Anwesenheitsgesellschaft* (face-to-face society). In this respect, the work of Rudolf Schlögl and his group is of primary interest for the present project.[98] The main idea here is that in the cities decisions are made as a result of interactions between members of a group, based on corporeal presence and direct communication. According to this historical narrative, after the Reformation new forms of interaction, and specifically written and printed media were to play a crucial role in urban decision-making. How this technological development changed urban politics is exemplified by the operation of the civic assemblies in these city-states. While earlier assemblies had important roles to play, based on the presence of as many of the citizen's body as possible, after the Reformation this institution either disappeared in imperial cities or lost its power. While earlier this transformation was interpreted as a growth of the autocratic rule of the council, Hoffmann-Rehnitz illustrates with the example of Lübeck and Cologne that it is historically more correct to understand it as part of the change from oral to mediated, written and printed forms of administration.

The capital of the Hansa cities, Lübeck has always been an important example of the development of cities in the Holy Roman Empire. The narrative of the vanishing significance of the city in the early modern period is based on the following three points: that the council became an independent agent in the thirteenth century, establishing an institutional hierarchy in the city, that communal participation weakened, and therefore the relationship between council and citizens became autocratic (*obrigkeitliche*) and oligarchic in nature. Finally, the fact that the constitution endured for a long time was also taken as a sign of a loss of the communal element, as it did not introduce new forms of participation in the affairs of the city. This is regarded in mainstream urban historiography of the city as a kind of ossification of the urban regime. A part of this tendency was the "prevailing conservative mentality among the citizens and particularly the urban elite."[99]

An alternative reading of the city's history assumes that the basis of the political life of the city was in fact the civic assembly and not the council.[100] More precisely, according to the ideology of the city, the key issue was the identity and consensus of council and communality (*konsensgestützte Herrschaft*). The main ways to seek a consensus were consultation with the distinguished heads of civic corporations or summoning a *Bursprake*. Such attempts at consensus-seeking, however, had to find different forms in the post-Reformation era, when printing and writing became more relevant as media of exchange between informal citizen bodies and the council.[101]

A more specific question is that of how to explain the short, unsettled period between 1528 and 1535. This is regarded as a return to earlier forms of communal rule, but was only as a short rupture in the otherwise continuous development. If this moment of citizen agitation and exceptional communal activity is compared with later periods of similar intensity (1598–1605, 1660s), instead of a civic assembly we find new institutions, "civic corporations of merchants and artisans (*bürgerschaftliche Kollegien*), as the main players of the political match of civic opposition."[102] The aldermen of these corporations were entitled to discuss the major issues with the council, and come to an agreement with it. This represents a transition from actual bodily presence during decision-making to participation in a corporation which was represented by its leaders. Instead of the whole community coming together to discuss issues of vital importance, Lübeck had by the early modern period a network of corporations (led by the four major guilds) engaging in communication to negotiate the future arrangements of the city. The mechanism of negotiations was partly formal, partly informal, creating a city which was less a corporate body, and more a legal abstraction of networks of citizen corporations in interaction with the council, which became the center of the network, representing the whole city. On the other hand, special significance was attached to the communication between the guilds behind the scene, outside the control of the council, creating a realm of public discussion. Thus in Lübeck there was both a centralized authority, the council with its principle of *Obrigkeit*, and a dispersed, decentralized network of communication or public realm, operating largely autonomously from the council. In other words, the earlier balance between council and community was replaced by a balance between the formal center of power and an informal network of dispersed power, ensuring that no authority could gain a monopoly on power.

To determine whether this development has more general relevance, one can compare Lübeck's example with its southern parallel, that of Cologne.[103] This city was also part of the Hanseatic league, but it had a well-defined, specific local institutional order in which the political corporations or *Gaffeln* had played a crucial role, together with the *Vierundvierziger* (a standing civic committee), in political decision-making since the end of the fourteenth century. Here, too, the civic assembly (called *Morgensprache*) had played the major role earlier, but it lost its significance around 1500. While earlier it was a forum for both discussion and decision-making, it ceded influence to the *Große Gottestracht*, a socio-religious ritual, whose function was to represent and visualize the communal aspect of the city. At the same time, the *Gaffeln* took over the negotiating power of the *Morgensprache*, through which citizens could exercise an influence on the council. In the political process interaction between them and the council ensured political consensus in difficult cases. Corporate participation could here, too, balance the centralized role of the council, resulting in a differentiated realm of public sphere.[104] Citizen complaints were communicated through institutionalized written channels, called supplications, which created a distance between council and corporations. On the other hand, the recipient of written messages could not be directly controlled (unlike with face-to-face communication), which made it more difficult to establish trust among agents within the city's administrative *Ordnung*. The trust between citizen's bodies and the council could, however, be ensured through the symbolic-ritual dimension, established by the Reformation, emphasizing the need for a cohesion of the *Gemeinde*, in its relationship of higher authorities, including the court of the centralized state and the spiritual realm of God's rule.

A specific feature of the life of post-Reformation early modern German urban centers is the consequence of the teaching of the Reformation of the special relationship of the secular and the religious power within a local community. Although the self-governance of the cities of Lutheran Germany was based on secular institutions, here, too, cooperation was required between the two realms, ensuring that the symbolic-ritual functions of the religious power could prevail. Another pattern is represented, referring to ancient Christian practices, by Calvin's Geneva, and more generally in the urban development of the territories controlled liturgically by the reformed church.

It is worth taking a closer look at Calvin's Geneva. The city was an independent city-state, with strategic links to nearby cantons, and Calvin's autocratic rule of the city is a telling example, although perhaps an extreme one, of how the new religious forces imagined this relationship. It may be revealing to examine at this point the developments of Calvin's relationship with the city, in particular with its councils, and how he took full control over the whole life of its citizenry through a long process of struggle with secular and theological opponents.

Traditionally, the triangle of power in Geneva consisted of the Bishop, the House of Savoy, and the citizens themselves. When Calvin arrived in town as a religious refugee from France in 1536, and wrote the first edition of his famous *Institutio*, republished in 1539, he was only twenty-seven years old. He was a young man full of religious zeal but also of political ambition.[105] The son of a lawyer, he had studied theology and law in France, and in Paris he also studied classical letters. His main interest as a young man, however, was in political ethics, which led him to write in 1532, at the age of twenty-three, his book on Seneca's *De Clementia*.[106] By the time he arrived there, Geneva had embraced the Reformation—more for political than for spiritual reasons, and in the decade before his arrival the city had got rid of both the rule of the bishops and the House of Savoy. In 1533 and 1534 the city had to defend its newly found independence, which they succeeded in with the help of their ally, Bern. In order to implement self-governance, two institutions of self-rule were established: a Little Council, consisting of twenty-five members, and a Council of Sixty. While the first body had administrative duties, the second dealt with the external affairs of the city. After 1527, the Council of Two Hundred took over the role of the Council of Sixty. The citizens were sometimes called together *en masse*—as we know from Rousseau—to deal with questions of general interest. As a result of it taking the Reformation seriously, the city magistracy adopted regulations which seriously hindered the license of city life. As the historian puts it, a spirit of intolerance was already characteristic of its leadership even before Calvin's arrival. Calvin had a great talent for giving form to religious life. His reforms, however, raised the suspicion of the civil magistrates that he wanted to take full control of the city. To prevent him gaining control of the city, at a certain point in the power struggle, in 1538 both Calvin and an older minister with whom he cooperated were expelled from the city. This did not ease the internal tension between rival factions of the city elite however, and the city was to see horrible scenes of mob violence as well. Geneva at this point was threatened with civil war. As a result of the temporal victory of the party which supported Calvin, in 1541 he returned to the city. After the city authorities accepted his Ecclesiastical Ordinances, later in 1541 he established a church body called the Consistory, consisting of twelve elders as well as the ministers of the city. The Consistory was under the close control of Calvin and met every week. There were four classes of officeholders in Calvin's institutional system: pastors, teachers, elders, and deacons. These bodies fought with the councils to realize Calvin's masterplan to take over the rule of the city, and introduce what may be judged by our own standards as a "tyrannical supervision of the lives of the people."[107] To be fair to Calvin, several other cities introduced regulations similar to those Calvin tried to enforce in Geneva. In fact, the inspiration came from Strasbourg, where Bucer had tried something similar, but had failed due to the opposition of the city councils.[108] One should also realize that the councils were even more severe with their regulations. The main reason why Calvin's rule is perceived as especially harsh is that he also tried to control the private life of the citizens. Not only did he ordain practices of religious worship, including obligatory church attendance, and determined moral standards for public meetings, including rules for behavior in pubs and other spaces of entertainment, but he also sought to supervise what happened in the citizens' families at home. He operated a system of surveillance, starting out from the ministers' activity, but also employing a network of spies which were active within the citizen body. Freedom of discussion on religious matters was strictly limited, forbidding to criticize the religious leadership, and in particular, Calvin. The severity of his conception of full control over spiritual affairs is proven by the trial which led to the condemnation and religious execution of Michael Servetus in 1553, managed by Calvin, but realized by the secular authority of the councils. Servetus had earlier been involved in a debate with Calvin (among others) on questions of faith, and he seemed to question the authority of Calvin. Although not a citizen of Geneva, when he spent some time there *en route* to Italy Calvin was informed of his presence and ordered his arrest. He was condemned to death as a heretic. This trial caused a degree of public discontent, not only in Geneva, but also in other Swiss cantons. A major criticism was published by Sebastian Castellio, former Rector of the *Collège* de Genève, expelled from Geneva by Calvin, under the title *Concerning Heretics, Whether They Are to Be Persecuted* in 1554. This was a work arguing in favor of religious toleration, and acceptance of different opinions in the Church and in the cities. As it turned out, the execution was quite advantageous politically for Calvin, helping him to solidify his power over the whole of the city, and in particular over the councils after 1555. This year was relevant for his takeover for two reasons. First, because people from his party were elected to positions in the councils, but also because a riot gave him a pretext to confront his enemies by force, causing them either to flee or to be prosecuted or killed. From that time onward until his death, Calvin was the supreme lord of the city, controlling both spiritual and secular affairs through his tremendous impact on the works of the councils. The regime he established determined the daily life of the citizens among whom the Protestant refugees were soon in the majority. To round out the picture it should be added that Calvin had a great success story in his final years with the establishment of an educational institution which became famous Europe-wide, the Academy, offering humanistic training initially for ministers, and after Calvin's death also in medicine and the law. Its first rector was Theodore Beza, a supporter of Calvin, and a great humanist theologian. It was only as a result of the success of the school that he was appointed to the head of the school, and attained the status of *bourgeois* in 1559, a privilege which allowed him to be elected to the greater councils. He never received, however, the status of *citoyen*, actual citizenship.[109]

Geneva under Calvin's leadership was a somewhat eccentric example of the new relationship between church and state, but in fact the secular struggles unleashed by the Reformation led to an unprecedented liberation of cities from the control of local lords, secular or religious, while bringing direct control of the ordinary life of the citizenry by spiritual leaders like Calvin in Geneva, or Althusius in the Geneva of the North, Emden.

A further point to be emphasized in connection with the development of German cities is the existence of city alliances. This was quite a popular format which enabled cities to enter a higher level of politics. For some time, urban networks promised to become a viable alternative or at least a counterbalance to the power of the centralized state. Thanks to their experience of material advantages of medieval forms of cooperation like the Hansa league, German cities were ready and able to cooperate in the troubled times of the different waves of Reformation, and these city alliances were able to keep control over the territory in their hands, even as centralized territorial authorities were appearing within the Empire. It can also be argued that the newly born Dutch and Swiss states, with their examples of voluntary alliances of provinces and cantons, and large-scale institutional mechanisms of self-rule, once again encouraged the formation of economically and politically lucrative forms of urban cooperation.

Generally speaking, the historical circumstances which did not allow the birth of a superpower at the center of the Holy Roman Empire were helpful for the survival of urban autonomy in the politically and economically divided territory, leading to a rather flourishing city life in the early modern period whenever war did not hinder commerce and industry. This new urban renaissance was supported by the constitutional arrangements of the Empire, as well as by the Reformation, which redrew the relationship of secular and religious power within the city walls as well between the city and other imperial constitutional agents. Although German cities only very rarely managed to achieve actual sovereignty, a large proportion of them were able to flourish in spite of, or because of the divided nature of political power within the empire.

If Calvin's Geneva illustrates how the Reformation transformed the rule of individual cities in the south, it might be worth examining a somewhat similar effort in the north. I have already mentioned the city of Emden in the north-west of the Holy Roman Empire. This was a city that was governed for decades by Johannes Althusius, the most erudite political theoretician in the German territories, one of the founders of the new genre of *Politica*, at the turn of the 1600s. It is instructive to dwell on his achievement, as both his political practice and his vision had a lot to do with the ideology of the European city.

Althusius was one of the new generation of dynamic professors at the newly established Academy of the Reformed Church in Herborn (Herborn Academy or Academia Nassauensis), an Academy which followed the Calvinist–Reformed theology, when he was invited through the family of one of his students to help Emden in its crisis of government.[110] Born in 1557 in an independent *Grafschaft* or county of the Holy Roman Empire, he first studied the writings of Aristotle in Cologne, before obtaining a doctorate in civil and ecclesiastical law in Basel in 1586. After teaching from 1586 to 1592 at the Academy, he went on to study theology in Heidelberg. In 1595, Althusius became councilor to the count, and within two years became the rector of the Academy. He published a volume on ethics in 1601 (*Civilis Converstionis Libri Duo*), while "the greatest achievement of his Herborn years was the publication in 1603 of the *Politica*."[111] This was the first work in this genre, in accordance with the new way of thinking, which caught the attention of the elders of Emden. Their city was experiencing an unparalleled crisis of political authority in this period. While Emden, close to the Dutch territories, had profited a lot economically from the war in the Low Countries against Spanish rule, the legitimacy of the government was questioned in an internal struggle of the city, which made the local lords think that they could take power into their own hands. The internal conflict was connected to the fact that Emden was regarded as "the Geneva of the North," because of its "strong Calvinist spirit."[112] Emden was a religious center, organizing the Synod of Emden in 1571, but it had a Lutheran provincial lord and a Catholic emperor. It was as a result of the "increasingly serious conflict with its provincial lord, as well as with various larger and more powerful units of the German Empire and Spanish Kingdom," that the elders of the city looked for an able leader to help the city out of the crisis.[113] It was "Althusius's growing juristic reputation," which "led the City Council to invite him to become the Syndic of Emden."[114] Between 1604 when he arrived there until his death in 1638, he served, effectively, as the political leader of the city. On top of this, from 1617 he also became an elder in the church of the city. According to Carney, it was this duality of being a secular and a religious leader in the city which allowed him "to exercise somewhat the same kind of influence in Emden as Calvin did in Geneva."[115]

What is exceptional in Althusius's achievement is that he excelled both as a practicing leader of his city and as a theoretician of post-Reformation urban political thought. As we have seen, his theory helped him to obtain a key position in the city, and his experience as an urban leader helped him to polish his theory—there are two later, rewritten editions of his *Politica*. This is in harmony with his own theoretical presupposition, according to which "(t)he exercise of government is tied to the particular kind of ethical training and cultivation required for 'magistrates.'"[116] This connection between character formation and political leadership was already established as a basic conviction of humanist political theorists, and Protestant educational theories only preserved that idea.[117] The similarities between Althusius's own practice and the theoretical backbone of his *Politica* are well known.[118] He also draws on the historical summaries of the political consequences of German *Schulphilosophie*, "designed to groom students in the moral and intellectual deportment required for the active life of the magistrate."[119] The birth of the genre of *Politica* is explained by the political requirements of an age of crisis. In accordance with the discourse on passions in the somewhat later British experience of revolutionary fervor, in the Holy Roman Empire, too, "rulers and ruled alike seemed driven by passionate excess."[120] It is particularly useful for us that the scale used by Althusius in his own theoretical construction is not that of the empire, but more on the local level, in other words at the level of urban communities.[121]

Althusius's work is an exercise in "the art of political preservation." Order and stability required "unity and the preservation of internal harmony," which excluded democracy, which was identified by Aristotle as bringing political chaos. Althusius regards "election by common men," as "riddled with danger for the unity of the body politic, and will trigger rebellion and sedition."[122] Unity, in his view, required the acceptance of hierarchy, and as he saw it, both Platonism and Christianity accepted the existence of natural and institutional hierarchy. While the community (*res publica*) was a legal person (*universitas* or corporate commonwealth), it was "represented by magistrates on various levels."[123] Althusius's own practice of leadership in Emden rejected democratic participation, instead restoring what he called aristocratic rule: "as syndic he himself restored aristocratic rule to Emden by using mercenaries to crush the institutions of increased popular participation that had developed during the 1590s."[124] Yet unlike Calvin he was not an (absolute) ruler, in that his idea of the public realm included the lower magistrates and the citizens' body. Althusius recognized that social consent or consensus was essential. He believed that a great deal depended on the virtue of prudence exercised by magistrates.

The analysis of prudence and government is the topic of chapters xxi to xxvii in the *Politica*.[125] Men are born with a sense of society, or sociability, but they also need to be taught how to become useful for society. In this respect, Althusius applies his own work on Ciceronian ethics, his *Civilis conversationis libri duo* (1601, second edition 1611). In that work, he was influenced by Catholic ideas on discipline such as those of Giovanni della Casa.[126] The main point about his teaching, however, is that ethics is no longer a moral philosophy—as in Melanchton—but an *ars decore conversandi cum hominibus* (the art of appropriate social interaction).[127] His ethics are Ciceronian in the sense that they seek *decorum*, but this latter term is taken to mean *rite facere* (to do the appropriate thing) and not *recte facere* (to do the right thing).[128] Althusius's key notion is symbiosis, or men bound together in society.[129] Althusius sets out to achieve social cohesion described in his *Politica* as "symmetria," "concordia," "symphonia," and "harmonia." However, his point is to show the requirements of governability, the ability to rule a community.

Althusius argues that the magistrate needs to be able to influence the behavior of subjects in such a way as to achieve his ends: public peace and prosperity. Althusius's ethics are highly rhetorical in the sense that he is trying to directly address the subjects. On the other hand, this effort can also be called pedagogical: like the humanists in general, Althusius strives to reform the character of the people in order to allow them to live together. The main doctrines of Althusius, the teacher, can be found in his inaugural lecture, delivered at Herborn in 1603. This text has the advantage that in it the rhetor chose the topic of university education—it is a meta-discourse on the relevance of teaching. Althusius's ideas in this address belong to the tradition of Calvinist *Schulphilosophie*. The aim of teaching for him is to reform the human character, in order to make it more sociable. One should not forget that he lived in the midst of heated religious disputes in the Holy Roman Empire. His idea of sociability and concord is to heal the Augustinian element in human nature. The role of political prudence or practical wisdom is a prerequisite for the magistrate—it is required to show him how society can be kept together. The magistrate's virtues can overcome human passions. This would be impossible, however, if there was no sociable element in our nature, and it is here that the Aristotelian overtones of Althusius's teaching become obvious, as we shall now see.

Althusius's inaugural lecture starts with a description of human nature. He asserts that human beings have an inborn capacity to live together, and their full potential can only be attained in a community. Human virtue can only flourish in a community and that the human being is a political animal. He also refers here to Cicero, when he speaks of politics as "the art of organising and keeping men in '*Coetus juris consensus and utilitatis*' (a consensual and beneficial lawful union)."[130] His notion of prudence is also Ciceronian, even if he also refers to Lipsius and Seneca. As he sees it, it is through prudence that human passions can be kept under control. One should be aware of the drives that can lead human actions in the wrong direction. The alternative is to behave prudently: to keep to the established customs of the community. In this Althusius is closer to a conservative position than anything else. The duty of the magistrate is to sustain sociability, the benevolent feelings of the subjects.[131] The magistrate can only achieve this aim if his community traditionally possesses the sociable virtues. It should be highlighted that Althusius is addressing here not only the prince or monarch, but primarily lower-level magistrates. He himself belonged to "the social middle ranks," and as such the audience for his theory consists of people preparing to assume these positions for local communities and not those who will rule sovereign states. He conceived of his book as guidance particularly for members of city councils. They, too, required training in understanding politics (*intellectus politicus*).[132]

His age is well known for the interest it took in the teachings of reason of state. Althusius claimed that the magistrate, as a political expert, also needs to learn certain prudential techniques, such as "the exercise of dissimulation and distrust"[133] Chapter xvii of the *Politica* is particularly concerned with such prudential behavior. His points of departure here are Cicero and Lipsius, who agreed that in practical politics theoretical knowledge is not enough, and that practical experience is required to become prudent. Civil prudence consists of both the prudence of the magistrate himself and the prudence he acquires through taking advice. Those giving advice to the magistrate should thus also possess a specific prudence: "he should be a friend to the magistrate and *imperium* who is wise in the customs and sentiments of the subjects of the realm, and well acquainted with public affairs. . . . A good counsellor's requisites are prudence, a liberal mind, a sound disposition and fidelity towards the commonwealth, and a capacity for silence."[134] In other words, caution must be exercised already at the stage of the selection of the councilor who can give advice to the magistrate on how to judge particular cases. Counseling itself becomes crucial in early modern politics, as the prerequisite for making right political decisions.[135] According to Althusius's teaching of prudence, it is not only the prince's court or the Diet for which this virtue is crucial in politics, but also for the circles around the king's court and the Diet, as well as for the lower (regional and local) levels of decision-making, together with the circles around the lower (regional and local) levels of county and urban rule.

This multiplication of the levels on which Althusius's *Politica* found political prudence to be relevant is a consequence of his Aristotelian concept of politics as the art of keeping men together in society, as demanded by the size or scale of the particular society concerned. This attention to the local was allowed by the specific circumstances of the Holy Roman Empire.

Althusius was one of the post-Reformation late humanists for whom both Aristotle and Cicero were crucial, and his *Politica* made use of the language of ancient political thought on all these different levels. Also significant for

Althusius's project was the fact that he wrote updated versions of his book while he himself worked as a local magistrate in Emden, which allowed him to concentrate on the practical necessities of this art, strengthening his own concept of practical wisdom. Finally, the specific situation of the post-Reformation and pre-Westphalia era had an impact on this theory, when internal crisis made political leaders alert to the imminent and direct consequences of letting passions lead one's politics. In such circumstances, there was a demand for calm and detached decision-making, which directed attention to the political role of counselors, and which gave birth to the idea of a professional educational program for the training of local, regional, or federal magistrates. It also facilitated the development of different forms of university curriculum which aimed at providing training in prudence, connecting the different levels of the *ars politica* and reason of state, between the highest imperial courts and the lowest local councils.

URBAN MAGISTRACY AND ROYAL COURT IN CENTRAL EUROPE

The refined structure of Althusius's political thought throws doubt on the usual narrative of early modern Europe, which regards local autonomy and the centralized power of the state as two polar opposite forms of politics. If the privileges of the cities come from royal power, which sustains the autonomy of the urban community against the immediate demands of the feudal powers, there is no reason to suppose that royal power is something which urban forces wanted to negate. This is specifically true in a Central European context, where the cities were never as powerful economically and financially as in the German or the Italian lands, and where the court itself was not so clearly the ultimate authority as was the case in őther parts of Europe.

The reason behind this historically specific state of affairs in the political stratification of Central Europe was that, compared to the general pattern, where the birth of the centralized territorial state led directly to the derogation of local autonomy, this phenomenon appeared later in Central Europe.[136] An example which illustrates the intricate relationship between town and court in the early modern Central European area can be found in one of the key figures of the town council of *Sopron*. Kristóf Lackner (1571–1631) was an exceptionally talented local leader, who was able to maintain a balance of power between local and national forces in a rather confused historical situation. His way of thinking and his own practice of leadership seem to embody the kind of well-educated local leader in the post-Reformation era who was able to keep his power and authority intact at home while successfully negotiating with the royal court externally.

Lackner had to confront several crucial challenges as a local town leader. To appreciate the scale of these problems one needs to understand the geopolitical situation of the city, which he governed for so long, certainly not with full autonomy, but preserving his space to maneuver throughout. Sopron (*Ödenburg*, Latin *Scarbantia*) lies on the border between the Hungarian Kingdom and the Habsburg lands. For most of its history its population was partly Hungarian, partly German. Lackner himself was sent to a nearby village to learn Hungarian as a child, a historical fact which suggests that he himself must have been German by birth, both ethnically and culturally. In his analysis of the mentality of late Renaissance Hungary, Tibor Klaniczay claimed that Lackner was a representative of the patrician caste of Sopron whose way of life was in a number of respects quite close to the feudal aristocracy of the country.[137] Lackner can be characterized by that sort of Stoic consciousness which was so pervasive in the elite of the late sixteenth century in this region. Perhaps the best known example of this way of thinking is, of course, the thought of Justus Lipsius, who was widely recognized in Hungary. Lipsius has long been seen as the leading light of representatives of the newly born Hungarian sciences of the state, including Lackner, whose "whole oeuvre is pervaded by the neo-Stoic way of thinking."[138] Yet interestingly, while Lackner's ethical ideas are close to those of Lipsius, his politics were not Stoic. Lipsius was a proponent of the centralized monarchical power and was not really anxious to defend urban privileges. On the other hand, Lackner, as a top leader of a free royal city of the Hungarian Kingdom, with an ancient Roman pedigree, was determined to defend the privileges of the city from local lords and the court. On the other hand, of course, full autonomy would not have been a realistic demand.

Stoic in his ethics, Lackner can be regarded as a representative of the typical urban republican "ideologist" of the early modern period in Europe. This way of thinking was not fully developed theoretically, but Lackner was able to articulate the main pillars of this perspective whereby urban republicanism embraces both the city as a political community (*civitas*), and the fatherland (*patria*). A mayor like Lackner works in the interests of the common good of the city (unlike the courtier, who works for the reason of state of the monarch). However, Lackner is careful to avoid regarding the interests of the city and the reason of state as contradictory. As the city's flourishing depended on commerce (which required peace and good external connections), and because the city was close to Vienna and the Habsburg court, he regarded politics as the art of compromise and tactical negotiations between city and court.

While compromise was not a new idea, Lackner's own version of it was unlike the political philosophy of Lipsius, whose main focus was on the hierarchical relationship between ruling and being obedient. Lackner himself chose, from the available discourses of the developing new disciplines of politics, the German type of Aristotelianism.[139] His version of Aristotelianism was, indeed, an art of compromise. A historiography has grown up according to which the seventeenth century can be regarded in Hungary as an age of compromises.[140] This is the century when the kingdom was divided into three parts, due to the Ottoman Turkish invasion of the central parts of the country, with the remaining parts having two competing rulers. One of them was a member of the House of Habsburg, ethnically non-Hungarian, and defending the Catholic cause, while the competitor was the prince of the newly proclaimed Transylvanian principality, himself ethnically Hungarian, and Protestant (in particular, Calvinist). In this divided situation, the political institutions of the country (the court, the principality, and the Diet), looked for compromises, negotiating a number of political agreements in the seventeenth century.[141] Lackner actively participated in the forging of two of these pacts (that of 1608 and 1622). In fact, as it turns out, Sopron was a locus of two of the five agreements, which suggests that not only its chief magistrate, but the city as a political community was indeed engaged in the process of creating systematic political settlements.

Sopron was a recurring location for the elites to meet and forge such compromises in the seventeenth century. I would argue that this is because the city had a very conscious strategy. One of the sources of Lackner's political success was that he was capable of winning the trust of the opposing parties to this compromise, and therefore he was crucial for the negotiations to start. Both his political activity and his written political pamphlets can thus be interpreted as part of the same clever strategy on his part. His art of forging compromises can be seen as an expression of the urban republicanism he was attached to, as undoubtedly the most experienced and influential political leader of his city. His political writings can also be explained in the context of this overall urban republican strategy. His art of compromise was paralleled by the newly born reason of state literature on the level of the city, a well-defined strategy of *ratio civilis* or *prudentia civilis*.

To understand the European context of this reason of the city, we have to consider the Italian background, noting that Lackner himself studied in Padova. It was in Italy in the late sixteenth and early seventeenth centuries that the literature of *ragion di stato* was born. It was a reaction to the work of Machiavelli from the representatives of the glorious counterreformation. Authors such as Ciro Spontone, Federico Bonaventura, Girolamo Frachetta, and Pietro Andrea Canoniero tried to adopt elements of Machiavellian political theory and insert them into the framework of Christian moral philosophy. As we shall see, Lackner's own urban politics of compromise can be understood in light of this Italian reason of state literature.[142]

Another genre can also be sensed in the background of Lackner's writings. This type of text was connected to late sixteenth-century German and Dutch authors, and it can be described as "advice on maintaining order" "merged into a new independent subject in the spectrum of the *artes liberales*. Its topic was politics, and the publication usually considered its prototype was the *Politica*, which drew together political philosophy, legal training and practical advice."[143] Usually it provided detailed suggestions on how to regulate economy and society, a task made easier in the context of a local community, "the middling and small jurisdictions of the imperial estates."[144] While Lipsius himself was crucial for this literature, another major author in this Aristotelian tradition was Johannes Althusius.

But did Lackner indeed have a connection to this literature of German culture and society? Beyond the fact that culturally Lackner belonged to a German urban community within the Hungarian Kingdom, his study in Padova might once again be relevant. After all, it was Padova where an openness toward the Holy Roman Empire was kept alive even after the Reformation, in order to attract as many students from that territory as possible. It was this German intellectual influence in Padova that can be detected in the way of thinking of Lackner.

He is known, for example, to have published a work entitled *Politia*. This work was written in the interest of his patria (*pro patria*), a term which in those days could still also mean the city rather than the country of the author. This text offered a full account of the tasks of a council member (*consiliariorum*), the specific method of free election of magistrates, and further details of processes in jurisdiction and elsewhere. His claims were supported with examples taken from legal regulations and principles, both from civil and criminal law.[145]

From the perspective of the present enquiry, however, a rather instructive work is his *Oration* about the glory of his city, Sopron. Although this address was published only recently, it was prepared for publication by its author. It is based on a public oration given in 1612 at the Learned Society (*Tudós Társaság*) of the city. This elite club of the city was established by Lackner, with only seventeen founding members. By the time the oration was given, it counted already thirty-six members, coming from rather different backgrounds, including noblemen as well as learned citizens and practitioners of such professions as merchant, chemist, notary, soldier, choir-master, schoolmaster, and so on.[146]

The genre of the oration itself goes back to the panegyric on the city of Italian humanism, the most famous example of which was Leonardo Bruni's *Laudatio Florentinae Urbis* (1404). This genre presents all the advantageous character traits of the city. Here the city is regarded as the patria, in the full sense of the term, as it was used in ancient Rome. It was Cicero who—referring back in *On Duties* to Plato—wrote that:

> it has been well said by Plato, we are not born for ourselves alone; since our country claims a part in us, our parents a part, our friends a part; . . . in this matter we ought to follow nature as a guide, to contribute our part to the common good, and by the interchange of kind offices, both in giving and receiving, alike by skill, by labor, and by the resources at our command, to strengthen the social union of men among men.[147]

Lackner explains this human attachment to the patria with the notion that the *patria* charms or enchants us, and that it does not let us forget about it.[148] Yet there is another rather obvious and well-known reason why a town can charm its citizens: it offers its citizens freedom. Sopron is presented by Lackner as a free royal city, which allowed the most autonomous form of urban self-government in the Hungarian Kingdom. The orator puts the phrase in a rather self-contradictory context, when he claims that a key merit of the town is that "it is obedient to royal power as a free royal city."[149] He knows that freedom and obedience do not often accompany each other, and therefore adds boldly that freedom "lives under the defence of the royal crown."[150] The royal crown in Hungarian political thought is a multi-layered concept. It is therefore not surprising that the Crown is referred to here as if it had a special power in itself, defending those who were under its jurisdiction. While in the customary historical constitution of Hungary towns had certain privileges, these were not extensive, and they could not always make use of these privileges. These privileges needed to be safeguarded by the crown itself. Lackner's point is that the freedom of the city is closely connected to the constitutional edifice of the kingdom. He carefully lists the duties of the king: "to avoid wars, to throw back the offensive of the enemy, this way thwarting his intention, to avoid the wind of storm with the help of the expanded sails of words."[151] He describes the citizens of Sopron as being famous for their love of freedom, linking urban freedom with certain rights of the city, including *jus gladii* and omnipotence, a term which he uses in the sense of Bodin's concept of sovereignty. Lackner's formulation of the liberty-loving nature of the citizens of his city, therefore, remains within the confines of loyalty to the crown, an idea which would remain with the city later in its history. Lackner most probably took over this form of devotion to liberty from the humanist laudations of the Italian city-states, and applies it to his own city. His oration states explicitly that "liberty has an inestimable value (*Libertas enim inaestimabilis res est*)."[152]

He associates other values with his city besides freedom. One of these values is undoubtedly wealth or (material) prosperity. He finds "the measure of wealth and opulence" to be crucial—and most historians would attest that in this period Sopron did indeed fare well economically. When explaining this opulence, Lackner refers to three factors: hard work, diligence, and concord. While the first two points connect him to the representatives of Protestant ethic in the spirit of Max Weber, the last point links urban politics with the state of economic affairs in the city. Apparently, Lackner is trying here to convince his own fellow citizens of the merits and individual utility of cooperation and of a close stewardship of order inside the city walls. This is the communal aspect of his laudation, a point which had much cogency in the troubled political context. As he saw it, the city should severely punish the free rider, who pretends to take part in a game of coordination but exits when doing so promises to be more profitable. Unlike Machiavelli, Lackner rests his argument on traditional Christian teaching, according to which wealth is "the pious grace and present of the Allmighty God."[153]

He also makes a very powerful defense of erudition, as a key factor in the growth of a thriving city. The German discourse on local government recognized the growing significance of public administration, and Lackner concurred with this. His terminology is telling: he refers to *politeia*, or public administration, also using the Latin version of the term, *administrationem Rei pub(licae)*.[154] By using this terminology he was implying that the success of administering the city was closely connected to the level of education of those who took part in that well-organized structure of administration. In his ideal city

> (p)owerfully flourishes the cultivation of the study of the liberal arts (cultus et doctrina liberalium disciplinarum), and the permanent education and civilization of the youth, all of which aims the better and better celebration of God's inexhaustible goodness towards men and the growth of the seeds of those in society who can manage the public affairs. (. . . *et seminarium reipub. pro capessenda adminsitratione educatur*).[155]

The most important body of the city, the council, by which he in fact means the whole assembly of the citizens, has a special legitimacy, according to Lackner: they are a corporate body due to the privileges of the city granted by Hungary's kings.[156] This exceptional and special royal preference, adds Lackner, was due to the loyalty which the citizens of the city manifested and pronounced toward the *patria* and its kings. This loyalty is, as he sees it, the secret of the city's right administration (*politeia*).[157] Lackner's political vision was similar to the communal thinking we detected in the ideology of late medieval German cities. Yet he was also aware of the city's vulnerability to external threats, and therefore he attributed a special significance to loyalty to the crown. His popularity among members of the elite was due to the fact that he did indeed manage to bring peace and prosperity to his city by his sense of diplomacy. On the other hand, as mayor of the city he took good care to win the support of the elite. That is why he does not spare laudatory words from the senate of the city. The council is "a guardian of the grace of the city, in accordance to its oath, searching the good of private and public interest," relying on "the two anchors of reward and punishment," "whatever might be helpful for the augmentation of the common good, it negotiates and fosters."[158] But he also expects loyalty to the crown even from the senate, as long as the crown attests the privileges offered to the town. This is how he describes the city council: "all royal decrees—if it is not beyond its capacity—it is ready to comply with."[159] Once again, in accordance with the practice of German towns in this period, Lackner's Protestant vision does not lose sight of a special care for the charitable functions of public administration: "the council itself takes care of orphans, orphanages, the abandoned and the widows, the schools and congregations."[160] A further proof of his Protestant ethic is that Lackner criticizes luxury, and claims that the council as a good steward or trustee of the public wealth, "has its own controllers and caretakers, from whom it expects a strict financial accounting."[161] It was István Németh who explained that during the seventeenth century the financial autonomy of the royal cities of the Hungarian Kingdom was later lost step by step, giving way to the royal inspectors, whose duty it was to ensure that the taxes and other financial obligations of the city were duly paid to the treasury of the court.[162]

Once again, it is crucial that in spite of his apparent popularity both among the elites and the wider population, Lackner did not promise full-scale urban autonomy in his speech. Rather, he concentrated on prosperity and peace, the free but controlled flow of goods and services, which can satisfy the demands of the city dwellers and especially, of the civil communities (this distinction once again showing his conscious policy of always preferring the interests of the citizens with voting power, the ability to pay taxes, and participate in the affairs of the city). The main point of his oration was the maintenance of social order by preserving the unavoidable hierarchy in assets and social prestige. He required—in accordance with the (reformed) Christian teaching—that "everyone should live satisfied with his own fate, adapting himself in accordance with his social status and his own condition, to the public interest."[163] This is quite evidently the sort of negotiation between private and public interest that is the hallmark of what is referred to as *Obrigkeit* in the historiography of early modern German urban history. Yet the argument also has a communal aspect: the social structure of the city did not change very much after the reformation, and therefore his main point was that in the city the individual was not opposed to the community, but on the contrary, his or her private interests were negotiated in the different communities, in which all citizens necessarily partook. Lackner's laudation is a good example of the way even the strongest local leaders had to refer to the good of the community in their own ideology. Unlike some of the more independent German cities, due to the special external political environment of his city, Lackner specifically stressed the relationship between the Crown and the cities, as a key to the success of the latter. Even in his most forward-looking ideas about public administration Lackner keeps emphasizing not only the mayor's, but the city administration's loyalty to the court. Yet this should not be seen as a decline of urban self-governance. In fact, we know from the historians' account of his activity that Lackner was able to very cleverly convince the power holders and decision-makers of both the national Diet and of the Royal court that he and his city were not against the interests of the territorial state. One can even make the stronger claim, that indeed, because of his clear views of the functions of administration at the various levels of power, and of the interplay between them, Lackner was in fact convinced of the necessity of cooperation between city and court. In other words, for him the city's autonomy was not, and should not be, absolute. No royal city can thrive if the country is not free and flourishing, and if the court cannot guarantee its privileges. The loyalty of his city, Sopron, to the crown was proven in 1605, when Bocskai's troops occupied a large section of the Western part of the Kingdom, and yet Sopron remained on the side of the crown.[164] It was the geopolitical reality of the day that supported this political choice of the city, as pointed out by Katalin Szende in her review of a monograph about the conflict between Bocskai and the city, which ended in an unsuccessful siege.[165] Yet one should also emphasize the statesmanship of Lackner who correctly measured the actual political weight of the particular political forces in the civil war waged between the Habsburg court and the principality of Transylvania. Lackner's diplomatic maneuvers were typical of Protestant city leaders' strategy and tactics in Central Europe, who governed cities whose freedom depended on royal privileges. Loyalty to the homeland and to the territorial state was in fact demanded by the ideology of the early modern city, as illustrated by Lackner's rhetorically phrased confession of why he undertook the project of writing in praise of his beloved city: "The whole work has broken out from the depth of my spirit in order to search the honour of the *patria*, and its benefits. . ," giving a true account of "his own attraction towards the *patria*."[166] Lackner's concept of public administration clarified the complex relationship between the court and the city that characterized the early modern division of power in this area of Central Europe. We have to understand that the longstanding success of Lackner as the head of the city administration depended on the complex *repertoire* of roles he played in the political life of Hungary: he was not simply a city mayor, but also took part in the political life of the local Diet of his county, as a nobleman, as well as a representative of his royal city in the national Diet; he could directly communicate in the royal court, as leader of a tax-paying city, and even went on diplomatic missions, to ensure the success of foreign commerce in his city. Finally, he was a patron of culture, a late humanist himself, who established an academy on the humanist model, as well as an ardent believer of his reformed Evangelical (Lutheran) Christian faith. As a city magistrate he had to cooperate on different levels of the political hierarchy of the territorial state, searching for cooperation, commerce, and compromise. In his speech, Lackner emphasized negotiation between individual and public interests and a consistently communal way of thinking, mediating between the local and the central, which was an unavoidable condition for cities to flourish in the early modern period.

CITY AND CENTRAL POWER IN THE EARLY MODERN PERIOD: AN OVERVIEW

One way of summarizing the conclusions that can be drawn from these stories of early modern urban life in Europe is to take an acquaintance of Lackner, Johannes Bocatius, as a paradigm case. The two of them were personally linked: Bocatius wrote a poem to welcome the publication of the school drama of Lackner, entitled *Cura Regia seu Consultatio Paterna* (The King's Worry or Paternal Consultation). This drama was staged in 1615 in the council room of the city hall of Sopron, a location which was quite in accordance with the pedagogical intentions of its author.

Who was Johannes Bocatius, the author of this poem, and why could he be taken as a good example to sum up the relationship between city and court in the early modern context, especially in the context of Central Europe? He lived between the troubled years of 1569 and 1621, and his life was mainly connected to the upper Hungarian city of Kassa. This was the city Szepsi Csombor forest off from on his European travels, the same city whose medieval struggles Sándor Márai was to dramatize. Bocatius can be regarded as a late humanist, a poet by vocation, but one who earned his living as a schoolmaster, and with his career and social standing was eventually appointed to the responsible position of the chief justice of Kassa. He was born into a bourgeois family with German and Wendish roots in the town of Vetschau in Lauschitz, Germany. His father was a merchant, which made him a representative of the new middle class.[167] He spent his early years studying in some of the most celebrated schools of Saxony, including Dresden and Wittenberg. It was in this environment of the early Reformation that he had discovered and fallen in love with poetry. He followed one of his masters in Iglau (Jihlava) to the town of *Körmöcbánya* in the Hungarian Kingdom. The town was a center of gold and silver mining in Hungary, with close connections to the

Lutheran territories of Silesia and Lauschitz, from where teachers and pastors arrived on a regular basis. Unlike the central part of the Hungarian Kingdom, which was occupied by the Ottoman Turks at this time, these lands were part of the Habsburg Empire, but enjoyed a certain degree of autonomy from the direct rule of Vienna, with their main political center being in Kassa. Bocatius found work as school teacher in 1593 in the nearby town of *Eperjes* (*Prešov*, Preschau) and was married, to Elisabeth Belsius. As a young man he was full of the new pedagogical ideas of the Lutherans but, being an erudite man, the writings of the ancient thinker Seneca also inspired him. His pedagogical program was to prepare his pupils, would-be local leaders and administrators, to live a meaningful life after they leave the school. Through his wife's family he also became acquainted with the political elites of his new country. His father-in-law, who died just before their marriage, was the secretary to the influential Catholic Churchman, Antal Verancsics. It was through these connections that, after the publication of a laudation of the archduke (*Ungaria gratulans*) he received the title of *poeta laureatus caesareus* (poet laureate of the emperor) from the Archduke Maximilian and was later ennobled by the Emperor, and King of Hungary, Rudolph II.

Bocatius very soon (in fact within a year), climbed the social ladder to become the Rector of the Gymnasium in Eperjes. Through his poetry, as well as his socializing capacity he obtained a number of supporters, among them major political actors (Zsigmond Báthory and Archduke Maximilian), aristocrats, and influential burghers. In the meantime, he received the title of magister from the University of Wittenberg, a remarkable achievement in that age, which allowed his administrative career to fly even higher. After seven years in Eperjes, he was invited by the council of Kassa, the major city in Upper Hungary, to take up the position of Rector of the Gymnasium of this larger and more powerful city. It was after moving to Kassa that he published his best known poetic work, entitled *Hungaridos libri poematum quinque* (Five Books of poems about Hungary) in 1599. Within half a year he was offered the position of city notary, for which position he gave up his post as head of the school, and received the citizenship of Kassa.

His career continued to flourish in Kassa. By 1601 he had become a senator or consul on the city council of twelve members. Then in 1603 and 1604 he was elected chief justice (*főbíró*, *judex*) of the city, the most important political position within the city. This, however, was the peak of his fortune—by 1605, he was only a senator, and by 1607 he would have been only a member of the *communitas* (the external council consisting of sixty to ninety members), had he not been imprisoned by that time. He was never ever able to regain a major position in the city administration.

It is at this point where his adventurous life becomes symbolically relevant for our story. So far, it might have been called typical of the age: a talented and motivated young man of German bourgeois culture and with a humanist education arrived from the Empire to Hungary and made his fortune as a town leader. In Bocatius's case, however, it was his exceptional renown that caused his ill fortune. As a town leader he was entrusted with important missions to and later from the Diet of Hungary, the most important self-governing organ of the Hungarian Kingdom. He took part in the Diet of *Pozsony* (Bratislava) in 1601, and later that year he took part in the deputation of the city to the court in Vienna and later to Prague, to ask for some allowances for the city after the great city fire.

His most important, symbolic struggle was in defense of the most important religious symbol of the city, the Saint Elisabeth church. In 1603 the Emperor ordered the Protestants to leave the church and return it to the Catholics. As the council declined to accept the order, the captain general of the imperial troops in Hungary, the Italian aristocrat Barbiano di Belgioioso, whose troops were lodged in the city, occupied the main square, threatening to destroy the whole city if he did not receive the keys of the church. Bocatius was not ready to comply, and only acquiesced the next day, expressing serious moral caveats at the injustice of this aggressive act. This injustice was followed by a number of hostile decisions against the Protestants, including the expelling of their preachers, prohibiting Protestant congregations, and also taking away from the city its twenty-eight villages which were vital for the supply of the city.

While the conflict was sparked by the denominational tension between the Catholic monarch and the Protestant city, the reason it became inflamed was the court's desire to show that it can have the final word in religious debates within cities, too. By this time, it was obvious that cities cannot compete with empires in maintaining standing armies—which was especially impossible in Central Europe, where the economic power of cities was not as strong as on the Italian peninsula. Furthermore, even the Italian city-states were losing the arms race with centralized states by then.

Instead of fighting a lonely and unpromising battle with the crown, Kassa tried to retaliate by the traditional methods: convening the five cities with which it had a longstanding alliance (the so-called *Pentapolitana* consisting of Eperjes, Bártfa, Kisszeben, and Lőcse besides Kassa).[168] It also petitioned the monarch, with a delegation from the city, led by Bocatius, traveling to Prague, where they spent four long months trying to impress some of the courtiers who might mediate between them and the king, but without success. The city alliance also tried to enlist the help of those county Diets in which there was a Protestant majority, also without success. Then, at the initiative of Bocatius, the city went one step further. When Barbiano took his troops to fight Stephen Bocskai, Prince of Transylvania, between 1605 and 1606, Bocskai was supported by the *hajdú*s, a specific group of Hungarian herdsmen. They even succeeded in winning a battle against Barbiano, and following their victory the city decided to support them. The city gates were opened for them, giving over the defense system of the city to Bocskai, instead of the royal army. The motivation behind this decision was rather obvious: while the legitimate Hungarian monarch, the Habsburg, Rudolph was Catholic, Bocskai was Protestant. This denominational division was present in the whole body of the local aristocracy, which was, therefore, divided in its loyalty between the royal court and the rebellious prince (*fejedelem*) of the Transylvanian principality.

The decision by Bocatius and his city to take the side of Bocskai was an obvious, but by no means an easy one. We have seen that Sopron, led by its mayor Kristóf Lackner made a different decision even if the majority of the citizens there, too, were Lutherans. This difference between their respective political commitments was partly due to the difference in their geopolitical position. Sopron was closer to Vienna, while Kassa was closer to the territory of the principality. Bocatius, who was not a native Hungarian, but part-German, part-Sorbian, had no other choice but to go along with the national line, instead of taking the side of the Habsburg dynasty. In any case, the rebellion of the city made Bocatius famous among the political elite of the Hungarian Diet, which was summoned in 1605 in *Szerencs* and later in the same year in *Korpona*. Bocatius answered this political summons in the delegation of the city. He also participated in the diplomatic meeting between the Turks and the Hungarians, before Bocskai had entered into peace talks with the Habsburgs. This meeting was recounted by Bocatius in his famous *Commemoratio* (1605), which gave a vivid picture of the run-down state of Pest-Buda under Turkish occupation.

The personal calvary of Bocatius really started, however, when he was elected to lead a diplomatic delegation to the secular electors of the Holy Roman Empire, to explain Bocskai's intentions to them. Although Bocatius was not keen to take this job, he could not turn it down. It was a total failure, because they were captured when they tried to cross the royal territory toward the Holy Roman Empire, and Bocatius was imprisoned by the king in Prague, to take revenge on the rebellious Hungarians. When they heard the news of his imprisonment the whole elite of the Hungarian nobility was appalled. Leading Church and secular figures made efforts to influence the king to release the council leader. Besides the leading figures of the Diet, including the palatine, György Thurzó, who tried to intervene, Bocatius's wife, Mrs. Elisabeth Belsius, also made exceptional efforts to rescue her beloved husband. But neither of these efforts proved successful. Yet in 1610, Bocatius got out of the prison, as far as we know, by actually escaping from the castle of Prague. As Bocatius wrote a full account of his imprisonment, all the details of it are available, except for those of his escape, which makes it an exceptional source of historical evidence. His unparalleled literary talent makes it difficult to verify that all the details which he provided in his narrative were historically correct. Compared to the legends which grew up about his escape, and more particularly about the self-sacrificing role his wife was supposed to have played in it, his account was quite objective, however. The general tenor of the tale told about his wife, was, for example, that she had had to make use of her female beauty in order to arrange for the escape which was, of course, a fabrication, and not the truth. Bocatius himself never used such narrative devices. Even so, his story was quite colorful, and the adventurous elements of it helped to keep his fame alive in Hungarian literature, up to the short story by the classic Hungarian writer, Mór Jókai, *The adventures of Bokácius* in the nineteenth century. Although some of the details of what actually happened are not clear even today, he probably had accomplices in his flight, but without his own active and courageous involvement in it the escape would not have been possible.

Perhaps the most surprising thing is how he was received in his hometown of Kassa, after almost two months of roaming from Prague to home. The magistracy of the city must have been in a sensitive political situation after his appearance: they certainly did not want to provoke the king once again by celebrating his return. They arranged a formal trial to clear up the legal status of the escape, in which Bocatius's case was defended by a preacher from the German part of the city, Georg Fabritius. Fabritius addressed his plea to the "respectable Senate" and the "noble Communitas," which shows that the case was taken rather seriously, as a matter for the whole community (*res publica*). The plea put the responsibility of sending Bocatius as an official delegate on the shoulders of Bocskai and the Diet. In order to avoid accusing the monarch of illegally arresting and imprisoning him, Fabritius claimed that false accusations had been made to deceive the king. As for his escape, the official version of the defense was that "as a result of his prayers was wonderfully set free," which was an acceptable explanation when pronounced by a preacher. As the palatine György Thurzó had released by that time a letter of protection (*protectionalis*) for Bocatius, Fabritius simply requested the affirmation of the letter by the Senate and the Community. But more importantly, he and his protégé requested the brotherly recognition of his loyalty to the city during his mission by his fellow citizens, which was more understandable, if we recall his earlier services to the community of citizens. Bocatius would have also welcomed financial restitution, but the basic point was to clear up his legal status, and regain his earlier reputation. In return he offered to write the story of the last few years, and in particular the miseries which had befallen the city, and more generally, on the country, explaining why they had no choice but to defend themselves in arms. This part of the defense was referring to the role played by the city and the country in the Bocskai affair, who in the Viennese peace treaty succeeded in stabilizing his position and even gained certain territories from the king, but died shortly afterward.

The interesting point for us here is not that the city allowed Bocatius to regain full membership of the community, but that they never elected him to any leading position in the council or elsewhere, offering him only his old position of the Rector of the school, which he was not in a position to decline. He remained in the service of the city, until Gábor Bethlen, the Prince of Transylvania, and later king-elect of Hungary arrived in Kassa. Bethlen offered him a job as something similar to a court historian, which was a prestigious position, and he accepted it, publishing two later works of historical narratives, *Mercurius historicus* (1620) and *Historia parasceve* (1621). Also, escorting his lord, he took part in the negotiations in Nikolsburg. Yet, he never regained his reputation in the eyes of the general public of his city.

Bocatius's story is interesting for us because of the unintended swings between city and country, which were so characteristic in an age when royal power was becoming centralized, and taking power away from the cities and placing it into the hands of court administrators. As an exceptionally influential intellectual of the age, Bocatius relied during his career on the services he could offer to his city. He was a rising star in the administrative and political circles of the city, and gained the most important position of the *iudex* very soon, but as such, was forced to take part in national politics, in which role he was sent on this rather dubious official diplomatic mission, and suffered violence, as the representative of his city, by the king.

Born and educated in the Empire, living his life as a native German speaker, he was also forced to make a difficult political choice between the opposing camps of the Transylvanian Prince and the Hungarian King, and opted to support both Bocskai and Bethlen against the Habsburg ruler—presumably due to the geopolitical realities of his town, and also because of his religious beliefs, which were being persecuted by the Catholic Habsburgs. His decision to accept the office of the court historian of Bethlen shows that by that time the court was a much more attractive sponsor and employer of an intellectual than a city council. Yet Bocatius continued to refer to himself as *civis cassoviensis*, the citizen of Kassa, and sometimes as *consularis* which meant that he was proud to have been a former mayor of his city. In the rather hectic political situation in early modern Upper Hungary, which had faced multiple threats from the Turks, the Transylvanian Prince, and the recatholizing efforts of the Crown, the city of Kassa lost much of its autonomy while trying to make the right diplomatic decisions. The competing courts of the Habsburg dynasty and the Transylvanian Prince determined the political balance of power, and in this stormy climate cities were destined to lose control over their fate. Bocatius, who was among the best minds of his age, with an unparalleled erudition, played a heroic role as the leader of his city, but the civil war-like situation proved to be a fatal obstacle to his mission and in the end his compatriots were not grateful for his services. Although Kassa remained an influential city for quite some time, it was not possible for the city to resist the major tendency of the age, which was growing royal control over the major cities of the country.[169] Due to its military, economic-financial, and administrative potential, the executive power of the centralized state won over the autonomous city. Yet, as we have also seen, it is not true that historically urban politics were no longer relevant after the birth of the Westphalian system, which is usually associated with the birth of a new form of the centralized state in Europe, generally. Cities kept much of their internal governance, even if the institutional structure of it became more complex, and the state administration kept a watchful eye on their activities, in order to collect in full the annual taxes from the town, and to uncover and pre-empt potential secret political coups. Yet, in spite of the close administrative control over the city, Kassa kept its important position in the politics of the day in Upper Hungary, revealing the continuing historical significance of urban centers even among the disadvantageous circumstances of early modern political life.

NOTES

1. William Shakespeare, *The Tragedy of Romeo and Juliet*, ed. Barbara A. Mowat and Paul Werstine, Folger Shakespeare Library, http://www.folgerdigitaltexts.org, 7–243, 243. https://www.folgerdigitaltexts.org/download/pdf/Rom.pdf

2. Ibid., 241.

3. *"Concordia parvae res crescunt, Discordia vero maxime dilabuntur"* (Salustius Crispus: *Bellum Iugurthinum*, 10.6).

4. Shakespeare, *The Tragedy*, 241.

5. Hendrik Spruyt, *The Sovereign State and Its Competitors: An Analysis of Systems Change* (Princeton: Princeton University Press, 1994), 135.

6. Ibid.

7. Ibid.

8. Ibid. Spruyt refers here, as often in other contexts, to Lauro Martines, *Power and Imagination: City-States in Renaissance Italy* (Baltimore: The Johns Hopkins University Press, 1988). This time to page 16.

9. Spruyt, *The Sovereign State*, 136.

10. Philip Jones, *The Italian City-State: From Commune to Signoria* (Oxford: Clarendon Press, 1997).

11. Ibid., 152.

12. Ibid.

13. Spruyt, *The Sovereign State*, 142.

14. Ibid.

15. Ibid., 143.

16. Ibid.
17. Ibid.
18. Ibid.
19. Ibid., 144. Spruyt relies here on Marvin Becker, "Some Aspects of Oligarchical, Dictatorial and Popular Signorie in Florence 1282–1382," *Comparative Studies in Society and History* 2 (July 1960): 421–39.
20. Hans Baron, "The Social Background of Political Liberty in the Early Italian Renaissance," *Comparative Studies in Society and History* 2 (July 1960): 446.
21. Nicolai Rubinstein, "Florence and Venice: Guicciardini," in *The Cambridge History of Political Thought, 1450–1700* (Cambridge: Cambridge University Press, 1991), 58–65. It might be relevant that Rubinstein himself came from a German Jewish background, and must have had a direct knowledge of the German tradition of interpreting Renaissance Italy, as exemplified by Jacob Burckhardt, among others.
22. Rubinstein, *Florence*, 55.
23. Alison Brown, "Introduction," in Francesco Guicciardini, *Dialogue on the Government of Florence*, ed. and trans. Alsion Brown (Cambridge: Cambridge University Press, 2002), vii–xxviii, x.
24. I call the rule of the Medici a kind of covered monarchy, because prior to 1537, the city remained formally a republic.
25. To be sure, Gaetano Lettieri has proven, that Machiavelli had the chance to take part in important missions for the Medici in 1525, through the mediation of Guicciardini.
26. Rubinstein, *Florence*, 59.
27. Ibid., 59, translation from Francesco Guicciardini, *Dialogo e discorsi del reggimente di Firenze*, ed. R. Palmarocchi (Bari: Laterza, 1932), 16. I myself will rely on the modern English language edition in the series of the Cambridge texts in the history of political thought. For details see notes below.
28. The first quote is the expression of Rubinstein, in *Florence*, 60, while the second one is the expression of the Italian author, in the *Dialogue*, trans. Rubinstein.
29. Rubinstein, *Florence*, 61, referring once again to the 1932 Italian language edition of the *Dialogo*, 118–9.
30. Rubinstein, *Florence*, 63. He quotes from Guicciardini, *Ricordi*, ed. R. Spongano (Florence: Sansoni, 1951).
31. Rubinstein, *Florence*, 63, translating Ricordi, C 218.
32. These are the words of Rubinstein, ibid., 63, but quoting Ricordi, A 119.
33. Rubinstein, *Florence*, 63.
34. Guicciardini, *Dialogue on the Government of Florence*, 39–40. A textual variant uses the expression about the plebs to riot, to make obvious the risks Guicciardini finds in the rule of the plebs—once again in harmony with Aristotle's dictum of the dangers of democracy and of the merits of balance and keep in the middle way.
35. Brown, "Introduction," xx–xxi.
36. Both of these quotes come from Guicciardini's "Considerations on the 'Discourses' of Machiavelli," in Francesco Guicciardini, *Selected Writings*, ed. C. and M. Grayson (Oxford: Oxford University Press, 1965), 65, quoted by Brown, *Introduction*, xxi.

37. Richard MacKenney, *The City-State, 1500–1700. Republican Liberty in an Age of Princely Power* (London: MacMillan, 1989), 5.
38. Ibid.
39. Ibid., 7.
40. Brian Pullan, "The Roles of the State and of the Town in the European Crisis of the 1590s," in *The European Crisis of the 1590s: Essays in Comparative History*, ed. Peter Clark (London: George Allen & Unwin, 1985).
41. MacKenney, *The City-State*, 8.
42. Ibid., 10.
43. Ibid., 15.
44. Ibid., 18.
45. Ibid., 22, referring to Peter Burke, *The Historical Anthropology of Early Modern Italy* (Cambridge: Cambridge University Press, 1987).
46. MacKenney, *The City-State*, 23.
47. Ibid., 25.
48. Fernand Braudel, *Civilisation and Capitalism 15th–18th Centuries*, trans. S. Reynolds, 3 volumes (London: Collins, 1982), Volume III: *The Perspective of the World*, chapter 2.
49. MacKenney, *The City-State*, 44.
50. Ibid., 45.
51. Ibid., 49.
52. J. G. A. Pocock, *The Machiavellian Moment* (Princeton: Princeton University Press, 1975), 281.
53. Ibid., 320.
54. James Hankins, *Virtue Politics. Soulcraft and Statecraft in Renaissance Italy* (Cambridge, MA: Belknap Press of Harvard University, 2019).
55. Pocock quotes the late sixteenth-century English translation of Contarini's book: Lewkenor, *The Commonwealth and Government of Venice*. Written by the Cardinall Gaspar Contareno and translated out of Italian into English by Lewes Lewkenor (London, 1599).
56. Pocock, *Machiavellian*, 322.
57. Lewkenor, *Commonwealth*, 7, quoted by Pocock, *Machiavellian*, 323.
58. Ibid., 323.
59. Lewkenor, *Commonwealth*, 11.
60. Pocock, *Machiavellian*, 324.
61. Pocock refers here to Felix Gilbert, "The Venetian Constitution in Florentine Political Thought," in Nicolai Rubinstein, *Florentine Studies: Politics and Society in Renaissance Florence* (London: Faber and Faber, 1968), 463–500, 468–70. Gilbert attributes this idea of connecting the perfection of Venetian institutional arrangements to Plato's *Laws* to Francesco Barbaro and his circle.
62. All these details from Gilbert, *Venetian Constitution*, 469.
63. Pocock, *Machiavellian*, 225.
64. Ibid., 226.
65. Ibid., 227.

66. Ibid., 277–8.

67. I am grateful to Maurizio Viroli for calling my attention to these two authors.

68. "He was a scholar, a scientist, a historian, indeed, a polymath, but he also played a leading role in the Risorgimento, the 'making' of Italy." Martin Thom, "City, Region and Nation: Carlo Cattaneo and the Making of Italy," *Citizenship Studies* 2, no. 2 (1999): 187–200, 187.

69. Norberto Bobbio, *Una filosofia militante. Studi su Carlo Cattaneo* (Turin: Einaudi, 1971).

70. Carlo Cattaneo, *Scritti letterari*, ed. Piero Treves, 2 vols. (Florence: Le Monnier, 1981), vol. II, 483–6, quoted by Martin Thom, "City and Language in the Thought of Carlo Cattaneo," *Journal of Modern Italian Studies* 5 no. 1 (2000): 1–21, 1.

71. This is the title of Giuseppe Armani's book: *Carlo Cattaneo. Il padre del federalismo italiano* (Milan: Garzanti, 1997).

72. Thom, *City, Region*, 188.

73. Charles Tilly, "Entanglements of European Cities and States," in *Cities and the Rise of States in Europe AD 1000–1800*, ed. C. Tilly and W. P. Blockmans (Boulder, CO: Westview Press, 1994).

74. Thom, *City, Region*, 193.

75. Ibid.

76. Ibid., 195.

77. Ibid., 197. Thom refers here to Adrian Lyttelton, "Shifting Identities: Nation, Region and City," in *Italian Regionalism: History, Identity and Politics*, ed. Carl Levy (Oxford: Berg, 1996).

78. Carlo Cattaneo, *Opere scelte*, ed. Delia Castelnuovo Frigessi, 4 vols. (Turin: Einaudi, 1972), vol. 2, 404.

79. Marino Berengo, *L'Europa delle città. Il volto della società urbana tra medioevo ed età moderna* (Turin: Einaudi, 1999).

80. Antony Molho, "Historians and Friends: Reflections on Some Contemporary Historians," *History of European Ideas* 45, no. 8 (2019): 1156–70.

81. Ibid., 1161.

82. Molho in this respect refers to Cantimori, who admitted that Berengo was "extraneous from schools and scholarly factions, of sects and small (ideological) churches, alien from abstract theories." Molho, *Historians*, 1161.

83. Quoted by Molho, *Historians*, 1161.

84. James Amelang, "The Europa delle città of Marino Berengo," *Rivista Storica Italiana* 113, no. 3 (2001): 754–763. I am grateful for Professor Amelang for sending me the typescript of this piece, and for his description of its context. I cannot give the exact page numbers, as I have no access to the published version (which, so I am informed, also mixed up some parts of the text).

85. Charles Tilly, "What Good Is Urban History?" *Journal of Urban History* 22 (1996), 702–19.

86. Amelang, *The Europa*.

87. Berengo, *L'Europa delle città*, xii–xiii.

88. Giorgio Chittolini, "L'Europa delle città secondo Marino Berengo," *Storica* 14 (1999), 105–27, 124.

89. In what follows, we shall rely on Philip R. Hoffmann-Rehnitz' chapter, entitled "Discontinuities, Political Transformation, Media Change, and the City in the Holy Roman Empire from the Fifteenth to Seventeenth Centuries," in *The Holy Roman Empire, Reconsidered*, ed. Jason Philip Coy, Benjamin Marschke and David Warren Sabean (New York, Oxford: Berghahn Books, 2010).

90. Ibid.

91. Ibid., 11.

92. Ibid., 12.

93. Ibid.

94. Ibid.

95. Eberhard Isenmann represented the first type, while Klaus Schreiner the second kind.

96. Ibid., 13.

97. Ibid., 14.

98. See Rudolf Schlögl, "Kommunikation und Vergesellschaftung unter Anwesenden. Formen des Sozialen und ihre Transformation in der Frühen Neuzeit," *Geschichte und Gesellschaft* 34 (2008): 155–224. About his workshop, see: Patrick Oelze, "Politische Kultur und soziale Ordnung in der frühneuzeitlichen Stadt. Das Projekt B4 im Kulturwissenschaftlichen Forschungskolleg/SFB 485 an der Universität Konstanz," *Jahrbuch der historischen Forschung 2004* (Munich, 2005): 77–87.

99. Hoffmann-Rehnitz, *Discontinuities*, 18.

100. Ernst Pitz, *Bürgereinung und Städteeinung: Studien zur Verfassungsgeschichte der Hanse-städte und der deutschen Hanse* (Cologne, Weimar, Vienna: Böhlau Verlag, 2001).

101. For this aspect, see Philip R. Hoffmann-Rehnitz, "Soziale Differenzierung und politische Integration. Zum Strukturwandel der politischen Ordnung in Lübeck (15–17. Jahrhundert)," in *Stadtgemeinde und Ständegesellschaft. Formen der Integration und Distinktion in der frühneuzeitlichen Stadt*, eds. Patrick Schmidt and Horst Carl (Berlin and Münster: LIT Verlag, 2007), 166–97.

102. Hoffmann-Rehnitz, *Discontinuities*, 19–20.

103. Robert Giel, *Politische Öffentlichkeit im spätmittelalterlich-frühneuzeitlichen Köln (1450–1550)* (Berlin: Duncker & Humblot GmbH, 1998).

104. Gerd Schwerhoff, "Apud populum potestas? Ratherrschaft und korporative Partizipation im spätmittelalterlichen und frühneuzeitlichen Köln," in *Stadtregiment und Bürgerfreiheit. Handlungsspielräume in deutschen und italienischen Städten des Späten Mittelalters und der Frühen Neuzeit. Bürgertum*, 7. eds. Klaus Schreiner and Ulrich Meier (Göttingen: Vandenhoeck & Ruprecht, 1994), 188–243.

105. In what follows, I rely here on the chapter on Calvin and Geneva, in William Gilbert, *Renaissance and Reformation*. (Lawrence, KS: Carrie, 1998), downloaded in April, 2020 from http://vlib.iue.it/carrie/texts/carrie_books/gilbert/14.html

106. Jean Calvin, *Commentary on Seneca's De Clementia, Books For the Ages, Ages Software* (Albany, OR: Version 1.0 © 1998), available at: http://media.sabda.org/alkitab-7/LIBRARY/CALVIN/CAL_SENE.PDF, downloaded in April, 2020.

107. Gilbert, *Renaissance*. See also the relevant chapters in Diarmaid MacCulloch, *The Reformation* (New York: Penguin Books, 2005).

108. MacCulloch, *The Reformation*, 231–32.

109. Ibid.

110. In what follows, I rely on the biographical and historical details of the "Translator's Introduction" in *Johannes Althusius. An Abridged translation of Politics Methodically Set Forth and Illustrated with Sacred and Profance Examples*, ed. and trans. with an introduction by Frederick S. Carney, foreword by Daniel J. Elazar, Indianapolis: Liberty Fund, 1964/1995), ix–xxxiii. See my chapter with the title: Ferenc Hörcher, "Overcoming a Crisis in an Early Modern Urban Context. Althusius on Concord and Prudence" to be published in a volume by the European Society for the History of Political Thought.

111. All the above details in Carney, *Althusius*, xi.

112. Ibid., xi.

113. Ibid., xii.

114. Ibid., xii.

115. Ibid., xii.

116. Robert von Friedeburg, "Persona and Office: Althusius on the Formation of Magistrates and Councillors," chapter 7 in *The Philosopher in Early Modern Europe*, ed. C. Condren, S. Gaukroger and I. Hunter (Cambridge: Cambridge University Press, 2006), 160–81, 162, 164.

117. In his monograph, James Hankins presents the views of Italian humanists, most of whom shared the view, that right leadership is not an institutional matter, but a matter of moral righteousness, which can be inculcated by the right sort of upbringing—by the insitutio defined by the humanists on the basis of the ancient Greek and Roman authors' heritage. See Hankins, *Virtue Politics*.

118. Instead of speaking simply about character formation, von Friedeburg brings in here the Roman notion of *persona*, as it is explicated by Cicero.

119. Von Friedeburg, *Persona*, 161.

120. Ibid., 162.

121. This is explained the following way: "Only the middling and small jurisdictions of the imperial estates provided the economy of scale to actually engage in the kind of detailed regulation of economy and society typical for the advice of the *Politica*." von Friedeburg, *Persona*, 164, n. 15.

122. Ibid., 166. The words used in the Abridged English translation I use is "tumults or sedition." Althusius, *Politica*, XVIII., 56§, 102.

123. Von Friedeburg, *Persona*, 168.

124. Ibid., 176.

125. He is following in this respect Paul Ludwig Weinacht, "Althusius – ein Aristoteliker? Über die Funktion praktischer Philosophie in politischen Calvinismus," in Karl-Wilhelm Dahm, Werner Krawietz, and Dieter Wyduckel, eds. "Politische

Theorie des Johannes Althusius," *Rechtstheorie, Supplementary vol. 7* (Berlin, 1987): 443–64.

126. Von Friedeburg, *Persona*, 171.

127. Ibid., 171, referring to Johannis Althusius, *Civilis conversationis libri duo: methodié digesti & exemplis sacris & profanis passim illustrati. Editi à Philippo Althusio*, Hanover, 1601, I.

128. Von Friedeburg, *Persona*, 171.

129. Michael Behnen, "Herrscherbild und Herrschaftstechnik in der 'Politica' des Johannes Althusius," *Zeitschrift für historische Forschung* 11 (1984): 417–72, 422. Behnen also calls attention to the fact that while Cicero speaks about the state with terms like these, Althusius defines with them *consociatio* and the *ius symbioticum*.

130. Von Friedeburg, *Persona*, 174, Referring to chapter I, 7 in the lecture, as well as to *Politica*, V, 4. and Cicero's *De re publica*, I, 25.

131. Von Friedeburg, 174–75.

132. Ibid., 177.

133. Ibid., referring to chapter xxvi, 5–9.

134. Althusius, *Politica*, xxvii, 157.

135. Joanne Paul, *Counsel and Command in Early Modern English Thought* (Cambridge: Cambridge University Press, 2020).

136. In this respect, I rely on the work of István Németh.

137. Tibor Klaniczay, "A magyar későreneszánsz problémái (Stoicizmus és manierizmus)," *Irodalomtörténet* 48, no. 1 (1960): 41–61, 50.

138. Ibid.

139. Sándor Bene, "Eszmetörténet és irodalomtörténet, A magyar politikai hagyomány kutatása," *Budapesti Könyvszemle-BUKSZ* 19, no. 1, 50–64, 54ff.

140. See especially the work of Géza Pálffy for this direction in history writing.

141. Géza Pálffy, "Egy elfelejtett kiegyezés a 17. századi magyar történelemben," in *Egy új együttműködés kezdete*, Annales Archivi Soproniensis (1) (Sopron: Magyar Nemzeti Levéltár Győr-Moson-Sopron megyei Soproni Levéltára; Budapest: MTA BTK, Történettudományi Intézet, 2014), 17–59, 19–20.

142. Endre Angyal, "Lackner Kristóf és a barokk humanizmus kezdetei," *Soproni Szemle* VIII, no. 1 (1944): 1–14, 3.

143. Von Friedeburg, *Persona*, 162, 164.

144. Ibid., 164.

145. Gergely Tóth, *Lackner Kristófnak, mindkét jog doktorának rövid önéletrajza* (Sopron, 2008), xxvi.

146. Tibor Grüll, "Lackner Kristóf beszéde Sopron város dícséretéről (1612)," *Lymbus Művelődéstörténeti Tár* 3 (1991): 45–97.

147. Cicero, *De Officiis*, Book I, 7. I used the Libethe enrichment of the community, Liberty Fund Online edition: https://oll.libertyfund.org/titles/cicero-on-moral-duties-de-officiis. I left out from the passage the part which concerns the Stoic universalist approach to human natural benevolence. Grüll, *Lackner Kristóf beszéde*, 74.

148. Ibid., 70.

149. Ibid., 79.

150. Ibid.

151. Ibid., 80.
152. Ibid., 79.
153. Ibid., 81.
154. Ibid., 83.
155. Ibid., 84.
156. Ibid.
157. Ibid.
158. Ibid., 86.
159. Ibid.
160. Ibid.
161. Ibid.
162. István Németh, "Állam és városok – A szakszerűsödés felé vezető első lépések a városi igazgatásban, 1670–1733" (State and Cities – The First Steps toward Professionalization in Urban Administration, 1670–1733), *Századok* 152, no. 4 (2018): 771–808.
163. Grüll, *Lackner Kristóf beszéde*, 92.
164. Péter Dominkovits, *"Egy nemzetek lévén..." A Nyugat-Dunántúl Bocskai István 1605. évi hadjárata idején* (Budapest: Martin Opitz Kiadó, 2006).
165. Katalin Szende, "Dominkovits Péter: 'Egy nemzetek lévén...' A Nyugat-Dunántúl Bocskai István 1605. évi hadjárata idején, Budapest, 2006" *Soproni Szemle* 1 (2009): 152–55, http://epa.oszk.hu/01900/01977/00242/pdf/EPA01977_soproni_szemle_2009_1_152-155.pdf
166. Grüll, *Lackner Kristóf beszéde*, 95.
167. In this summary of his life, I rely on the afterword by Ferenc Csonka, in János Bocatius, *Öt év börtönben (Five Years in Prison) (1606–1610)*, trans. with notes and afterword by Ferenc Csonka (Budapest: Európa Publisher, 1985), 187–236, as well as István H. Németh, "A Many Sided Intellectual on the Stage of Poetry and Politics: Joannes Bocatius," published in the blog of the Hungarian National Archive, https://mnl.gov.hu/mnl/ol/hirek/egy_sokoldalu_ertelmisegi_a_kolteszet_es_a_politika_szinpadan
168. Jaroslav Miller, *Urban Societies in East-Central Europe, 1500–1700* (Farnham: Ashgate Publishing, 2008; London: Routledge, 2016), 169.
169. See the monograph and articles by István Németh about this development.

Chapter 3

The City of Ancient Greece and Christian Europe

Both the Renaissance and the Reformation were returns to an earlier form of thinking—the Renaissance to the ancient Greek and Roman way of thinking, the Reformation to the teaching of the Bible and the early Church. This motif of repetition with variation gives a special character to European thinking—which is itself a recurring theme, analyzed in a detailed fashion in Rémi Brague's book on Rome.[1]

This chapter returns to the origins of the specific urban way of thinking in ancient Athens and Rome. Yet the present author—not being an ancient philologist—is constantly aware of his limitations in attempting to do so. One should be aware of the inherent difficulty of such an enterprise, in any case: it is impossible to truly pass beyond one's own horizon, back to the original, and build a bridge between present-day and earlier forms of thinking and living. Our own way of thinking cannot be erased of the consequences of the process which led to the present moment. It is, therefore, more honest to admit that even though we are interested in the ancient forms of urban cohabitation, in order to better understand our own predicament, we will never be able to fully comprehend them as the ancients did, and will necessarily remain chained to our own historical moment. In other words, this reconstruction of the original will be an early twenty-first-century effort, from a perspective determined by a region of the old continent, called Central Europe, with all the consequences that go with it. A further dimension of the complications of what is called the hermeneutic situation of historical understanding is that we are going to concentrate here on a few selected thinkers who were able to articulate their views of urban politics in that age—which means that we shall gain an insight into the historical situation through a very narrow window: with the help of political thinkers who themselves looked back on what they were talking about from a later period, once again warning us that our account does not provide a direct access to the reality of the historical period we are concerned with.

THE INSTITUTIONS OF ANCIENT ATHENS

Centuries of European thought are built on the works of Plato and Aristotle, writing about ancient Athens and its contemporary rivals, such as Sparta. When dealing with the heritage of ancient Greek political thought, one should be aware of the internal tensions between the different thinkers' respective ideas. Aristotle, the main protagonist of our story, was a student of Plato, but he became a thinker in his own right. In the traditional narrative, they are represented as embodying two different ways of thinking. This contrast is reflected in the visual narrative of Raphael, in his famous picture of the *School of Athens*.[2] A realistic cast of mind is traditionally associated with Aristotle, while Plato—in connection with his theory of forms or ideas—is usually considered to have been an idealist. The European urban experience, which was often incompletely articulated, drew more on Aristotle than on Plato in its own narrative. This fact justifies the choice to focus here chiefly on Aristotle, and only in passing on Plato. Our own story thus itself becomes biased toward the Aristotelian legacy. Yet as soon as we admit the constructed nature of the historical reconstruction we are attempting, we also admit that it is a partial picture of the historical whole. The European way of urban political thinking itself is also a series of recurring efforts to make sense of the original experience of ancient Athens and Rome, and certainly the ways in which it varies can be explained by the particular inclinations of the storytellers themselves.

In what follows, we shall first focus on the remarkable achievements of the political institutional machinery of ancient Athens, with the help of a historical reconstruction by an ancient historian, Wilfried Nippel, which itself examines the Athenian achievement in order to make sense of later developments. The English title of the book makes it explicit that this is a comparative narrative of the past, which has the purpose of explaining the events which determine our own political predicaments.[3] The term *democracy* itself, that Nippel uses to describe our own present-day European political model, is a Greek one, a sign that our world of politics is based on the ancient Athenian experience. While we will not concentrate on democracy, but on what we call urban republics, that term, again, comes from an ancient Greek word, *politeia*.

The etymology of our own political terminology makes such a comparison an unavoidable exercise. Clearly, then, discussing present-day political concerns by reference to the past, or investigating the past through our own experience, is an accepted and regular feature of political theory in Europe.

An well-known recent example of the genre is a volume edited by John Dunn, the historian of political thought and political theorist entitled: *Democracy: The Unfinished Journey, 508 BC to AD 1993*.[4] A further example is the philosopher Pierre Manent's book: *Metamorphoses of the City. On the Western Dynamic*.[5] All three of these authors, Nippel, the German ancient historian, Dunn, the British historian of political thought and political theorist, and Manent, the French philosopher, offer this wide perspective because they believe that a reliable analysis of present-day political phenomena requires an understanding of the long-term historical developments which led to them.

Here we shall concentrate on some of the chief innovations of Athenian democracy, both in its actual institutional structure and in the conceptual framework of its politics. We are interested in the framework of thought of the people who made the claim that politics requires a shared responsibility for the fate of the community by each of its citizens.

A key problem of any political community is the relationship required to unite a network of neighborhoods without creating imbalance. Nippel claims that in the peninsula of Attica this unification "created a political centre, but not the rule of a city over a surrounding area and its inhabitants."[6] Although this description is perhaps overtly critical the point is clear: in the process of the birth of a city, its dependence on its surroundings is crucial. In other words, there must be a balance between the city and its environment. Another recurring theme of this tale of the origins of Athens is the role of its lawgivers, such as Solon. Solon, the legislator, had a specific mission to serve as a mediator between the conflicting interest groups of the leading nobility and the mass of farmers. The way he mediated was to draw up laws which can serve as a basis for negotiating in debates. The spirit of his laws established political institutions which were able to channel and formalize conflict, creating that specifically Greek element of shared responsibility. In order to pacify conflict, institutions were created. "Popular assemblies became more important; magistrates were elected by all citizens with the same voting rights, and the assemblies also functioned as courts in which citizens could appeal against judgements made by magistrates."[7] These institutions secured the legal status of the Athenian citizen. Citizenship had "its own specific value as a guarantee of personal freedom."[8] It was in Solon's time that the concept of *Eunomia* (good order) came into use, which described the smooth operation of the established institutions, in the interest of mediating conflict. This was only achievable through the concept of shared responsibility—even if it was not yet a democracy in the sense attributed to the term by Plato, Socrates, or Aristotle: "Solon expressly emphasized the principle of the responsibility of each citizen for the fate of the commonwealth, the welfare of which depended upon their own conduct, and not the will of the gods."[9] It is important not to view the relationship between the city and its gods as a contrast. A few lines later Nippel points out that the sphere of the Gods was also invoked—if not by Solon, but by Peisistratos, in the form of encouraging the organization of festivals to celebrate divine power. In the case of Athens this meant the cult of Athena, which "furthered a sense of belonging to the polis."[10] Solon's point was, rather, to show that the support of the gods depended on individuals' own contribution to the common cause.

Another point to consider about the Athenian experience was that it saw the beginning of a systematic public administration. While the people of Athens and their surroundings consisted of more than 100 local communities, or demes, public administration was not based on them. Instead, the artificial units were created, called *phylai*. Each *phyle* consisted of urban, coastal, and interior territories, and as such they were cross-sections of Athens, artificial entities created mainly for military purposes. While each local community, or *demos,* had the task of maintaining a list of citizens for military purposes, it was in fact the *phyle*, the artificial administrative unit, which organized the raising of military units. This division by Cleisthenes of the territory of Athens and its surroundings into *phylai* helped to involve the whole population, which is the first condition of internal order . It is also necessary to defend the area from external threats. The main advantage of a well-functioning public administration is to make use of all the resources of the community, as a healthy body will make use of all its bodily organs in order to survive. It is, therefore, not an exaggeration to state that Cleisthenes made it possible for Athens to mature, through the interconnections of its parts with the help of a smoothly functioning public administration. It was Cleisthenes, in other words, who "gave the Athenians their tribes (*phylai*) and democracy."[11]

A further measure which encouraged participation in common affairs was ostracism, the institution which allowed the people to exile a member of the elite on a regular basis. It is interesting to see an early nineteenth-century commentator, Benjamin Constant, express his hatred for this institution, because he regarded it as a weapon against individual liberty. However, one should be aware that he was writing after the worst experiences of the French Revolution, which saw large sections of the earlier elite of the country tortured, killed, or exiled. However, Nippel's reconstruction of ancient Athenian institutions, in contrast, finds ostracism to be "an ingenious arrangement."[12] He argues that this institution created the popular assembly (*ekklesia*), perhaps the most important single institution of Athens, the *polis*, where citizens took responsibility for public affairs long before the establishment of democracy. The public vote involved in the institution of ostracism enabled the people to make a choice between two competing leaders, defending themselves against the arrogance of any growing power. According to the narrative of Nippel, the institution had a stabilizing effect, making "the preservation of a constant line possible," or, if needed "to make a clear change of course," in accordance with the will of the majority.[13]

Breaking the power of strong individuals by the general assembly was crucial for the birth of democracy in Athens. Yet the crucial aspect of this development is to allow the evolution not only of a strong sense of belonging, but also of an awareness of one's own role in public affairs, a cognizance which is crucial for a city to be regarded as a *res publica*, a republic. This shared responsibility defines both the Athenian *polis* and the later Roman republic, the forms of political community which have served as constant reference points for European cities to this day, irrespective of the specific larger political entities of which they were constituent members.

A further step in the process of the birth of democracy was the rearrangement of the role and functions of the ten *archon*s, who had earlier recruited the elite. In the age of democracy, they lost their power and prestige, as the individual governing offices themselves became less powerful, compared to the popular assembly, or the *boule*, the new organs of the Athenian people. This loss of prestige of the *archon*s was the result of changing the rules on how to recruit it, from election to drawing lots. As the office of the *strategoi*, or the commanders of the military units, however, continued to be elected, election as a method of public decision-making preserved its prestige: at the election to this function "both military ability and qualities of political leadership were put on trial."[14]

Yet, in practice, democracy meant that the popular assembly was conceived of as the most significant institution, because the number of cases they handled increased dramatically. This body also made its decisions according to the majority principle. To accept that principle, the *demos* had to learn that if one belongs to the minority, which was voted down by the majority, one is still required to accept the majority decision as one's own. This was only possible because the number of decisions made was indeed high, so one could easily escape from a minority position. The city itself paid close attention to avoiding internal schisms and longstanding conflicts within the *demos*: "the symbolic integration of the entire citizenry was again and again secured by public festivals and rituals."[15] In parallel with the growing power of the popular assembly, the *Areopagus*—the council consisting of earlier *archon*s—lost both a number of its earlier offices and its prestige. With it, the popular political appeal of the elderly, who earlier had a reputation and authority because of their experience and wisdom, were lost.

The real importance of the popular assembly was expressed by the introduction of payment for public service. This was a measure introduced by the most outstanding figure of the democratic age in Athens, Pericles. The importance attributed to this measure is clear from Aristotle's Politics and Athenian Constitution, as well as from Plutarch's Pericles. This measure had the effect of encouraging and making it possible for the poorest strata of society to become genuinely involved in the decision-making process. Participation was thenceforth not simply a luxury allowed to those citizens who could afford it, but a condition of the smooth operation of a symbolically relevant common activity. From that time onward, this participation was expected from every member of the lower orders. This measure was crucial for broadening the basis of democracy and make it a general principle of the political regime of the *polis*.

Pericles also introduced new legislation which helped to define Athenian citizenship, requiring that both of a citizen's parents be citizens of Athens. This regulation was required to keep participation in public affairs under control, which was, of course, a heavy burden on the exercise of public authority of the *polis*. The fact that both renumeration for political involvement and this balancing measure of defining (this way also confining) citizenship were introduced by Pericles proves that he was the kind of politician who deliberately utilized the *demos* to build up and preserve his own power. We do not need to go into the details of the different subgroups of the Athenians, including the role and rights of women, *metics, hoplites*, and slaves—but one should stress that exclusivity remained an important part of the Athenian concept of citizenship, which differentiates it from the less selective modern concepts of democracy—even if selectivity will always remain a feature of democracy.

It is also worth emphasizing that, in the age of Pericles, Athenian democracy bore a close resemblance to what Weber called a plebiscitary leader democracy.[16] Of course, Weber's primary historical reference is not to Pericles's Athens, but to Caesarism in ancient Rome. Yet Pericles seems to be an early example of a populist leader, who was able to remain in power for a long time and exercise that power with an exceptional authority, by surfing on the waves of public opinion. Concentrating power in his hands excluded any other competitors from the realm of power, with the help of the majority of the *ekklesia*. This must be the reason why Thucydides, who had a realistic sense of politics, appreciated the rule and power of the single-handed leader of Athenian democracy.[17] While Pericles determined Athenian politics for almost four decades, his unquestioned leadership lasted in the final part of his life from at least 443 until 429, when he died. But no matter how we evaluate his leadership, it still served as an influential precedent. At the same time, however, the long-term lack of rivals for Pericles remains a riddle of Athenian democracy. The most probable explanation seems to be that he was indeed a "populist" leader, in which case Athenian democracy can be understood as being in close proximity to populist rule. The talent of Pericles must have been to defend himself against the aristocratic elite by giving a political voice to the people. On the other hand, Thucydides's claim that Athenian democracy in the age of Pericles was a "rule (*arche*) under the principle man" was usually understood to mean that even Athenian democracy needed guidance, in other words, "that ultimately only a 'guided' democracy can be successful."[18] The translation of Thucydides's phrase by Hobbes about Athens, quoted in Nippel's analysis is rather instructive: "It was in name a state democratical, but in fact a government of the principal man."[19] One should always keep in mind the cautionary remark that if the principal man cannot maintain a fine balance between the different parts of the body politic, democracy can easily turn into tyranny. In fact, Nippel elsewhere quotes the Hobbesian edict that Pericles too had excessive power: "it is said that Pericles once made thunder and lightning in his speeches and threw all Greece into confusion."[20] This sort of criticism should always be remembered in connection with democratic "populism": "in a democracy, a leader of the people can end up as a tyrant." Yet Nippel's final judgment is that we have no evidence which would verify convincingly that there were real instances of democracies turning into tyrannies in Athenian history.[21]

ARISTOTLE ON ATHENS

Having examined certain features of the institutional framework of Athenian democracy, let us now turn to the political theory of Aristotle, and his interpretation of Athenian democracy. Besides *Politics*, in which he presents his teachings about the ideal and the best possible *poleis*, we shall also draw on the *Athenian Constitution*, discovered only in 1880, and attributed either to Aristotle himself or to someone from his school.[22] Hopefully, the two texts will present Aristotle's specific way of thinking about the Ancient Greek *poleis*, and in particular, about Athens.

Aristotle himself was not Athenian.[23] His father was the physician of the king of Macedon, and he himself was also raised there, only moving to Athens at the age of seventeen. He attended Plato's Academy, which had a determining influence on him. He returned to the court of Philip, the king of Macedon, to serve as the tutor to his son Alexander. He stayed there for eight years, after which he returned to Athens, founding his own educational institution, the Lyceum. After thirteen years at its head, he had to leave Athens, and died a year later, in 321, in Chalcis.

The most important fact about Aristotle's life in connection with his political thought is the internal tension between his own civil status as a legal alien in Athens and his claim that "citizenship in a state and participation in its political life was a precondition of achieving human flourishing—a precondition denied to Aristotle himself."[24] We cannot be sure about his own political convictions, as his surviving texts do not offer a clue to it. However, Athens' participatory model, which inclined toward democracy, is in direct opposition to the intentions of Alexander, whose imperial aims included the occupation of the Greek city-states. Aristotle seems to have been connected to Philip by his childhood friendship, and in *Politics* he referred to his ambition to educate Philip's son as best he could.[25] Even at the Macedonian court, though, he seems to have intervened in the interest of Athens, which is especially surprising considering the suggestions that when he first left Athens it was apparently due to the anti-Macedonian feelings there. We know that, while teaching the duties of a ruler and the art of governing, he wrote a text for his pupil on monarchy and another one on the colonies, both of them crucial for a would-be conqueror. He remained in contact with Alexandros for the remainder of his life, even if it was not an emotional friendship. His close friendship in Macedon also connected him to the regent of Macedon, Antipatros, who was its most influential politician after Alexandros occupied Greece, and continued with his expeditions. His interest in politics was piqued by his acquaintance with these influential people, and his Lyceion, the school that he established near to Athens, was a center for researchers into ethics and politics, influencing the Athenian politics of the day. After the death of Alexander in 323, the anti-Macedon feelings led to accusations against him, claiming that he was atheist. As Aristotle was aware of how the city had condemned Socrates to death, he escaped to Chalcis, which was regarded as the center of Macedon support in Greece, where he died the next year.

Aristotle clearly had a lifelong attachment to Macedon, but his heart was fully engaged with Athens. More importantly for our present venture, he seems to have thought that the proper scale of human politics was not the empire but the *polis*. He himself seems to have been an admirer of city-states. This preoccupation can explain his efforts to collect examples of as many constitutions of Greek city-states as he could—according to tradition he and his disciples collected 158 different constitutions. There were two important aspects of the *polis* that seem to have been of primary importance for him. One was its size or scale. He did not believe that a *polis* can function effectively if it becomes too large—where too large seems to be the size where a herald cannot make himself heard to all or the citizens are too numerous to know each other's characters.[26] The reason for this limit of scale is that a city which is too large is "almost incapable of constitutional government."[27] The second major aspect of his admiration of the *polis* was constitutionality. Although he was aware of the two dimensions of a city: its physical location (this is what the Romans call *urbs*) and the community of its inhabitants (the Roman *civitas*), he does not accept either as the foundation by which a city-state can be identified. Instead, the key to such an identification is the constitution of the *polis*: "the polis is a partnership, and is a partnership of citizens in a constitution."[28] Although the city is built up of its constituents, the families and tribes of citizens, its identity depends on the particular structure of the constituents, in other words on its constitution. The European tradition of the city would also preserve this particularity of having a constitution, written or simply customary, which determines the relationship between different institutions and offices. All the communities of citizens have to find their places in that constitution, as citizenship in this tradition means the same thing as it meant for Aristotle: "a right to participate in the administration of justice and government."[29] In other words, neither the *polis* nor the European city is just a collection of citizens, but it is rather "a society unified under a government," or, a political community.[30]

If the particular pattern of its citizens defines a city, is the community or the individual its primary unit, its proper scale? This is the age-old question of whether the whole or the part is more important. Aristotle seems to be unequivocal in answering this question. As Everson puts it, "A state is thus, as Aristotle claims more than once, prior to its citizens, as 'the whole is of necessity prior to the part.'"[31] This prioritization leads Aristotle to argue that the responsibility for the education of the individual belongs to the city, as the knowledge and culture of the individual will have a major impact on the performance of the city as a whole. We should not, therefore, "suppose that anyone of the citizens belong to himself, for they all belong to the state, and are each of them a part of the state."[32] This order and hierarchy of the whole and of the individual is supported by Aristotle's assertion that the individual is naturally, or one could say necessarily, a citizen of a state. This leads him to the conclusion that although the family comes first historically, and it is from families that the state develops, the state is actually "by nature prior to the family and the individual."[33] If belonging to the *polis* is a necessary attribute of the individual, it is important that the particular form of constitution of the *polis* is "indeed the result of deliberation and choice, and so a matter of artifice, rather than nature."[34] The decision will be determined, of course, by the particular circumstances (natural and social) in which a city exists. Furthermore, once the decision is made to belong to the *polis*, a tradition starts to grow up, and after a while the traditional form of the constitution will develop a natural advantage over new, untried alternatives.

If the whole is privileged over the individuals which it is composed of, the purpose of the whole accordingly cannot be defined in isolation from the purpose of the individuals of which it consists; "the purpose of the state" is understood by Aristotle as being "to enable its citizens to lead the good life."[35] The purpose of each being is to bring to perfection the potential which lies latently within it. The purpose of human life for Aristotle is *eudaimonia*, usually translated as human flourishing, which belongs to the individual. The *raison d'etre* of the state, then, is individual flourishing, even if it also has to ensure the *eudaimonia* of all its citizens.

The connection between ethics and politics in Aristotelian practical philosophy is this: ethics defines the conditions which allow the individual to flourish, while politics concerns the conditions of the political community to safeguard the *eudaimonia* of all its citizens. Ethics is therefore preliminary to politics, while without success in politics, individual *eudaimonia* is not achievable, either. Moral decisions, in other words decisions as to good and evil, and even the decisions of the just and the unjust, all belong to the community: "the association of living beings who have this sense makes a family and a state."[36] This sort of common sense, or as the Romans would put it, *sensus communis* is an important feature of Aristotelian politics. "A large collection of individuals may exercise better judgement than a small group, even if the individual members of the latter are each wiser than those of the former. Their claim to authority rests on their collective expertise."[37] This communal aspect of knowledge in politics is also connected with the requirement in a community that "all the citizens alike should take their turn of governing and being governed,"[38] that is to say, each individual should share the burden of political decision-making, even if the particular form of government is not majoritarian, that is, democratic. It is human flourishing which requires political participation. Once again, we should remember that Aristotle did not gain Athenian citizenship.

Finally, two more themes were addressed by Aristotle in connection with Athens. One is the role and function of the middle classes, the other his views on Pericles, probably the best known leader of Athenian democracy. Making a connection between his *Ethics* and his *Politics*, the philosopher starts out from the claim that "a happy life is the one that expresses virtue," and adds that "virtue is a mean," which brings him to the point that "the middle life, the mean that each sort of person can actually achieve, must be best."[39] As he sees it, this is true not only of an individual's life, but also about cities and their constitutions, which implies that the mean is the best in cities as well. As he sees it, the citizenry of each city consists of three elements: the rich, the poor and "those in between these." According to his ethical considerations, the third was the most advantageous of the three financial situations, because it allows for moderation and "it most readily obeys reason."[40] Most importantly, this middle station of life can mediate in the agonistic struggle between rich and poor, which recurs in every city, a struggle which leads to a city "not of freemen, but of slaves and masters."[41] As opposed to a city divided by faction, the citizens of the middle are similar, and therefore a city is easiest to govern when "constituted out of those from which we say the city-state is naturally constituted" who "survive best in city states," "because they are neither plotted against nor engage in plotting, they live out their lives free from danger."[42] He draws the following conclusion from all these considerations: "the political community that depends on those in the middle is best

... city-states can be well governed where those in the middle are numerous and stronger ... tyranny arises ... much less often from middle constitutions ... That the middle constitution is best is evident, since it alone is free from faction."[43] There is of necessity an opposition between the fight between factions and the dominance of the middle classes, which is central to Aristotle's moderate political convictions. Interestingly, when he has to choose between democracy and oligarchy, he opts for democracy for the very reason that "Democracies are also more stable ... because of those in the middle (for they are more numerous in democracies)."[44] Also, he is of the opinion that "the best legislators have come from the middle citizens"[45] and he explicitly mentions Solon and Lycurgus in this regard.[46] Interestingly, he makes use of the metaphor of balance in a city: the extremes should be balanced by the middle, in order to prevent major swings—like the keel in a sailing ship, "it will tip the balance when added to either and prevent the opposing extremes from arising."[47] Yet this political emphasis on the middle classes is also confirmed by another metaphor, that of the arbiter: the middle class is the arbiter between the rich and the poor: "The arbitrator is most trusted everywhere, and the middle person is an arbitrator."[48]

Interestingly, Aristotle also employs the imagery of balance in his early theory of a division of power, when he speaks of three elements, which all constitutions consist of, and to which the lawgivers must pay due regard. The three elements are as follows: "One of the three parts deliberates about public affairs; the second concerns the offices ... and the third is what decides lawsuits."[49] We know that the separation of powers would play a crucial role in early modern constitutional theory, mostly due to Locke and Montesquieu, but it is more important for us here that it would go on to also have a major impact on city constitutions, where the assumption was that a mixed constitution can safeguard balance and stability, regulating the relationships between the one, the few, and the many as groups of citizens.

Finally, let us consider Aristotle's relationship to Pericles, the personification of Athenian democracy. There are references in the *Politics* to Pericles, but also in the *Constitution of Athens*, which it is not certain was by Aristotle's own hand. However, most experts agree that it is most probably at least from Aristotle's school, so one can use it as a convenient way to summarize the views on Athenian democracy in Aristotle's milieu. In *Politics* it is in connection with Solon that Aristotle mentions the name of Pericles. As he saw it, Solon is not responsible for the establishment of the institution of the council and the elected magistracy, both of which predated him. He is responsible, however, for establishing the law courts. "That, indeed, is why some people criticize him."[50] He was regarded, according to Aristotle, as a popular leader, who "flattered the common people like a tyrant," and it was for this reason that he, along with Ephialtes, "curtailed the power of the

Areopagus," and "introduced payment for jurors."[51] In this way he, too, like other popular leaders, "enhanced the power of the people," contributing to the birth of "the present democracy."[52] Yet he does not seem to believe that Pericles truly wanted to establish a fully democratic regime, since his actions, just as much as those of Solon, were dependent on political circumstances, and not undertaken on their own inherent merits.

The curtailment of the Areopagus is also crucial according to the account given in *The Constitution of Athens*. The Areopagus is generally considered to have been the main instrument of the defense of aristocracy. It was attacked by Ephialtes, first by removing many of its members, but also by stripping it "of all its additional powers including the guardianship of the constitution."[53] He shared these powers "among the *Boule*, the *Ekklesia* and the *dikasteria*."[54] After these constitutional changes Ephialtes was murdered, but by that time the Areopagus "lost its supervisory powers."[55] These developments liberated political debate in Athens. It was commonly accepted by contemporaries that the Athenian people did not care any more about the laws, which were formerly strictly observed. It was at this moment that Pericles took power. This is the description of him in the text: "Pericles became one of the leaders of the people."[56] With the rise of Pericles, the state became still more democratic, as he deprived the Areopagus of some more of its powers and turned the state into a naval authority. It gave "the masses the courage to take more into their own hands in all fields of government," and they "decided to run the state themselves."[57] A further move by Pericles was to introduce "pay for those serving in the dikasteria," in order to counterbalance his wealthy rival, Cimon. This was fatal both because the level of "the quality of the *dikastai* declined," but also because with it came "the beginning of corruption of the *dikastai*."[58] The text also mentions a further measure by Pericles, that of narrowing down the status of Athenian citizenship. All in all, however, the judgment of this work on Pericles is not absolutely negative, even if the effect he had is judged to be fatal: "Throughout the period of Pericles' ascendancy the state was run reasonably well, but after his death there was a marked decline."[59] This decline is due to the fact that the people's leader was no longer approved by the respectable citizens (i.e., the Areopagus, and through that, the aristocracy), and also because the people of Athens and its leaders forgot their obligations to follow the rules. The text is decidedly in favor of Pericles's opponent, the leader of the aristocrats, Thucydides, who is acclaimed here, along with Nicias as "not only true gentlemen and good politicians, but also that they looked after the city like fathers."[60]

All in all, the judgment of the Aristotelian corpus of Pericles is not a direct condemnation of his actual rule, but an indirect criticism of the consequences of that rule, for preparing the grounds for mob rule. It turned out to be detrimental due to the constitutional downgrading of the Areopagus, and also because it gave an undue regard to demagogues, who would play only too well the role of populist leaders. Apparently, Pericles's own personal charisma kept the people under control during his own rule, but his regulations prepared the ground for the uncontrolled and corrupt power of the people after him.

In spite of Aristotle's criticism, the heritage of Athenian democracy in the age of Pericles proved to be crucial for the European tradition, first through the example of Rome, and in particular of the Roman republic, and later via the republican regimes of the Italian city-states. This is, I think, because participation in political affairs really is an attractive prospect for most people, and because it also has its own logic—a logic which will prove to be crucial for European cities. Yet it is worth considering two reservations. On the one hand, one should take note of the role played by Pericles in keeping Athens under control—the role of individual leaders would similarly be crucial in the city republics of Europe. On the other hand, criticisms of Aristotle (as well as of Plato) would also continue in that tradition, with their emphasis on the importance of control over the people, which includes both the formalized or informal authority of the urban aristocracy, as well as due regard to the laws and the constitution of the city. Athens, therefore, remained both a major example of the Golden Age of ancient Greece, but could also be used by historians and rhetors to point out the dangers of the revolution of the masses.[61] In fact, as we have seen, the German city paid attention to both sides of this coin—both participation in public affairs and a strong control of authority over the life of the citizen body. One should consider the European city, therefore, as heir both to Pericles and to Aristotle's criticism of him.

BENJAMIN CONSTANT ON ATHENS

Aristotle, as we have seen, had certain doubts about the long-term stability and sustainability of Athenian democracy, and worked out in its place his own theory of a mixed, or at least a balanced constitution. One of the most famous modern accounts of Athenian democracy, the lecture by Benjamin Constant in 1819, later published under the title *The Liberty of the Ancients Compared with that of the Moderns* offered a criticism of ancient democracy from another point of view. Written shortly after the long years of violence of the French revolution, and before a succession of revolutionary episodes in nineteenth-century French politics, Constant made a famous conceptual distinction in this work.[62] He claimed that liberty for the ancients meant something totally different than it does for us. While the ancient Greeks considered liberty to be participation in the decision-making process, for us, moderns, liberty means personal freedom from the tutelage of political power.[63] According to Constant, the experience of collective freedom went together with "the complete subjection of the individual to the authority of the group" turning him into "a slave in all his private relations."[64] Moderns seek to defend their individual liberty against the community and the state. This is the result of cultural progress, which made available benefits that were not available earlier, and opened the eyes of the people: "the progress of civilisation, the steady increase of commerce, the communication among peoples, have infinitely multiplied and varied the means of personal happiness."[65] The distinction between the two notions is a difference in the relationship between the community and the individual who is a member of it: in the ancient paradigm, "the individual was in a way lost in the nation, the citizen lost in the city."[66] It was the French Revolution which awakened in the individual the need to be free from the community.

One should be careful, however, about how to interpret Constant's own view about these two different conceptions of liberty. The usual interpretation, according to which he is simply in favor of modern liberty, suggesting that we leave behind liberty as participation is in fact a misunderstanding. Also, if someone claims that Constant prefers contemporary France to ancient Athens, this explanation also misses the point. First of all, because according to Constant's reconstruction of the story, Athens is quite similar to modern Western societies. As we have seen, he attributed the modern concept of liberty to the success of commerce, which makes it possible for the individuals to change their specific way of life. He does not find such a major difference between the commercial spirit of the moderns and that of the ancient Athenians: "Athens . . . engaged in trade far more than any other Greek republic; so it allowed its citizens infinitely more individual liberty than did Sparta or Rome." Therefore, his explicit conclusion was that: "The spirit of the Athenian merchants was like that of merchants today."[67] In this sense, the distinction between the ancient and the modern paradigm of liberty was preceded by the difference between the Athenian and the Spartan relationships between the individual and the community.

However, taking a further step may blur the sharpness of the contrast, or at least may redefine its relevance. At the very end of his lecture, Constant admits that his conceptual distinction is not meant as an either-or choice. On the contrary, "far from renouncing either of the two sorts of freedom that I have described, it is necessary (I repeat) for us to learn to combine the two."[68] In a very influential final passage, Constant makes explicit the relevance he attributes to social institutions. He refers to Sismondi, claiming that there is a need for political education, and it is through institutions that a society can carry out "the moral education of the citizens."[69] In this sense, he does not idealize individual freedom as the final state of social development. He also seems to be returning to the idea of the common good, or of public interest, when he claims: "By respecting their individual rights, securing their independence, refraining from troubling their work, institutions must nevertheless dedicate themselves to influencing public affair, calling on the people to contribute to the exercise of power through their decisions and their votes."[70] In present-day terms, Constant is defending both the liberal value of individual liberty, and the republican value of participation and communal decision-making.

It is at this point that Constant's topic becomes crucial for us. The strong argument we can and should make on the basis of his lecture is that the European city represents a combination of the two values, the home of both the liberal and the republican ideal of liberty, and that this combination is the heritage of ancient Athens and of republican Rome. Compared to the systematic forms of domination of external forces of the individual both in the ancient world and in feudal Europe, to become a citizen of a city meant liberation. A medieval saying expresses it as, "*Stadtluft macht frei.*"[71] Within the walls of the city the individual was defended from external domination, and had the chance to pursue his own happiness. On the other hand, to become a citizen meant to take on certain duties, which amounted to a rather heavy burden on the individual, but one without which the community could not have defended its citizens. The great idea of the citizens of the European city was that individual liberty and the power of the community depend on each other: citizenship makes one free, but only if one's freedom is guaranteed by the community, consisting of individual citizens. The causal link, however, also works in the opposite direction: the community could not have expected citizen's active participation in the common affairs if it was not able to provide a kind of freedom which was not available any other way. In this sense, the European city cherished and often achieved both the values of individual liberty and individual responsibility for communal affairs at the same time. It prepared the ground for later efforts to widen the republican experience so that it could also function at the level of the state.[72] The so-called republican notion of liberty, made popular today by Quentin Skinner and Philip Pettit, becomes crucial in the context of the state. The reference point for modern republicanism is more like *libertas*, the Roman notion of liberty.

THE INSTITUTIONAL FRAMEWORK OF THE ROMAN REPUBLIC

If ancient Athens was one of the reference points of the European city, then ancient Rome is clearly the other one. Yet there is an important difference between these two references. Ancient Athens remained a city-state for all its known history, even when it became the leader of a city alliance. While Alexander certainly occupied the whole of Greece, and the Hellenistic period oversaw empire in Greece, the identity of Athens still remained that of a city-state. The history of Rome, on the other hand, was traditionally divided into a narrative of the city's political life in a Republican and an imperial period. This division derives from a particular understanding of the concept of the republic, yet it is vital for us here. We shall concentrate below on the republican identity of ancient Rome. Once again, it will be necessary to examine the institutional framework of the city, before discussing its most important theoretician, Cicero, the politician and political theorist.

First of all, we need to address a crucial point. As mentioned, Rome's development, and particularly the development of its republican character, was not independent from the perception of the political life of ancient Athens, and in general of Greek thought. While Rome had its own special character, it always remained crucial for Rome to refer to the achievements of its Greek predecessor, Athens. In this respect, one should keep in mind the theory of Rémi Brague in his book on the Roman model.[73] The idea of this book in a nutshell was that European history is based on repetition and variation: the Romans imitated, in their own way, the Athenian example, while Christian Europe repeated with variations the Roman example. One can, of course, concentrate on the differences between these civilizational paradigms, yet it remains true that if we want to make sense of the Roman example, Athens will always remain there, in the background.

Also of crucial importance for fully assessing the Roman heritage was the birth and development of Roman law. While law (*nomos*) played a crucial role for the Athenian city-state, its role for the Greeks was rather different from the concept of *ius* for the Romans. *Nomos* referred to the accepted norms of behavior of the *polis*, in other words, it was not sharply divided from customs and other types of unwritten, uncodified ethical norms. The concept of *ius*, however, defined a specific discourse or paradigm, which was called law, or legal thinking. The concept of *ius* lay at the center of Roman legal thinking, defining the specific rights of the Roman citizen (*civis*) within the political community of Rome (*civitas romana*). For the Roman citizens citizenship was the most valuable, because it gave them certain rights which were not available to the citizens of other cities. All in all, Romans were kept together by their concept of Roman law, which prescribed the rights and duties of the Roman citizens.

Now let us try to identify what is meant by the term *Roman republic*. This was a form of communal organization that grew out of the rule of kings in Rome. It is generally agreed that the birth of the republic dates back to 509, when the office of the king was replaced by the offices of elected magistrates and certain well-defined assemblies. There were two major differences between the earlier regime and the later form of rule. One is that instead of being a form of individual rule, a system of shared responsibilities was put into practice. In other words, from that time onward the citizens of Rome were required to participate in the governance of their city. This commonality or public dominion was expressed by the Latin term *res publica*, the common affairs. This meant that there was a division of power (rights, duties, and offices) from the very beginning of the history of the Republic. A second point is that rules (*leges*) defined the powers of the political institutions and offices, excluding the possibility of arbitrary rule or transgression of one's entitlement for an extended period of time. Interestingly, even when the office of the emperor was established from the time of Octavian (Augustus), for a long time it was operated along the rules of the *res publica*, with all new entitlements voted for by the senate and the popular assembly. This fact—that arbitrary rule had to be hidden behind the veil of legality—is a proof that the concept of the Roman law was closely associated with the idea of politics, even in the age of the principate and of the later emperors.

It is worth describing at this point the basic institutions of this political-legal framework so influential in later European history. The main source used will be *Lectures in the History of Political Thought* by Michael Oakeshott.[74] The relevance of this account by a conservative political thinker (originally trained as a historian in Cambridge) is that he introduces the Roman institutions from the perspective of the history of political thought, the same perspective as our own. In the chapter on *The Political Experience of the Ancient Romans* Oakeshott gives an account of the basic legally defined political institutions of the Roman Republic. He presents political life in the city-state of Rome as a centuries-long struggle between a hereditary nobility (representing the aristocratic principle in the political community, or *civitas*), and "the claims of a non-noble class of free landowners, called *plebeians*."[75] These competing political forces had to live together in the community which entailed maintaining a dynamic balance, what he calls a "temporary *modus vivendi*" of a complicated set of institutions. The Roman political architectonic had four pillars: (1) "two ancient assemblies of the populous Romanus," (2) "the ancient patrician senate," (3) "a new assembly of the plebeian class, the *concilium plebis*, controlled by tribunes," and (4) "two consular magistrates, elected for one year."[76] Oakeshott refers only briefly to the functions of these pillars, to show the role they might have played in the operation of the republic. The two ancient assemblies were involved in making legislative proposals (they had the right to veto them), as well as in the election process of what is called by

Oakeshott "the executive government," which was made up of two consuls. The ancient patrician senate had earlier been composed of the sons of the traditional noble families, and they met on a regular basis as a "deliberative assembly." The *concilium plebis* was able to draw up specific legal acts, called *plebiscita*, which were to be applied to the whole *populus Romanus*. Finally, the actual executive power (*imperium*) was in the hands of the consuls, "elected by the popular assemblies and by the senate" usually from the noble families.[77] In Oakeshott's account the struggle between the two power groups generated immense social tension, but an inevitable tendency of its development was that the *plebeians* were gradually gaining ground.

In order to show how this complex web of institutions was able to work together (and without giving a detailed account of all their magistrative functions), Oakeshott introduces a basic distinction in Roman legal-political thought. This is the distinction between power (*potestas*) and authority (*auctoritas*). While the first one described the realm of political action, the second would, for a long time, have tremendous influence on the political life. *Potestas* meant "to hold a particular office and to have the right and the duty to exercise the 'powers' which belonged by law to that office."[78] It is important to note that the office and its powers were conceptually distinguished—as Oakeshott explained, this allowed Octavian to surpass the traditional division of labor when he took the powers of all the major offices, without taking the offices themselves, which would have been understood as trespassing the legal regulations organizing the traditional division of power. Besides power, another element emerged in the Roman system, that of authority. Authority did not give explicit powers into the hands of those who enjoyed it, but it was crucial for the smooth operation of the system. Those who had authority were expected to think in an autonomous manner, and, based on that, give their opinions on the political questions which had to be addressed. While *potestas*, obtained by the tribunes or magistrates such as the censor (and even more the *imperium*, the form of power the consuls had) consisted of well-defined competences. These competences were precisely circumscribed in order to ensure that they were not exceeded. On the other hand, the senate, which was the traditional organ of the city-state, obtained *auctoritas*. In other words, it did not have actual power in its hands, but its members had authority, a special mandate not circumscribed by anything, which could thus cover all possible fields of politics. What Oakeshott was implying was that there was a kind of division of power within this institutional mechanism between those who wielded power and those who possessed *auctoritas* in Rome. This division played a major role in maintaining the balance of this system. The power of the assemblies and the *imperium* of the consuls were in a way counterbalanced by the *auctoritas* of the patrician institution of the senate.

The aim of this division was stability. The varying functions of the different members of the systems were designed to exert countereffects, in order to balance each other. Yet there is an even more complex connection and correlation between them, the famous idea of the mixed constitution. The idea behind the term was the view that while the Roman political system depended both on the popular assembly of the senate and the consuls, neither of these institutions could take the lead exclusively. This is because the system was not based on the dominance of one of the three kinds of power (the rule of one, of the few, or of the many) over the others. Instead, there was a division of power as well as an internal balance of power between these divided elements of power. In the next section we will see how the different elements of this mixed constitution actually worked.

CICERO'S ACCOUNT OF THE MIXED CONSTITUTION

The starting point is what one of the historical accounts called the Platonic-Aristotelian framework.[79] This framework was based on four basic assumptions. The first of these was that the purpose of a political philosophy is to discover the perfectly just regime. Yet because of the impact of chance and fortune in politics, this was judged to be unattainable in practice, so people had to make do with the non-ideal conditions of politics. Due to the unstable character of human nature, we have to expect different non-ideally just regimes for different people in different (historical, geographic, etc.) conditions. Furthermore, in all of these regimes it will be the case that conflict is politically risky, and therefore the aim is to establish "civic harmony" or "likemindedness" (*homonoia*); while "faction" and "civic conflict" (*stasis*) is to be avoided. It is through the mixed constitution that *stasis* will be minimized.

Plato and Aristotle clearly had different approaches to solving this problem of *stasis*. For Plato a mixture of democratic and monarchic elements might work—producing freedom, friendship, and intelligence in the *polis*.[80] On the other hand, for Aristotle "the best practical alternative for most Greek states was the polity, a mixture of oligarchy and democracy."[81] The explanation is that democracy brings freedom and oligarchy brings wealth, while at the same time democracy means numerical equality whereas oligarchy entails equality according to merit. Both these aspects are needed, which is why a mixed constitution is the most rational solution.

Before turning to Cicero, it is worth recalling the theory of mixed constitution of Polybius, the Greek historian and analyst of the Roman system. As a historian he was not looking for ideal conditions. He was interested in what actually happened and not in the ideal state of affairs. A second point of difference compared to the Platonic-Aristotelian scheme is that his account of human nature was "far more uniform and transparent than Plato and Aristotle would allow."[82] Basically, in his view "constitutional degeneration can be predicted with almost exact precision."[83] As self-interest is only restrained by humans when they feel fear, the constitution needs to bring about a state of mutual fear. The solution—which he attributes to Lycurgus, the Spartan lawgiver—is to let the one, the few, and the many have their share of power. Their fear of each other can be controlled by the elders (the few, the aristocratic element), who will switch sides when either the monarch or the people grow too powerful.[84] Polybius's language is that of mechanics, when an impulse comes from one direction and there is a reaction to it from the opposite direction.

Rome was different from Sparta, however. Therefore, in Rome Polybius does not find the middle stratum keeping the balance. The key to balance here is to keep the fundamental powers separate.[85] The consuls control the military, while the senate is responsible for revenue. The people directly administer the judiciary function, and the people can "veto the Senate's decrees" "through the office of the tribune."[86] In other words, besides separating administrative functions, governing organs can "aid and obstruct the actions of the others."[87] This way "ambition checks ambition."[88] Polybius, then, rejects the fourth principle of the Platonic-Aristotelian framework: to his mind the aim of the offices is not to deliver justice, but only to reach a kind of momentary standstill. Opposing powers are made productive here, through the operation of a system of mutual checks and balances between the administrative units.

Cicero's own account of the Roman republican system is told by his fictionalized version of Scipio, who was a friend of Polybius. In fact, Scipio's words are interpreted along Polybian lines, except that his argument is not based on opposition, but instead presupposes the value of cooperation. This is not a sound interpretation, as Cicero never claims to follow Polybius. On the contrary, his Scipio seems to accept as a first principle the Platonic-Aristotelian model, to the extent that he has a scheme for an ideal constitution, that is, for a just regime in ideal conditions. The parallel which helps him to establish this ideal regime is the natural world, and therefore the ideal state is ruled by a monarch who is just and wise. A further difference between Cicero's narrator, Scipio, and Polybius is that the former "restores political culture to its central position in constitutional analysis. Education, law, custom, and religion are all important components of the Roman regime."[89] Cicero's Scipio appreciates the educational efforts of Numa to "civilize" the interpersonal activity of Romans: "he recalled to humanity and gentleness the souls of men which had previously been savage and wild with desires of war."⁹⁰ By domesticating human aggression and selfishness, the Romans were usually able to avoid revolution. A further step in this direction is Scipio's account of the constitutional role of *auctoritas* and *libertas*, along with that of power (*potestas*). The equitable balance of the state is achieved by a division of power, authority, and liberty: the first goes to the magistrates, the second to the senate, while the third one belongs to the people. To be sure, this is an all-important move, anchoring a conservative element in Cicero's system. In his account the senate, the council of the elderly, does not have direct power but it can teach and give guidance with the help of the experience of its members in political questions. These members are "men steeped in the tradition which joined the present generation to its roots in the original foundation."⁹¹ In other words, the senate is the tradition-based, conservative element in the system, whose authority comes from their experience. Their authority gives them a mandate to influence decision-makers and the general public on whatever question arises. This conservative element gives stability to the system, by connecting present-day dilemmas to the dilemmas of the past, and helps to avoid major revolutions (which in this context would mean a change of the system).

A further novel expect of Scipio's account is the liberty of the people, to which he attributes a normative role: it functions to counterbalance the *potestas* of the magistrates and the *auctoritas* of the senate. Here the main concern is to disarm the *populares* (the populists), the breed of politicians who play to the crowd, and who were the opponents of the *optimates* (the best ones), who tried to win the support of the best men. While the populists preferred numerical equality, the *optimates* were in favor of the equality of merit. The populists craved the support of the mob because they also had an irrational impulse in them. This irrationality manifested itself in the fact that they were ready to earn the recognition of the ordinary people even by paying the price of sacrificing their respect (*dignitas*), which would have been regarded by an ordinary educated Roman not as gaining liberty (*libertas*) but "a perversion of liberty (*licentia*)." For the *optimates*, even a general ballot was associated with license.⁹²

Cicero himself based his political thought on *dignitas*, which he interpreted as "the esteem and standing enjoyed by an individual because of the merit that was perceived to exist in him."⁹³ If liberty makes sense, it needs to be understood in the context of an arrangement which does not endanger the respect of the individuals who enjoy that liberty. As the *Republic* puts it, numerical "equality itself is inequitable because it takes into account no degrees of worth (*gradus dignitatis*)."⁹⁴ Scipio was concerned about the risks incurred by a democratic concept of liberty, which can directly lead to tyranny. However, he was not uncritical of the aristocrats, either, and regarded liberty as an important requirement of human nature, as it presented itself in the thoughts and actions of free men. It is for this reason that "the mixed constitution incorporates an element of democratic freedom, even while maintaining the authority of the senate and 'something outstanding and kingly.'"[95] This is, in fact, in harmony with Plato's account of an ideal regime, in *The Laws*, where again some provisions are made to provide a degree of numerical equality. This is the reason why Plato favors a system representing a mixture of democracy and monarchy. Importantly, there, freedom is counterbalanced by friendship (*philia*), wisdom (*phronesis*), and intelligence (*nous*).[96] These counterweights to freedom in Scipio's case include affection (*caritas*) and judgment (*consilium*), where *caritas* is associated with the monarchical principle, *consilium* with aristocracy, and *libertas* with the democratic element.[97] Scipio, just like Plato in *The Laws*, and unlike Polybius, does not rely on a mechanism of checks and balances, but achieves balance by establishing a mixed system which includes both freedom (*libertas, eleutheria*) and prudence (*consilium, phronesis*).[98] This is, in other words, a system based on firm pillars, and one which therefore achieves harmony and stability without effect and countereffect from the different parts of the mix. As Scipio puts it, with an almost cosmic musical analogy: the state "sings by the agreement (*consensus*) of the very different groups." What is called harmony (*harmonia*) by musicians is concord (*concordia*) in the state."[99] In other words, Scipio's system incorporates the democratic element "for the sake of concord" (*hominum concordiae causa sapienter popularium*).[100]

Scipio's whole structure is one from which conflict needs to be eliminated. It is for this reason that concord and affection become crucial for its working, and this is the reason behind the demand for a "political culture with an enduring connection to customs and traditions of the past,"[101] a past which is shared by all the citizens, and from which the resources of concord and affection can be recovered.

Whenever the European urban tradition referred to Cicero, it would be along these lines, based on human nature, accepting diversity between the different components of society, but requiring harmony (concord) between these parts, to be achieved by prudentially safeguarding justice. Scipio's message would be taken seriously:

> the state, through the rational regulation of the highest and lowest and the intermediate orders, sings harmoniously with the agreement of very different groups, for what is called harmony by musicians with respect to choral music is called concord (*concordia*) in the state—the tightest and best bond of security in every commonwealth. And that concord cannot exist at all without justice.[102]

ARISTOTLE, CICERO, AND DANTE: ITALIAN URBAN HUMANISM

The names of Aristotle and Cicero also occupied a special place in the urban culture of Christian Europe. This simple statement will be illustrated in this section.[103] One way to do so is by describing a series of portraits on the walls of the council hall of the communal palace of a small Italian commune. The location is Lucignano, south of Florence. The story of the decoration of its town hall started in 1438 when the council of the small town under the dominion of Siena started a program to decorate the walls of their Sala del Consiglio in the Palazzo del Comune with a series of famous, symbolic figures (*uomini famosi*). While the intention behind these frescoes was entirely political—to assert the independence of the city from Siena, their overlord—they did not follow existing examples, like that of the Palazzo Publico in Siena, designed by Taddeo di Bartolo, using established Roman republican themes. Rather, Lucignano employed what is known as a Dantesque approach to the past. The series consists of thirty-one figures, whose selection was inspired by Dante, as explained at the outset by the quotations taken from Dante, explaining the first four figures, but in fact all thirty-one figures on the walls express the political views offered in Dante's works or letters. In their choice of their heroes, most of them secular, the commissioning members of the council of the city (*conciglieri*) followed the original intention, reassuring the viewer of the continuing relevance of the concept. This loyalty to the plan during a long process of creation resulted in an exceptionally well-defined and expressive artistic output—in spite of the fact that it was gradually created over the course of almost half a century. Its basic message can be characterized as a "Dantesque iconography of justice."[104]

For our purposes, I will concentrate on two figures, as the main protagonists of this subchapter. The series represents both Cicero and Aristotle, making it a fitting illustration of the main theme of this chapter. It serves to vindicate the claim that the two ancient thinkers both had a very definite and distinct political philosophy, and a well-established position in the canon of political heroes of Italian humanism. What is more, Italian humanism specifically applied that tradition to Italian local political thought, as is demonstrated in the symbolism in the decoration of the town hall of this small town, Lucignano, in late medieval Italy.

Let us first focus on the second lunette of the south wall, representing Cicero, supported by the figures of Gaius Mucius Scaevola and Lucius Junius Brutus. Cicero is at the center of the composition with the two others complementing the message conveyed by his figure, as indicated by the representation of a book which he is pointing at with a "didactic gesture":

presumably his own theoretical work. His two companions represent the republican values promulgated by Cicero. One of them, Mucius Scaevola was the legendary hero who put his hand into the fire to show his loyalty to Rome. He was presented in the Quattrocento as an example of "the most ancient Roman example of self-sacrifice for the Republic."[105] We do not need to go into the detailed analysis of the figure on Cicero's other side, Brutus, but notably his figure does not match the descriptions of him by Cicero, but—as the inscription tells us—he is painted as described by Dante. As the art historian puts it, "The virtues of prudence, justice, fortitude, and temperance are associated with Brutus."[106] In particular, justice is symbolized by the figure itself, "Brutus holds the scales of justice in his left hand and the sword of justice in his right."[107] An inscription close to him can be translated thus: "take all who pray Brutus, first consul of Rome, prudent, strong and moderate, as their example."[108]

Cicero stands between Mucius Scaevola and Junius Brutus, in a central position. Not only is he guarded by the two, he is also larger than them. Dante, indeed, had a high opinion of him, referring to him both in his *Convivio* and *Monarchia*, as well as in his long letter to Cangrande della Scala. It is no exaggeration to say that Cicero was the object of a cult in medieval Italy, but even so Dante is exceptionally engaged with him. One can even say that the most important aspect, of Cicero's figure in the Quattrocento, his committed patriotism and his civil activism, were in a way the aspects which Dante's work popularized. In this respect, one can compare Petrarch's and Dante's own ways of interpreting Cicero—a topic to which we shall return in the subchapter on Cicero in the late medieval and Renaissance period. For our present purposes, it is enough to say that Petrarch was still pictured in the earlier tradition as a scholar who enjoyed to work alone in his country villa on his theoretical works, and who was relieved to be able to get out of the mess of politics. In contrast to this picture, Dante presented him as a contemporary humanist engaged both in intellectual endeavors and political responsibilities, who embodied the socially cohesive aspects of Roman law. In the following quote, Dante was ready to interpret Cicero as the best spokesperson of the law: "Cicero says this very well at the beginning of his Rhetoric: 'Laws should always be so interpreted as to promote the good of the commonwealth.'"[109]

The figure on the wall of the Council Hall is still wearing the robes of a medieval scholar, but the comportment of his body suggests his military capacities. It was Cicero who identified virtue as a *habitus*, and this figurative representation has the tokens of the virtue of justice. This is made obvious by the fasces held by Mucius Scaevola and by Junius Brutus with scales and a sword in each hand, on his two sides. Justice and a high regard for the law are closely connected in Cicero's teaching, as understood in the late medieval period, drawing on *De Officiis*, where following the law is presented as the most straightforward way to liberty. Even Aquinas was ready to build his notion of virtue in the *Summa* on Cicero's works on duty and on invention.[110] Dante himself understood Cicero's notion of justice as "duty encompassing all human values."[111]

It is on justice that the specific political regime associated with Cicero by his late medieval readers was built: the idealized Roman Republic. In this respect, again, the words of Cicero in the book he is holding in the picture are explained by the two figures standing on each side of him, both of whom represent patriotic attachment and justice, the basic requirements of an ideal republic in the sense that Cicero is supposed to have attributed to the term. In this respect, the inscription under Brutus might be crucial.[112]

Brutus was not alone in representing the classical republican virtues as the values behind the whole project of the Council Hall. Judith was also represented among the thirty-one surviving heroes. She was to be found at the side of the only Greek historical or mythical figure in the series, the philosopher, Aristotle. The third figure in the group was King Solomon, again a Biblical figure.[113] King Solomon represented wisdom (in the Latin translation *sapientia*) in the Bible. The books in which he appears are called wisdom literature in Hebrew. Two further adjectives are usually associated with Solomon. From an Apocrypha, he was associated with righteousness, while Byzantine commentators called him "*prudentissimus*."

As we shall see, prudence is a recurring theme of this triad. Not only was Solomon labeled the most prudent, but Judith, too, with a sword in her right hand, and the head of Holofernes at her side, exemplified the virtue of prudence. Judith did not merely represent female chastity, as Lucretia, another famous female Jewish heroine did, but also prudence. Most of the medieval literature also called her prudent, including Petrarch, who "praises her prudence in his *Trionfo della Pudizia*."[114] Latini attributed to her the virtue of courage.[115] Dante himself described her in a passage which symbolizes "the Church Triumphant of Paradise." She is elevated in his writings to the heights of Virgin Mary, and the meaning he attributes her is that she was "an instrument of God in humbling the proud."[116]

Both of these Biblical figures, Judith, the prudent heroine, and King Solomon, the just king, function in the composition to explain the specific character traits of Aristotle, the main figure in this triad. He, too, like Cicero, is dressed in the typical garb of the medieval scholar, and he, too, holds a book in his hand. This clearly connects him to Cicero in the earlier composition. The message of the book can be read on the page of the book: PRUDENTIA EST RECTA ACTIONEM (Prudence is the right action).[117] Prudence stands here for the ancient Greek term of *phronesis*, which was indeed crucial for Aristotle's practical philosophy, connecting as it did the sphere of rationality and the practical field of action. As prudence is crucial for the individual, so is justice crucial for the community. Both are virtues in the Aristotelian sense. As the philosopher implied, we have to find the mean between the two opposite extremes.

While in his *Ethics*, practical wisdom is the major virtue, in his *Politics* it is justice. Aristotle's interpretation in the medieval context was determined by the commentary of Boethius. As we shall see, a number of important authors of the Middle Ages drew upon his ideas, including Aquinas, Lucas de Penna, and Marsilius of Padua. This last author, for example, followed Aristotle in his claim that goodness presupposes prudence, and prudence presupposes moral virtue.[118] This interest in Aristotle was universal in the medieval era, especially in the late medieval period.

Dante, too, was deeply involved in Aristotelian ideas. He himself planned to write a treatise on justice, as he thought that justice, not power, should serve as the basis of political rule. In *On Monarchy*, Dante "refers to Aristotle's words describing action as the mirror of prudence."[119] It is even possible to interpret the structure of the *Divine Comedy* as a huge machinery of justice, distributing punishment and reward according to merit and demerit.

Once again, the art historian concisely sums up the message of the composition: "Aristotle, alone among all the ancient Greeks, takes his place in the essentially Roman assembly at Lucignano. Like Judith, he represents prudence, and like Solomon, wisdom."[120]

If we compare the ways in which Cicero and Aristotle are represented on the walls of Lucignano, we can indeed assert that there was indeed a Ciceronian-Aristotelian tradition of political thought in late medieval and humanist Italy. This intellectual package also had a major impact on the thought of local politics in Italy. This is expressed in the town hall symbolism of Lucignano, representing the basic values of the political community, the cardinal virtues of prudence, justice, courage, and moderation. Let us next take a closer look at both these traditions, starting with the earlier, Aristotelian heritage, before briefly considering the Ciceronian legacy.

THE SCHOOLMEN AND THE CHANCELLOR: THE RECEPTION OF ARISTOTLE

Aristotle, "the philosopher" had a major impact in Christian Europe, even if some of his major works were preserved in a rather adventurous manner, through the transmission of Arabic culture. It is important moreover to distinguish between the reception of his theoretical and practical philosophy.

The reception of the latter, which is the interesting part of the story for us, was perhaps even less straightforward than the former. Before embarking on that story, let us stop for a moment to ponder the distinction between theoretical and practical philosophy. In fact, this division is itself a specifically Aristotelian teaching, perhaps the crucial distinction to understand the impact of Aristotelianism in the urban environment—as Nederman argues in his article on the meaning of medieval Aristotelianism.[121] According to Nederman, it was not much more than "one way . . . of arranging and ordering knowledge (especially moral and political knowledge) in a systematic fashion."[122] This arrangement distinguishes between theoretical knowledge, which is valuable for its own sake, and practical knowledge, a field of study which is valuable because it leads us to take the right action. Two major components of practical knowledge are ethics and politics, the first of which allows the individual to as an individual, while the second enables the individual to flourish in a community. The relevance of practical philosophy is to bring scientific enquiry out of the cells of the monks, or the classroom of the medieval university, and help people to make efforts to learn how to actually live their lives. Aristotelian practical philosophy leads directly to medieval and early modern urban humanism, an intellectual enquiry with definitive practical, political, and ethical aims. Together with practical philosophy comes the teaching that knowledge has an educative function. Human capacities are such that we require education in the practical sciences of ethics and politics in order to live a happy life, and develop our sociable nature as *zoon politikon*. Italian city-states particularly, but the paradigmatic European cities all over Europe learned to educate their citizens in ethical and political matters, according to the Aristotelian principle, although sometimes substantially changing the content of the teaching material, for example, by introducing characteristically Christian elements into that package.[123] As we shall see, both medieval and a large portion of the humanistic form of Aristotelianism was Christianized.

If we want to distinguish between the different periods of the reception of Aristotle's ideas, we can differentiate the following phases: his reception before the Latin translations of his practical philosophy (and most importantly of his *Nicomachean Ethics* and his *Politics*), the influence of the two translations of *Politics*, and the impact of the most important commentators of the translations. One should also take into account the vernacular reception of Aristotle's texts, as Italy witnessed the earliest signs of a vernacular reception. This was in the last phase of the renaissance, and its relevance lies in the fact that it made the intellectual content of this philosophy available to the wider public of the citizenry of the Italian city-states. However, according to recent interpretations, drawing a rigid demarcation line between the scholastic and humanist phases of the reception is historically inaccurate, as these interpretations were in constant interaction with each other.[124] The interesting moment for us, once again, is when Aristotle's texts are taken out of the monastic cells and the halls of the schools and academies, and begin serving as points of references in the everyday discussion of the citizens about politics.

There are certain key moments in the reception process.[125] Particularly important for the development of urban thought is the appearance of the Latin translation of the text of Aristotle's *Politics*. Two important translations were made in this era, one by William of Moerbeke in the first half of the 1260s, the other by Leonardo Bruni in 1437.[126] Moerbeke's achievement is unparalleled: in an age when knowledge of ancient Greek language was rare, he managed to produce a word-by-word translation of Aristotle's text. Besides this translation he also rendered into Latin a number of further Aristotelian works, including a recasting of Grosseteste's translation of the *Nicomachean Ethics*, as well as the *Poetics*. Before the advent of this translation, thinkers had to fill lacunae in the content of *Politics* by various circumspect methods, such as Roger Bacon in his *Opus Maior* (1267), who referred to the work of Avicenna on how the legislator educates the citizens, and to certain Roman Law ideas, or Brunetto Latini, who in his *Livres dou Tresor*, "drew upon Cicero's ideas to supplement the political dimension of the Aristotelian framework of practical knowledge."[127] These examples show us how closely the literature of political thought of the Greeks and the Romans were intertwined in the minds of their medieval readers. Aristotle and Cicero, being perhaps the two best known authors, were regarded as the main thread of the ancient Greco-Roman tradition.

In order to see how much easier it was in Bruni's time, some 150 years later, than for Moerbeke, to make such a translation into Latin, it should suffice to list some of the scholars engaged in interpreting the Aristotelian corpus between Moerbeke and Bruni. One of them, and in the long run, the most influential, was Saint Thomas of Aquinas, who wrote his commentary on the *Politics* some time between 1269 and 1272.[128] A number of key terms from his notes on Aristotle's political philosophy were reused in political discussions in the age. According to Aquinas, Aristotle "lays out the true relationship between the city and other communities."[129] This is most probably a reference to the relevant passage in the first book of *Politics* on family, village and *polis*, but the issue has a different ring in an age when medieval monarchies were dominant, and when in Italy the communes were in the process of growing into autonomous city-states.

A further point might be regarded as crucial in Aquinas's interpretation, namely Aristotle's discussion of the best (possible) form of government.

Himself not having had direct experience of politics, Aquinas is not fully consistent in this respect. Sometimes he seems to prefer a system where a single ruler takes the lead, for he can be "more effective . . . in preserving the unity of peace."[130] This judgment is underlined by Aquinas's criticism of what might be labeled as urban democracy: "Provinces and cities that are not governed by one labour under dissentions and are tossed about without peace," while "provinces and cities that are governed by one king rejoice in peace, flourish in justice, and are gladdened by their affluence."[131] One should note in this respect that Aquinas originated from the south of Italy, Naples, which was ruled in his day by the Kingdom of Sicily. As Aquinas was not specifically concerned with politics, it was his logic which helped him to spot the relevant issues in the Aristotelian practical philosophical treatise. He did not specifically concentrate on the city-state, as he had spent most of his professional life as a theologian on the continent, in various cities including the seat of the French royal administration, Paris and in the free imperial city of Cologne. He had, therefore, the possibility to verify the Aristotelian claim in European (as well as in the Roman) courts, that a kingdom is a best form of regime, if and when it was steered away from corruption by checks and balances: "A kingdom is the best form of government of the people, so long as it is not corrupt. . . . Hence from the very first the Lord did not set up the kingly authority with full power, but gave them judges and governors to rule them."[132] Yet he is not totally negligent of the problems of self-governing cities. In his *Summa* he is happy to take into account the arguments in favor of the mixed constitution, a typical arrangement in the Italian late medieval communes. These are the arguments he presents in favor of this political arrangement: "all should take some share in the government: for this form of constitution ensures peace among the people, commends itself to all, and is most enduring, as stated in *Politics* Book Two."[133] He is careful not to push the case too far, and looks instead for the golden mean among the different regimes, which for him is the mixed constitution: "For this is the best form of polity, being partly kingdom, since there is one at the head of all; partly aristocracy, in so far as a number of persons are set in authority; partly democracy, i.e. government by the people, in so far as the rulers can be chosen from the people, and the people have the right to choose their rulers."[134] Finally, Aquinas wrote specifically about the city in the Aristotelian sense (*polis*), as ideally sized, but he also added that in fact the region is perhaps even more ideally scaled than the city. It can be argued that he thus "altered one of Aristotle's most characteristic doctrines."[135] In fact, Aquinas was referring here to the Italian example of the commune, which always meant a city together with its larger environment, over which it had a kind of dominion: "in a city, which is the perfect community, there is sufficiency with respect to the necessities of life, and it is even more present in a province, since there is a necessity of fighting together and giving mutual aid against the enemy."[136]

To summarize his views on the issue: Aquinas did not focus exclusively on the Italian city-state, and therefore was ready to offer all the Aristotelian alternatives for the best possible regime, including a monarchy ruled under legal constraints, a mixed constitution, and the self-rule of a city commune.

The next Latin translator of Aristotle's *Politics*, however, was himself a city magistrate, and therefore his sole focus was on the rule of the city-state. It is perhaps in connection with his more functionalist approach to the Aristotelian legacy that Leonardo Bruni (1370–1444) felt he had to correct Moerbeke's translation of *Politics*. Bruni's own experiental horizon helped him to translate the text, as "the world of the polis described by Aristotle was much more familiar to Bruni, who lived in the city-state of Florence, than it would have been to William."[137] He translates the names of forms of regime with the help of Latin phrases which made sense in his own city-state, Florence: he offers "'respublica' for polity and 'de populari statu' for democracy."[138] He made use of Aristotle to substantiate his own city's ideology and hence to support and legitimize his own activity.

Bruni is also a very convenient example, to illustrate how the two elements of the urban communal traditions, the Aristotelian and the Ciceronian, converged, to establish a huge and solid basis for Christian humanist urban ideology. Along with his translations of the Aristotelian package of practical philosophy, including not only *Politics*, but also *Nicomachean Ethics* as well as the pseudo-Aristotelian *Economics*, he was also engaged in updating the Ciceronian Roman heritage. His *New Cicero* was not simply a biography of the Roman statesman and thinker, but presented Cicero as a role model for the city magistrate in Renaissance Italy. To establish Cicero as his hero, Bruni in fact relied on the classical Latin terms of *otium* and *negotium*. Bruni presented Cicero as not only a great scholar, making major contributions in private, as a result of having withdrawn from public life, as Petrarch did, but also as a great citizen, ready to fight and even to die for what he believed was the best form of government, the republic, for his native city.[139] Bruni's achievement of combining the two legacies is a good example of our next topic: that there is a rich reception of Cicero in the medieval and Renaissance urban context. Before beginning that subchapter, let us add one more episode to the history of Aristotelian reception. As pointed out earlier, we cannot leave unmentioned the large body of literature in vernacular Italian on the Aristotelian heritage, which shows indeed a very bold adaptation of Aristotle to the local needs of urban politics.

When the Italian communes had reached a certain level of development, communal government became a popular form of political regime, and the elected officials of these regimes needed an education in politics.[140] They were not familiar with Latin, and they did not have the necessary university education to acquire that skill. The specific vernacular literature which arose to help them was to a large extent Aristotelian either in its origin or in its spirit. The typical genres which served this function were advice-literature, "mirror-for princes" literature adapted to the new circumstances, and rhetorical handbooks, explaining the art of public speech and writing. As the city-states were based on the assumption of communal government, the starting point of Aristotle's *Politics* (man's social/political nature, his birth into natural communities, the idea of the common good) "resonated with the late medieval political experience."[141] The burghers of the Italian city-states were ready to create a culture (narratives, norms, and mythology), which expressed these basic convictions. Besides the written evidence of this intention, which we shall introduce here, one can also point to paintings like the frescoes of *Buon Governo*, in Siena, painted by Ambrogio Lorenzetti, as expressions of these kinds of political ideals. We shall deal with these frescoes later, along the lines suggested by Skinner in his analysis of the frescoes, but we can already establish that two alternatives are proposed in the relevant literature about the sources of the painting's underlying ideology: while the classic work of Nicolai Rubinstein claims that they represent Aristotelian ideas of virtues and vices, Skinner doubts this attribution, and argues in favor of a Ciceronian inspiration.[142] For us here, the interesting thing is not which of the alternatives is actually correct, but that the two alternatives are Aristotle and Cicero, which is ample proof that their respective legacies were rather close to each other by that time.

One of the most obvious signs of the adaption of Aristotelian ideas to local urban circumstances is the vernacular translation by the Florentine Taddeo Alderotti (1215–1295) of the *Nicomachean Ethics*, from its translation into Latin by Hermannus Alemannus. Taddeo distorts the famous distinction of the three types of rule, presenting communal government as the best of all possible regimes: "There are three types of rule: one is the rule of a king, another of good men, and the third is the rule of the community. And this is the best of all."[143]

This translation is linked to Brunetto Latini's own *Li livres dou trésor*. Latini is important in this context for two reasons: first, because he himself was a notary and an influential politician of Florence, thus embodying the ideal of the magistrate who backs his political activity with an ideology enriched with ancient wisdom, and second, because he is presented in Dante's *Commedia* as Dante's teacher, which indicates the central position of Dante in this Italian vernacular Aristotelianism. Latini's work is dedicated to the instruction of Florentine *podestà* and other city officials.[144] It is Latini who paraphrases Aristotle's *Ethics* in the following way: "it is a natural thing for a man to be a citizen and to live among men and among other artisans."[145] As

Allen notes, Latini's work "is unmistakeably influenced by Aristotle, with Ciceronian rhetoric used to fill in the gaps created by the absence of a full translation of the *Ethics* and of any knowledge of the *Politics*."[146]

A further source for the vernacular Aristotelian discourse was the Italian translation of the French version of Giles of Rome's *De regimine principum* (1277–1280); the vernacular version was entitled *Del reggimento de' principi di Egidio Romano* (1288). Giles was a friar of the Augustinian order who had direct access to Aristotle's *Ethics* and *Politics*, to Latin translations of the Greek texts, as well as to Aristotelian commentaries by Aquinas and Albert the Great.[147] However, the author lacked the direct political engagement that Latini had. His work was a more typically scholastic product of a monk. Also, while Latini's *Trésor* was meant to address urban magistrates, Giles's work was meant as book of advice for the French dauphin, the future Philip IV, and therefore served as an ideological backbone of the French monarchy of the age. Yet the idea behind the Italian translation was the conviction that "the people can nevertheless take instruction from this book."[148] This was true because it relied on the Aristotelian notion of the common good: "Public utility and the common good are better and more worthy than the individual good and than one's own benefit; true and natural reason teaches that man must love God, the common good and the benefit of the people more than his own good or his own benefit."[149] The vernacular version also included an original passage added to Giles's Latin text, addressing the specific issues of the Italian cities, where, according to the text, "all the people are to summon and elect the lord and punish him when he does evil."[150] The difference is not so great between a monarchical and an elected communal government because for both the ultimate standard is the common good: "all towns and all cities are ordered and established for some good."[151] In this sense both of them are republics, serving the *res publica*.

Although Giles's text was popular, both in its Latin and vernacular rendering, and helped to disseminate Aristotelian ideas of politics, the major force in this respect was none other than Dante himself. Both his *Monarchy*, written in Latin, and his *Commedia* and *Convivio*, written in the vernacular, were rich sources of Aristotelianism for the contemporary reader. It is true that Dante's direct knowledge of the *Politics* itself was once in question. More recently, however, there is a tendency to argue that he must have known Moerbeke's Latin rendering of the text.[152] Of his vernacular works it was the *Convivio*, which was closest to the Aristotelian perspective. Most importantly, it offered Dante's philosophical anthropology which, like Aristotle's own thought, was based on the idea that humans are social and political beings by their very nature. Friendship, too, is crucial for him, however, as a Florentine exile, not only within the city, but among cities, too: "For the sake of trade and defence, the city in turn needs to cooperate with, and have friendly relations with, surrounding cities."[153] In the ideal scenario, which for Dante, too, was the kingdom, "cities would be at peace, neighbourhoods in this peace would live in friendship, and households through this friendship would obtain all they need."[154]

The major influence of Aristotle in these ideas is difficult to miss, but Dante makes his debt to the philosopher even more explicit in the *Commedia*, where he is labeled the "maestro" (by Carlo Martello, Charles Martel of Anjou, prince of Hungary).[155] Moreover, the commentaries played a major role in transmitting Aristotelian ideas to a larger public. In this respect, the earliest commentary on the whole *Commedia*, composed by Jacopo della Lana is crucial. This work was written sometime between 1323 and 1328. It explains the above scene in the following way: "it is necessary to be a citizen and political, for (as Aristotle says in the *Politics*) man is a social animal, and it is impossible for him to live in a solitary manner."[156] A further commentary by Francesco da Buti, from between 1385 and 1395, also comments on this specific part, claiming "perchè l'uomo è compagnevile animale e naturato a vivere acompagnato."[157]

To summarize the major Aristotelian themes present not only in Dante, but more generally in the vernacular reception of Aristotle, and which were used in the city-states for specific educational and advisory purposes, the key issues were the priority of the community, the natural sociability of human beings, a natural outcome of them having been born into a community, and the notion of the common good as the main purpose of one's political life, as well as the glorification of the city, which was free, and which elected its lord by the citizenry, or which was ruled by the community directly (for example, in Latini). The widespread application of these ideas reflects their relevance to the political thought of the Italian city-states, especially in the North of Italy.[158] Interestingly, this interest in Aristotle's community-based politics went very well in that context with the cult of Roman republicanism, as preserved in the works of Cicero, who was also frequently read by the magistrates of the city-states.

THE MONK AND THE CLERIC: THE CICERONIAN HERITAGE

The text of Cicero's *Republic* remained unknown for centuries after the decline of the Roman Empire. Yet the fame of its author's name survived, as did the existence of his great work, by excerpts quoted from it by other writers. But the palimpsest to which we owe much of the present text was not discovered until 1819. So, if one wants to make sense of the influence he exerted on the medieval period, we have to rely on other works by the Roman statesman and rhetor.

One of the most meaningful narratives about the impact of Cicero, and through it that of the Roman public spirit on the Christian world was told by Hans Baron. Although some parts of the meaning he attributed to this story were questioned later, the historical facts he uncovered are still useful. In what follows, I will draw upon a classic essay by him about this very topic.[159] Besides the primary story which he tells in this article, we shall try to interpret the meaning of Baron's own dogged research into Italian humanism, and more importantly, the specific "message" he attributed to the story he uncovered, which was not unrelated to his own standing and fate in the tragic history of the twentieth century.

Probably the most important question about the afterlife of Cicero is how his reputation managed to survive in the Christian Middle Ages. Although there is a continuity between the late Roman empire and the early Church fathers—as is evident from the oeuvre and life story of St Augustine—it is not obvious how this Republican celebrity survived in the context of Christian thought. Baron is confident that there is an almost unbroken line of reception of Cicero's work and intellectual standing. The context in which he was discussed in those centuries revolved around the moral questions of how to lead one's life in a meaningful way. The potential answers to this question had to choose between the options of *otium* and *negotium*, two opposite terms, describing two idealized ways of life. While *otium* means leisure, its meaning has been colored by the Greek philosophical background where private leisure (*skhole*) was originally connected to philosophical dialogues. *Negotium*, on the other hand, was connected with an active life lived in the service of a given community. This ancient philosophical meaning was transformed in the Christian context into the seclusion of the hermit, praying to God, and attending to intellectual activity.

It is in this context that a famous, but textually fragmented part of Cicero's *Republic*, the so-called *Somnium Scipionis* (The dream of Scipio) was commented on, for example, by Macrobius in about 400 CE. That Neoplatonic heathen author commented on Cicero by way of excerpting large portions of this sixth book of *De re publica*, which is how it was saved for us. The Platonic contemplation of Plotinus, to which he was attached, taught that the human mind should "rise as quickly as possible to religious contemplation and the purification of the soul."[160] For him, certainly, the life of contemplation (of God) was much more valuable than the lower grade of a life of civil activity, which could just as well lead to happiness, while the best possible solution was a combination of wisdom and activity. However, it is very important to note that Macrobious also highlights a Ciceronian slogan, making it available for centuries of Christian culture in Europe: "nothing in this earth is more agreeable to God" than life as lived in the "civitates."[161]

A further reference point in the early Middle Ages is the work of Saint Ambrose, who adapted Cicero's *De Officiis* for medieval "clerics and laymen."[162] It is very telling that although the intention of Ambrose was to destroy all references to the political way of life as virtuous, in order to direct all attention to *sapientia–prudentia*, due to the fact that Ambrose himself was "a Roman at heart, expressions of Cicero's Roman patriotism and civic spirit of activity frequently survived in the details of his book."[163] This line of interpretation, also strengthened by St. Jerome and John of Salisbury, led to the conclusion that Cicero was an example of "monastic seclusion," "of misogyny and flight from active life" even in the humanist ideals described by Petrarch.[164] The famous collection of *Moralium Dogma Philosophorum* gives precedence to the virtue of *temperantia* as opposed to *iustitia* and *fortutido*, because the latter help one to rule in the circle of a family or a state, while the former helps one to rule oneself, and "it is better for man to govern himself than to exercise any external dominion."[165]

Before turning to the humanist revival, there is one more preliminary step, however. As we have already seen, the birth of the medieval university also helped to reawaken ideas about the practical life, including the ethics and politics of Aristotle. "Seen from a certain distance, Cicero's teachings were now compared with those of Aristotle, the Fathers, and the new medieval philosophers."[166]

It is in the context of the thirteenth century that Baron introduces his all important distinction between the points of view of "the secular cleric and of the monk."[167] While the major thread of his narrative so far emphasized the medieval interpretation of Cicero as a man of seclusion, the concept of civic humanism which interests him so much in the Italian context leads him to refer to the new civic duties of the cleric: "A cleric, writing in civic surroundings, would contemplate his studies in quite a different light from a writer in a monastic cell. . . he would consider his own literary work as a service to the community—as a parallel in the intellectual sphere to the politico-social work of a citizen."[168] His examples include Guido, a Pisan cleric, who, as early as 1118, considered that human study should be most importantly devoted to the service of human society, and the judge, Albertano da Brescia, who in 1238 quoted Cicero's *De Officiis*, that a life lived in *cose communali e grandi*, is to be considered "more fruitful" than one lived in the service of a life of *otium*, that is sheer contemplation. According to Baron, this "civic revival of the Roman Cicero" led to Cicero's *De Officiis* finding a place in the curriculum of practical philosophy in the scholastic university.[169] Even Aquinas refers to it in his *Summa*, when writing about the distinction between the active and the contemplative way of life. Certainly, the angelic doctor was still clearly on the side of a life spent in silent meditation rather than activity, even if his own life did not allow him this luxury.

This reawakening could not have been stopped by scholasticism, either. Baron's first example is an Italian biography of Cicero, written not much after 1300, presenting Cicero as "a Roman statesman as well as an author."[170] Besides his written output, this biographer emphasized how much "Cicero devoted himself so whole-heartedly to administrative affairs and the protection of the Republic."[171] Yet even Petrarch's own interpretation is not fully divorced from the medieval picture of Cicero. Hans Baron's Petrarch remains the captive of an internal struggle between the Christian interpretation and that of the new culture of the city-states of Italy. He builds his reading of Petrarch on the episode of his finding Cicero's personal *Letters to Atticus* in 1345 in Verona. This is what he finds in those letters: "He saw the historical Cicero. . . a Roman citizen. . . who, from his rural retreat, followed political events feverishly." As Baron describes the episode : "Petrarch, the semi-cleric and hermit of the Vaucluse, shrank back in horror from this discovery," because "Cicero's civic spirit was to him nothing but an offence against all the traditions of the Middle Ages."[172] This is not because he fully identified his position with a hermit. It is because Petrarch was in favor of a kind of "humanistic solitude" comparable to "monastic seclusion."[173] Yet he struggled with what he understood from Cicero, through his interpretation of Scipio. He presented an ideological construct of *otium* which connected the world of the humanists of the Italian city-states with Roman citizenship.

Beyond this point Baron's story is well-known. He revived the world of the values of political activity as exemplified by the great heroes of what he calls civic humanism (*Bürgerhumanismus*) in a notably German fashion, from 1925 onward. His aim in this was to intellectually counterbalance—as an intellectual of a German Jewish background—the frightening prospect of a Nazi takeover. His heroes were Coluccio Salutati, the chancellor of Florence between 1375 and 1406 (who discovered the *Epistolae Familiares*) and Pier Paolo Vergerio, a pupil of Salutati, who, in a fictive letter, answered the criticism of Cicero in Petrarch's famous letter addressed to the Roman citizen. Vergerio's story quotes Cicero as saying that my philosophy and culture "were not meant to serve my own self-gratifying leisure, but to be used for the benefit of the community."[174] His Cicero adds to this that he admires the citizen "who takes upon himself work for the state and the cares which are demanded by the '*salus omnium*.'"[175]

The next hero of Baron's civic humanist pantheon is Leonardo Bruni Aretino, Salutati's pupil and Vergerio's friend, who himself as we saw earlier, held the position of chancellor of Florence. His biography of Cicero, entitled *Cicero Novus*, has become the standard reference work on this theme. This biography says nothing about a contradiction between *otium* and *negotium*. Rather, it admired "the ideal union of political action and literary creation in Cicero's life."[176] As he saw it, these were "two parts of one and the same task: the work of a Roman citizen for his 'patria.'"[177]

Next, Baron cites humanists from Venice. His example is Francesco Barbaro who, he claims, stated in 1417 that the Venetian aristocracy seemed to be following the footsteps of their Roman precursors, by being engaged both in political activity and high culture. Another example is Leonardo Giustiniani, and his funeral speech of Carlo Zeno, a leading politician of the age. According to Giustiniani, the Venetian political leader is expected to combine in his own career the values of *otium* and *negotium* simultaneously.

After this Venetian digression Baron's lineage of civic humanism returns to Florence. A close follower of Bruni, Matteo Palmieri is next in the line, as the author of a piece *On Civic Life* (*Della Vita Civile*), a parallel to Cicero's *De Officiis*.[178] According to Baron, in it the author combines *Somnium Scipionis* (from Cicero's *Republic*) with certain ideas of *De Officiis*. Baron cites the following example of Palmieri's glorification of civic activity: "No human work can be better than care for the welfare of the *'patria'*, the maintenance of the *'città'* and the preservation of unity and harmony in a rightly ordered community."[179]

Let us conclude this short summary with the end of Baron's civic humanist lineage, the other great poet of the age, Dante. For, just as the beginning of Baron's civic humanist paradigm was represented by a poet, Petrarch, so his story also closes with a poet, the Florentine exile, author of the *Divine Comedy*. The interesting thing is that Dante lived earlier than Petrarch. Hence Baron's story distorts historical continuity. But while he had up until this point been interested in how his heroes read and interpreted Cicero, this time he does not deal with Dante directly, but instead discusses the reception of him, by certain authors Baron identified as civic humanists. While earlier Dante had had the prestige of a medieval thinker "who kept aloof from the common world,"[180] it was Leonardo Bruni, who—according to his civic humanist, Ciceronian understanding of the ideal life of citizens—rediscovered the political significance of Dante's career in Florence. For him, Dante's participation in the Battle of Campaldino, for example, was crucial. Also, in his *Vita di Dante*, which was written in 1436, the title of which echoes the title of Dante's own work *Vita Nuova*, of 1294, he regarded the fact that Dante established a family, and had children, as crucial in understanding his role as a citizen of Florence. By interpreting him in his family context, Bruni attempted to connect him to a line of the greatest philosophers, such as Aristotle, Cicero, Cato, Seneca, and Varro, who all were fathers of families, and citizens of their *poleis*. Bruni criticized Petrarch for not following this pattern. Imitation thus gained a new significance: the figure of Dante is to be understood in accordance with the Ciceronian paradigm. According to Bruni, in Dante "the ideas, even the words of the Crassus of *De Oratore* had reappeared," in an "extended and transformed" form.[181]

Tellingly, this model of imitating and rephrasing an earlier model was repeated when it came to Bruni himself. The many writers who later wrote about Dante would similarly imitate Bruni's Ciceronian interpretation of Dante. This is true of Gianozzo Manetti, of Ristoforo Landino and even of Alessandro Vellutello, who was the most prestigious Dante scholar of his age, the first half of the sixteenth century. They all read Dante as a protagonist within the framework of "the civic spirit of Cicero's *De Oratore*," understanding him "as a symbol of the union of thought and action, of studious and civic life."[182]

In the present analysis, Baron's detailed civic humanist genealogy was important not only for the historical connections that he made, but also because he himself seems to embody that very tradition, within the context of the twentieth century. Even if his story is heavily anachronistic, as pointed out by some of his later readers, including the Cambridge historians or James Hankins, the fact that Baron himself embodied the very tradition he recounted is proof of the viability of the civic tradition. The historical inaccuracies that Baron's thesis may indeed include are connected to the relevance which he attributes to the story, in a twentieth-century context. In other words, his anachronisms are proof of the meta-historical relevance of the idea, transforming his own writing exercise from a pedantic academic exercise, within the paradigm of *otium*, into a practical activity as a citizen of the twentieth century, ready to do in the intellectual realm whatever is required to defend his own values and traditions. Born in Berlin at the turn of the century, Baron tried to live the life of a German Jew, studying—just like Felix Gilbert, another twentieth-century student of Italian Renaissance humanism—with the liberal Protestant theologian, Ernst Troeltsch and the influential historian of the interwar period, Friedrich Meinecke. In their chapter on Hans Baron, entitled "Humanism and Republican Liberty in an Age of Tyranny," David Weinstein and Avihu Zakai keep emphasizing the dual meaning of Baron's story.[183] As they present him, he was not "an unbiased, detached historian," but one whose work "portrays in the most vivid terms a tremendous political crisis. . . with consequences reaching to the modern world."[184] They quote one of his contemporaries, who characterizes Baron as someone who "sought to preserve and consolidate his own identity with respect to a tradition. . . that became further and further removed by exile, the catastrophes of Nazism and of war."[185] It is for this very reason that they find him to be a "very political historian," embodying the tradition he wrote about, reading "our twentieth-century calamity into a fifteenth-century crisis."[186] In so doing, he was, the authors claim, part of a group of "exiled German-Jewish *Bildungsbürgertum* (cultured middle class intellectuals)," "who invoked the values of Renaissance humanism against the horrors of Nazism."[187] Along with the medievalist Walter Goetz, Baron's orientation was greatly inspired by his professor, Ernst Troeltsch, a Protestant liberal theologian and professor of philosophy in Berlin. Although quite pessimistic about the future of Western civilization, like Goetz, Troeltsch was politically active, with a political orientation toward the new Weimar Republic, like Weber, Meinecke, Rathenau, and Thomas Mann. In 1919 Troeltsch published a series of essays, entitled *Deutschland und Westeuropa* (Germany and Western Europe), which "pleaded for a synthesis of the German and the West European intellectual traditions."[188] Although Troeltsch died too young to have a major impact on the intellectual life of his nation, his political activity in the liberal cause and "his ideas, Western orientation (*Westorientierung*), and enthusiasm for republicanism had a crucial effect on Baron."[189] It was Troeltsch who encouraged Baron to write his dissertation on Calvin's views of the state, and who not only showed Baron the contrast of the atrocities of the twentieth-century German history and their conceptual opposite, the sense of common good in the Italian renaissance, but also led him to the specific early modern German tradition of Protestantism. The importance of this historical triangle—construed from the Italian tradition of city-states, early modern German urban experience and twentieth-century historical experience—will emerge in our story, in connection with the rise and decline of the German *Bürgertum*.

FROM THE ANCIENT *POLIS* TO THE ITALIAN CITY-STATE AND BEYOND

This chapter has attempted to summarize a long story, the classical part of the history of the European city. It started out from the birth of the self-governing ancient Greek *polis* and arrived at the autonomous Italian Renaissance city-state. This story consisted of four episodes: ancient Athens, ancient Rome, the medieval, and the renaissance city. A certain pattern recurred throughout the story: each step was built on the memory of the former. Ancient Rome was aware of the achievements of the Greeks, medieval Christian Europe was aware of the civilizations of Athens and Rome, and the Renaissance grew out of the medieval city, while it was also a reappraisal of the ancient world. These four episodes left a lasting legacy in Europe, one which was elevated to the level of an ideal which could never again be reached, but which could be used as a standard by which the present moment could be measured.

This story has been told through analyzing the political ideas of two city-states, of Athens and Rome, and their political thinkers, Aristotle and Cicero, embodying the Greek and Roman ideals, respectively. This is of course an almost unacceptable simplification of a rather long story, but hopefully one which had helped to portray an overall view of the *longue durée* developments of the narrative we are interested in, that of the political philosophy of the European city in its classical—that is pre-modern—period. In this last subchapter, I will try to summarize the essence of this paradigm.

At least since the time of Lord Acton's interest in the European history of political liberty, European history has been envisaged as an ever-growing realm of individual liberty, which is regarded as its *differentia specifica*.[190] As we tried to show in the subchapter on Benjamin Constant's essay on the ancients and the moderns, this first phase of the history of the European city was also to a large extent connected to the birth of the concept of individual liberty. Yet if we try to identify European urban political thought with the ever-growing realm of individual liberty, we are reading this story along the lines of what has come to be called Whig historiography, following Herbert Butterfield. This is certainly a distortion of the past, reading it in the shadow of the painstaking fears of the twentieth century, as we find it in Isaiah Berlin's *Two Concepts of Liberty* (1958), recently claimed to be the single most influential essay in contemporary political philosophy.[191] Berlin (1909–1997) was another exiled Jewish intellectual, whose family escaped from the old Hanseatic city of Riga, in his days part of the Russian empire. He was forced to leave his hometown as a child in 1921 after living through some of the unparalleled events of his century, including the horrors of the Russian Revolution. Yet his generation had to live through another political apocalypse, too, that of the Second World War. His essay, distinguishing between negative and positive liberty, was a *memento*, facing the problem of how to avoid totalitarian rule, written from the perspective of an idealized European citizen. If we draw parallels between the stories of Jewish *émigrés* such as Hans Baron (1900–1988) and Isaiah Berlin (1909–1997) (we could also point to Leo Strauss (1899–1973) and Hannah Arendt (1906–1975) in this respect), we see Jewish intellectuals trying to make sense of the European past and building up an ideal from the past, which they can use to measure the present. One can criticize their historical analysis for becoming at times anachronistic, and hence distorting their writing of history. This, however, is not my point here. Instead, I would suggest that they, too, be seen as part of the very same story of Europe, which they so robustly told us, in which the experience of the city dweller and his love of liberty is crucial. Strauss used the symbolic names of Athens, Jerusalem, and Rome. Like these historians, the present author is not an objective, neutral story teller, scrutinizing the details of a neutral past, but one who is trying to make sense of his own way of thinking, as well as of the vexing challenges of the future of Europe, in light of the story he is in the process of narrating.

Yet we should also remember Quentin Skinner's point, elaborated in a famous British Academy lecture, of a third concept of liberty.[192] The lecture was one of the Isaiah Berlin series of lectures, which was especially apt as it addressed the famous distinction drawn by Berlin, arguing that there is a third concept without which negative freedom could not be enjoyed. Himself well known as an advocate of republican liberty, this direction of thought is appropriately called the *republican critique of liberalism*.[193] Skinner's argument involves an elaborate defense of the causal link between negative liberty and this third concept, which he defines as liberty from "living in subjection to the will of others."[194] Interestingly, Skinner points out that this common law definition of liberty comes straight from Roman law, and also links it to those great Roman historians, Sallust, Livy, and Tacitus, "who had traced the subversion of the republican *civitas libera* and its collapse into the servitude of the principate."[195] It is only one step from this Roman republican history writing tradition to arrive at Cicero, who ("though a heathen yet a wise man") is referred to, together with Tacitus, with the help of Sir Thomas Hedley in Skinner's narrative.[196]

Skinner does not explicitly mention in this work the fact that this medieval tradition of the *civitas libera* also survives in the context of urban governments. To see this connection between the Roman concept of *civitas libera*, as made famous by the Roman republican historians, and Cicero and the Italian city-states, it is worth turning to another of his works, Skinner's piece on Ambrogio Lorenzetti's *Buon governo* frescoes in Siena. Skinner returned to this topic more than once, first in 1986 and later in 1999, which shows that he found this pictorial representation of good governance crucial to his own concept of republican liberty.[197] In the first piece professor Skinner opens with the claim that Lorenzetti's masterwork refers to the Italian late medieval, early modern city-republics: "Between the early thirteenth and mid-fourteenth centuries, the city-republics of the *Regnum Italicum* engendered a distinctive political literature concerned with the ideals and methods of republican self-government."[198] Lorenzetti's frescoes were ordered by the nine ruling officials of the medieval commune of Siena, for the walls of the Council Chamber of the Palazzo Pubblico in Siena. They are therefore directly concerned with visually representing the values of that form of community, the late medieval, early Renaissance city-state. Lorenzetti's chief virtues are famously Peace, Concordia, and Justice, ensuring a peaceful communal life through "the effects of just government" in town and countryside.[199]

Skinner challenges Rubinstein's classic interpretation of the scene. The key difference between their interpretations is in their identification of the central figure, a "mysterious regal figure," identified by Rubinstein as "the Aristotelian concept of the common good as the basis and criterion of good government."[200] Skinner, on the other hand, discovers two layers of meaning in the representation of his figure: first, he stands for the city, but at the same time, he is also characterized as a supreme judge. This leads Skinner to conclude that—as he quotes from Latini's *Li livres dou trésor*—"the good of the people" requires that "*signorie* should be held by the commune itself."²⁰¹ Skinner paraphrases this medieval wisdom in the following words: "the supreme ruler or judge of Siena must be the Sienese themselves."²⁰² According to Skinner, this is a statement of his third concept of liberty as being not subjected to the will of others.

Skinner has a further question about the frescoes, concerning the identity and meaning of the dancing young ladies. He agrees with a recent interpretation, according to which they are not ladies at all, but were originally meant to be men.²⁰³ They might not look exactly manly, but that is because they are meant to be youthful, who do not have as yet the fully developed manly characters. They are dancing a special dance, the *tripudium*, according to Skinner, in order to express their joy about the "scenes of civic peace and glory."²⁰⁴ The group consists of nine youngsters, which alludes to the Signori Nove, the nine administrative leaders of the city of Siena. Their significance is that they function "as elected representatives of the citizens as a whole."²⁰⁵

It is, however, in Skinner's other work on Lorenzetti's frescoes that we learn about the relevance of the Roman tradition as represented by Lorenzetti. It is there that he speaks of faction as a key problem to be avoided in a well-governed city. The historical question he poses is where this assumption comes from. One possible explanation is that this is an Aristotelian element in the way European cities thought about their inner order. If so, it might have become common knowledge after "the reworking of Aristotelian categories by Aquinas and his disciples."²⁰⁶ Yet Skinner thinks that the idea was already in common currency by that time, originating first from the Roman authors Cicero and Seneca. Specifically, he names "Cicero's celebration of the ideal of the *bonum commune* at the start of *De Officiis*" as the source of this insight into the value of concord in civic government.²⁰⁷

Cicero composed a general dictum about human nature: "We are not born simply for ourselves, for our country and friends are both able to claim a share in us. People are born for the sake of other people in order that they can mutually benefit one another. We ought therefore to follow Nature's lead and place the *communes utilitates* at the heart of our concerns."²⁰⁸ Later, however, he specifies his general norm, applying it to the case of "those who aim to take charge of public affairs."²⁰⁹ The requirement from leaders is to "care for the good of the whole citizen body," because "anyone who considers only one part of the citizenry, while neglecting the rest, will be introducing sedition and Discordia into the city, the most pernicious danger of all."²¹⁰ Skinner cites as contemporary sources of this idea the names of Giovanni da Viterbo and Brunetto Latini, both of whom quoted Cicero's *De Officiis*. At this point Skinner distinguishes the Ciceronian element from the Aristotelian legacy, what he refers to as *Thomistic Aristotelianism*.²¹¹ This might be relevant for him partly to support his claim that the pre-humanist origins of this city ideology included ancient Roman sources, and partly to separate this tradition from scholasticism and the Aristotelianism of the medieval Christian university, as exemplified by the teachings of Aquinas. This may be why he questions the orthodoxy of art historians and historians of ideas, including Rubinstein, Smart, and Baxandall. Yet this distinction is less relevant for us, as we are more interested in the *longue durée* narrative, or grand narrative, which aims to link the Renaissance humanist Italian context with its Greek, Roman, and Christian sources. In fact, perhaps the most telling for us is the difficulty Skinner had trying to distinguish between these traditions, which came to be mixed up in the ideology of existing cities from medieval to early modern times. We are perfectly happy, then, to reconcile the two positions of Rubinstein and Skinner, claiming that both of these traditions were present in the formally much less conceptually clarified views of the members of the *signorie* of Siena, who ordered Lorenzetti's frescoes for their council hall.

It is more important to stress that it was within the experiential horizon of the medieval cities that the Aristotelian-Ciceronian package became crucial. Its elements include human sociability, the active life this implies in the interest of the whole city, the service one owes to one's city, a strict prohibition of discord, as illustrated by Shakespeare's Romeo. The best regimes of governance are some sort of mixed constitutions, where each part is taking responsibility, thus balancing each other, yet there are specific virtues to be possessed by the leader of a city. These necessary qualities of a city leader include the cardinal virtues of Cicero, which can also be traced back to Greek origins: practical wisdom, justice, courage, and moderation. To be sure, liberty does not seem as crucial for Aristotle as it is for Cicero (as proven by the latter's concept of *civitas libera*). It can be argued, however, that this last concept referred to "cities or communities" which, in return for services rendered to Rome, were permitted to administer their own affairs without interference from imperial officials, and as such it was quite close in its meaning to the Aristotelian notion of self-sufficiency (*autarkeia*), the basic criterion of the happy life one can attain in the *polis*, as he understood it.[212] The definition of *self-sufficiency* can be found at the beginning of the *Nicomachean Ethics*: "what is self-sufficient is what, on its own, makes a life choiceworthy and lacking in nothing, and this, we think, is what happiness is like."[213] The important thing about this concept of *eudaimonia* as self-sufficiency is that it is closely connected to the basic characteristics of the human being for Aristotle, so that his explanation of self-sufficient happiness chimes with the famous Aristotelian definition that "a human being is by nature political."[214] In fact, Aristotle's own explanation of self-sufficiency identifies it with a communal life which allows the individual freedom, equality, justice, and being subjected to the rule of law, a description which is fully shared by Cicero. It is in the context of explaining the politically just that Aristotle makes the crucial claim: "the latter is found where people share a communal life with a view to self-sufficiency and are free and equal, either proportionally or arithmetically. So those who are not like that have nothing politically just in their relations with each other . . . For what is just can exist only among people whose relations with each other are subject to law."[215]

I would argue that this whole Aristotelian-Ciceronian ideological package, which is analysed by Skinner, serves as the basic ideology of the European city, a credo which was well developed by the time a version of it flourished in the high medieval Italian city-states. I would also suggest that this package was meant so seriously, that a basic command was passed on from generations of city burghers to further generations of citizens to preserve the values celebrated in that tradition, and to keep order and stability in the city by cherishing the wisdom of their forefathers. Finally, an important element of this package is reverence to (the) God(s), as the source of human flourishing, and the attendance to the divine commands, where it is the cult of its founding God(ess) in the ancient variant, and of its patron saint in its Christian version, which guarantees the survival of the city. In fact, it is this whole package and the honorable preservation of it, that I call the conservative urban republican heritage of the European city.

NOTES

1. Rémi Brague, *Europe, la voie romaine* (Paris: Criterion, 1992).
2. The contrast is described in Ferenc Horkay Hörcher, "Prudencia, kairosz, decorum. A konzervativizmus időszemléletéről," *Információs társadalom* 6, no. 4 (2006): 61–80.
3. Wilfried Nippel, *Ancient and Modern Democracy. Two Concepts of Liberty*, trans. Keith Tribe (Cambridge: Cambridge University Press, 2015). The original German language version was published in 2008. It is important to note here, that the original German language title presents the relationship of ancient and modern democracy as an either-or relationship, while the English language translation presents the two in a complementary relationship.
4. John Dunn, *Democracy: The Unfinished Journey, 508 BC to AD 1993* (Oxford: Oxford University Press, 1992).
5. Pierre Manent, *Metamorphoses of the City. On the Western Dynamic*, trans. Marc Lepain (Cambridge: Harvard University Press, 2013).
6. Nippel, *Ancient*, 10.
7. Ibid., 11.
8. Ibid.
9. Ibid.
10. Ibid., 12.
11. Herodotus, 6.131.1, quoted by Nippel, *Ancient*, 13.

12. Ibid., 15.
13. Ibid., 16.
14. Ibid., 18.
15. Ibid., 20.
16. For the present-day renaissance of the term, see András Körösényi, "The Theory and Practice of Plebiscitary Leadership: Weber and the Orban Regime," *East European Politics and Societies* 33, no. 2 (2019): 280–301.
17. Thucydides, 2.65.9.
18. Nippel, *Ancient*, 32.
19. Quoted by Nippel, *Ancient*, 32, n. 94 from Hobbes, 1629.
20. Thomas Hobbes, *De Cive*, Ch 5, §5, *On the Citizen*, ed. Richard Tuck and Michael Silverthorne (Cambridge: Cambridge University Press, 1998), 71–2, quoted by Nippel, *Ancient*, 81.
21. Nippel, *Ancient*, 81.
22. We cannot be sure that this text was actually written by Aristotle, but the historical reconstruction in it indeed shares an Artistotelian view of politics.
23. In the biographical details, I rely on the "Introduction" by Stephen Everson, in *Aristotle: The Politics and The Constitution of Athens* (Cambridge: Cambridge University Press, 1996, 2017), ix–xxxvii.
24. Everson, "Introduction," xi.
25. Here I rely on Sir David Ross, *Aristotle* (London: Routledge, 1995). See the chapter entitled "Life and Works."
26. Everson, "Introduction," xvi, 1326b6, 1326b14-15.
27. 1326b4–5.
28. 1276b1–4, quoted by Everson, "Introduction," xvii.
29. 1275a22–33, referred to by Everson, "Introduction," xviii.
30. Ibid., xix.
31. i.2, 1253a20, quoted by Everson, "Introduction," xix.
32. 1337a27–9, quoted by Everson, "Introduction," xix.
33. I.2 1253a18–19, quoted by Everson, "Introduction," xix.
34. Ibid., xxi.
35. Ibid., xxv.
36. 1253a15–18, quoted by Everson, "Introduction," xxx.
37. Ibid., xxxi.
38. 1332b25–7, quoted by Everson, "Introduction," xxxi.
39. *Politics*, 1295a35–40.
40. 1295b1–4.
41. 1295b22–23.
42. 1295b25–33.
43. 1295b 34–1296a8.
44. 1296a14–17.
45. 1296a17–18.
46. 1296a19.
47. 1296b37–39.
48. 1297a4–5.

49. 1297b41–1298a3.
50. 1274a3–4.
51. 1274a8–9.
52. 1274a7–10.
53. Aristotle, *The Constitution of Athens*, in *Aristotle: The Politics and The Constitution of Athens*, ed. Stephen Everson (Cambridge: Cambridge University Press, 2017), 229. xxv.2.
54. Ibid.
55. Ibid., xxvi.1.
56. Ibid., xxvii.1.
57. Ibid., xxvii.1–2.
58. Ibid., xxvii.3–5.
59. Ibid., xxviii.1.
60. Ibid., xxviii.5.
61. This is the title of a work by the Spanish political thinker Ortega y Gasset in the early twentieth century.
62. The lecture was originally addressed to the audience in the Athénée Royal of Paris in 1819.
63. The terminology went back to a longstanding debate in early modern France about the artisitic and scientific achievements of the ancients, in comparison with the art of the Renaissance and Baroque era and the new science of Bacon and Descartes.
64. I use the following translation: Benjamin Constant, *The Liberty of the Ancients Compared with That of the Moderns*, trans. Jonathan Bennett, in 2010, online version published in 2017, https://www.earlymoderntexts.com/assets/pdfs/constant1819.pdf, 2.
65. Ibid., 6.
66. Ibid., 3.
67. Ibid., 5.
68. Ibid., 13.
69. Ibid., 14.
70. Ibid.
71. Appr. urban air makes you free.
72. For a defence of this connection between the two notions of liberty (individual and communal), see Quentin Skinner, "A Third Concept of Liberty, Isaiah Berlin Lecture," *Proceedings of the British Academy* 117, The British Academy (2002): 237–68.
73. Brague, *Europe*.
74. Michael Oakeshott, *Lectures in the History of Political Thought*, ed. Terry Nardin and Luke O'Sullivan (Exeter: imprint-academic.com, 2006).
75. Ibid., 193. According to Oakeshott, this "struggle for poer" lasted for three and a half centuries.
76. Ibid., 193.
77. Ibid., 193–194.

78. Ibid., 195.
79. In what follows, I rely on Jed W. Atkins, *Cicero on Politics and the Limits of Reason. The Republic and Laws*, (Cambridge: Cambridge University Press, 2013). See especially chapter 3, entitled "Constitutional Change and the Mixed Constitution," 80–115.
80. Atkins, *Cicero*, 83 refers to Plato, *Leg*. 3.693d–e.
81. Atkins, *Cicero*, 83, referring to Aristotle, *Pol*. 4.8.1293b33–1294a29.
82. Atkins, *Cicero*, 87.
83. Ibid., 88.
84. Ibid., 91.
85. Ibid., 92.
86. Ibid., 93.
87. Ibid.
88. Ibid., referring to Polyb. 6.18.
89. Ibid., 106.
90. Cicero, *Republic*, 2.27, quoted by Atkins, *Cicero*, 106.
91. Oakeshott, *Lectures*, 108.
92. Cicero, *Pro Sestio*, 103, referred to by Atkins, *Cicero*, 110.
93. Thomas N. Mitchell, *Cicero, the Senior Statesman* (New Haven: Yale University Press, 1991), 47, quoted by Atkins, *Cicero*, 110.
94. Cicero, *Republic*, 1.43.
95. Atkins, *Cicero*, 112, quoting Cicero, *Republic*, 1.69.
96. Atkins, *Cicero*, 113.
97. Atkins, *Cicero*, 113, referring to Cicero, *Republic*, 1.55.
98. Atkins, *Cicero*, 113.
99. Cicero, *Republic*, 2.69, quoted by Atkins, *Cicero*, 114.
100. Cicero, *Republic*, 2.54, quoted by Atkins, *Cicero*, 114.
101. Ibid., 115.
102. Cicero, *Republic*, 2.69, quoted by Atkins, *Cicero*, 115.
103. In what follows, I rely on the excellent introduction to the series by Christiane L. Joost-Gaugier, "Dante and the History of Art: The Case of a Tuscan Commune." Part II: The Sala del Consiglio at Lucignano, *Artibus et Historiae* 11, no. 22 (1990): 23–46.
104. Joost-Gaugier, *Dante*, 24.
105. Ibid.
106. Ibid., 26.
107. Ibid., 27.
108. "DA BRUTO P(RIMO) CONSULO / DE ROMANI SILSTO PRU/DENTE FORTE E TEPPE/RATO PIGLI ASENPLO ON/GNI DI FESORATO"
109. Dante, *De monarchia*, II:5, quoted by Joost-Gaugier, *Dante*, 27.
110. For a detailed account of Aquinas' own reading of Cicero, see: E. K. Rand, *Cicero in the Courtroom of St. Thomas* (Milwaukee: The Bruce Publishing Co., 1946).
111. Dante, *Convivio*, Joost-Gaugier in this respect refers among others to Hans Baron, as he writes about Cicero in *In Search of Florentine Civic Humanism*, I, (Princeton: Princeton University Press, 1988), 97–100.

112. As we saw, Brutus is labelled as the first consul of Rome, endowed with the virtues of prudence, courage and moderation. According to Joost-Gaugier, this description of him should be connected to Dante's *Inferno*, IV:127.

113. It might be explained with the form of the field where they are represented, that the three of them are not lined up side by side, but King Solomon is placed below Aristotle and Judith. Aristotle's importance is expressed by the fact that he is the first in the row, if we look at them as we read, from left to right.

114. Joost-Gaugier, *Dante*, 45, n. 124.

115. Ibid., 37.

116. Joost Gaugier refers to Dante, *Divine Commedy*, Purgatorium, XII: 59–60.

117. Joost-Gaugier, *Dante*, 37.

118. Joost-Gaugier refers in connection with this claim to Marsilius of Padua, *The Defender of Peace*, ed. Alan Gewirth (New York: Columbia Hard Cover, 1951), 2 vols., esp. II, 60.

119. Joost-Gaugier, *Dante*, 38.

120. Ibid., 38.

121. Cary J. Nederman, "The Meaning of 'Aristotelianism' in Medieval Moral and Political Thought," *Journal of the History of Ideas* 57, no. 4 (Oct. 1996): 563–85.

122. Ibid., 573.

123. A magnificent summary of practical education in Renaissance Italian city-states is James Hankins, *Virtue Politics*.

124. For this point, see Luca Bianchi, "Continuity and Change in the Aristotelian Tradition," in *The Cambridge Companion to Renaissance Philosophy*, ed. James Hankins (Cambridge: Cambridge University Press, 2007), 49–71.

125. I rely here on the D. Phil. thesis by Grace Allen, entitled "Vernacular Encounters with Aristotle's *Politics* in Italy, 1260–1600" submitted at the Warburg Institute and the University of London, in 2015.

126. See chapter 4. Bruni's translation of Aristotle's *Politics*, in Eckart Schütrumpf, *The Earliest Translations of Aristotle's Politics and the Creation of Political Terminology*, Morphomata Lectures (Cologne: Wilhelm Fink, 2014), 33–8.

127. For these references see Nederman, *The Meaning*, 582.

128. Grace Allen, "The Latin and Greek *fortuna* of Aristotle's *Politics* in Europe, 1260–1600," in *Vernacular Encounters*, 17–43, 26.

129. Thomas Aquinas and Peter of Auvergne, *In octos libros Politicorum Aristotelis expositio*, I.i.12, trans. from *Medieval Political Theory: A Reader: The Quest for the Body Politic 1100-1400*, ed. Cary Joseph Nederman and Kate Langdon Forhan (London and New York: Routledge, 1993), 139. This quotation seems to refer to *Politics*, 1252a9–22.

130. Thomas Aquinas and Ptolemy of Lucca, "De regno ad regem Cypri," I.3.17, trans. James M. Blythe, in Ptolemy of Lucca, *On the Government of Rulers: De Reminie Principum* (Philadelphia: University of Pennsylvania Press, 1997), 66, quoted by Allen, 29.

131. Ibid., I.30.20, quoted by Allen, "The Latin and Greek *fortuna* of Aristotle's *Politics*," 29.

132. *Summa theologiae, Prima Secundae*, 105.1. the English form taken (but slightly modified by Grace Allen) from Thomas Aquinas, Summa Theologica, Part

I-II, trans. Fathers of the English Dominican Province, Project Gutenberg, accessed 14 October, 2014, Allen, "The Latin and Greek *fortuna* of Aristotle's *Politics*," 31.

133. *Summa theologiae*, quoted by Allen, "The Latin and Greek *fortuna* of Aristotle's *Politics*," 30.

134. *Summa theologiae*.

135. Allen, "The Latin and Greek *fortuna* of Aristotle's *Politics*," 31–2.

136. Aquinas-Lucca, *De regno*, I.2., in Lucca, *On the Government of Rulers*, 64. Grace Allen also gives the locus in the *Politics*, 1252b10–1253a2.

137. Allen, "The Latin and Greek *fortuna* of Aristotle's *Politics*," 37.

138. Ibid., 38. Aristotle, *In hoc libro contenta. Politicorum libri octo...*, trans. Leonardo Bruni, comm. Jacques Lefèvre d'Étaples (Paris, 1526), f. 58r. Allen also mentions, that Garin was careful to emphasize that Burni's Latin took over a lot more from medieval sources than he was ready to admit. Also, one should be aware of the continuity between the medieval commune form of the city and its Renaissance city-state format.

139. It is important to note here, that beside being an equivalent of Aristotelian democracy, republic in the Renaissance had a wider meaning, referring to any kind of well-ordered political community, in which the rulers took care of the public good. See about this: Hankins, *Virtue Politics*.

140. Jones, *The Italian City-State*.

141. Grace Allen, "The Earliest Reception of Aristotle's *Politics* in the Italian Vernacular: 1260–1400," in *Vernacular Encounters*, 44–72, 45.

142. Nicolai Rubinstein, "Political Ideas in Sienese Art: The Frescoes by Ambrogio Lorenzetti and Taddeo di Bartolo in the Palazzo Pubblico," *Journal of the Warburg and Courtauld Institutes* 21 (1958): 179–207; Quentin Skinner, "Ambrogio Lorenzetti's Buon Governo Frescoes: Two Old Questions, Two New Answers," *Journal of the Warburg and Courtould Institutes* 62 (1999): 1–28.

143. Enrico Fenzi, "Brunetto Latini, ovvero il fondamento politico dell'arte della parola e il potere dell'intellettuale," in *A scuola con Ser Brunetto. Indagini sull ricezione di Brunetti Latini dal Medievo al Rinascimento*, ed. Irene Maffia Scariati, Atti del Convegno internazionale di studi Università do Basilea, 8–10 giugno 2006 (Florence, 2008), 323–372, 335.

144. On Latini, Grace Allen refers to Giorgio Inglese, *Latini, Brunetto, Dizionario biografico degli italiani (1960–2014)*, LXIV, 4–12. See Allen's explicit claim, that Latini's work "was a text designed for practical use by those in government and, in particular, those governing an Italian city-state." Allen, "The Earliest Reception of Aristotle's *Politics*," 48.

145. Brunetto Latini, *Li livres dou tresor* (Italian) f. 46v. quoted by Allen, "The Earliest Reception of Aristotle's *Politics*," 47–8. Grace Allen's translation of the text was made after consulting J. M. Najemy's own one, in John M. Najemy, "Brunetto Latini's Politics," *Dante Studies* 112 (1994): 33–52, 41.

146. Allen, "The Earliest Reception of Aristotle's *Politics*," 48.

147. Ibid., 49–50.

148. Giles of Rome, *Del Reggimento de' principi*, I.i.1., 4, quoted by Allen, "The Earliest Reception of Aristotle's *Politics*," 51.

149. Ibid., I.iii.3, quoted by Allen, "The Earliest Reception of Aristotle's *Politics*," 52.

150. Ibid., III.ii.2, quoted by Allen, "The Earliest Reception of Aristotle's *Politics*," 51.

151. Ibid., II.i.1, quoted by Allen, "The Earliest Reception of Aristotle's *Politics*," 53.

152. For the denial see Allen Gilbert, "Had Dante Read the *Politics* of Aristotle?" *PMLA* 43, no. 3 (1928): 602–13. For the affirmation see for example Enrico Berti, "Politica," in *Enciclopedia Dantesca*, 6 vols. (Rome: Istituto della Enciclopedia Italiana fondata da Giovanni Treccani, 1970–1978), IV, 585–87.

153. For this and the next quote, see Dante, *Convivio*, IV.iv, 275–77, trans. Christopher Ryan, *The Banquet*, 127–28.

154. Dante, *Convivio* IV.iv, 275–77. Translation from Dante, *The Banquet*, trans. Christopher Ryan (Anma Libri, 1988), 127–28, quoted with slight modifications by Allen, "The Earliest Reception of Aristotle's *Politics*," 65.

155. Allen, "The Earliest Reception of Aristotle's *Politics*," 66, referring to Paradiso 8, from Dante, *Paradiso* I., Italian Text and Translation, trans. Charles S. Singleton (Princeton: Princeton University Press, 1975), 90–1.

156. Jacopo della Lana, *Commento alla 'Commedia,'* ed. Mirko Volpi and Arianna Terzi, 4 vols. (Rome, 2009), II, Paradiso 8, 1931–33, quoted by Allen, *Chapter Two*, 67.

157. It translates into English: "humans are sociable beings and they live naturally in company." Francesco da Buti, *Commento... sopra La Divina Commedia di Dante Alighieri*, ed. Crescentino Giannini, 3 vols. (Pisa: Fratelli Nistri, 1858–1862), III.i, Paradiso 8, 270.

158. Allen, "The Earliest Reception of Aristotle's *Politics*," 72.

159. Hans Baron, "Cicero and the Roman Civic Spirit in the Middle Ages and Early Renaissance," *The Bulletin of the John Rylands Library* 22, no. 1 (Manchester: University Press, 1938): 72–97. This piece was an edited version of the talk he gave on this topic in Manchester in 1938.

160. Ibid., 77.

161. Baron takes this description from H. van Lieshout, *La Théorie Plotinienne de la vertu. Essau sur la génèse d'un article de lasomme Théologique de saint Thomas* (Freiburg i. Switzerland, 1926), 124ff.

162. Baron, *Cicero*, 77.

163. Ibid., 78.

164. Ibid., 78, 79.

165. *Moralium Dogma Philosophorum*, ed. John Holmberg (in Arbeten utgivna med understöd av Vilhelm Ekmans Universitetsfond, Uppsala, vol. 37), 53.

166. Baron, *Cicero*, 81.

167. Ibid., 82.

168. Ibid.

169. Ibid., 83.

170. Ibid., 85.

171. Epythoma de vita, gestis, scientie prstantia... Ciceronis, in the Cicero Codex from Petrarch's library, as published in P. de Nolhac, Pétrarque et l'humanisme, 2nd edition, 1807 vol. I, 227ff.

172. Baron, *Cicero*, 86.

173. Ibid., 87.

174. Ibid., 89, quoting *Vergerio's Epistolario*, ed. L. Smith, 1934, in Fonti per la storia d'Italia, 439ff.

175. Baron, *Cicero*.

176. Ibid., 90.

177. Ibid.

178. Matteo Palmieri, *Della vita Civile* (Milan, 1830).

179. Baron, *Cicero*, 93, quoting *Della vita civile*, 220ff, 228ff.

180. Ibid., 96.

181. Ibid., 97.

182. Ibid.

183. David Weinstein, and Avihu Zakai, *Jewish Exiles and European Thought in the Shadow of the Third Reich* (Cambridge: Cambridge University Press, 2017), 20–70.

184. Ibid., 20.

185. Riccardo Fubini, "Renaissance Historian," *Journal of Modern History* 64 (September, 1992): 542–44.

186. Weinstein, and Zakai, *Jewish Exiles*, 20, 26.

187. Ibid., 31.

188. Wolfgang J. Mommsen, *The Return to the Western Tradition: German Historiography since 1945* (Washington: German Historical Institute, 1991), 37.

189. Weinstein, and Zakai, *Jewish Exiles*, 41.

190. See Lord Acton's two famous essays on liberty, the remnants of his unfinished venture to write the history of liberty in Europe.

191. For this claim see Adam Swift, *Political Philosophy: A Beginners' Guide for Students and Politicians* (Cambridge, Polity Press, 2001), 51.

192. The lecture was read at the Academy on 21 November 2001. It is available at the following link: https://www.thebritishacademy.ac.uk/documents/754/11-skinner.pdf

193. Alan Patten, "The Republican Critique of Liberalism," *British Journal of Political Science* 26, (1996): 25–44.

194. Quentin Skinner, *A Third Concept*, 262. This form is a simplified version of the one to be found in the work of the medieval legal scholar, Henry de Bracton's *De Legibus et Consuetudinibus Angliae of c.1260*. As Skinner points out earlier in his essay, Bracton identifies as slave someone who "lives in subjection to the dominion of someone else." Skinner, *A Third Concept*, 248, n. 54.

195. Ibid., 249.

196. Ibid., 252, n. 76, referring to Elizabeth Read Foster, ed., *Proceedings in Parliament, 1610*, 2 vols. (New Haven, Conn.: Yale University Press, 1966), II. 192.

197. Skinner, *Buon Governo*. Skinner's two essays on Lorenzetti were republished in his 2002 collection of essays, under different titles.

198. Quentin Skinner, "Ambrogio Lorenzetti and the portrayal of virtuous government," in Skinner, *Visions of Politics*, I-III. (Cambridge: Cambridge University Press, 2017), vol 2. Renaissance Virtues, 39–92, 39.

199. Skinner, *Buon Governo*, 6.

200. Ibid., 10, referring to Rubinstein, *Sienese Art*, 184.

201. Francis J. Carmody, ed., *Li livres dou trésor de Brunetto Latini* (Berkely and Los Angeles: University of California Publications in Modern Philology, 1948), 211.

202. Skinner, *Buon Governo*, 14.

203. Jane Bridgeman, "Ambrogio Lorenzetti's Dancing 'Maidens': Case of Mistaken Identity," *Apollo* CXXXIII, no. 351 (1991): 245–51.

204. Skinner, *Buon Governo*, 27.

205. Ibid., 28.

206. Skinner, *Lorenzetti and the portrayal*, 46. Rubinstein is given as the source of the view that it is the reception of Aristotle which serves as the origin of this idea. Rubinstein, 1958, 186–7, as referred to in Skinner, *Lorenzetti and the portrayal*, 43, n. 26.

207. Ibid., 46.

208. Ibid., 47, quoting Cicero, *De Officiis*, 1913, I. VII. 22.

209. Ibid.

210. Ibid., quoting Cicero, *De Officiis*, 1913, I. XXV, 85–6.

211. Ibid., 40.

212. This explanation of the *civitas libera* comes from: Harold Whetstone Johnston, *Selected Orations and Letters of Cicero; To Which is Added the Catiline of Sallust*, rev. Hugh MacMaster Kingery (Chicago and New York: Scott, Foresman and Company, 1910), 268.

213. NE, 1097b14

214. NE, 1097b10

215. NE, 1134a25–27.

Chapter 4

From the Megalopolis to the City of Human Scale

This survey of the political philosophy of the European city has taken its paradigms from the Renaissance and the early modern period. The second and the third chapters of the book aimed to describe this phase and its prehistory, examining ancient Athens, Rome, and the medieval city as major steps in the evolution of the archetype of the European town. The present analysis contends that the coming of the modern era did not witness a real break in the nature of urban dwelling. On the contrary, urbanization proved to be a key factor in European modernization, leading to an unprecedented boom in the growth of cities and the birth of large areas of urbanized territory. The chief difference was that the key political agent in modernity became the state: the modern city was controlled by external state authorities. Therefore, compared to those of the court and the capital, the local politics of individual cities became a peripheral affair.

The modern city was a highly contentious form of habitation in other respects, too. This chapter will provide a short summary of some of the most important episodes in the story of the modernized city, with the newly born urban bourgeoisie at its center. While the growth and size of cities will be crucial in this period, our real question will be how the overgrown and overpopulated modern megalopolis can be transformed into the sustainable city of the postmodern or late modern age.

The modernist city is the megalopolis. The driving force of the megalopolis is not quality of life, but simply size, both in terms of its territory and in its number of inhabitants. The critical term itself is attributed to Patrick Geddes, and his pioneering work on urbanism, *Cities in Evolution* (1915).[1] The title of his great book reflects Geddes's background as a biologist, who viewed the city with the eyes of an evolutionary biologist, trying to make sense of its rapid progress. The term he coined, *conurbation*, relates to whole urban regions, built up of overgrown cities, where unprecedented new urban challenges had to be confronted, leading to the establishment of the new discipline of urbanism.

The new phenomenon of excessive growth was viewed from the very start with contempt by critical theorists. And it was not only Geddes who was highly pessimistic. The German historian Oswald Spengler's famous *The Decline of the West* (1918, 1922, 1923) was also a product of the years of and after the First World War, and it expressed serious doubts about the future of Western civilization, based on the devastating experience of World War I. Spengler's undertaking was, in fact, a highly politicized and rather artificial historical narrative. As he saw it, since the Thirty Years War Europe had witnessed an unbalancing of the great powers: France and Britain were guilty of overthrowing the German empire—a historical transformation which needed to be redressed in the twentieth century in order to reintroduce the balance of power.[2]

But beyond this political message, the real focus of Spengler's story was on cultures, understood as living organisms. Even in this respect, he had a rather pessimistic vision of modern historical developments, which he saw as the transgression of normality. "The defining component of the civilization stage is the 'megalopolis' or 'world-city.'"[3] In his pessimistic narrative, the shift from culture to civilization, which had led to a fatal value deficit, was generated by the abrupt centralization of industry, commerce, capital, and political power in urban centers: "From these periods onward three or four world-cities . . . have absorbed into themselves the whole content of History, while the old wide landscape of the Culture, become merely provincial, serves only to feed the cities with what remains of its higher mankind."[4] His understanding was based on the conceptual opposites of the world-city and the provinces. As he saw it, "In place of a world, there is a city, a point, in which the whole life of broad regions is collecting while the rest dries up."[5]

While Geddes criticized overgrowth from a British perspective, and Spengler offered a Germanic interpretation of modern urban development, it was Lewis Mumford who introduced a less biased, external, Northern American analysis on modernist developments. He fell under the spell of Geddes as a student, and their relationship was for a long time that of master and student.[6] It was through Geddes that Mumford's way of thinking became connected to the history of the European city. Mumford's approach to the city was based on a historically founded sociology, but his approach was no less critical, not to say skeptical, in many respects than that of Spengler. He, too, thought in terms of a conceptual opposition. As he saw it, the ideal city of the medieval period gave way to the modern city, the megalopolis, which was in fact a late version of ancient Rome, in its imperial period, and will therefore end the same way, in collapse. Beyond this historical narrative, however,

Mumford's real target was the typical American version of urban development, the sprawling suburbs of the metropolitan areas. An important aspect of his philosophy of the city was his criticism of the lack of spirituality in the modern city, a theme of cultural criticism which paralleled Spengler's attack on civilization as opposed to culture.

The following section will examine a single example of the modern megalopolis, nineteenth-century Paris. It is in Paris that we can meet the modern bourgeois, a key protagonist of the history of the European city. After this encounter we jump to the twentieth century, focusing on the tragic consequences of the totalitarian impulse in urban growth, the Holocaust and the Communist persecution of the middle classes. Both of these events played a role in the eradication of bourgeois urban culture from European life. After this gloomy perspective, a selection of contrasting intellectual efforts will be introduced, which aim to imagine alternatives to the totalitarian impulse in urban development.

THE DARK SIDE OF THE INDUSTRIALIZED CITY

"Old Paris is no more (the form of a city / Changes more quickly, alas! than the human heart)."[7] This famous quote about the transformation of the nineteenth-century Paris was written by Baudelaire, arguably the most representative poet of the age. It is instructive to consider this poet and his poetry, in order to reconstruct some of the sentiments which accompanied the major transformations in social structure as well as in the way of life and habitus of the people of Paris.

Baudelaire's *Fleurs du mal*, first published in 1857, can be read as a great diary of the changes taking place in the heart of France, especially the series of poems entitled *Tableaux Parisiens* (Parisian scenes) which reveal a great deal about this mental revolution, and which includes this poem, entitled *Le Cygne* (The Swan). The poem is dedicated to Victor Hugo, who was forced to leave Paris for political reasons during the regime of Napoleon III. The poem's speaker addresses an ancient Greek mythological character, Andromache. The title of the poem is a metaphor: the Swan is a symbol of change (metamorphosis, with the word of the title of that work by Ovid also mentioned in the poem). This animal seems ridiculous when moving on the ground, while in the air it flies beautifully. The change which the swan represents is reversed, however, from beauty to ridicule, with the disappearance of the old Paris and the birth of another, misshapen Paris. In this new megalopolis the speaker cannot feel at home. He is inclined to preserve the remnants of old Paris in his memory, which he regards as the monuments of ancient beauty and glory: "I see only in memory that camp of stalls, / (. . .), /The huge stone blocks stained green in puddles of water, / And in the windows shine the jumbled bric-a-brac."[8]

The reason for recalling here Baudelaire's reminiscences of old Paris, together with his descriptions of a new, albeit fearful, out-of-shape Paris, is to underline the public sentiments which followed the unparalleled industrialization and urbanization of the period, which made the city into the capital of modernity. Paris is perhaps the most representative of the nineteenth-century industrial, political, and cultural centers, and Baudelaire was the representative poet of its counterculture. Indeed, Walter Benjamin, a twentieth-century German-Jewish literary critic, who was partly brought up in Paris himself, claimed that Paris was nothing less than the capital of the nineteenth century. An essay with just such a title, *Paris, Capital of the 19th century*, was published as an exposé for his great panorama of mid-nineteenth-century Paris, the famous Arcades Project, together with an accompanying piece, *The Paris of the Second Empire in Baudelaire* (1938). We will focus instead on a third essay by Benjamin, however, *On Some Motifs in Baudelaire* (1939), which has been deemed "the culmination of Benjamin's engagement with modern urbanism in general."[9]

Benjamin's unsystematic introduction to the life of the metropolis "creates what is now one of the single most influential studies of the modern city through a sustained reading of Charles Baudelaire's lyric poetry."[10] According to Benjamin, much more can be learned by reading Baudelaire's poetry than from sociological studies, and most importantly it reveals the secret, inner life, and the underworld of the metropolis.

The figure made famous by Benjamin's analysis of Baudelaire's poetic "behavior" is, of course, the *flaneur*. The *flaneur*, the hero of Baudelaire, which is perhaps also his self-portrait, is a hunter in the metropolitan jungle who gets acquainted with the new city by strolling through its streets, chasing new experiences. Benjamin makes it clear that this *déclassé* version of the dandy is to be understood as the opposite of the man of the crowd, who inhabits the giant city of the nineteenth century.[11] Benjamin describes the difference between them in the following way: "The man of the crowd is no flaneur. In him, composure has given way to manic behavior. He exemplifies, rather, what had to become of the *flaneur* after the latter was deprived of the milieu to which he belonged."[12]

Baudelaire's description of Paris is in fact a description of a loss of home, a loss of belonging, according to the narrative of Benjamin, an *émigré*, writing in Paris. Just like Benjamin, the poet, too, recalls his experiences of the city in the good old days of his childhood: "Baudelaire's Paris preserved some features that dated back to the old days."[13] Yet in order to be able to uncover those hidden treasures, the poet has to sacrifice his own present self. It is this attitude of self-negation which lends the poetry its magic. Baudelaire himself was a cultural critic of the freshly born megacity—writing as he did in the period when Haussmann restructured Paris. Yet he decided to support the new sensibility, modernity, but only at the price of glorifying its underworld, the dark side of the glamorous capital. This is his specific, cultural form of rebellion. Not for nothing is his poetry book entitled *The Flowers of Evil*.

Benjamin wants to help us understand the psychological process taking place within the poet, which inspires his poetry. In order to fully identify himself with the modern city, Baudelaire has to detach himself from his earlier, childhood self, and present a life of detachment, or alienation. The crowd described in the famous poem by Baudelaire is the swarm of people who inhabit the metropolis, in a blind and deaf manner, disregarding pain, cruelty, and moral corruption, striving for commodities, the new fetishes of society. The poet is someone "on whom, in his cradle, a fairy has bestowed the love of masks and masquerading," in order "to take a bath of multitude," and with that also "the hate of home, and the passion for roaming."[14]

This loss of (feeling at) home is a crucial experience of the inhabitants of the giant city. It was the end point of a lengthy procedure, however. Paris, the capital of France (and the long-time seat of the French king) had a political relevance which in Baudelaire's day went way beyond that of any other sizable city. In other words, the city operated indeed as the heart of the whole country, representing French grandeur and glory, beyond the particular interests of its ever-growing number of inhabitants.

Reviewing the urban history of Paris, the first flourishing of the city came in the thirteenth century. The population of the city grew to around 160,000 inhabitants by 1250. By the end of the fourteenth century, great losses were suffered as a result of the Black Plague, which afflicted the whole of Europe. Further major influences on population numbers were the Hundred Years' War, and then the losses caused by the fierce religious wars and power struggles of the sixteenth century. A period of unprecedented growth started in the seventeenth century—in other words, after the Peace of Westphalia—in the days of King Henry IV and Richelieu. Paris kept growing until the French Revolution, when it passed the threshold of 600,000 inhabitants. To govern such a monster caused enormous difficulties not only for local authorities, but also for the centralized state. Whenever there was trouble—popular uprisings or other forms of social unrest—in the capital, it was not only a problem for Paris, but also for the whole country. By 1800 the city had lost almost 100,000 inhabitants in the revolution and the subsequent wars, initiating an unprecedented period of urbanization and urban conflicts. Indeed, the nineteenth century can be labeled the century of revolutions in Paris.[15] After the Great Revolution, which lasted for about quarter of a century, causing serious problems in the life of the city, at least three major popular revolts took place within the city walls: in 1830, 1848, and 1871, respectively. "Only with the establishment of electoral democracy within a relatively stable Third Republic after 1877, in the words of François Furet's famous quip, did 'the French Revolution finally enter the harbour' and bring revolutionary upheavals to a close."[16] According to the major narratives of this history, these revolutionary upheavals were caused by the surviving radical elements of the revolution, the *sans-culottes* and the post-revolutionary elites, who sought a return to earlier modes of controlling political power. Although this narrative has been challenged by recent historiography, which keeps emphasizing that the ever new revolutionary movements did not simply repeat the messages of the earlier ones, it is an undoubted fact that nineteenth-century Paris experienced a series of political turmoils, while the transformation of the political regimes during this period was caused by fundamental changes in its society and economy. The basic narrative of post-1789 France is the emergence of a new form of republican identity, based on the self-conscious French (and Parisian) concept of citizenship (in those days mainly of men). The changes caused by further urbanization doubled the population of the capital, resulting in an expansion of the huge exploited masses that came to be called the proletariat. Famously, Haussmann's daring urban reconstructions in the mid-century created the stage for Paris to represent the center of nineteenth-century European progress. However, as Baudelaire's poetry reveals, a counter-narrative also developed, decrying a loss of values in the megapolis. This mental shift was underpinned by troubling social phenomena: a rise in criminality, including juvenile delinquency, a breakdown of public hygiene—and with it the growing chance of epidemics—unprecedented levels of poverty, together with an unimaginable moral corruption as a result of the enjoyment of luxury, prostitution, alcoholism, and other forms of drug use. It was most probably because of the shocking pace of urbanization that cities like Paris (and the other major megacities of the continent) were conceptualized as centers of an underworld in the mental map of the people of the countryside. The contrast between modernity in the city and conventional ways of life in the countryside had socio-political and cultural consequences, and this was expressed in sharply different forms of life, fashion, dialect, and popular culture both inside and outside the capital. All of this led to an escalating political conflict between bodies of public administration and to the revolt of the masses, a term made famous by Ortega in the early twentieth century, but also based on the experience of the former century. The series of political revolutions were painted in dark colors by the new artistic sensibility of the age, giving voice directly or indirectly to the suffering caused by the cruelty of the new alliance of big business and state authorities against the urban proletariat. It was in this context of social unrest that theoreticians of social change such as Marx and Engels, and disillusioned artists such as Baudelaire and Dostoyevsky and Balzac and Dickens famously took the side of the masses.

While Paris as an urban center has had a reputation for moral decline and corruption since the Middle Ages, it was only after the Industrial Revolution and the introduction of a capitalist system of economy that sin and immorality became strongly attached to Paris in the public imagination of ordinary countrymen. This was an almost unavoidable consequence of the appearance of an urban space which was too big to get a grip on in one's mental map, since the unknown is easily associated by men with the dangerous and the threatening. While one should not underestimate the suffering of the urban poor, the fact is that the standard of living of the average Parisian was growing rapidly in the nineteenth century. Yet the cultural impression left by the abrupt social, economic, and political changes, and the birth of a megalo-city was a frightening and disillusioning prospect. Modernity, championed by the urban bourgeoisie, found its other in the coalition of the urban masses and the revolutionary vanguard of the new art and social prophecy.

THE GLORY AND THE DECLINE OF THE BOURGEOISIE

After encountering the dark side of the city, let us now turn to the bright side of nineteenth-century European urban life. Paris took the lead in giving a role in world history to the third order of European feudal society, the bourgeoisie. In the English-speaking world, too, certain economic and political factors prepared the ground for the takeover of the bourgeoisie, and this development proved to be crucial for the evolution of a new mentality. The term and concept of the *bourgeoisie* were to play a more important role on the continent, however, as demonstrated by recent continental historiography. This chapter will refer to two continental historians for whom the issue of the new role of the bourgeoisie was crucial: Jürgen Kocka and John Lukacs. Before turning to them, it is first worth examining the word *bourgeoisie* itself.

The adjective bourgeois and even more the noun bourgeoisie still have a somewhat foreign ring to them in English, as they sound French (one might even guess, Parisian). Yet it is not a newly borrowed term. The word "bourgeois" is claimed to have appeared in English in the 1560s, with the meaning: "of or pertaining to the French middle class."[17] It was later extended to cover the same class in other countries. It certainly derives from Indo-European versions of the term "burgh." The bourgeois, then, is the early modern and modern town dweller, "citizen or freeman of a city." Soon, however, a further dimension of its meaning was added to this, that of "tradespeople or citizens of middle rank in other nations." A newer connotation is the aesthetic dimension of its meaning, which dates back to the nineteenth century.

Two important German authors had a major impact on the transformation of the meaning of the word: Hegel and Marx. It was Hegel who created the conceptual opposition of *citoyen* and *bourgeois*.[18] Although the distinction is, of course, French, and Hegel himself borrowed it from Rousseau, and while Schiller also recognizes this duality, the relevance attributed to it is Hegel's own conceptual innovation. The *bourgeois* is the individual's name in the context of commerce and civil society in general. He is the *homo economicus* who is only concerned with private profit. This is an important activity for Hegel, as it creates civil society, an insight he took from the Scottish Enlightenment. However, this activity has a limited radius of action, excluding both politics and culture. According to his critics, the *bourgeois* entrepreneur is exclusively interested in profit, disregarding the common good. It is the *citoyen*, the citizen of the state, the *homo politicus*, who is able also to take into account the common good, and who is himself an agent of the state, whose activity is in the interest of the whole. In Hegel's hierarchy, to act for the state represents a higher reality, a more developed form of activity than that represented by the action for private profit.

The other key theoretician of the term *bourgeoisie* was, of course, Karl Marx, who put the term into the framework of a deterministic philosophy of history.[19] Marxist historical determinism led from less developed to more developed forms of social systems, always defined by class conflicts. Modernity, as he saw it, was determined first by the *bourgeoisie's* fight against retrograde feudalist forms of rule, as seen in what he called the *bourgeois* revolutions (meaning in particular Cromwell's revolution in Britain and the French Revolution). "The modern *bourgeois* society that has sprouted from the ruins of feudal society has not done away with class antagonisms."[20] This is a society based on industrialization, the market, and capitalist forms of production and exchange. Its wealth is based on exploitation, and more precisely on the unjust exploitation of the wage worker, the class known in Marxist terminology as the proletariat. As Marx saw it, a key development in capitalist society occurred when "(t)he *bourgeoisie* has subjected the country to the rule of the towns. It has created enormous cities."[21]

Hegel and Marx had a tremendous influence on social thinking in the nineteenth century. We will not dwell here on their respective theories. Instead, we will jump to that part of twentieth-century history writing which described modern German historical development during the nineteenth and twentieth centuries. One of the main preoccupations of this history writing was attempting to answer the tantalizing question: how could Nazism have taken over the imagination of the German people so overwhelmingly? It is in this context that the idea of a German *Sonderweg* was born. At this point it will be useful to first summarize this German historiographical context, and to explain the significance of the German *Bürger* (*bourgeois*).

Jürgen Kocka was one author who connected the problem of the German *Sonderweg* with the historical role of the *bourgeoisie*.[22] Kocka proved to be an influential historian who was able to give a more nuanced account of German history in a European context than earlier accounts, as represented by Ralf Dahrendorf. To simplify his argument, Dahrendorf claimed that a key factor in the birth of Nazism was that Germany did not have a fully developed form of *bourgeois* society. Dahrendorf was referring to *bourgeois* society in both senses of the term used by Hegel. He also referred to the deterministic scheme of Marx. As he saw it Germany's historical development was delayed, or belated, which meant that "neither in the sense of a society of citizens or in that of one dominated by a confident *bourgeoisie* did a modern society emerge."[23]

The research into social history which has been written since the 1970s and 1980s has made it clear, however, that in the social life in the *Reich* a large set of *bourgeois* values had emerged, in the fields of "taste, fashion, and the everyday conduct of affairs." Where earlier generations of scholars saw a *Defizit an Bürgerlichkeit* (a lack of *bourgeoisie*), more recent research has found *bourgeois* values dominating among "the prevailing views of the law, morality, and the social order; the notions of private property and social obligation, and the general principles of public life."[24] Besides the research on social history associated with Werner Conze and the reconstructive work of urban history led in Frankfurt by Lothar Gall, it was the work of Jürgen Kocka, working in Bielefeld, which has had the strongest influence on the professional discussion of this topic.[25] The "Bielefeld School" of historical writing included such towering figures as the leftist social historian Hans-Ulrich Wehler and the more conservative Reinhart Kosselleck, a key figure of conceptual history. It says much about the atmosphere of the school that in one interview, Kocka refers to the political differences between himself and Koselleck, but keeps emphasizing their agreement on certain professional issues.[26]

Kocka himself defined his research topic in 1986–1987 as the question of the *bourgeoisie* in the senses of both *Bürgertum* and *Bürgerlichkeit*, a form of conceptualization which is difficult to translate into English. His research was a comparative exercise, drawing on the findings of invited researchers from all over Europe, and from a number of disciplines, resulting in a monumental, three volume collection of essays entitled *Bürgertum im 19. Jahrhundert: Deutschland im europäischen Vergleich*.[27] While this collection was published in German, a selection of that material was made available in English in 1993.[28] This volume sought to identify the term *middle class* in a European context, focusing specifically on the German-English and German-French comparison, with these two societies taken as the most developed forms of social development, but also providing a comparison with such belated societies as those in Hungary or Italy. It also addressed the sensitive issue of the status of the Jewish bourgeoisie in Germany. Kocka's own piece in the English language volume takes a socio-historical approach, which identifies three types of *bourgeois* class in the German *Reich* of the nineteenth century: "the traditional burgher class of the towns," the *Bildungsbürgertum* (the bourgeoisie endowed with cultural capital), and the economic *bourgeoisie*.[29] This classification seems problematic in itself: it reflects the shortcomings of the German discussion of *Bürgerlichkeit*. Kocka also made an effort to distinguish these types from two other urban strata: the petty *bourgeoisie* or *Mittelstand*, and the working class.[30] Kocka's social history is also colored by his interest in intellectual history—most probably influenced by the work of Reinhart Koselleck in the field of conceptual history (*Begriffsgeschichte*). It is this interest which helps Kocka to describe the everyday culture of the German *bourgeoisie*, "the broader *bourgeois* norms and values that became culturally dominant," making use of the notion of the public sphere, made famous a few years before by Jürgen Habermas.[31] According to one critic, Kocka's approach was based on a rather vague and rosy notion of civil society (*bürgerliche Gesellschaft*), which seemed to combine a vision of liberal politics and an idealized reconstruction of the early capitalist economy. This duality is expressed in the two possible interpretations of the term, either as a "society of citizens" or a "society dominated by the bourgeoisie."[32]

The concept of civil society was a crucial notion for Kocka. In his etymological overview of the term, he makes it explicit that its meaning is connected in his mind with the specific political sense attributed to the term before and during the transition period which followed the fall of the Berlin Wall in 1990. In his essay entitled *Civil society from a historical perspective*, Kocka made use of what he learned from Koselleckian conceptual history.[33] In this essay, he relies on a longue durée grand narrative which refers back to what he calls "the *societas civilis* in Aristotelian tradition" and forward to the 1980s, when it was used in a fully positive meaning, as "the central expression in anti-dictatorial critique, especially in East Central Europe—in Prague, Warsaw and Budapest, where dissidents such as Václav Havel, Bronislaw Geremek and Györgi (sic) Konrád used the term."[34] In this latter context, he also refers to leftist social theorists, who again used the term in their own politically motivated research, including "social scientists such as John Keane, Charles Taylor and Jürgen Habermas."[35]

For Kocka, however, the real task was to distinguish civil society as a nineteenth-century middle class *bourgeois* culture from the progressive vision of civil society in and after the age of Enlightenment. According to the traditional account, thinkers such as Locke, Kant, and others referred to it in a vision "in which the people would live together in peace as politically mature, responsible citizens—as private individuals in their families and as citizens in public."[36] Compared to this vision, the long nineteenth century brought a dead end with the domination of "a 'middle class (*bürgerliche*) society' of the *bourgeoisie*" and not "a 'civil society' made up of citizens (Bürger)."[37] It was simplified accounts such as this one which led to Dahrendorf's critical account. Kocka presented a more elaborate picture of German society and culture in the long nineteenth century. He started out from a notion of the *bürgerlich* "in German-speaking Central Europe," which is close to what is labeled in art history as *Biedermeier*.[38] In the early nineteenth century, "in German-speaking Central Europe, the terms *Bürgertum* and *bürgerlich* referred to the small urban social formation of businesspeople, industrialists, bankers and directors on the one hand, and to academically educated officials, professors, secondary school teachers, layers, physicians, clerics and journalists, on the other."[39] This is the root of what came to be called the middle class. Members of this group were characterized by what was known as "a middle class culture (*bürgerliche Kultur*)."[40] This culture did not equate simply to what would be called high culture: it encompassed "general education, certain values such as self-reliance, a specific family model and certain forms of communication."[41] This class was still a potent historical force in the first half of the nineteenth century, according to Kocka, because it held a vision of a civil society as a potentially liberating political project. As Kocka saw it, however, by the second half of the century, "parts of the middle class became conservative and defensive, turning away from essential aspects of civil society."[42]

Obviously, Kocka's criticism is based on a comparative historical analysis, referring to England and France as the positive examples, where "the middle class and nobility became much more closely intertwined," resulting in "broader social bases of the developing civil society."[43] For him, Poland (and possibly also Hungary) was the negative example, where "the gentry took the place of the poorly developed, sometimes ethnically foreign middle class."[44] Between these two extremes, the liberal British and the feudal Central European paradigm, Germany seemed to strike a middle way, at least for a time. Unfortunately, however, the political activity of the German *Bürger* in the newly born German *Reich* was unlike that of the middle ranks in Victorian England or of the French *citoyens* of the France of *Napoleon III*. This difference in attitudes, together with the antisemitic tendencies of German society, politically exploited by its ruling elite, led to the deadlock of German history in the first half of the nineteenth century, and to the Nazi regime of Hitler. A similarly apolitical attitude of the *bourgeoisie* in Central Europe led to the birth of authoritarian regimes in the region, like those of Piłsudski and Horthy, and later to the political tragedies and sins of some of these political regimes during World War II.

As is perhaps evident from this comparative exercise, this is still an abstract narrative, based on a particular conception of the revolutionary and post-revolutionary French citizenry, and on a somewhat anachronistic interpretation of twentieth-century history. Kocka's narrative of a turn toward conservatism by the German *bourgeoisie* is, I believe, mistaken. As this book has demonstrated, the German middle classes were natural heirs to the mentality of urban dwellers of the early modern German cities, a tradition which is continuous, even if it is an undercurrent. They certainly had their own, sometimes rather critical judgments of political developments but they were never revolutionary as a historical force. In this sense, they did not turn *more* "conservative and defensive," because a conservative attitude has always been their political inclination, for centuries. This is not to deny their responsibility for the birth of a shallow nationalist rhetoric in the period of the First World War, or even later, at the time of Hitler's takeover before the Second World War. The crux of the matter is that unlike the citizens of the French capital, they did not have an activist political inclination, and their concept of civil society was much more peaceful, following the patterns of what Weber identified as the Protestant ethic. While politically engaged, this bourgeoisie was more interested in local politics and running its own cities than in large-scale politics, for good reason.

Clearly, the above characterization of Kocka's view of the German and Central European summary is a rather simplified one, which cannot do justice to all the details of his research findings. For us, the key conclusion to be drawn is that in spite of these failures of the metahistory of civil society presented by Kocka, the philosophy of the European city can and should make use of the research into the culture and social life of the middle classes in German-speaking central Europe. This period of the classical German *Bürgerlichkeit* remains an important phase in the modern development of urban thought.

The next section will focus more specifically on the Central European scene. We shall concentrate here on a single city, Budapest, at a single political moment, 1900, as described by the conservative historian John Lukacs.[45] Lukacs was a generation older than Kocka, and belonged rather to Koselleck's generation. Politically, too, John Lukacs was closer to Koselleck: he admits his conservative inclinations, though he prefers to call himself reactionary and not simply conservative. A Hungarian citizen of Jewish descent, Lukacs deserted the Hungarian army after the German occupation of the country in 1944, as he was forced to serve in the labor service (*munkaszolgálat*), under the anti-Jewish legislation of the country, although he was brought up as a Catholic. During the last months of the war, he hid in a cellar in order to avoid deportation to the death camps, which was the fate of the majority of the Hungarian Jews. Obtaining his degree in history from Budapest University, he left the country for the United States soon after, just before the full communist takeover.

In America, John Lukacs was able to pursue a career as a university professor of history. Besides teaching, he published a great deal: he was a social and cultural conservative, critical of mass culture in the United States and the West, in general, and he published his famous portrait of his hometown, Budapest, in 1988 at the comparatively advanced age of sixty-four. His intention was to show that besides Vienna, Budapest, too, represented a remarkable achievement at the turn of the century. Beyond providing the historical facts, he wished to offer an artistically phrased assessment of the achievements of the generation of his parents, the world of *ancien régime* Hungary, the happy peacetime in the thriving capital of the pre-WWI Hungarian Kingdom, within the larger political complex of the Dual Monarchy.

He published the book before the fall of the Berlin Wall, when interest in Central Europe was on the rise, for a mainly American audience. Lukacs wrote the book partly as a social historian, and partly as a cultural critic of modernity. His basic insight was that in the last quarter of the nineteenth century, Budapest became one of the fastest growing metropolises of the world. Yet Lukacs was much more an intellectual historian than a historian of sheer numbers. As well as providing a "physical description" of the city, he presents a "description of the lives of its various classes of people," including their "political views" as well as "their intellectual lives and art" together with "their mental and spiritual inclinations."[46] The most daring aspect of the book is that it concentrates on a mere ten years in the life of the city, from 1896 to 1906, a brave decision based on the assumption that this moment was the highlight in its life.

Himself an admirably cultured character, Lukacs had an individualized style of history writing. His language is close to the prose of fiction writers, turning his portrait into something resembling literature. The starting point of his narrative is, in fact, literature and he keeps returning to it later. He introduces a novel by a today less-known Hungarian writer, Ferenc Körmendi, born in 1900.[47] The novel has a symbolic title: *The Happy Generation* (*A boldog emberöltő*), and was published in 1934.[48] Lukacs reminds us that this was when Hitler took over the power, an event which would force the author himself to leave the country. He characterizes the book as a "great Budapest *haut-bourgeois* novel," chronicling a class not far removed from the life of the Paris or Berlin *bourgeoisie*, or that of Thomas Mann's *Buddenbrooks*, although Mann's family saga was published somewhat earlier, in 1901, at the time when the story of Körmendi's novel starts. In spite of its title, the book only presents half a generation, in its decline. The crucial issue for Lukacs is to present the life of the ancien *régime*: his hero was born in 1900 so his own heyday expresses the spirit of the age, "suffused with the optimism of security, respectability, cultivation and progress."[49] The novel was written more than thirty years later, in a gloomier age, and its retrospective view is "painful and melancholy"—a feeling and atmosphere which is not far from Lukacs's own views of the age he describes in his work, from the perspective of the 1980s. In this respect, another comparison can be drawn, alongside Mann's *Buddenbrooks*: that of Stefan Zweig, author of *The World of Yesterday*. In both Körmendi's and Zweig's novels, Lukacs claims that we encounter the values of the turn of the century.

One of Lukacs's main aims was to reconstruct the basic value system of his heroes, the *bourgeoisie* or middle class of Budapest, "the presence of the solid *bourgeois* virtues of personal and civilizational probity."[50] Recalling Goethe, one of the most important classical reference points on the reading lists of this German-speaking *bourgeoisie*, he speaks of a "world of protective affinities."[51] In other words, his historical point is that while this is a value system in which individual responsibility is crucial, there is also a communal dimension to it, which comes from the social functions of the elite in this important capital city. Their patrician patterns of life resembled those of the German patricians in many other cities of the Holy Roman and the Habsburg empires.

The typical *bourgeois* way of life in Hungary was characteristic of other newly arrived groups in Hungarian cities, due to the policies of its kings and queens of inviting foreign merchants and artisans to populate its often depopulated cities. This was also necessary because "the national disdain for commerce and finance lasted for a long time."[52] On the other hand, the crown traditionally largely depended on the taxes collected in the royal cities. As a result of the conscious policy of its kings to bring in an urban element, "by 1900 the tone of Budapest was that of a bourgeois city. Perhaps in all of Eastern Europe it was the *only* bourgeois city."[53] By this statement Lukacs means that Budapest was closer to the original German model of the bourgeois city than any of the other cities in the area.

Lukacs's explanation of this *bourgeois* character of the city is, of course, historical. When giving a description of the city, both *urbs* and *civitas*, he looks at the way it grows, instead of only presenting a static sociographic panorama. As he presents it, the dynamics of the development of the two historical parts of the city, Buda and Pest were different. "Buda... was largely German speaking, conservative, Catholic and loyal to Habsburg rule."[54] Pest, on the other hand, had a less well-established and well-off population, which is why Lukacs speaks of "the Magyar nationalism and the radical enthusiasms of Pest."[55] Besides this internal division, Lukacs also gives a detailed picture of the social stratification of the whole country, mirrored to a large extent, but not fully, by the population of the metropolis. He continually emphasizes the feudal traits of this society, led by its traditional aristocratic elite, with its cosmopolitan culture, which was constitutionally balanced by a wider stratum of the nobility, out of which, by the last quarter of the century, the so-called gentry had arisen. This is a class which preserved much of its feudal mentality, having lost their estates, a growing proportion of its members' income derived from what they can earn from the state, taking jobs in the state bureaucracy. The gentry were the heir of the nobility, the privileged class, supported by the centuries-old constitutional traditions of the country, based on the assumption that they were the safeguard of national autonomy and self-governance. Accustomed to their life of (tax-free) independence, members of this *petite noblesse terrienne*[56] wanted to keep their life of leisure.

In his description of the gentry, and of the role they played in the life of the metropolis, Lukacs draws on the work of Győző Concha, whom he regards as the best observer of the gentry. Concha was an important voice of turn-of-the century Hungarian social science, educated as a lawyer, who was both historically and sociologically well informed about Hungarian life in the late nineteenth century. The point Lukacs wants to make about the gentry and Budapest is that by this time the income of this gentry was coming less and less from their estates, which were not run properly, and which they had lost anyhow over the centuries, and more from the jobs offered by the state, which they got much more easily in the age of nationalism than the foreign elements of the cities. For this reason, the gentry moved to Budapest, the center of public administration, in this way determining its atmosphere. They became the new urban middle class, labeled variously in the historical literature as the "gentlemanly middle class" (*úri középosztály*) or "the Christian middle class." The first label was used to distinguish this class from the other constitutional elements of the country, the aristocracy, the *bourgeoisie*, the peasantry, and also from a new class, created by the growing industrialization, the working class, the lowest and least privileged class of this late feudal society.

The gentry felt the need to distinguish itself also from the historical German urban element, which they regarded as alien, and whom they distrusted for their loyalty to the Habsburg crown. The gentry middle classes were also anxious to distance themselves from the Jewish population. The culture of the gentry was provincial, while the *bourgeoisie*, either German or Jewish, had a much more cosmopolitan style, which connected them more to the aristocracy than to the Christian middle class, which remained often pathetically nationalist. One of the great merits of Lukacs's reconstruction is to show how all these elements found themselves in a precarious balance in the last quarter of the nineteenth century, at the time of economic boom and prosperity in turn-of-the-century Budapest. This balance depended not only on the settlement with Austria, but also on a compact between the different layers of the Budapest *bourgeoisie*: the historical German-speaking patriciate, the gentry middle classes, and the new Jewish bourgeoisie. This latter settlement depended on the compromises made by the foreign elements with the supporters of Hungarian nationalism in the city. Lukacs's feelings about this compromise are not one-sided. He admits that "the extraordinary rise of Budapest depended on the extraordinary force of Hungarian nationalism in the nineteenth century."[57] On the other hand, he is rather clear about the inbuilt social, and later political conflicts between the different elements of the population of the capital. While in Buda this conflict was less tense, between the historical German patriciate and the nationalist gentry population, in Pest there were more pronounced conflicts between the nationalist and the non-Hungarian, in this case to a large extent Jewish inhabitants. For a long time, the compromise was still able to cool down passions and heal conflicts, while the city was flourishing, but the balance broke down amid the tragic events of the First World War, and the painful consequences of defeat for Hungary. The year 1900 was indeed an exceptional moment, then, perhaps the last peaceful one in the history of the city: "In 1900 the elements of a fatal discord and division between the urban and the populist . . . between the cosmopolitan and the nationalist, between the non-Jewish Hungarian and the Jewish-Hungarian culture and civilization of Budapest were already there. But the break had not yet come."[58] The exceptional achievement of the city depended on this atmosphere of precariously balanced compromise and an unstable and unsatisfactory integration, which lasted as long as the economic boom endured.

Among the achievements of these doomed, and yet idyllic years, Lukacs is perhaps most interested in the urban culture of the city. Himself a son of the city, he recalls his childhood memories when he tries to reconstruct the general atmosphere, what he calls the tone of the city. Let me pick out two types of institutions of Budapest, beloved by the author, and described with great analytical and historical accuracy. One is the gymnasium, the historically established secondary school; the other is the coffee house, one of the most important theatrical stages of the protagonists of the culture of the city. As he saw it, the generation of Budapest in 1900 was a particularly successful generation, producing five of the six Nobel Prize winners to have come from Hungary—although all of them had to leave the country at a certain point in their professional careers. Besides the Nobel Laureates, this generation produced a plethora of artists, writers, musicians, and scholars, who achieved worldwide fame, a list of whose names covers a whole page, including Béla Bartók, André Kertész, and László Moholy-Nagy. The reason behind their success, claims Lukacs, is the specific form of secondary education, characteristic of Budapest, offered in the specific educational institution of the classical gymnasium. This institution followed the Austrian and German models, as did basically the whole modern educational system—except for one of the best of them, Eötvös College (*Eötvös Kollégium*), modeled largely after the *Ecole Normale* in Paris. The excellence of the gymnasium was due partly to its teaching program, "requiring, among other subjects, Latin and Greek, and attendance for eight years."[59] Teaching was strong both in the humanities and the natural sciences. There was also "a thorough march through the history of Magyar literature and of Hungarian (and also of Greek and Roman) history."[60] The number of such gymnasiums grew from three in 1876 to twelve in 1896 in Budapest. Matriculation (*érettségi*), the "final and severe examination" upon leaving a gymnasium, further contributed to the social prestige of the institution.[61]

The other favorite institution of Lukacs is the coffee house. Although many other urban centers had nice coffee house cultures, Lukacs might be right in claiming that there was something rather specific about the coffee houses of Budapest. These were even more numerous than the gymnasiums. He claims that nearly 600 such places of public entertainment existed in Budapest around 1900. He quotes the ironic words of one of the most popular journalists in those years, connecting the life in the coffee houses with that of other institutions of education: "every intelligent person had spent a part of his youth in the coffeehouse."[62] As a historian, Lukacs is able to draw on a developed historiography of this topic, in this case on a three volume history of the cafés of Budapest, by Béla Bevilaqua-Borsodi. In his description of its social functions and of its role in the life of the metropolis, Lukacs compares the typical café of Budapest to English and Irish pubs. The difference is that the cafés of Budapest offered more amenities and were, if anything, even friendlier to their guests than the pubs. They were open for long hours, offering food for the stomach but also sweet fruits for the mind, including newspapers and journals, as well as sometimes even music. With these functions they resembled more the British clubs than pubs. Different groups and networks of the cultural elite congregated in different cafés, all of them having meetings on a regular basis in their favorite haunts, including "journalists, playwrights, or sculptors and painters."[63] A coffee house, in this sense, served as a stage for the protagonists of culture: young artists, often arriving from the countryside to Budapest, had to get initiated into one of these circles in order to win honor and reputation.

Taken together, the education system and the rich social life of the coffee house in Budapest, it is amazing how this institutional framework resembles the days of the Enlightenment both on the continent and in Britain. It recalls the daily lives of authors such as Shaftesbury and Addison and Hume and Goethe, members of the Scottish Enlightenment in Edinburgh, Glasgow, or Aberdeen or in Weimar, for that matter. One should note the function of the clubs, pubs, and coffee houses in Enlightenment culture. While these were forms of public entertainment and education, they also had what a social anthropologist might call civilizing functions: they spread the ideas of civility and cultural refinement, the education of a cultivated taste. This infrastructure of sociability was the cradle of *bourgeois* culture in Europe, together with institutions such as salons, theaters and operas, dance halls, and academies and museums, from the Renaissance through the Baroque and the Enlightenment, up to the age of Romanticism and Biedermeier. It was also connected to print culture, since many writers, editors, and other professionals of the literary world worked in such settings rather than in their often small and uncomfortable editorial offices. Lukacs frequently returns in his narrative to the literature which depicted the lives of its representatives, together with a description of their environment and preoccupations such as the rivalry between the elites of modern newspapers and cultural journals.

Taken as a whole, Lukacs presents the Budapest *bourgeois* as a *Bildungsbürger*, a type of urban dweller characterized by a refined interest in the arts and the sciences. In the longest chapter of the book, entitled *The Generation of 1900*, Lukacs argues that the identity of this generation was formed by high culture and sociability. A line which serves to summarize all this reads: "Budapest in 1900 had a tremendous respect for intellectual achievement of all kinds."[64]

That this culture was *bourgeois* in the sense of representing the urban middle classes of this late Victorian era, known in Hungary as the Age of the Monarchy (that of Franz Joseph), is also made obvious: "That precocious cultural appetite came not only from the schools but, even more, from the homes of Budapest."[65] Although these middle class families in the capital were having fewer children, these children of the *bourgeoisie* "had become the subjects of increasing attention. More interest and more money could be spent on their education."[66] Jewish families, similarly to the families of German-speaking Budapest citizens, were eager to assimilate, imitating the family life of the gentry in certain respects, but also themselves setting examples in other areas—such as in their educational, cultural, and professional choices. Due to the nature of wealth accumulation, families in the era operated like economic units, preserving and burnishing the name of the family from generation to generation. Emphasizing the cosmopolitan atmosphere of the capital, Lukacs introduces famous families of different ethnic backgrounds (Greek, Swiss, Rumanian, Serbian, as well as German and Jewish families). All these non-*magyar* elements were happy to identify themselves with the national cause, leading after 1867 to developments such as the "emancipation of Jews in Hungary," a law which was "passed with a large majority."[67] According to Lukacs, this piece of legislation, "guaranteeing civic and legal equality to Jews in Hungary," was exceptional in Central and Eastern Europe.[68] Discrimination against them at earlier times had taught them strategies for rising socially with the help of education, the professions, and the banking sector, as in other European centers of the turn of century, of which Lukacs specifically names Berlin, Vienna, and Paris.[69] Yet the eagerness of Jewish families in Budapest to assimilate—some of them forming part of the financial elite—was quite remarkable: "The ambitions, habits and even manners of the financial aristocracy conformed to those of the gentry. . . rather than to the nobility."[70]

Lukacs, himself of Hungarian-Jewish background, being brought up in Budapest, also mentions cases of "popular anti-Semitism" as well, as the proportion of Jews jumped to 21.5 percent in 1900, leading to the city's nickname of Judapest. While the respected patrician families of Jewish descent earned "a respect, which continued for a long time," "lasting, in some ways, through the worst years of the Hitler period,"[71] popular anti-Semitism was also growing (as in other European cities, including Paris). The historian notes the conflicts between the German-speaking guilds and the newly arrived Jewish artisans, merchants, and entrepreneurs. He makes two major points about anti-Semitism. One is that from the 1880s onward both popular and political anti-Semitism was on the rise. The second point is that at the happy moment of 1900 in most cases Jews were still honored members of Budapest society, and this social peace had a major role to play in the success of the city. Its achievements were to a large extent due to "the extraordinary symbiosis of Hungarian Jews and non-Jewish Hungarians in Budapest in 1900 and after."[72]

Lukacs's narrative even becomes nostalgic at times in this respect: "(i)n few, if any, cities of the world had Jews prospered as freely and as much as in Budapest toward the end of the nineteenth century."[73] He calls this social peace an "inseparable and lasting" "compound of the older Hungarian and the newer Jewish aspirations."[74]

The break with this specific *concordia*, or as he calls it, this "harmonious accord," quoting Antal Szerb, the author and literary critic of Jewish descent from the 1930s, was, he argues, a modern phenomenon.[75] As he points out, the new political anti-Semitism paralleled the split between Budapest and the country in public discussions, in Parliamentary debates, and outside of it, in literature and journalism just as much as in the discussions of the ordinary people. Lukacs illustrates the breakdown of that "symbiosis" once again with three consecutive examples taken from the literary oeuvre of a Hungarian writer. The Catholic Mihály Babits, who had come from the small provincial city of *Szekszárd* to the capital, depicted the relationship between Christian and Jewish members of the society through the symbolic friendship of two young men at the turn of the century, in his novel *Halálfiai* (The Children of Death). His novel *Kártyavár* (House of Cards) recounts the life of two working-class suburbs of Budapest, presenting a breakdown of social trust and peace. Finally, the novel *Timár Virgil fia* (The son of Virgil Timár) tells the story of a "shy, celibate Catholic religious teacher and his favorite student . . . a half-Jewish boy who eventually becomes an intellectual in Budapest."[76] These three examples of Babits's novels serve to show how the split between the two ethnic (and cultural) groups took place in Hungary, and how far Budapest remained a safe home for Jews, before the anti-Semitic laws in the interwar period.

The last chapter of Lukacs's book summarizes the history of the city from 1900 up until the time when he wrote the book in the 1980s. He mentions the two world wars, in which Hungary took part on the side of the losers, the break-up of the Dual Monarchy, the revolutions after the First World War, the Trianon peace settlement which led to what he calls "the wholesale amputation of Hungary," the Second World War, leading to the deportation and death of more than half a million Jews from Hungary, an official ally by that time of Nazi Germany, the German and the Russian occupation of the city, and the 1956 rising against Russian occupation and Stalinist rule.[77] This summary introduces in a nutshell all the unspeakable suffering the twentieth century brought to the city, cataclysms which could not have been predicted in 1900. As Lukacs points out, "(i)n 1945 the three capital cities of Europe that had suffered the greatest destruction were Budapest, Warsaw and Berlin."[78] This is what happens when totalitarian powers occupy the capital cities of the region, or—in the case of Berlin—when they finally collapse under the pressure of a coalition of Western freedom and eastern totalitarian barbarism.

THE TOTALITARIAN STATE AND THE GLOBAL POLIS

American readers can hardly imagine the life of Central European urban centers under totalitarian rule if they had no relatives in the area. They may be familiar with famous scenes in popular Hollywood films about the war. Perhaps a better guide to what happened was the literature produced mostly by *émigré* writers and thinkers who criticized the totalitarian régimes from abroad. The best known authors in this respect include Arthur Koestler, who published his *Darkness at Noon* in 1940, Czeslaw Milosz's Captive Mind, which appeared in 1953, and Hannah Arendt, who traced the *Origins of Totalitarianism* in 1951. A special case was Aleksandr Solzhenitsyn, whose *One Day in the Life of Ivan Denisovich* (1962) was still published in the Soviet Union, but whose later work could only be published outside his home country, and who was forced to emigrate to the West in the 1970s.

We shall now examine the totalizing tendencies as they related to urban phenomena, without giving a detailed account of the background of political history. I will first discuss the architecture of the totalitarian powers, then in the second half of this chapter I will also look at the Western type of Megalopolis, famously criticized by Lewis Mumford in his *The City in History* (1961), as the afterlife of totalitarian rule.

Narratives of the Megalopolis usually start from the example of ancient Rome, as a prefiguration of the Rome of the first half of the twentieth century, in the hands of the Fascists. Mumford himself considers this option: "Cities like Rome, which historically came to the full end of their cycle before resuming growth again at a lower stage, afford an abundance of data for studying the rise and fall of Megalopolis."[79] If this is true, the Megalopolis itself is a characteristically European phenomenon. This might be true, even if European cities, generally speaking, long resisted the temptation to grow oversize. The fact is, however, that both Europe and America, showed similar symptoms of a growing urban cancer as the cities under totalitarian rule: "the fact that the same signs of overgrowth and overconcentration exist in 'communist' Soviet Russia as in 'capitalist' United States shows that these forces are universal ones, operating almost without respect to the prevailing ideologies or ideal goals."[80]

There is something inhuman about oversized cities. Europe as a continent is a small territory, and the limits to growth of European city were discussed as early as in Aristotelian theory. Yet absolutist rule is not an alien, Asian, or Eastern element: ancient Rome spawned Neros, who took over half the known world, and who—by the way—were also dangerous to their own hometowns as well, as Nero proved, burning down Rome on a whim. Totalitarian power is associated with destruction, but its external output is capture and conquest. In Mumford's terms, the Megalopolis is a conquest over nature, which is carried out by the technology of a refined civilization. In this sense, it is not a thing of the past, but has a modernist aspect to it. A prime example of this is Fascist urban planning, one of the most progressive in its age, yet a true inheritor of imperial Rome's effort. The same is true of those efforts to unify Europe which determined early modern politics on the continent, and in particular, the ambitions which captured the imaginations of French emperors, from the time of the Sun King onward, who built the geometrically conceived artificial city of Versailles, influencing urban planners all over the world, including those of Washington City. Another such figure was Napoleon, the paradigmatic French emperor, who built an oversized empire, connecting destruction and modernity. Both Mussolini and Hitler would build on that tradition, combining the stylistic elements of centralized rational planning and a classical architectural style based on regular and symmetrical geometrical forms. The grand designs of totalitarian architectures can be exemplified by the work of Marcello Piacentini in the fascist EUR district in Rome, or by Albert Speer's plan for *Germania*, the capital of the world, which bore traces of both ancient Rome and modern technology. In both cases, the idea was to be oversized, in spatial, populational, and technical terms. As the official program of the Nazi party formulated it, the aim was to exercise "an impression of simplicity, uniformity, monumentality, solidity and eternity."[81]

In the heart of Europe, however, such projects could only succeed for limited periods of time, over a limited territory. It was in Soviet Russia that urban planning had the bad fortune of having enough space to grow truly oversized. There it was the example of great, often Westernizing czars which showed the way, enlightened despots who were also great builders, including Peter the Great and Catherine the Great (note their names already). Even so, Stalin's projects were indeed unparalleled in their colossal size. He borrowed the name of a specific style, called Stalinist Empire, which again combined classicist and modernist elements. This arrogant architectural language can be recognized in the famous buildings of the seven sisters in Moscow and similar skyscrapers in various cities of the Communist realm, which themselves served as autonomous settlements within the city, of which the most important example is the building of Lomonosov University in Moscow.

The governing idea of Stalinist architecture was a radical transformation of the face of Russian cities, expressing the new spirit (or to be more precise, the oppressive ideology) of the totalitarian state, and the perverse desires of its ruler. As the state was already based on a desire to grow, so the dreams of the architects of the cities of communist Russia centered on growth. A superb account of this is given by the architect-artist, Artur Klinau, in his book entitled *Minsk, the Sun City of Dreams*.[82] It tells the story of the hometown of the author, the ancient city of Minsk, which has been transformed into a monster by Soviet Communist architecture. A revealing episode from this story is when the author recalls his childhood days, when he played at home with toy building blocks, building wonderful cities. But whenever he finished his construction, he would wage wargames against these cities, as he was not interested anymore in building. "If I had only one city, rubber dogs and empty perfume flacons attacked us, and plush teddies and the rabbits were valiantly defending the walls. Sooner or later, the city had to give in. . . it seemed to have been condemned to wither away, as I was not interested in the city after it had been ready. I wanted to demolish it, to be able to build a new one."[83]

Totalitarian rulers had the same, clearly Freudian desire to build on a superhuman scale, and therefore the Megalopolis is rightly associated with an inhuman *Wille zur Macht*, as Nietzsche puts it. As it happens, though, this enchantment with size is characteristic of cities in America just as much as of those in the Communist parts of the world. Money, just as much as totalitarian power, has the capacity to build oversized cities. It will be instructive to examine how Mumford describes the Megalopolis, this typical feature of the modern landscape, both in the West and in the East.

First of all, in Mumford's grand narrative, the Megalopolis turns out to be the final phase in the historical transformation of the city, following the chapter of suburbia. He links suburbia to Tocqueville's analysis of American democracy in the early nineteenth century. Democracy was directly connected by the French traveler to a new kind of despotism.

> He sought to "trace the novel features under which despotism may appear in the world." "The first thing that strikes observation," he writes in his book on America, "is an uncountable number of men, all equal and alike, incessantly endeavoring to produce the petty and paltry pleasures with which they glut their lives. Each of them living apart, is a stranger to the fate of all the rest."[84]

Mumford, the cultural critic, finds the French aristocrat's analysis interesting because that narrative connects specifically American spatial relationships with certain ways of life, and through that with certain interpersonal relationships. In other words, the Frenchman derives the physical nature of the *urbs* from the customs and manners of the *civitas*.

The last chapter of Mumford's great book adds a further dimension to this American way of life, which created the phenomenon of urban sprawl. He starts out from forced urbanization, as a consequence of the fact that the "dominant economy is a metropolitan economy, in which no effective enterprise is possible without a close tie to the big city."[85] As a result of the demands of this spatial disposition of the productive units of the economy, technical innovations detach human communities from their natural environment. Demography certainly also played its role in this development, which, together with the technical development of urban infrastructure, led to the rise of "undifferentiated, formless urban mass, or 'conurbation.'"[86]

Mumford ascribes the Megalopolis to the human inspiration which he labels "giantism." This is the result of a forced industrialization and the specific economic-financial innovations which also led to the globalizing tendencies of capitalism. Mumford's heroes are those who saw the dangers this development meant for the city, in its original, European sense. He refers to Patrick Geddes, Pyotr Kropotkin, Ebenezer Howard, and Max Weber, as examples of those who warned of "urban disorder and decay."[87] It is clear that Weber is the source of the significance Mumford attributed to the bureaucracy in managing these gigantic urban networks. Mumford describes the consequences of the ever more complicated transactions which make possible the management of life in the Megalopolis, employing language which resembles Marxist descriptions of alienation or Orwell's account of the impersonal mechanisms employed by Big Brother: as "transactions become more complicated, mechanical bureaucratic processes must replace direct human contact and personal intercourse."[88] Building on the work of early practitioners of cultural criticism, he presents the modernist urban project as a shift from quality to quantity. In a chapter significantly entitled "The Removal of Limits," he claims that this "urban explosion" is the result of "the removal of quantitative limits."[89] The title of the relevant subchapter is once again telling: Mumford talks about the phenomenon of "Sprawling Giantism."[90] This is, in fact, an admission that the liberal part of the world produces the same totalizing tendencies as we have seen in the totalitarian state, even if it is not done as a result of the command of the Führer, the Duce, or of the First Secretary of the Communist party, but as a result of impersonal economic-financial demands. In a subchapter with an apocalyptic vision, entitled "The Destiny of Megalopolis," Mumford lays down a severe judgment in the language of the critics of the Cold War, but at the same time he connects the American developments with Russian totalitarianism: "The metropolitan regime now threatens to reach its climax in a meaningless war, one of total extermination. . . . Thus absolute power has become absolute nihilism."[91] He despairs that both the United States and the Soviet Union are characterized by "collective mechanisms of destruction."[92]

Even at this point of decay and absolute power, however, Mumford's narrative offers an account of a positive alternative to this scenario. In order to show this alternative, it turns back to the organic birth of the city—out of the village. He finds that it is from the village that the city learns to provide a "mothering and life-promoting environment."[93] It is this that assures stability and security for the human community, and harmony with its natural and communal surroundings. Alongside this organic element of the *urbs*, the village also lends the city the key feature of the *civitas*. The city derives from the village "the ways and values of an ungraded democracy in which each member plays his appropriate role at each stage in the life cycle."[94] This emphasis on the kinship with a lower level of social organism helps, of course, to balance another tendency, which is also present within the germ of the city: its inclination to invade, to overtake, and to dominate its surroundings, including the natural environment and the social context.

Apparently, in the modernist project the demand of balance is often forgotten. There are, however, positive examples, which show that it is not impossible, even in the midst of the most advanced capitalist environment, to counter the unbridled growth of urban centers. What is required are the virtues of moderation and sobriety. As Mumford sees it, "only in scattered and occasional instances do we discover political power well distributed in small communities, as in seventeenth-century Holland or Switzerland"—in cities, where "the ideals of life /(are) constantly regulating the eccentric manifestations of power."[95]

Mumford's insights into how to find the right proportions of growth, and the results and conclusions of his grand narrative of urban history are in perfect harmony with the findings of the current work's reconstruction of the political philosophy of the European city, even if we have derived these conclusions from different sources. The present reconstruction has traced these developments back to the Aristotelian theoretical heritage of the Greek city, as it was reborn in the republican phase of ancient Rome, and later in Italian communes and the medieval commercial centers of the north. But even the early modern Dutch and Swiss examples are based on the same assumptions: a city can keep its form as long as it insists on the proper scale: that which fits human life. The alternative is a form of urban life resembling the symptoms of a growing cancer—the modern, totalitarian Megalopolis or its late modern, capitalist counterpart.

A counterargument that may be raised is that technological development, and the context of a post-industrial advanced economy might be a challenge to maintaining a properly proportioned European city. No doubt, Mumford is aware that there can be no Rousseauist return to nature, away from advanced technology and concentrated power. However, while he does not use the term, he seems to suggest that subsidiarity might be the key to creating an environment which can resist the all-encompassing forces of conurbation. He believes in the capacity of the intellectual virtues of urban dwellers, in other words in the cultural function of the big city, to keep growth under control. Our present-day civilization enables cooperation over large territories, and we only need to find the right forms of that cooperation. This cooperation depends on subsidiarity: nothing needs to be centralized so long as it can be handled in a coordinated fashion locally. This is the idea behind the following suggestion of Mumford's: "we must seek a reciprocal relation between smaller and larger units, based upon each performing the sort of task for which it is uniquely fitted."[96] The key to facilitating such a division of labor within a network of cities is the survival of the smaller unit, in cooperation with the larger one—which is only possible if all the participating urban centers remain sovereign, and decide their own fates. This would function in a subsidiary form of hierarchy, as described by the Catholic social teaching, and taken over by the original ideas of European unification. It is only within such a self-reliant smaller or larger unit that inhabitants can amass the interpersonal experience which is crucial for the preservation of the *zoon politikon*. The guarantee of the preservation of a humanly proportioned city is the life of its inhabitants lived in a *civitas* which governs itself. A humanly proportioned city should remain "a place where meetings and encounters and challenges, as between personalities, supplements and reduces again to human dimensions the vast impersonal network that now spreads around it."[97] This is what I have called, in the present account, the face-to-face society of the European city, with its concept of friendship, of which Aristotle spoke in the *Nicomachean Ethics*. Friendship is required within the city, while peaceful cooperation is necessary for intercity collaboration.

The preservation of a network of urban functions shared among the different layers of forms of cohabitation is a conservative program, as shown by

Mumford's own example. He describes, in a lively manner, how the network of early fresco paintings is preserved in remote places in France, while replicas of these works are collected in urban centers. A multi-layered cooperation between the scattered samples preserved in localities and the replicas in the centers made it possible for visitors to learn about the whole network in the center, or go out and see the individual samples where they are still locally guarded and stored. This is the ideal form of what Mumford calls "inter-urban co-operation," which he encourages also in industry and business, noting that there are "indications that similar processes are at work, extending and diffusing, to some degree decentralizing, functions that were hitherto highly concentrated in a few centres."[98] It is crucial, for ecological reasons, to make sense of the logic inherent in these scattered examples, and to try to formulate their general principles, in order to share this wise knowledge among the participants in economic life and public administration, that is, to teach these examples of good practice, in order to save the local aspect.

SMALL IS BEAUTIFUL: KOHR AND SCHUMACHER

While the Megalopolis is the unfortunate general direction of urban planning in the twentieth century, this mainstream trend has encountered opposition from the beginning. Mumford himself is one of the most important voices of this opposition, but the theoretical foundations of this opposition were laid by the so-called "Small is beautiful" movement. While this term was coined by the German-born British economist E. F. Schumacher, his story begins with his master, Leopold Kohr. The relationship of Schumacher to Kohr is comparable to the passionate relationship between Mumford and Geddes. In both cases, it was the student who made the ideas of the master widely available to the general public. Both Mumford and Schumacher recognized the extent to which they were inspired by the work of their respective forerunner. While Mumford was much younger than Geddes, Schumacher and Kohr came from the same generation, which helped their ideas to grow together in a more organic way than in the former case. Mumford was not only much younger than Geddes, but they lived far away from each other, making it impossible for them to embark on a common project. In contrast, Kohr and Schumacher came from the same German-speaking, Central European urban culture, which is the reason why their sources of inspiration also had much in common.

Both Kohr and Schumacher studied economics, or national economics, as it was earlier called. In fact, it was due to their early experience of life in small urban units that their way of thinking went against the mainstream thinking of economic theory, based as it was on a rationally egoistic individual as its starting point. Just as Geddes and Mumford recognized the inherent problems of modern or modernist urbanism in the first half of twentieth century, so did Kohr and Schumacher recognize the internal conflicts within the system of post-1945 economic theory, which was based on Keynesian ideas of social organization, and which resulted in the birth of the welfare state. Although this latter was a promising effort it eventually led to the oil crisis in the 1970s and the birth of the Green movement. Kohr himself was perhaps the more radical and the more daringly anarchist of the two, inviting and accepting criticism and sometimes even fiasco. Schumacher, on the other hand, succeeded in bringing their common ideas to a breakthrough with the publication of his iconic book, *Small Is Beautiful* in 1973. The following account concentrates only on some of the main phases of their common story, in order to give an insight into the undercurrent of ecologically sustainable development within post-1945 European urban thought.

Kohr was born in a small town called Oberndorf, near Salzburg, in those days within the decentralized empire of the Austro-Hungarian monarchy. Arguably, this social and family background played a major role in determining the way of thinking of the economist, political scientist, and lawyer. Fittingly, the foreword to the flagship of his publications, *The Breakdown of Nations*, by Kirkpatrick Sale, starts with the following quote:

> There seems only one cause behind all forms of social misery: bigness. Oversimplified as this may seem, we shall find the idea more easily acceptable if we consider that bigness, or oversize, is really much more than just a social problem. It appears to be the one and only problem permeating all creation. Wherever something is wrong, something is too big.[99]

This criticism is based on his early experience of how his birthplace was managed in Austria. "It remained his regulative ideal for the proper size and reach of a political unit."[100]

Yet, paradoxically, Kohr must have had an adventurous soul, which led him away from his hometown, never allowing him to return and settle down back there, even though he had always planned to do so in his old age.[101] He studied first in Central Europe, both in Innsbruck and in Vienna, but later he had the good fortune to study at the London School of Economics, one of the major new centers of economic thought in the century. As a journalist, he had a similar formative experience in his youth as did George Orwell, the famous British writer: the Spanish Civil War. He was particularly struck by the small Spanish anarchist city-states of Alcoy and Caspe. "That is when it started." he remembered later, adding: "I'll never forget reading the sign, Welcome to the Free Commune of Caspe."[102] He became a lifelong friend of Orwell and with other authors such as Hemingway and Malraux in Spain.

With his Jewish background, Kohr decided to leave Austria after Hitler's annexation of the country, and moved to the United States. First, he taught economics and political philosophy at Rutgers University from 1943 to 1955. He later craved more adventure, and moved to teach and live in Puerto Rico. Naturally, he had a theoretical argument for this choice: the form of life and way of thinking the people of this "unincorporated territory of the United States" had been built on a mixture of rather different cultural roots, including indigenous, Spanish, African American, and native American elements. Besides teaching economics at the local university, he worked as independent advisor for city planning initiatives. He also became interested in the independence movement of the nearby island of Anguilla. However, the local population was not really open to his innovative ideas. In the meantime, he finally succeeded in publishing his first book in Britain, *The Breakdown of Nations* (1957) with the help of Herbert Read, the poet, art historian, and philosophical anarchist who was working in those days at a publisher, as an editor. While all of Kohr's earlier efforts to get the book published had proven futile, Read, a fellow-anarchist, swiftly recognized the significance of the work of the Austrian-born critic of concentrated political and economic power.

Kohr had to find another cause of smallness for which to fight. He had by that time taken a firm philosophical position: he was in favor of the underdogs in a world of big business and global politics. After his retirement he moved to Wales, to fight for Welsh autonomy and devolution, as well as finding time to return for periods to his hometown in Austria. His impact was felt among a small circle of friends and fellow thinkers, including Ivan Illich and E.F. Schumacher, who himself found fame with the publication of his book *Small is Beautiful*, an idea he certainly owned to Kohr. The success of his book led to Kohr becoming better known in British academic circles. He was invited by students to university campuses to talk about his initiatives. He received the Right Livelihood Award in 1983, "for his early inspiration of the movement for a human scale."[103]

What, in essence, is the idea that drove Kohr's work and guided his life? It was an idea that was already known to the Greeks: that human societies can only be successful and happy as long as they can preserve, or return to, the human scale. A short summary of the main idea of Kohr, can be found in his acceptance speech at the award-giving ceremony, in 1984, itself a symbolic year, the title of the famous book of his friend, George Orwell, cautioning his readers in 1948 of the dangers of totalitarianism. It was in this acceptance speech that Kohr claimed:

> The primary problem thus being one of excessive size, of unsurveyable dimensions, of cancerous overgrowth and bigness, the only practical solution must logically lie not in still larger units which make every problem commensurate

to their enlarged scale, but in the opposite direction: in smallness. This alone can solve the host of secondary problems which are derived from the primary problem of excessive social size. And it solves them not by their abolition but by making them manageable through the reduction of their scale.[104]

While this is a theoretical thesis, it is based on an investigation of the history of ideas and research into historical forms of human cooperation. Kohr refers to Aristotle and Saint Augustine, among others, as his major heroes. As he saw it, Aristotle presented smallness "as a cure for social ills," and his ideal city-state was only as large as "can be taken in at a single view." In a community of the size of the city-state "all is translucent, the connections are transparent, and nothing can stay hidden." The ideally sized state, according to this Aristotelian principle, is tiny Lichtenstein. Kohr regards Saint Augustine as an "apostle of smallness," because of his criticism of the fragility of imperial Rome. In connection with Augustine, he cites John Neville Figgis, an Anglican priest and monk of the turn of the century, a student of Lord Acton and a political philosopher of the Middle Ages, who was influenced by the corporate theory of Gierke.[105] Kohr quotes Figgis's book, *The Political Aspects of St. Augustine's City of God*, published posthumously in 1921.

Among his examples of political history, Kohr points to the example of the Holy Roman Empire, divided itself into small units, to the cantonal structure of the small Switzerland, and also to the United States—the United States which was described in de Tocqueville's *Democracy in America*. The most important historical example he cites in this speech, however, is the network of medieval monasteries, the network of which he interprets as an "Owenite co-operative network of small cells, loosely linked together," referring back to the Welsh utopian philanthropist of the nineteenth century, Robert Owen. For Kohr, the crucial aspect of the geographic network of monasteries—beside the fact that they did not grow larger than a certain size—is their connection with each other, creating a "glittering network of practically sovereign communities." It was important for Kohr that these communities had a close relationship to their immediate surroundings, which he characterized thus: they were ready to "use intensively the material and intellectual resources of their immediate neighbourhood," and in return they helped to raise the quality of life of those living around their community by producing marvelous works of art, "sponsor(ing) literature, architecture, and the arts." Kohr calls this relationship between the monastery and its surroundings "a limited but strong and independent gravitational field of its own." Surely, for Kohr, who also studied the life of Buddhist monasteries, and who returned to traditional Christianity at the end of his life, it was important that monks had a special discipline of living their life. This is evinced by the fact that a recurring expression in the speech is the German term *lebensrichtig*, which is similar to what is referred to as "right livelihood" in English, which was the name of the prize he actually won. He borrowed this term from an old friend, who lived in Lichtenstein, Josef Haid.[106]

Kohr connects small, humanly scaled habitation with life reform movements, citing further historical examples of this besides the medieval Christian monasteries. He refers to the "enchanting regional city-state patterns of Mexico," which were developed on the orders of Philip II of Spain, the settlements of the Amish communities and the Kibbutz communities of Israel. He perhaps stretches the point somewhat when he includes the rural communes of communist China. To avoid being misunderstood he stresses that "the Chinese development device for the local communes was not the extension of government control." His idea is not political, it is an "alternative to both right and left." Another example he cites is the small town in Wales, Aberystwyth, where Kohr had been living for some time, and where he was able to avoid using a car in his daily routine, but instead went everywhere on foot, as all the places he needed to visit in the town were within easy reach of the center. It was in this context that Kohr referred to another winner of the Right Livelihood Award, the founder of what he called "barefoot" economics, Artur Manfred Max-Neef. This Chilean economist of German descent also envisaged revitalising small and medium-sized communities through 'barefoot economics.'"[107] This barefooted way of thinking is crucial to the economics of smallness, referring as it does to the Biblical example of David's fight against Goliath. Kohr, of course, admits that "smallness is just the irrational dream of a romantic," but he claims that life is only worth living as a romantic. It is therefore very apt that he recalls two authors of fiction at the end of his speech, quoting André Gide's final words "I love small nations. I love small numbers. The World will be saved by the few," as well as citing Orwell again.

What Leopold Kohr initiated was brought to fruition by Fritz Schumacher. While Kohr was a son of provincial Austria, Schumacher was born in the city of Bonn, which chance—or perhaps its middle size—had made the capital of Germany. His father was also a professor of political economy so the young Schumacher received a world-class education. He studied initially in Bonn and Berlin, going on to become a Rhodes Scholar at New College, Oxford, and completing his education by receiving a PhD in economics from Columbia University, New York. His primary profession was economics, but he also gained practical work experience in business, farming, and journalism. He left Germany for England, to avoid Nazi rule. During the war he was classed as an enemy alien, and detained. It was during these years that he published an article which caught the attention of John Maynard Keynes, the famous and at that time quite fashionable economist, whom he had met earlier in Cambridge in 1929. The articles enthused Keynes so much that he borrowed some of its ideas to reuse them in his own work, although without giving references where they came from. While the young Schumacher adored Keynes, who helped him to find a position at Oxford, he later grew critical of his master's ideas. He himself had a rather rich and varied career, early on exercising a remarkable influence by becoming "chief editorial writer on economics for *The Times*, a Kissinger-like achievement for a native German so early in post-war England"—as Leopold Kohr would put it.[108] Two other factors of his biography are also relevant. First, the fact that he worked as a chief advisor for such giant organizations as the UK National Coal Board (with its 800,000 employees), which taught him the difficulties of managing such overgrown administrations. Second, as an influential economist of his day, he became advisor to certain underdeveloped third world countries, such as Burma and Zambia. He not only learned ways of life which were wholly different from the Western model, but also witnessed poverty and Western oppression, as well as learning Buddhist religious and social teachings. These formative experiences led him to publish his book *Small is Beautiful*, which finally caught the attention of the world. The *Times Literary Supplement* ranked it as one of the 100 most influential books of the post-WWII era. By the time of the publication of his book, his spiritual search had led him "to the astonishment of Schumacher's Marxist and Buddhist friends alike," to the Roman Catholic Church, and he converted to Catholicism.[109]

If Schumacher's great idea is that of scale, that is, the problem of finding the right size of the basic units used to solve a problem in economics or politics, is would seem to be a contradiction that he ended up joining the most universal and global of religions. The word Catholic itself means general or universal. Yet I feel that there is in fact no contradiction here. It was Catholic Social Teaching that invented the notion of subsidiarity in the social encyclical of *Quadragesimo Anno* (1931). The term *subsidiarity* is defined in the following way by the Catechism: "a community of a higher order should not interfere in the internal life of a community of a lower order, depriving the latter of its functions, but rather should support it in case of need and help to coordinate its activity with the activities of the rest of society, always with a view to the common good."[110] While subsidiarity has since become one of the main ideological principles of the European Union, largely due to the fact that it was established by influential Christian democrats, the tendency of the growth of that supranational organization is the opposite: as it is becoming larger and larger. However, the notion of subsidiarity seems to have been crucial for Schumacher, who must have been aware of the Catholic sources of this principle of subsidiarity or, as originally phrased, subsidiary function. The idea is raised in the sixteenth chapter of his famous book, which addresses the problem of large-scale organizations. Subsidiarity is the first of the five principles the author explains here, to form the basis of a theory of large-scale organizations. He quotes directly from *Quadragesimo Anno*, the

Encyclical of Pope Pius XI, *On Reconstruction of the Social Order*, which was issued in 1931, during the world economic crisis known as the Great Depression. This is the quote he takes directly from article 79 of the encyclical, between quotation marks, but without giving the source: "it is an injustice and at the same time a grave evil and disturbance of right order to assign to a greater and higher association what lesser and subordinate organizations can do. For every social activity ought of its very nature to furnish help to the members of the body social, and never destroy and absorb them."[111] While Schumacher applies the principle of the relationship of the higher- to the lower-level units to matters of economic organization, he admits that the principle was originally meant to be applied to society. This makes it all the more useful for our present purposes. Let us see how Schumacher interprets the Catholic doctrine: as he understood it, the higher unit should not consider itself to be wiser or more efficient at solving the problems of lower units. He does not explain fully why this should not be the case, however, as he must have found the principle to be self-evident. After all, it is obvious that the lower unit is closer to the particulars of the case to be solved, thus making it more suited to tackling it.

Beyond this, there are further aspects which support the principle, according to Schumacher. First if we wish to encourage loyalty between the levels, that is, a lasting relationship, the connection should always build up upward from below, from the smaller and lower units to the higher and larger one. It will always work against loyalty if a higher unit wants to absorb the functions of a lower one. As Schumacher puts it: "the burden of proof lies always on those who want to deprive a lower level of its function."[112] Second, he refers to the freedom and responsibility of the lower unit, claiming that to deprive a unit of its freedom and responsibility is counterproductive and detrimental. To underline this point, he once again quotes from the encyclical: "those in command should be sure that the more perfectly a graduated order is preserved among the various associations, in observance of the principle of 'subsidiary function,' the stronger social authority and effectiveness will be the happier and more prosperous the condition of the State."[113] The original Catholic document uses the term *authority* instead of *loyalty*, used by Schumacher, but the meaning is the same: the connection between the gradually arranged elements of the whole should be kept strong, and that is only possible if the lower unit's freedom and responsibility are respected and preserved.

Taking into consideration that the original encyclical described the norm of subsidiarity in a social context, we can also apply it to society. In other words, we can easily translate Schumacher's description of this relationship between the lower and the higher units of economic organization to the problem of the local administration of the centralized early modern state. In other words, it can be applied to the relationship between the court and the (royal) city. Consider Schumacher's organogram of state administration: "The large organisation will consist of many semi-autonomous units. . . . Each of them will have a large amount of freedom, to give the greatest possible chance to creativity and entrepreneurship."[114] Translated to the relationship between court and cities, this means preserving a large amount of freedom and responsibility for the semi-autonomous units of the cities, in order to ensure that they will be creative and will produce new initiatives—the benefits of which include them being able to pay more tax to the central treasury of the state. One cannot help but notice behind this scheme the Weberian recapitulation of how capitalist commercial ventures originally enriched the cities, and how the cities enriched the state—for example, in the case of Holland. Schumacher's symbolic representation of this connection is of "a man holding a large number of balloons in his hand," which he explains thus: "Each of the balloons has its own buoyancy and the lift, and the man himself does not lord it over the balloons, but stands beneath them, yet holding all the strings firmly in his hand."[115] What this example is meant to communicate is that the profit realized by the center depends on the achievements of the subsidiary unit, in our case the richness of the state treasury depends on the success of the "semi-autonomous" cities.

Of course, due to the nature of the metaphor, this image cannot express all the details properly. Nonetheless, it is clear from this image that the size of the balloons matters a lot. One would suppose that the larger they are, the easier they can elevate the man. Yet one can also argue that there is a certain size beyond which the balloons will burst. Indeed, in another chapter of the book, Schumacher investigates the optimal size of the cities (balloons) as well as the optimal size of the country (the man). He asks some very Aristotelian questions: "What scale is appropriate? It depends on what we are trying to do. The question of scale is extremely crucial today, in political, social and economic affairs just as in almost everything else. What, for instance, is the appropriate size of a city? And also, one might ask, what is the appropriate size of a country?"[116] The reason I call this question Aristotelian is that Aristotle asks the same question in relationship with the ideal polis in his *Politics*.[117] And just like Aristotle, Schumacher found that a city has a certain natural limit, beyond which it is not advisable to grow. Like the Greek philosopher, the German economist is hesitant to prescribe a fixed proportion of population density, claiming that: we "can recognise right and wrong at the extremes, although we cannot normally judge them finely enough." Unlike his ancient forerunner, however, at the end he does suggest a number: "I think it is fairly safe to say that the upper limit of what is desirable for the size of a city is probably something of the order of half a million inhabitants."[118] Considering that he was born in Bonn, it is perhaps not too courageous to claim that his definition of the *right size of the city* might have something to do with his original perception of his birth place. Bonn grew from its original size in the childhood years of Schumacher (just below 100,000) to 300,000 when he was writing his book, yet its growth seems to have been limited.

As he puts it, a growth in population beyond the size of half a million adds nothing "to the virtue of the city," taking the term *virtue* from ancient moral philosophy. Schumacher uses even stronger words about what he also calls the megalopolis, giving the examples of London, Tokyo, and New York. He speaks about "enormous problems" and "human degradation."[119] He also borrows from the language of theology, when he mentions "the idolatry of giantism," and the organic language of health, referring to "pathological growth."[120] All this rhetoric expresses the Aristotelian view that everything living, including human settlements, has an ideal size, and therefore the economic consensus of the day, that growth is preferable among all conditions, does not hold unconditionally.

Yet Schumacher is not preaching a return to the small. On the contrary, he would do everything against "a prevailing idolatry of smallness."[121] Instead, what he suggests is a kind of scale-awareness: we need to be aware of the costs of growth and choose a size that fits the particular activity. What he searches for is the balance between the too large and the too small. Smallness is balanced in his ideal world by largeness and largeness by smallness. Both of them can embody a valuable principle. As he understands it, smallness gives us freedom, while the large-scale brings order into human affairs: "we need the freedom of lots and lots of small, autonomous units, and, at the same time, the orderliness of large-scale, possibly global, unity and co-ordination."[122] This description is in accordance with the earlier teaching of subsidiarity by the Catholic Church: Schumacher here shows that smallness is not to be understood as antagonistic with largeness. Rather, they should be seen as mutually dependent elements. Active human beings need both the freedom and autonomy of small urban units and their coordination on a state or global level. We need to act freely, in our immediate environment, working together with those whom we know and therefore trust. That is why, as in Aristotle, the proper scale of human activity is a kind of face-to-face society.[123] In our particular societies, however, we have to be able to communicate with other units in a peaceful and effective manner, which requires order on a larger scale. We also need a kind of enlarged thinking, "when it comes to the world of ideas, to principles or to ethics, to the indivisibility of peace and also of ecology."[124] It is not a stretch to refer to the historical experience of the German empire in the medieval and early modern period: a large realm, which guarantees peace within its own borders, but allows certain autonomy to each of the minor units, the small principalities of the realm, which most often organically develop around a properly sized urban center.

Schumacher's remarkable achievement was not the invention of an idea out of the blue: he did nothing revolutionary. Rather, what he did was to try to make sense of the particular historical experience of the environment he knew best, and to build a theory on that basis. His message was not a cult of the small, even if he succeeded in highlighting both the creativity and effectiveness of the activity of small human groups as well as the aesthetic quality of small size. This aesthetic quality can be understood as the sensual property of being in balance or in harmony.

Instead of arguing for another kind of one-sidedness, Schumacher encouraged a search for a division of labor between the small and the large, a division which is ideal when properly tailored to a particular function. His great contribution to the political philosophy of the European city was to show that there is no inherent contradiction between the interest and reason of the city and that of the state. On the contrary, he showed that each depends on the other. As he saw it, the smaller unit cannot properly function without the counterbalance of the larger unit. The freedom afforded by smallness requires the safeguard of order provided by the larger unit. City and state are not competitors but units which are destined to work together. It was for this reason that Schumacher favored "an articulated structure that can cope with a multiplicity of small-scale units."[125]

THE PRINCE, THE PHILOSOPHER, AND THE ARCHITECT

Once again, it is important to stress that Schumacher did not want to create a dogma of smallness. His whole idea was a division of labor between larger and smaller units. This was a theory built on firm, historical foundations and on actual experience, taking into account all the necessary constraints the human world has to confront. In this sense, his approach was not only a realistic, but a conservative idea: to try to preserve, to accommodate, and to follow best practices, *mutatis mutandis*. His horizon was the historical experience of the medieval and early modern German Empire, and he remained loyal to that particular experience while also presenting the big picture. We will now turn to another example of a conservative theorist who was able to build his philosophy on his own country's historical experience. While Schumacher approached the problem of scale from the point of view of economics, Sir Roger Scruton was originally a philosopher of art. He confronted the aesthetic problem of a politics based on a disproportionate amount of power, the totalitarian state in the eastern part of Europe, as well as the ugliness of destruction in the name of progress and even revolution, in the leftist ideology of the 1960s in the western part of Europe. It was this aesthetic sensibility and awareness, which, incidentally, needs to be distinguished from the pedantry of the *bel esprit*, which led Scruton to study the politics of his own country with historical depth. The British tradition led him to a political philosophy of conservatism, based on immemorial constitutional customs and a finely tuned balance of power based on functional distinctions.

Scruton, who was probably the most influential conservative thinker of the late twentieth and early twenty-first centuries, had a tremendous output, focusing on two fields of philosophy: aesthetics and politics, which he practiced by turns. Where his two fields of interest overlapped was in the problem of the city, in its original, complex sense. In the final years of his life, he concentrated on that field, not only in theory, but also by taking part in the political decision-making process on a national scale as an expert, and also as a political advisor: in the work of the Building Better, Building More Beautiful Commission.

Here we will examine another project, however: a large-scale urban development undertaken by the Prince of Wales. Poundbury, the traditionalist urban development projected by the prince as an extension of the historical English city of Dorchester, saw the cooperation of the royal investor, an architect, and a philosopher, as advisor. In what follows, we will consider this venture, which can be regarded as an effort to concentrate all the knowledge of the historical experience of the European city into one location, and one model experiment.

The basic idea of Poundbury is that a city should be built in accordance with the human scale. Léon Krier, the architect who planned the city, write that: "the right form of the city exists only in the right scale."[126] But what is meant by the *right scale* here? It refers first of all to the physical size and proportions of the human body which determines the appropriate physical size of the *urbs*: "Tiredness sets a natural limit to what a human being is prepared to walk daily and this limit has taught mankind all through history the size of rural or urban communities."[127] It also refers to the natural frequency of human interactions with others, determining the scale of *civitas*, which should not exceed, according to Krier, a population of 15,000. Roger Scruton expresses this idea of proportionality in the following terms in his documentary *Why Beauty Matters*: "the proportions are human proportions; the details are restful to the eye. This is not great or original architecture, nor does it try to be; it is a modest attempt to get things right by following patterns and examples laid down by tradition. This is not nostalgia, but knowledge passed on from age to age."[128] The principles which the experimental city was built on include the use of local material for the buildings as well as the classical vernacular, as opposed to the faceless style of modern architecture.

At this point it is worth recapitulating the ideas of the late Sir Roger Scruton about architecture and the city.[129] In order to do so, it is necessary first to characterize his collaborators, the developer, Prince Charles, the Prince of Wales, and the architect, Léon Krier. Their work made it possible that Poundbury is close to completion as a building development.

It may perhaps come as a surprise that the prince himself has put his own ideas into words, in a book published under the title: *A Vision of Britain. A personal View of Architecture.*[130] The book was published in 1989, at the time when the planning of Poundbury had already begun in accordance with these principles, leading to the start of actual construction works in 1993. In his book, Prince Charles urged a return to tradition, as modern architecture, as he saw it, had arrived at a deadlock: "we seem to have forgotten some of the basic principles that have governed architecture since the Greek."[131] What he envisaged was a return to "our own heritage of regional styles," "to rediscover our architectural past, as well as the basic principles which allowed our much-loved towns and villages to develop as they did."[132] His long list of the standards which need to be complied with included, among other principles, (such as place, hierarchy, harmony, and community) the idea of scale. His elaboration of this concept begins with these words: "Man is the measure of all things. Buildings must relate first of all to human proportions and then respect the scale of the buildings around them."[133] In order to achieve this proportionality, he is in favor of height limitation. Horizontally, too, he is in favor of "an enclosed and contained city."[134] The idea of scale is followed in his vision by the idea of harmony, "the playing together of the parts," which can be achieved by recognizing the principle that "each building that goes beside another has to be in tune with its neighbour."[135] This principle also requires humility on the part of the architect. One can also add that such humility was a virtue of the developer as well. Rulers and emperors have always liked to build grandiose structures. In this respect, it is a moot point whether the idea of building a city is a modest proposal, or once again, the hubris of a prince. My suggestion is that while rulers usually built castles and palaces for their own use, to develop a city for the use of the public is an act of self-discipline, even if the gesture may also have aristocratic overtones. After all, not all of us are in a position to initiate such a project: it needed a royal prince to get the whole thing started.

Humility, I would like to argue, is present in the description of the architect who submitted the general plan for Poundbury, Léon Krier. He writes that: "The function of architecture is not, and never has been, to take one's breath away: it exists to create a built environment which is habitable, agreeable, beautiful, elegant and solid."[136] While he has clearly become an international celebrity, this is partly the result of the fierce criticism which his projects received, among them that of Poundbury.

Krier is aware of the fact that Poundbury will not be an autonomous city, but rather a quarter of Dorchester. As he understands European cities, they always consisted of smaller units, which he calls quarters. Each quarter has a life of its own, and each of them is a city within the city, as "each quarter must have its own center, periphery and limit." For town dwellers most of their daily functions are of the kind that can be carried out within these limits, on foot. This is because the city deliberately concentrates its basic functions within a confined territory: "a city is a geographical center of limited size, integrating all periodic and aperiodic urban activities, functions and uses, whether private or public, commercial or productive, religious and political in nature."[137] Krier directly refers to Aristotle's limits on the size of the city or of the townquarter. With this reference, he, too, makes it clear, that he wants to continue the great tradition of the European city, as has been passed down from the time of the ancient Greek polis.

By now, even most of its skeptics have had to admit that the cooperation of Prince Charles and Léon Krier was successful. Poundbury, the newly built, but tradition-based city within the city of Dorchester, has become popular, attracted inhabitants, and begun to live its own life. Yet it is the philosopher who can explain this rather exceptional experiment. While both Prince Charles and Léon Krier were well informed in theory, their real merits were not theoretical. Krier did the planning, while Prince Charles made the whole thing happen by providing the initial impetus and even some of the starting financial resources as well as the publicity for the project. As we have seen, both the Prince and Krier published books on their principles. Yet it was the late Roger Scruton who was able to make the theory fully explicit. There is no room here to fully trace the development of Scruton's urban ideas, from his phenomenologically inspired early book *The Aesthetics of Architecture* (1979) to his *Classical Vernacular* in 1994, and the fully developed theory of aesthetics, *Beauty*, published in 2009. Similarly, this is not the place to analyze in a detailed fashion the relationship of his conservative political philosophy to his ideas of beauty. Rather, I shall draw on two short pieces from his later years, when he was already in a position to reflect on the Poundbury project. But before doing so, let us stress here, as a preliminary, that Scruton's career as a philosopher can be regarded as deeply embedded in art and aesthetics, leading straightforwardly to his final role as first the chair, and—after a short and humiliating interval—later the co-chair of the independent committee set up by the Conservative government, the Building Better, Building Beautiful Commission, whose very name was the target of fierce criticism. The interim report of the commission, entitled "Creating Space for Beauty," recognizes the major impact of Scruton on the work of the commission.[138]

Of greater relevance to us, however, are two shorter publications by Scruton. In the first one, published in 2008 in the *City Journal*, Scruton directly addresses the work of Léon Krier, and his Poundbury project.[139] The second is a very late piece, a lecture he gave in late 2018, and that can be regarded as a true summation of his principles of urban aesthetics.[140] In the first text Scruton glorifies the European city as an institution and as a certain way of life: "Nothing is more precious in the Western heritage, therefore, than the cities of Europe, recording the triumph of civilized humanity not only in their orderly streets, majestic facades, and public monuments, but also in their smallest architectural details and the intricate play of light on their cornices and apertures."[141]

He directly contrasts European cities with those of the United States, to show the importance of their historical dimension, including their Roman and medieval heritage. He takes a stand against the position of the prophets of modernism, Le Corbusier and Walter Gropius, who, in his interpretation, wanted to destroy the traditional texture of the inner cities. His position is not simply that of the antiquarian. Part of his argumentative strategy is linguistic. For example, he redefines what the modernists called "slums" as "the harmonious classical streets of affordable houses, seeded with local industries, corner shops, schools, and places of worship, that had made it possible for real communities to flourish in the center of our towns." Nor does he shrink from political arguments. As he saw it, the work of, or rather the destruction wrought by modernist urban planners was comparable to the way of thinking of totalitarian leaders: both of them made dubious universal claims to substitute or even to exclude the accepted ways of handling urban matters. Both the modernist planner and the modern totalitarian politician are led by vast ideological dogmas, disregarding reality, or the particular contingencies they confront, during their "liberating" efforts. He disagrees with the modernists' exclusive concern with the function of buildings, and employs a criticism of a cultural nature when criticizing building technologies characteristic of modernist urbanism. Interestingly, he agrees with Jane Jacobs, when she criticizes the functional zoning of cities in the United States.[142] Instead of that method, he prefers Krier's model of a policentric city. According to this model, the city is a combination of a number of autonomous quarters. As Scruton interprets this model, the proper relationship between quarter and city can be exemplified by the relationship of Poundbury to Dorchester. London, too, consists of independent quarters such as the City, Westminster, Chelsea, Kensington, Bloomsbury, Whitechapel, and this relationship of the part and the whole seems to be crucial to Scruton in urban structures. In order to ensure that the city does not begin to grow excessively in a cancer-like manner, he advocates strict rules, including prohibitions and prescriptions. In this respect, Scruton compares urban planning to the use of natural language, as Wittgenstein did earlier. Both the city and natural language can be seen as forms of human communication, which require a vocabulary of well-defined words and a grammar of stable rules, in order to function properly. As he saw it, while the modernists liberated themselves from the control of classical vocabulary and grammar, Krier returned to them. In this way the urban plan of Krier is much easier to decipher for its would-be inhabitants, making it also at once more homely.

A further point the philosopher makes is that in a city (*urbs*) people live together (*civitas*)—which makes rules important in another respect, too. Without rules, no political community can endure. Through the known rules, members of the community can identify themselves with the community and their behavior becomes readable for others. Common rules of behavior are thus, and here he quotes Krier: "the foundation of civility and civilisation."[143] When following the rules of the community, individual citizens are ready to give up some parts of their acclaimed liberty, and accept the priority of the community. In particular, the common good will have a basic effect on their behavior, instead of taking into account only their private interests, as individuals living in a megalopolis would be expected to behave. In an interview, Hans Maes paraphrases Scruton's claim, "the business of architecture is the building of a home – not my home and your home only, but the home of the community."[144] In this respect, too, civility turns out to be crucial. For Scruton, a good building does not distinguish itself but instead finds its place in the community, the same way as a good citizen's virtue can be found in conforming to the rules which take care of the common good. This is what he calls "good manners," the "key virtue of architecture."[145] As he saw it, the famous figures of modern architecture, Le Corbusier and Gropius committed a basic "mistake"—they tried to revolutionize architecture rules by their theoretical manifestos, exciting people to riot, instead of remaining "modest and discreet."[146] Convinced that such bad manners are politically dangerous, revolutionary, and socially destructive, Scruton is delighted with what he calls "pattern-book architecture," as patterns make available the best achievements of "millennia of slowly accumulating common sense," connecting architectural and community rules to the customary rules of politics in the conservative idiom.[147] Both architecture as human cohabitation and good politics, require "a practice bound by a publicly accepted grammar," in the Wittgensteinian judgment of Scruton.

As he interprets it, this link between urban architecture and politics explains why Poundbury, the tradition-based city, is being developed around its town hall, the center of the city(quarter). This is the age-old way of the European city, which has always centered around the town hall, the center of its political life as well as around the church, its spiritual center. The social texture of the city is expressed by the physical space thus created. The town hall represents the community of the whole city and this is expressed in the idea that the town hall marks its political center.

Instead of trying to present all the fine and nuanced details of Scruton's analysis of the traditional (as opposed to the modern and postmodern) European city, I will concentrate here on only two specific ideas. One is

Scruton's remarkable term, *oikophilia*, apparently coined by him, the other is his view of the relationship of the city to God.

It is in his ecological thought that Scruton works out the concept of *oikophilia*. In his book *Green Philosophy*, he describes our loving relationship to our homes, and he coins the term *oikophilia* to express the human being's basic need of home.[148] Scruton emphasizes that our archetypical attachment to our home—to the place where we were born or where we spent the most formative part of our lives—is not explainable by standard economic explanations like "cost-benefit analysis" or "by the theory of preference orderings."[149] He had to resort to forceful language, sometimes approaching poetry, to explain what is at stake here: "It is an existential yearning, wrapped up with the metaphysics of space and time."[150] The reason for the deep roots of our attachment is conveyed by the original sense of the Greek notion of *oikos*, which means not only the house but also the family attached to it. The Greek term also explains why it is more than a bond to a physical environment—after all, the human being in his early years is most directly (i.e., existentially) dependent on his or her family. An even closer relationship also plays a role, one that is truly existential: it is "the imprint left by our primary attachment to the mother."[151] Scruton refers to psychological research by the psychoanalyst and attachment theorist John Bowlby on childhood attachment. As Scruton interprets Bowlby's "deep psychology," *oikos* means "not only the home but the people contained in it, and the surrounding settlements that endow that home with its lastingness and its familiar smile."[152] The term describes the specific character of the family home: it is something that you share with others. While it provides the human being with all the "lasting safety" that she requires, it also helps to educate her in her duties as a member of a community, which enables her to become a citizen of a political order. Scruton refers to great works of art, from the poetry of such ancient poets as Hesiod and Theocritus, to modern novelists like Proust and filmmakers like Edgar Reitz, director of the *Heimat* trilogy about his home region of Germany, Hunsrück.[153] Scruton cites these artworks to underline that the home is not simply a spatial geographical location but also an aspect of time, which reveals the connection between different generations of a family, allowing one to feel "the presence of others, not only the living but also the dead and the unborn."[154] Again, this feeling helps people to develop their social capacities. Scruton quite naturally connects the supragenerational dimension of the family to the account of society given by Burke, in his famous criticism of the French Revolution. The comparison of society to the family plays a major role in Burke, when he claims: "A flourishing society is a fabric of historical loyalties and expectations, shaped by the free dealings of people over many generations."[155] The relevance of that fabric cannot be calculated mechanically, on a merely utilitarian basis. It also bears a metaphysical stamp. When

Burke criticizes the French revolutionary who squandered the wealth of the nation, his point is that the "sudden waste of accumulated savings was a desecration of the dead; it was also a theft from the unborn."[156] Desecration and theft are rather strong words, drawing attention to the legal-metaphysical dimension of the intergenerational relationship. The difference between other places and home is that it is only at home that one can bodily feel the "unseen bonds of obligation," while performing everyday activities, like "washing up, stoking the fire, or changing a nappy—a sudden recognition that others to whom I belong and who belong to me are present in my action."[157]

It is in connection with these "homely" feelings that we learn to appreciate the problem of scale in politics, too. In contrast with the French revolutionaries, but also with French absolutism, Scruton believed that the state cannot be built from above, only from below. In particular, he stressed the significance of small communities—what he called "face-to-face interaction."[158] Like MacIntyre, he defended the modes of small communities (family, local clubs and societies, school, church, team, and university), on the basis that they provide the individual agent with the necessary experience of living together. He quotes Burke, when explaining the significance of the civil society as helpful for fostering a responsibility to the community in individuals. Scruton also cites Burke's famous phrase about local attachment, and in particular, the concept of the famous "little platoon": "To be attached to the subdivision, to love the little platoon we belong to in society, is the first principle (the germ as it were) of public affections. It is the first link in the series by which we proceed towards a love to our country, and to mankind."[159] It is remarkable that to express this emotional attachment, Burke uses the expression "public affections," which can be interpreted as an alternative to the notion of common sense, in accordance with some sort of emotion-based moral or public philosophy—quite common in eighteenth-century Britain, if one recalls the sympathy theory of the Scots. This commitment in Burke is not based on contract, it is not a conscious choice, but rather a sentimental, almost unconscious identification and attachment to a locus, which we know by heart and love. This is how Scruton substantializes his claim that the wisdom of a community cannot be summed up in the form of a doctrine or a plan, but rather in its customs and traditions. Citing such traditions, Scruton succeeds in linking small community engagement with the conservative philosophy of politics. He also refers to the Austrian economists and to Hayek, who wrote about the spontaneous order created by markets, as well as to Oakeshott's concept of civil association, which Scruton sets in opposition to political rationalism. Through these steps, Scruton succeeds in delineating the culture of belonging, which makes it possible for him to talk about trust, gift, and good will in connection with one's homeplace, and to describe the conditions of local communities' "eudaimonia" or human flourishing.

This culture can be endangered by the growth sustained by modernism, which reached cities at the beginning of the twentieth century. Scruton recalls successful British public (or civic) endeavors such as The Town and Country Association and the Campaign for the Preservation (subsequently Protection) of Rural England, which were instrumental in the adoption, after the Second World War, of the policy of Green belts, which preserved the face of the countryside, maintaining the traditional relationship between the human settlement and its environment.

As he saw them, these movements were inspired by a sense of beauty and of love of home. They also guaranteed that the inhabitants of cities did not spread into the countryside.[160] Scruton draws on literature evoking old England such as the description of rural market towns by Thomas Hardy. The important thing for him was to remind his readers that England was able to oppose the urbanist vision of modernism, which would have wiped out both people's attachment to local places and their sense of history by destroying neighborhoods and the accompanying feeling of homeliness. These early movements to defend local communities were reflected in Nicholas Boys Smith's initiative, Create Streets, which once again raised the idea of the self-contained cities which existed in the pre-modern era. According to Scruton, the idea of the self-containment of the city meant first of all that cities are able to close down, their borders being well-defined (in opposition to the various forms of suburbanization). A second meaning of the term is moderation or self-discipline—that the city does not seek to occupy the surrounding environment.

A final defining feature of the European city, as analyzed by Scruton, was that both the ancient polis and the medieval city were sacred places. Scruton also addresses this issue in connection with Poundbury. As he saw it, the new quarter had a range of public buildings, including a town hall, offices, and the headquarters of public administration, factories, and warehouses—yet it was still missing one vital kind of building: a church, or a place of public worship. Scruton shares with his readers his memory of the discussion he had with the architect about this kind of building. He himself brought up this theme because of the discussion of the ancient city in Fustel de Coulanges's book, which claimed that new cities were born originally when the citizens came together to mark off a place which was consecrated, and there they raised a church to worship the gods. To quote the French author: "As soon as the families, the phratries, and the tribes had agreed to unite and have the same worship, they immediately founded the city as a sanctuary for this common worship, and thus the foundation of a city was always a religious act."[161] In other words, they had certain rites to mark the event. The Romans, as Fustel describes it, summarizing the foundation stories of the ancient historians, first cleaned themselves ritually by leaping through a sacred flame. Then

"Romulus dug a small trench, of a circular form, and threw into it a clod of earth," taken from his earlier city, Alba, and his example was followed by all the others.[162] Ancient Romans considered it their religious duty to take with them the sacred soil of their ancestors when they decided to establish a new city. In doing so they made the new place symbolically the land of their fathers, "terra patrum, patria." "When placing in the trench a clod of earth from their former country, they believed they had enclosed there the souls of their ancestors." "At this same place Romulus set up an altar, and lighted a fire upon it. This was the holy fire of the city."[163] From this celebration was born the temple of Vesta.

The church also remained the center of the city in Christian culture. In this regard the twentieth-century Hungarian poet, János Pilinszky, wrote that: "Among the private and public houses the church belongs to eternity, even if we simply evaluate it formally. A city in the classic sense of the word cannot be envisaged without it."[164]

To find a place for one's home both the ancients and the Christians followed the wisdom of the god(s), in order to ensure that he/they should take care of the city and its inhabitants. The god(s) had to find his/their home there in order for the inhabitants to find their home there, too. Scruton claimed that this consideration of the sacred is missing from the approach of (post)modernist urbanism. Krier largely agreed with him, but he drew his attention to the fact that with the tools of architecture it is scarcely possible to change the way of life people pursue, or their specific way of thinking. If he or his fellow architects wanted to force something on the people, they would be committing the same mistake as they charged the modernists with.

In practice, however, the problem was solved in 2018 when the first church building of the new city quarter was consecrated, the Dorchester Community Church.

Yet the theoretical problem remains. How can cities return to the traditional ways, without convincing their inhabitants of the mistaken views they have embraced under the spell of modernism? As soon as one tries to share one's views, as an intellectual or even more as an architectural critic, one commits the error of misunderstanding one's role. This is the typical attitude of the modernist artist who seeks to force his views on his audience. This was also the essential problem of Socrates. The ancient Greek philosopher was aware of the mistaken views of the people of Athens, but he could not simply state those mistakes, because that would not convince his interlocutors. They had to recognize their errors and find the solutions by themselves. His strategy was called the elenctic method, or midwifery, a form of argumentation based on cross questioning in order to bring out the implicit underlying assumptions of the positions of the discussants, and to show that they are untenable. While this method, popularized by Plato, is indeed tricky and rhetorically very powerful, Socrates finally paid with his life for the subversive views that he spread. Scruton himself was accused by his critics severely, and had to suffer public shame for false accusations, which shows that indeed politics is always involved in such issues of public worship. However, he had the courage to summarize his position by quoting Krier with approval:

"By creating cities, we create ourselves. When we despoil our cities, we despoil ourselves. Our most cherished memories will henceforth generate the poison of regret, of irretrievable loss, even of hatred of what we prized most. We then flee from the world and from ourselves. A beautiful village, a beautiful house, a beautiful city can become a home for all, a universal home. But if we lose this aim we build our own exile here on earth."[165]

NOTES

1. Patrick Geddes, *Cities in Evolution. An Introduction to the Town Planning Movement and to the Study of Civics* (London: Williams and Norgate, 1915).

2. See: W. Reed Smith, "Megalopolis versus Social Retardation: The Continuing Relevance of the Views of Spengler and Toynbee on the Variability of the Rate of Cultural Change," *Comparative Civilizations Review* 61, no. 61 (2009): Article 8, 119–46.

3. Smith, *Megalopolis*, 121, quoting from Spengler, *The Decline of the West*, One-Volume edition (New York: Knopf, 1932).

4. Smith, *Megalopolis*, 122, quoting Spengler, *Decline*, 25.

5. Ibid.

6. For Geddes' and Mumford's relationship, see Paul Goldberger, "Mumford and the Master," *New York Times*, November 19, 1995, Section 7, 28. It is a short review of the volume: *Lewis Mumford and Patrick Geddes, The Correspondence*, ed. Frank G. Novak Jr. Illustrated. (New York: Routledge, 2014), 383. Goldberger writes: "Geddes, 41 years his senior, a biologist, urban planner, sociologist and determined outsider to the academy, . . . argued passionately that all subjects were intertwined and spent much of his life trying to formulate a rational system for the synthesis of knowledge and human experience."

7. Charles Baudelaire, *The Swan*, trans. William Aggeler, The Flowers of Evil (Fresno, CA: Academy Library Guild, 1954).The original French version is as follows: "Le vieux Paris n'est plus (la forme d'une ville / Change plus vite, hélas! que le coeur d'un mortel)."

8. Ibid.

9. Walter Benjamin, "On Some Motifs in Baudelaire," trans. Harry Zohn in *Illuminations: Essays and Reflections*, ed. Hannah Arendt (New York: Schocken, 1968), 155–200. Zohn's translation can also be found in *Selected Writings* Volume IV, 1938–40 (Cambridge: Belknap, 2003), 313–55. The quotation about the essay is from John Phillips's commentary, entitled, *Walter Benjamin "Some Motifs,"* available

at: https://courses.nus.edu.sg/course/elljwp/benmotifs.htm#_edn2 (approached May, 2020).

10. John Phillips, *Walter Benjamin "Some Motifs,"* available at: https://courses.nus.edu.sg/course/elljwp/benmotifs.htm#_ednref2

11. The parallel of Baudelaire's flaneur at home in Paris is Poe's own one, who dwells in nineteenth-century London, according to Benjamin.

12. Benjamin, *On Some Motifs*, 188.

13. Ibid.

14. Charles Baudelaire, "Crowds," in Baudelaire, *Paris Spleen*, trans. Louise Varèse (New York: New Direction Books, 1970), 20–21.

15. See Peter McPhee, "The Revolutionary Century? Revolts in Nineteenth-Century France," in *Crowd Actions in Britain and France from the Middle Ages to the Modern World*, ed. Michael T. Davis (London: Palgrave Macmillan, 2015), 193–207. For the perspective of 19th century Paris and France as a revolution, see: Malcolm Crook, ed., *Revolutionary France 1788–1880* (Oxford: Oxford University Press, 2002); Roger Magraw, *France 1815–1914: The Bourgeois Century* (London: MacMillan, 1983); François Furet, *La Révolution: de Turgot à Jules Ferry, 1770–1880* (Paris: Hachette, 1989).

16. Furet, *La Révolution*, 516–7, quoted by McPhee, *Revolt*, 193.

17. See the term bourgeois in the Online Etymology Dictionary.

18. For a description of the distinction, see: Sonia Arribas, "Bourgeois and Citoyen. Struggle as the Mediation of their Tragic Conflict in Hegel's Jena Manuscripts," *Hegel-Jahrbuch* 1 (1999): 213–9.

19. For a condensed form of this view of societal developments, see *Manifesto of the Communist Party* by Karl Marx and Frederick Engels, February 1848, Part. I. "Bourgeois and Proletarians."

20. Marx and Engels, *Manifesto*, 14.

21. Ibid., 17.

22. See Jürgen Kocka, "German History before Hitler: The Debate about the German Sonderweg," *Journal of Contemporary History* 23, no. 1 (January, 1988): 3–16.

23. Ralf Dahrendorf, *Society and Democracy in Germany* (London, 1968), 397. Quoted by Geoff Eley, "Introduction 1: Is There a History of the Kaiserreich," in *Society, Culture, and their State in Germany, 1870–1930*, ed. Geoff Eley (Ann Arbor: The University of Michigan Press, 1997), 1–42, 5, n. 5. https://books.google.hu/books?id=xXgsNh4QnQwC&pg=PA5&lpg=PA5&dq=J%C3%BCrgen+kocka+bourgeoisie&source=bl&ots=jUMvM_MiwP&sig=ACfU3U3i9am9yGOIzfk05XeYgwgAdeFCpg&hl=hu&sa=X&ved=2ahUKEwjB49e476rpAhXk_CoKHanfDDIQ6AEwBHoECAoQAQ#v=onepage&q=J%C3%BCrgen%20kocka%20bourgeoisie&f=false

24. Eley, "Introduction 1," 5.

25. I am relying here on the review by Geoff Eley: Jürgen Kocka and Allen Mitchell, ed., *Bourgeois Society in Nineteenth-Century Europe* (Oxford/Providence: Berg, 1993), in *Central European History* 27, no. 4 (1994): 518–23.

26. See Conversation with Jürgen Kocka, 12-14-2017, *Politika*, where he said about his relationship to Koselleck: "I admired him and I still do. He was a historian who politically was different."

27. Jürgen Kocka, ed., *Bürgertum im 19. Jahrhundert: Deutschland im europäischen Vergleich*, 3 vols. (Munich, 1988).

28. Jürgen Kocka and Allen Mitchell, ed., *Bourgeois Society in Nineteenth-Century Europe* (Oxford/Providence: Berg, 1993).

29. Eley, *Review*, 520.

30. Ibid.

31. Ibid.

32. Ibid., 521. It quotes Kocka's own essay in Kocka and Allen, *Borugeois Soicety*, 8ff.

33. Jürgen Kocka, "Civil society from a historical perspective," *European Review* 12, no. 1 (2004): 65–79.

34. Ibid., 66, 67.

35. Ibid., 67.

36. Ibid., 66.

37. Ibid., 67.

38. See the work of the Hungarian author, Béla Zolnai on what he calls the Hungarian Biedermeier.

39. Kocka, *Civil Society*, 72.

40. Ibid.

41. Ibid.

42. Ibid., 73.

43. Ibid.

44. Ibid.

45. John Lukacs, *Budapest 1900. A Historical Portrait of a City and Its Culture* (New York: Grove Press, 1988).

46. Ibid., xiv.

47. To be sure, the novel we are going to deal with is considered as "one of the main works of Hungarian literature before the second world war." (Géza Hegedűs, *A magyar irodalom arcképcsarnoka*, available at: https://mek.oszk.hu/01100/01149/html/index.htm).

48. According to Lukacs, the French and English translations were of poor quality. Lukacs, *Budapest*, 17.

49. Ibid., 18.

50. Ibid.

51. Ibid.

52. Ibid., 92.

53. Ibid., 75.

54. Ibid., 70.

55. Ibid.

56. Ibid., 87.

57. Ibid., 69.

58. Ibid., 91.

59. Ibid., 142.

60. Ibid., 144.

61. Ibid., 142.

62. Ibid., 148.
63. Ibid., 150.
64. Ibid., 146.
65. Ibid.
66. Ibid., 73.
67. Ibid., 92.
68. Ibid., 188.
69. Lukacs specifically mentions the large proportion of the Jewish families in the leadership of banks, resulting in a boom in the financial sector as well: "By 1900, . . . Budapest had become the largest financial center of Europe east of Vienna." Lukacs, *Budapest*, 93.
70. Ibid., 94.
71. Ibid., 94–95.
72. Ibid., 188.
73. Ibid., 189.
74. Ibid.
75. Ibid., 190.
76. Ibid.
77. Ibid., 211.
78. Ibid., 221.
79. Lewis Mumford, *The City in History: Its Origins, Its Transformations, and Its Prospects* (Boston: Mariner Books, 1968), 526.
80. Ibid.
81. Hartmut Espe, "Differences in the perception of national socialist and classicist architecture," *Journal of Environmental Psychology* 1, no. 1 (1981): 33–42.
82. Artur Klinau, *Minsk, the Sun City of Dreams* (Berlin: Suhrkamp, 2006). A summary and analysis of this book can be found in Ferenc Hörcher, "The Dark Night of the City. Solar Construction and Urban Destruction in Communist Minsk," in *Conservative Critics of Political Utopia*, ed. Máté Botos (Budapest: L'Harmattan, 2019), 75–95.
83. Quoted in Hörcher, *The Dark Night*, 90.
84. Mumford, *The City in History*, 513, quoting Tocqueville without references. The quote can be found in Alexis de Tocqueville, *Democracy in America*, 2 vols. (New York: Schocken, 1961), vol. 1, 380.
85. Mumford, *The City in History*, 525.
86. Ibid., 529.
87. Ibid., 532.
88. Ibid., 535.
89. Ibid., 540.
90. Ibid., 543.
91. Ibid., 555.
92. Ibid.
93. Ibid., 558.
94. Ibid.
95. Ibid.

96. Ibid., 563.
97. Ibid.
98. Ibid., 564.
99. Kirckpatrick Sale, "Foreword," in Leopold Kohr, *The Breakdown of Nations* (1957, 1978), available at: http://www.ditext.com/kohr/foreword.html
100. Steven Yates, "Who Was Leopold Kohr?" *American Daily Herald*, Saturday, January 21, 2012, https://web.archive.org/web/20120124010516/http://www.americandailyherald.com/steven-yates/who-was-leopold-kohr
101. In this respect, he resembles Sándor Márai, mentioned earlier in this book, the herald of his historical hometwon, Kassa (today Kosice), who, however, could never return to his birthplace in his life, which he left as a young man.
102. Quoted by Sale, *Foreword*.
103. From the explanation of awarding Leopold Kohr the Right Livelyhood Award. The relevant homepage of the Award is: https://www.rightlivelihoodaward.org/laureates/leopold-kohr/
104. Leopold Kohr, Acceptance speech, the eve of 1984, https://www.rightliveli hoodaward.org/speech/acceptance-speech-leopold-kohr/
105. Figgis refers to certain passages specifically to III.10 and IV.3, 15. John Neville Figgis, *The Political Aspects of St. Augustine's City of God* (Altenmünster: Jazzybee Verlag Jürgen Beck, 2017), 41.
106. Josef Haid, *Lebensrichtig – Ein neuer Weg für unser Denken und Handeln* (Chur: Asama Verlag, 1983).
107. This is from the homepage of the award, dedicated to Manfred Max-Neef, who got the prize in the same year as Kohr.
108. Leopold Kohr, *Tribute to E. F. Schumacher, The Schumacher Lectures*, ed. Satish Kumar (New York: Harper and Row, 1980).
109. For this expresssion, see: Diana Schumacher, "Who Was Fritz Schumacher?" *The Gandhi Foundation*, November 25, 2011, https://gandhifoundation.org/2011/11/25/who-was-fritz-schumacher-by-diana-schumacher/
110. Cathecism of the Catholic Church, 1883. It also refers to *CA* 48 § 4; cf. Pius XI, *Quadragesimo anno* I, 184–186.
111. *Quadragesimo Anno*, 1931, 79, quoted in E.F. Schumacher, *Small Is Beautiful* (London: Abacu, 1974, 1987), 203.
112. Schumacher, *Small Is Beautiful*, 204.
113. *Quadragesimo Anno*, 80.
114. Schumacher, *Small Is Beautiful*, 204.
115. Ibid.
116. Ibid., 55.
117. Aristotle, *Politics*, 1326.
118. Schumacher, *Small Is Beautiful*, 55.
119. Ibid.
120. Ibid.
121. Ibid., 54.
122. Ibid.

123. Aristotle: "each citizen must know what sorts of people the other citizens are. For where they do not know this, the business of electing officials and deciding lawsuits must go badly." (*Politics*, 1326b15–18.)

124. Schumacher, *Small Is Beautiful*, 54.

125. Ibid., 62.

126. Léon Krier, *The City Within the City*, http://zeta.math.utsa.edu/~yxk833/KRIER/city.html, 2.

127. Ibid., 1.

128. Louise Lockwood, dir., "Why Beauty Matters," television production, 28 November 2009, United Kingdom: British Broadcasting Corporation. Event occurs at 50:02.

129. For a detailed account see my earlier study: "A léptékhelyes város dicsérete. A herceg, az építész és a filozófus beszélgetése," in *A Kisváros dicsérete*, eds. Ferenc Hörcher et al. (Balatonfüred: Tempevölgy Könyvek 37, 2019), 111–31.

130. HRH The Prince of Wales, *A Vision of Britain. A Personal View of Architecture* (London, etc.: Doubleday, 1989).

131. Ibid., 76.

132. Ibid., 77.

133. Ibid., 82.

134. Ibid.

135. Ibid.

136. Krier, *The City*, 1.

137. Ibid., 3.

138. "Creating Space for Beauty." The Interim Report of the Building Better, Building Beautiful Commission, July 2019, https://assets.publishing.service.gov.uk/government/uploads/system/uploads/attachment_data/file/815495/BBBB_Commission_Interim_Report_Appendices.pdf

139. Roger Scruton, "Cities for Living. Antimodernist Léon Krier designs urban environments to human scale," *City Journal* (Spring, 2008), https://www.city-journal.org/html/cities-living-13088.html

140. Roger Scruton, "The Fabric of the City," The Colin Amery Memorial Lecture by Sir Roger Scruton for Policy Exchange, 14 November 2018, https://policyexchange.org.uk/wp-content/uploads/2018/11/The-Fabric-of-the-City.pdf

141. Scruton, *Cities*.

142. Jane Jacobs, *The Death and Life of Great American Cities* (New York: Random House, 1961).

143. The quote is now available in Léon Krier, *The Architecture of Community*, ed. Dhiru A. Thadani and Peter J. Hetzel (Washington, London: Island Press, Covelo, 2009), 439. Though Scruton does not quote longer, the next sentence connects architecture once again to politics: "Without their common acceptance there can be no constitution nor maintenance of a normal civilized life."

144. Hans Maes, "Sharing a Home in the World. A Conversation with Roger Scruton," in Hans Maes, *Conversation on Art and Aesthetics* (Oxford: Oxford University Press, 2017), 179–204, 200.

145. Roger Scruton, *Gentle Regrets. Thoughts from a Life* (London: Continuum, 2005), 209.

146. Ibid.

147. Ibid.

148. Another author who called attention to the significance of our home in our life was Gaston Bachelard, in his *The Poetics of Space* (Paris: Presses Universitaires de France, 1957).

149. Here I rely on Scruton's late essay with the title "Settling Down and Marking Time," *CUSP Essay Series on the Morality of Sustainable Prosperity*, no. 2, published February 2017, at: https://www.cusp.ac.uk/themes/m/rs_m1-2/

150. Scruton, *Settling Down*, 9.

151. Ibid.

152. John Bowlby, *Attachment*, 2nd ed. (New York: Basic Books, 1999), *Separation* (New York: Basic Books, 2000), *Loss* (London: Pimlico, 1998).

153. His name is misspellt in the published version of the essay.

154. Scruton, *Settling Down*, 9.

155. Ibid., 10.

156. Ibid.

157. Ibid., 11.

158. Ibid.

159. Edmund Burke, *Reflections on the Revolution in France*, ed. Iain Hampsher-Monk (Cambridge: Cambridge University Press, 2014), 47–48.

160. Scruton, *Settling Down*, 15.

161. de Coulanges, *The Ancient City*, 177.

162. Ibid., 180.

163. Ibid., 181.

164. János Pilinszky, "Egy város ürügyén" (On the pretext of a city), *Új Ember* (12 June, 1966).

165. Quoted in Scruton, *Cities*. Though Scruton does not give his source, it can be found in the following collection of Krier's writings: Krier, *The Architecture of Community*, 439.

Conclusion

The City as a Work of Art

We have almost finished our excursion into the forgotten heritage of the political thought of the European city. The final ritual before departing is to try to sum up our findings. In order to do so, we shall make use of two modern works of art, based on the assumption that artistic creativity can convey more about the European urban heritage than any other form of communication. The first of these artworks is well known all over the world—it is a composition of statues entitled *The Burghers of Calais* (1889) by probably the most famous modern French sculptor, Auguste Rodin. The second one is a work of prose fiction by a novelist practically unknown outside Hungary, Antal Szerb (1901–1945). His novel about classical Italian art, *Journey by Moonlight*, was published in 1937. We shall single out one city from the restless journeys of the novel's hero across the peninsula: Siena. The hope is that through these recollections of the artistic presentations of two European cities, the French port city of Calais and the Italian city republic of Siena, we can gain an insight into the essence of what a European city is. It will be necessary also to recall the urban historian's view of Siena, and finally we will outline our own ideal type of the European city, in a somewhat Weberian vein. This final description might not fit any of the European cities precisely, but hopefully its major features will help the reader identify the essence of the European city as a political entity.

RODIN'S CALAIS

Les Bourgeois de Calais, (The Burghers of Calais) is a six figure sculpture by the most influential modern French sculptor, Auguste Rodin, commissioned by the city of Calais in 1884, and finished in 1889. Although it exists in twelve "original" copies and a number of replicas, the "real one" stands in front of the town hall of Calais to this day, representing, or more precisely embodying the city. According to Rilke, the one-time secretary of the artist, "the silent group was to stand, raised by a low step above the common life of the market place as though the fearful departure were always pending."[1] This final section of the book will consider this representation of a group of burghers to try to decode the message they convey about being a burgher, a responsible citizen of a European city.

Rodin's composition of six somewhat larger-than-lifesize figures refers to probably the most well-known, tragic episode of the history of the city, as recounted in the chronicle of the contemporary court historian from the Low Countries, Jean Froissart. The incident happened during the Hundred Years' War, in 1346–1347. Edward III, the English king, besieged the city while the French King, Philip VI ordered it to hold out. The city resisted the foreign army for eleven months until hunger compelled them to surrender. The English king demanded that the city sacrifice six of its burghers in order to save the lives of the members of the community. The statue presents six of the wealthiest members of the citizenry, led by Eustache de Saint-Pierre, who volunteered to sacrifice themselves, in accordance with the chronicle. They had to humble themselves and were ordered by the English king to "wear sackcloth and halters, carry the keys of the city, and present themselves at his camp, ready for the execution."[2] As a full narrative of the story has survived, although the historical truth of it is doubtful, the artist decided to remain faithful to its wording. Yet his art form forced him to make an important decision: he had to choose one single moment of the dramatic line of events to express the essence of the story, and with it, the essence of the city as well. Rodin selected the moment when the burghers set out from the city for the English king's camp. At that moment, they thought they would have to die, not knowing that the pregnant queen would convince her husband to pardon them.

Let us try to make sense of the moment the statue presents. This is a moment of utmost despair, when the six of them had to leave their home, through the gate in the city wall which had defended them for almost a year against the enemy. Although it was their own choice to make this sacrifice, at this instant they felt the exact weight of their fate. It is now that they recognize what it feels like to be all alone, without the security and support of the community, preparing for a cruel death. Rodin did not want to present six super human heroes, whose virtues are far above our own doubts and anxieties. Rather, he wanted us to be able to enter the perspective of the burghers, with the agonizing inner struggle to persevere to be able to complete the mission. Rodin, as a rebellious modernist artist, did not accept the standard academic aesthetics of national monuments, which traditionally presented superhuman values in order to encourage the onlookers to be able to transcend their ordinary human conditions. He refused to make use of symbols and allegories, instead simply presenting fear, anger, and determination, as the natural impulses of his protagonists.

The basic question Rodin's statue poses concerns the relationship between the individual and his community at a moment of crisis, in this case a military defeat. This question is all the more pressing in the context of modernity—a fourteenth-century story was being interpreted at the end of the nineteenth century, when this relationship between the individual and the citizen body was itself crucially changing. As we saw in the case of Baudelaire, mid-nineteenth-century French art was focusing on the inner world of the individual, pushing into the background the demands of the community upon him. Rodin is presumably himself struggling with this problem. He himself took part in the defense of the French capital as a member of the National Guard in the Franco-Prussian War, when the French were defeated and had to suffer the shame of total surrender. As a result of his own personal participation in the lost battle Rodin was presumably able to imagine the emotional state of the burghers, and he wanted to convey their tumultuous feelings with the help of the body language which is the most important artistic tool of the sculptor, in the realistic and mimetic tradition of modeling which characterizes Rodin's art.

The artistic task Rodin undertook was a complex one. The citizens of Calais wanted to see the heroism of their ancestors in the figures. Interestingly, the commission for the statue came at a moment when Calais seemed once again to be gaining real national significance. In 1882 "the English Parliament announced its decision to build a tunnel under the Channel to connect Dover with Calais."[3] Calais, in the process of being united with the neighboring settlement of Saint-Pierre, was on the threshold of becoming a "maritime, industrial and commercial center: a large city whose prosperity will be even greater after the union."[4] Yet once again, they had to make a sacrifice: its historical walls had to be pulled down to make the unification possible. It was in this context that the city council decided to erect the monument, although it took a decade to be realized.

Rodin, anxious to create his first great masterpiece in the genre of the public monument, was struggling to achieve something artistically exceptional. His composition went through several different phases. His problems had at least two different layers. First, he wished to characterize his heroes individually. He had the names of all six of them (the first four were mentioned by the chronicler, while the names of the final two he got from recently revealed historical documents), and he made every effort to individualize them. This was crucial to gain a sort of psychological credibility. By presenting six different protagonists he also offered the onlookers the opportunity to make their own minds up about the six "secular martyrs."[5] They comprised:

- the leader of the group, Eustache de Saint-Pierre. In the final version, he is "an old man, tired and desolate."[6] In his representation, it is claimed, Rodin made a step forward toward the modern anti-hero.
- the second to volunteer, Jean d'Aire. According to Froissart, a "greatly respected and wealthy citizen, who had two beautiful daughters."[7] His hands, feet, and the key he clasps are all oversized. His head and gestures both express power and resolution.
- Pierre de Wiessant. He is the younger of the two brothers, Pierre and Jacques. He has probably the most expressive gesture, which greatly inspired Rilke: "he turns back to himself. His right arm is raised, bent, vacillating. His hands open in the air as though to let something go, as one gives freedom to a bird. This gesture is symbolic of a departure from all uncertainty."[8] Rilke, who lived fifty-one years, adds one more memorable sentence to this description: "This figure, if placed by itself in a dim, old garden, would be a monument for all who have died young."[9]
- Pierre's older brother, Jacques, who is also holding a key in one of his hands, while the other hand makes a strange gesture, something like that to "dispell a terrifying nightmare."[10]
- Jean de Fiennes, the youngest of the group.[11] Though Rodin changed his figure many times, his function within the composition remained the same, as the youngest, he has a "doubting disposition" and "looks back toward the town he may never see again."[12]
- Andrieu d'Andres, who remains unknown. His face is covered by his hands, expressing despair at the moment when he realises his fate. The hands fully covering his face are eloquent, as is the back of the head, making the figure expressive without the help of a facial expression.

In spite of their individuality, the six of them had to relate to each other and to the community which they left behind but for which they were ready to sacrifice their individual lives. The development of the composition led from the first maquette presenting them as a collective, almost as if they were merged together, to the second and the final maquette, where the individuals stand alone, each of them struggling to make sense of his own personal fate. Rodin's artistic innovation was his realization that, being part of the same artistic composition, the individuals would anyhow be compared by the onlookers. At the same time the artistic composition succeeds in connecting them, creating a group of indissoluble unity. In this wholeness, the very ordinary human beings, in the midst of their moment of weakness and vulnerability, can become more than a collection of individual selves. Together they are able to suggest the survival of their political community, of the city, their final source of identity, and their final center of belonging.

Let us now consider what Rilke, the poet, writes about the unity of the composition. He starts out from the most obvious first sight: "It seems at first as though Rodin had done nothing more than gather them together."[13] And yet Rilke is quite explicit about "the unity of the group, which, although it consisted of single figures, held closely together as a whole."[14] Rilke, the poet, uses a metaphor which expresses perfectly how the individuals are able to stand for the whole: "The figures do not touch one another, but stand side by side like the last trees of a hewn-down forest united only by the surrounding atmosphere."[15] This is an exposition of an artwork which only a poet could write. With his refined linguistic sensibility, he makes use of the fact that we do not think about the trees of the forest as trees standing side by side each other, but as a united whole, the ensemble of trees, which is also the home to many other plants and animals. Similarly, the burghers are more than well-formed individuals—they are, taken together, the community of the burghers of Calais, the *civitas* which belongs to the *urbs*, the home of burghers from time immemorial.

The city and its burghers—that was the subject of Rodin's statue. The artistic challenge was to find a valid answer to the following question: how can he represent both individuality—each burgher on his own—and the group which is composed of the burghers, and which represents the whole city of Calais. While the first maquette of the monument presents the figures grown together, the final version leaves them alone. Each burgher is within his own bubble, representing his own fate. The artistic marvel is how each of the burghers becomes a member of the burghers' community. Rilke paid special attention to the artistic technique which makes this possible. He was aware of the different views provided by the different perspectives the observer can take when looking at the group. This dynamic aspect of the viewer interacts with the dynamism of the group. Through the gestures of the figures Rodin succeeded in expressing movement: the group seems to be moving from the city toward the camp of the enemy. But there is an internal movement within the statue, too: the ensemble is "pulsing", as if it were a living creature, consisting of six men: "a pulsating world enclosed within its own boundaries."[16] One can compare the effect of this unity in diversity, of movement within a static order, to the cover page of Hobbes's *Leviathan*: the observer can confront each individual of the group, identifying him and appreciating his individuality, while still sensing their collective identity, the unity which they had build up together. Rilke asserts that Rodin makes us realize that "Contact may exist between objects far distant from one another."[17] This contact is made possible between distant figures by the atmosphere Rodin is able to create, which envelops the figures, bringing together the whole statue. Yet the atmosphere itself is not a static element—it also moves and pulses. It is the task of sculptors, like architects, to rearrange space: the physical objects they create have spatial dimensions and they reorder the space around them by the simple fact that the built object is separated from its environment. The relationship between the artistic object and its atmosphere, or the space which is occupied by it, is crucial for the artist, as this will determine our sense of the object. As Rilke puts it: "He enhanced the relationship of the atmosphere to his work to such a degree that the surrounding air seemed to give more life, more passion, as it were, to the embraced surfaces."[18] This intensity of the relationship between the artistic object and its atmosphere is compared by Rilke to an architectural effect: to "the animals on the cathedrals to which the air relates itself in a strange fashion."[19] The comparison between Rodin's statue and a Gothic cathedral is very telling, as is the comparison of the sculptor to the architect and the builder: Rodin does not simply imitate the earthly forms of human beings with his statue, but the links between his heroes turn into the lines of force which hold together a whole cathedral, and finally a whole city. In other words, Rodin's ensemble represents not only the exaggerated forms of six individual human beings, but the whole *civitas* of Calais. Furthermore, Rodin also builds the *urbs*: the physical space which the burghers create together and in which they dwell, and which by now has over a century of history, turning it into a kind of natural phenomenon. Each European city has its own distinguishing mark, its own specific local atmosphere, which turns the physical environment into a living creature which survives the death of its inhabitants. As Rilke puts it: "The atmosphere has traced deeper lines upon these monuments, has shadowed them with veils of dust, has seasoned them with rain and frost, with sun and storm, and has thus endowed them with endurance so that they may remain imperishable through many slowly-passing dusks and dawns."[20] Rodin's monument is a living, autonomous creature, like Hobbes's *Leviathan*, just as each and every European city is an autonomous unit. He succeeded in giving the group of his figures a life of its own, as was the case with Pygmalion, whose story was told by Rodin's contemporary, the playwright George Bernard Shaw. A work of art becomes a natural, in fact a living creature, a creature of God. This is expressed by another metaphor of the poet: "These sculptural forms seen from a distance are not only surrounded by the immediate atmosphere, but by the whole sky."[21] So it is, too, with the famous *vedutas* of European art history, from El Greco's *Veduta of Toledo* to Canaletto's depictions of Venice: all these paintings emphasize the relationship between the city and the Gods, transforming a number of buildings and their environment into a huge phenomenon, both natural and supernatural, that is beautiful and sublime. There is a similar resonance in the famous last two lines of Mihály Babits's long, narrative poem, *The Book of Jonah*, which represents the Biblical Nineveh, the sinful city, as one huge living creature, surviving everything, but struggling to do so: "The monstrous town, like to a panting and exhausted beast, lay stretched out on the sand."

Calais, too, after almost a year under attack, was a living creature, struggling to survive. Its six burghers were able to help the city to do so by offering their lives as six sacrifices on its altar, and the artist is able to give eternal life to the city by presenting this ensemble as a group of priests, saying mass together, celebrating God and the patron saint of the city. Whenever we hear the name of the city, we associate it with Rodin's famous work of art, just as whenever we look at the figures of his statue, we recall the life struggle of the whole city, and the mercy of God who saved the city.

ANTAL SZERB'S SIENA

Rodin's art celebrated the French city of Calais at the moment of its deepest existential crisis. The genius of Rodin was to turn this moment of loss and despair into a celebration of the common "raison," the common sense of the *civitas*. The burghers of Calais are compelled by their individual reason to sacrifice their own individual lives in order to save their community. The decision of each of the burghers of Calais is a rational choice, and presents the morality of the burgher in the French tradition at its best. The interesting thing is the way that Rodin is able to show individuality in action in the service of the community, and to show the rational nature of the burghers' choice through their body language and through the force of artistic composition, when they make the greatest sacrifice of their lives.

Rodin was inspired throughout his career by Renaissance Italian art. We shall now turn again to the Italian city, this time from the perspective of a Central European author. If Rodin, the Parisian, was the paradigmatic modern sculptor, who was capable of representing the whole of his culture, Antal Szerb, born in the magical atmosphere of turn of the century Budapest, was a cultural historian of his country as well as of Europe. He wrote a history both of Hungarian and of European literature. He could have become as famous as Rodin, had he not perished like so many of his contemporaries because of his Jewish ancestry during the Second World War. Yet his art survived him, and it is a stunning celebration of Western culture. His death and the survival of his work is a symbol of the strength of art in face of the vulnerability of the perishing human body.

Perhaps the most celebrated novel by Szerb was based on his own wanderings in historical Italy. Having spent years in Europe in his youth, he was a lover of Italian cities and of traveling. His most famous novel, *Journey by Moonlight* (1937) is a fictional version of his own travels in Italy, an account of which was published as a travelog just one year before the novel, in 1936.

The novel tells a story of a young man, named *Mihály* (Michael), whose honeymoon trip to Venice with his newlywed wife turns out to be a real pilgrim's progress: a life-changing experience. Szerb, who was born into an assimilated Jewish family in Budapest, but who was baptized, sets the story's turning point in Rome, the eternal city. Yet the whole book is essentially the confessions of a lover of Italian cities, his journey being a ritual pilgrimage, or—from another perspective—the customary study tour of the Central European intelligentsia of the first half of the twentieth century.

It will suffice to concentrate on his description of a single city in the novel: Siena. As we have seen earlier, describing a city is one of the great challenges of the art of language: the architectural ensemble is a three-dimensional object which is hard to describe in its unity, the more so as its essence is the interaction between parts of its physical body and its soul, the citizenry.

Szerb was convinced that a city has—beside its tangible body—both a temporal dimension and a spirit, which needs to be addressed if one wishes to grasp its essence. His nuanced descriptions of European cities have been compared to those of Georg Simmel, Walter Benjamin, Lewis Mumford, and Michel Certeau.[22] This might be true of his essays, but the novel is a different genre: here his erudition combines with his artistic inspiration resulting in feasts of language which magically put on the stage the cities of which we have heard so much, but which are given a new life by the artistic rendering in Szerb's novel. His own aim with his novels was to achieve something similar to the art of Cocteau and Alain-Fournier, two famous writers of his generation. The real topic of the book, however, is, nostalgia, a nostalgia which is hard to explain, decadent, which goes beyond mere mannerism, creating a register of language which illuminates the real life of the European city.

The story can be interpreted on two main levels. One is the genre of the *Bildungsreise*, of which much has been said in this book. The *Bildungsreise* is the modern form of the pilgrim's progress: it is a journey which provides a sentimental education, as found in the stories of Stendhal or Laurence Sterne, or those of Goethe, for that matter, who is repeatedly referred to by Szerb. This spiritual growth is achieved by rather exceptional forms of learning. It is realized through the hero's encounters with cities, his journey turning into a calvary, a *via crucis*, a procession of the believer to celebrate Easter, the death and rebirth of Christ in Rome.

Through one of the novel's main protagonists, the brilliant art historian and archaeologist, Professor Rudi Waldheim, the writer is able to communicate his intention to investigate the nature of travel as a journey into the past in at least three senses: it is a journey back into the depth of history, into one's childhood, and into the archaic-mythological date of the Italian cities.[23] It is the third dimension of this time travel that we need to target here: his artistic reconstruction of the myths of the Italian cities, which are not necessarily historically true, but which reveal much more of real significance than sheer historical data. The lengths Szerb goes to in order to lend this mythological dimension to his narrative is comparable to the efforts made by Freud in *Totem and Tabu*, Bachofen in his *Gräbersymbolik*, Frazer in *The Golden Bough*, and Jane Harrison in *Themis* and in the *Prolegomena to the Study of Greek Religion*.[24] All of these theories of the role of myth in the life of human communities are connected to death rituals, a crucial element of Etruscan religious cults, and of Szerb's modernist novel.

A *précis* of the plot is necessary to show how the past—of the dead— becomes a crucial dimension of the novel's temporal horizon. Mihály, an oversensitive arts student, is haunted by the extraordinary friends of his youth, the Ulpius family, who grew up in an old house in the old town of Buda. While *Tamás*, the son of the family, is already dead, *Éva*, Tamás's beautiful sister, who was the center of their small friendly circle, and who apparently helped Tamás to commit suicide, is still alive. Mihály, who recently got married to rid himself of the fantasies of his youth, and who travels to Italy on his honeymoon trip, becomes separated from his wife in Italy, and during his sojourn in different Italian cities returns to his *temps perdu*, is haunted by meetings with two friends from his old circle, and in Rome he finally encounters Éva as well. They agree to meet again soon and Mihály hopes that he can find death in the arms of Éva, thus reappropriating the death of Tamás, to whom he is still attracted by a kind of homoerotic affinity. Yet in the meantime he fortuitously becomes the godfather of a newly born child in the slum of Rome, and after celebrating the christening of the child he gets drunk and misses his meeting with Éva. It turns out that Éva did not turn up either, claiming in a letter she sent to him that Mihály needs to find his own death. Mihály is fetched back to Budapest from Rome by his father, who saves him from suicide by bringing him back to the normal life of the middle classes in Budapest.

The cities that Mihály visits become important stations of his calvary, or phases of his rite of passage. His culture and his extraordinary sensitivity enable him to read buildings, cities, and landscapes as if they had specific meanings or as if they carried symbolic messages, or indeed as if they were the mirrors of his own soul. In other words, he reads cities with a psychoanalytical interpretation of architecture. Italian cities clearly contain the remnants or mementos of different ages, the external manifestations of the inner lives of earlier generations, which sit side by side, horizontally, or layer under layer, vertically. Freud, whose imagination operated on similar lines to Szerb, always dreamed of arriving in Rome at Easter time, to meet his friend, Wilhelm Fliess. He, too, used Rome to describe the workings of the subconscious.

Christopher Bollas reconstructed the description of Rome by Freud in *Civilisation and its Discontents*, in his essay on architecture and the unconscious.[25] In this thought experiment Freud presents the city of Rome as a place where everything which has once existed could survive and exist side by side, synchronically, in order to describe the operation of the subconscious, claiming that "in mental life nothing which has once been formed can perish." Bollas quotes the following Roman archaeological example employed by Freud: "Where the Colosseum now stands" he writes "we could at the same time admire Nero's vanished Golden House."[26] The aim of the thought experiment is of course to show what it might be like to see and sense all these things, these different layers of history and memory, together and at the same time. Bollas goes one step further, radicalizing the Freudian comparison of the city and the unconscious. He claims that if Freud looked at his own example more closely he would have gained a more realistic account of the workings of the unconscious, too. After all, just as in a city, in the human unconscious, too, there are necessarily obliterations and examples of evanescence. In fact, "obliterations are indeed part of the unconscious, so much so that depending on how one wished to look at the Rome of one's unconscious life, we could see both the preserved and the destroyed."[27] In other words, through archaeological excavation, one can identify what has been lost and what has survived, both in the unconscious and in the city, making the connection between the two, the unconscious and the city, much closer and more realistic.

Rome is, of course, special in this respect, even among Italian cities. Through centuries of archaeological research we indeed know much more about its past than about that of most other cities. What is more is that it is a sacred city, the center of a world religion. Yet what Szerb's hero, Mihály is looking for is not simply knowledge about the past for its own sake. Rather, what the novel aims to show is that through the layers of the architectural remnants of so many different generations, through the cultivation of the memories of the forefathers, the community of a city is able to preserve a communal identity which can be sensed even by foreigners, if they take sufficient care of it. This is because the external remnants, parts of the city's architectural heritage, are able to communicate that identity to the visitor. The atmosphere of the city, which can be sensed by a special sense which we might call the sense of the city, can convey some explicit messages, but most often more of the implicit messages of the dead.

Szerb is a late Romantic, and a poet, too, in this respect. As such, both he and his arts student hero have the ability to tap into this spiritual dialogue between the generations. For both the writer and his hero, travel in Italy is undertaken for more than simply cultural enjoyment or as a social activity. Szerb's hero, Mihály, is on a spiritual journey among the historical reservoirs of Italian cities. For him, each city represents an occasion to make a further step in his own spiritual development, and the writer is happy to describe explicitly or implicitly those steps forward, as the steps of a visitor to a city. Cities can thus teach not only the writer and the hero, but finally us, the readers, how to live. Let us explore this point through the example of the novel's references to Siena.

The first time the city is mentioned is just before the physical separation of Mihály and his wife, when Mihály, most probably as a form of escape from his marriage, boards another train at a small provincial train station where their train had stopped. This radical separation is explained by the fact that, before getting off the train, after mentioning Goethe and the earlier tradition of grand tour and pilgrimage to Italy, Mihály expressed his wish to see Siena. His wife, not sensing the danger, thought it must be the paintings of the Sienese primitives that he would like to see, and she fails to realize Mihály's real motives. She is unable to recognize that Mihály would like to go to Siena in order to reorder his life: "just to say the name Siena gives me the feeling that I might stumble across something there that would make everything all right."[28] His wife, of course, called him a fool for this supposition—which resulted in her losing him.

The next time the name of the city comes up is in a discussion between Mihály and his acquaintance and short-time lover, Millicent, an American who is art history student. She was encouraged to travel to Siena to see the primitives by her professor in a letter, and Mihály is afraid that he might lose her. Millicent is ready to lend him money, which enables Mihály to accompany her on her journey to Siena. They therefore leave Foligno, where they had been staying—a small, historical city, which served as a railway junction and was therefore heavily bombed during the Second World War, just a few years after the novel's narrative, and the book's publication. Szerb, the writer, according to the testimony of his documentary travelog, already sensed something of the disaster approaching, as he keeps referring to the fascists. His novel does not repeat those references, but cherishes the cult of death, instead, rehearsing the exceptional values of the cities. For his hero, the cities of Italy mean "a great delicate treasure he might at any moment let slip from his hands."[29]

Of the cities he had seen so far, for Mihály, Siena turns out to be the most beautiful, when he finally has the chance to see it. "It was more beautiful than Venice, finer than aristocratic Florence, lovelier than dear Bologna with its arcades. Perhaps an element in this was that he was there not with Erzsi, officially, but with Millicent, and on the loose."[30] Szerb's description is remarkable. On the one hand he repeats some of the words of the Baedekers of the age. But beyond this snobbish rhetoric, or rather below it, which he introduces to keep in balance the overtly poetic parts of his prose, we can feel the power of his attraction, which captivates both the narrator and the hero of the novel. It is worth quoting parts of this description of the beautiful Siena, which have the magisterial touch of a *veduta* in words, to show the sense of magic he can invoke in his readers, when really inspired by the beauty of the Italian city.

A key to the beauty of Italian cities is that they were built on hills. This choice is, of course, understandable from the point of view of self-defense: It is easier to defend your city, if geography and gravity are on your side. Enemy soldiers will have to climb the hill if they want to attack you, while you are above them, as the defender, which also gives you symbolic power beside the practicalities of the fight. Siena's streets are precipitous, covering the hills along the forms of a star. Interestingly, however, the highest point is not occupied by the citadel, or fortress, which could defend the inhabitants in times of attack but by the cathedral. "The city had the quality of a fairytale, a happy fairytale, lent it by the fact that from everywhere you could see, at its highest point, the cathedral hovering over it like a towered Zeppelin, in the livery of a pantomime zebra."[31] The location of the dome proves the religious origins of the city—its position can remind one that the last hope is not the physical strength of its defenders but the spiritual power of its divine patron. This fabulous tone creates the illusion that when it is in danger the city can fly away from its besieging enemy with the help of God.

The fact that the hills play a major role in the physical layout of the city keeps returning in the description. Mihály explains the proportion of hills and city to Millicent in the following words: "'This is the landscape of humanity' he told Millicent. 'Here a hill is exactly the size a hill should be. Here everything is to scale, tailored to the human form.'"[32] This is clearly a reference to the mathematical foundations of Renaissance aesthetics, following ancient examples. His partner, the somewhat air-headed Millicent, however, cannot make sense of Mihály's claim, and in asking for clarification she makes his serious (and snobbish) claim appear to be somewhat pompous and ironic: "How would you know what size a hill should be?"[33]

This playful presentation by the narrator does not detract from the author's effort to let us see and sense the sheer beauty of the city, and to show that its relationship to its geographic environment is crucial. How the two of them, city and landscape, relate to each other is also illustrated to the reader in a scene at dawn. The next morning when Mihály woke up, he got out of bed and looked out of the window toward the hills outside the city. "Slight, lilac-coloured clouds were sailing over the Tuscan landscape, and a tinge of gold slowly and timidly prepared for dawn. And nothing existed but lilac and the gold of first light over distant hills."[34] No wonder that Mihály is enchanted by the magic of the moment, a moment of twilight and distant perspective. He realizes that this is a turning point in his life.

It is at this moment that the narration is on the verge of turning into poetry. Szerb's narrator changes his voice to that of a poet, the most highly esteemed one in his time, by letting his hero recite aloud a poem, the best known verse of Rilke, one-time assistant to Rodin:

"Denn da is keine Stelle/ Die dich nicht steht. Du musst dein Leben ändern."[35]

This is indeed a quotation from a famous poem, written by the poet in Paris, when he worked for Rodin, and was inspired by classical statuary, which had an honored place in Rodin's workshop. The "places" mentioned in the poem, which look at the speaker, were in the context of the poem different parts of the body of the Apollo statue the poem described. This reference in the original Rilke poem is transformed by the dramaturgy of Szerb's novel: here, these places are elements of the magical landscape at dawn, viewed from a window in the city.[36] It is this humanized landscape that enchants the hero and that reminds him at the same time of his existential challenge.

Beside the unparalleled landscape of and around the city, the beauty of which is hard to resist, there is one more element that Szerb's novel makes explicit: the special character of the inhabitants of the city. The narrator compares the faces of these people to the face of the city: as he perceives them, both of them are smiling. This is how the inhabitants are characterized: "On the faces of its people you could see that they were very poor, but very happy—happy in their inimitable Latin way."[37] This is how the hero sees the main square of the city: "They went down to the Campo, the main square, the scallop shape of which was like the city's smile."[38] The smile on the face of the people as well as on the face of the city is, of course, more than an observation by tourist. The ability to smile becomes a secret knowledge of the Siennese, like the smile of Leonardo's Mona Lisa: the narration suggests that through it the city and its inhabitants can communicate with eternity.

Finally, let us recall Szerb's reference to the message of one of the gates of the city. He quotes the inscription of Porta Camollia directly, in the original language: *"Cor magis tibi Sena pandit"* (Siena opens up to you a heart that is greater [than the gate through which you are passing]). He does not mention that this was historically a less-than-sincere address to the new ruler, Ferdinando I de' Medici (1587–1609). The Medicis were, of course Florentine, centuries-long enemies of the city of Siena, and this inscription served to welcome Ferdinando, the son of Cosimo, who bought the city. Szerb does not mention these unfortunate political circumstances. Instead, he lets his hero dive into history: Mihály identifies the raising of the ghost of the dead as the new mission of his life. This is a mission on which we can no longer accompany him.

THE POLITICAL PHILOSOPHY OF SIENA

Instead, let us dive into history. We leave the twentieth-century novel, and turn to another authority: that of the historian of Siena, Mario Ascheri. What does he have to say about the specificity of this city? First of all, the historian's mission is to deconstruct all the historical illusions or misconceptions about the past of "democratic communes," like Siena. According to such myths "the Italian communes were political societies of equals, and thus the very antithesis of feudal society with its hierarchical structures."[39] Instead of being *"bourgeois"* or "egalitarian," as *"bourgeois* historians of the nineteenth century" claimed, Ascheri, the urban historian, stresses that "the Italian cities which fostered communes harboured all manner of unmodern horrors, clan loyalty and the desire for ennoblement included."[40] This is the tone of the realist historian, who wants to blow the whistle on all sorts of idealizations of the past. This is because "the greatest risk any historians runs is the risk of importing into his account of the period with which he is concerned the preoccupations of periods nearer his own."[41] Conversely, he claims that the historical material is not gone, but is still there in the form of the "live tissue" for those whose history it is. Is this not also true, however, of the illusions concerning those historical materials?

More generally we may ask: what exactly does the reality of the past mean? It seems to be, in fact, a combination of historically verifiable "facts," together with the narratives we build upon them. According to Ascheri, the Italian city-state was "a particular species within the broader genus of 'commune'"[42] While *civic autonomy* is a term of a nineteenth-century lawyer, in a certain sense we can ascribe this term to cities like Siena, he argues, where "among particular groups of citizens" the idea was born that "the time had come for them to take the government of their cities into their own hands even more purposefully."[43] This was made possible by the specific professionalism of the lawyers and notaries in the service of the city, who were ready to provide the documentation required for this sort of self-government. Although a full concert of cooperation among the members of the community was never realized, by interpreting certain Roman law texts people realized that "the coexistence of the prince's general law and local laws specific to individual cities was actually possible."[44] To be sure, in most cases, full autonomy was not achieved by the city. However, something approaching it seems to have been possible.

While in the high medieval period the city worked as a "coalition of factions," during the fourteenth century it gave way to the *signore*, and by the fifteenth century "it transformed itself into a 'regional state': a regional state which might even go so far as to proclaim itself sovereign, as, for example, the Commune of Florence."[45] More important than full sovereignty was what Ascheri calls attention to communal "constitutionalism": "regarding all social problems the communes came up with the most wide-ranging and far-reaching legislation known to the medieval West."[46] This wide-ranging local legislation made it possible to define the details of the institutional operation of the local authorities, as well as to safeguard the citizens against encroachments by different sources of power (ecclesiastical or secular, imperial or regional), on the "autonomous" body of the citizenry.

Ascheri does not hesitate to compare the ideology which enabled these major innovations in the administration of local affairs to the English rule of law, or to the eighteenth-century Enlightened continental model of the *Rechtsstaat*: "the separation of political powers from judicial and administrative powers" which made it possible "to create checks and balances, protect the citizen and guarantee the impartiality of the administration."[47] A crucial issue in this ideology was the fundamental principle of the citizen's participation in the legislative process of the polis.[48] He uses the word *polis* intentionally: the historian is eager to emphasize that this ideology was legitimized with reference to ancient cultural traditions, such as the Ciceronian and the Aristotelian heritage. An important aspect of these ancient influences was the encouragement to rely on "general parliaments of the whole population" as well as on "frequent and well-attended councils" as these could serve as "sources of legitimacy for both communal government and communal life," which led to an "enfranchised citizenry to a degree never previously conceived and in all likelihood never since achieved."[49]

It is at this point that Ascheri returns to the problem of the role of public art in the organization of everyday life in the city. He cites the best known example of art serving the ideology of the city—Lorenzetti's *Buon Governo*, in the Palazzo Pubblico in Siena. In his interpretation, the painting presents the city "as a political entity with its own physiognomy, distinct from its separate members," embodying the "idea of the legal person," long before the cover page of Hobbes's *Leviathan*.[50] Besides expressing and spreading the official ideology by their authorized program, art works had a further function in these city-states. They helped to establish or strengthen the reputation of the particular city where they were commissioned and housed, in the closely fought battle for recognition in an Italian, or sometimes even in a European-wide arena of competition. This is because, when they were not actually engaged in wars with each other (and they were masters in that art as well[51]), city-states were "in never-ending competition with every other for the best works of art in order to affirm the *honor civitatis*."[52] In other words, fine art, as well as literature, music, and theater were regarded as public affairs, with serious roles and functions to keep alive the ideology of the city internally, and to spread the prestige of the citizenry externally.

As a result of the activity of its artists in the service of the city, artworks produced a "self-image of the city as a culturally homogeneous monolith capable of absorbing and abating its internal social conflicts, thereby encouraging a remarkable degree of social harmony."[53] This ideology of the role of art in keeping the *civitas* together, and allowing the *urbs* to take part in the intercity competition for prestige, is captured by the term *campanilismo* in late medieval, Renaissance, and in some exceptionally lucky cases, in early modern Italian urban history. While it is usually understood as a kind of almost irrational competition between localities, from our point of view it is more important to emphasize the cohesion which it generated among those who belong to the same local community. In another essay on Siena's republicanism by Ascheri the historian calls the cohesion achieved by the city's sponsoring activity of art and culture "an incredibly strong collective identity."[54] As the most widely known expression of the survival of this strong collective identity, far beyond the actual political form of the city-state, Ascheri refers to the Palio, perhaps the most important public event, or one may even call it a cult, which is associated with the city of Siena. As a sign of its "lasting prestige," he refers to the legislation from the Fascist era, which assigned "the privilege of the Palio race to Siena."[55] Ascheri also quotes Mario Luzi, "the peerless bard of Sieneseness," who described it as a "celebration of identity that has . . . become essential to Siena," but which was nevertheless "entirely irrational. . . and totally unintelligible even to the Sienese themselves."[56]

The further examples he gives are still more surprising. One would hardly think of the institution of a city bank or of a music academy as a form of the expression of a strong collective identity. Yet this is Ascheri's claim—that they, too, enhanced that particular collective identity. All of these, and many more, should be interpreted as a historical manifestation of "the long-term pre-eminence of the deeply-rooted civic sentiment that underpinned the city-state of the 12th to 14th centuries."[57] This civic sentiment found its external embodiment in the perception of the community of the city dwellers as forming n "unum corpus" since earliest times.[58] Ascheri repeatedly emphasizes that this cohesion was not achieved by famous thinkers, as is claimed in Florence. His only example of a powerful ideologist is Francesco Patrizi, whose *De institutione rei publicae* (c. 1465–1471) is more of an exception and not the norm. This is how Ascheri explains the phenomena as the unintended consequences of rather specific spatial and historical circumstances: "The small population of the city, combined with a highly favourable geographic position and an ancient civic culture strengthened by the mortal dangers ever close at hand, enabled the formation of a collective cultural structure so pervasive that it was scarcely perceptible even to its living complex."[59] It was the survival of this collective cultural achievement in architecture that ensured that "broad participation remained a constant in the city's politics" even after the loss of its actual political autonomy.[60]

Despite admitting all these components of the solidity of Sienese identity, Ascheri refuses to idealize it. He refers to the internal social tensions between the city's two classes, the *casati* (magnates) and the *popolo*. Even so, he claims, that this internal agonism "did not exclude civic solidarity," which is proven by the fact that the *casati*, too, could gain important offices in the magistracy and the city council.[61] The fact is that centripetal forces proved stronger than centrifugal ones, and this tendency was due to the accepted wisdom of the community, which identified two basic principles of cohabitation:

1. "the intention to officially guarantee 'justice' to all citizens irrespective of political status," expressed in the language of virtues: "justice, the queen and mirror of all the virtues necessary for political life, is perpetually in force, and . . . through it, the good citizens who love their sweet Siena homeland may repose in peace and unity."[62]
2. "the peace and unity to be assured. . . derive from the fair distribution of the honours (and burdens) of government among those admitted to full political rights," a principle established in 1356, by the council of nine, or Nove.

These two principles seem to have underpinned the strong and longstanding official ideology of the unity of the city—also reaffirmed by the constant challenge represented by Florence—which was preserved even in the age of the *signori*, and even after the collapse of the city after Spanish and later French occupation, in 1555. The institutional framework survived the disappearance of its actual *raison d'etre*, and its official ideology lingers on, expressed through works of art such as "monuments, frescoes, statues or statutory and legislative texts."[63] The result of this unison of cultural production and surviving ethnographic practices (of its "myths and rituals"[64]) is proof of the survival of a powerful communal or civic identity, unparalleled even among the historical Italian cities, well into the period of the nation-state, and perhaps even beyond it.

SUMMARY

Let us sum up the major findings of this enquiry into the ideal type of the European city.[65] A *city* is a collection of buildings in a particular area arranged in space in a well-defined order to house a group of people. While the architectural ensemble used to be called the *urbs*, the group of people living together in it is called the *civitas*. Cities are different in different cultures.

This book has tried to reconstruct the specific political thought characterizing urban communities in Europe.

The major idea which defines the European city is that the political community which lives together within the walls of the city is regarded as a basic unit of politics, to be understood as operating according to its own terms. City walls are crucial in the military respect because for centuries they not only made the area of the *urbs* and its inhabitants, the *civitas,* defendable from external enemies, but also made visible the borders of the jurisdiction of the local authorities. While cities could not have survived without the surrounding territory, with which they built up a larger unit, called in Italian and in some other languages a *commune*, the city walls separated the area and its population from the outside world, defining the property (and its owners) which belonged to the city in a narrow sense—those ones who happened to be within the walls—and that other area and that other part of the population which did not belong to it in a narrow sense—those outside the walls. The walls also had a symbolic function: they defined a realm with a specific jurisdiction, in other words, a group of people with specific entitlements, enabling the members of that group to live a way of life characteristic of that area, and even—as we saw in the example of Siena—building up a certain mindset in the community which distinguished the members of the community from others. Finally, the walls served as a political and religious border, defining the area and the group of people who belonged to a specific political arrangement and a particular religious denomination and practice.

European cities have visible signs which identify them. Most of the time cities are of a rather limited size—their radius defined perhaps by the point from where the tower of the church is still visible, or from where the sound of the church bells can still be heard. They may have certain geographical attributes such as being built on the seashore, on a river, or on a hill. The buildings are typically arranged following the well-ordered shape of a grid, delineated by open public spaces, called *streets*, which people living there use for transportation, and squares, connected by streets, which give home to a number of people for longer stays, both those living there and foreigners. The closer a building is built to the centers of the network of streets, in other words, to the main square, the more prestige its owner had. Squares could be distinguished from each other according to the activities associated with them: there were market squares, where food and other products were sold and bought, squares with a political or military function as well as squares which were the venues for open air religious rituals.

The buildings of a city fell into two basic categories. First there were those which had a public function. These buildings served various public functions, including religious, military, political, professional, commercial, financial, educational, social, hospitable, and entertainment purposes. As their forms were meant to express their function, the formal architectural vocabulary could easily define *public buildings* such as a citadel, a city fortress, or the military barracks, the main church(es), the city hall, the market hall, the school, the cloister, the hospital, the poor house, the hotel, the pub, and so on. Further buildings had the primary function of housing the inhabitants of a city, or, if they obtained certain rights and privileges, its citizens, and their families and households. As most of the inhabitants were artisans, each with a specific craft, their house also had to contain a workshop and showroom.

Both the way the buildings were built and maintained and the way citizens were expected to behave and think and feel were determined by more or less exact rules or conventions. The nature of these rules and conventions were usually customary, and based on the knowledge and wisdom of earlier generations. The key to the success of the city depended on close attention being paid to these rules by all the inhabitants, that is, by all citizens, as well as by anyone else when they were staying within the walls of the cities. If someone was unaware of or neglected one of the rules and regulations any other member of the community was authorized to draw his or her attention to their trespassing the rules. This was a relatively soft means of policing, but one which succeeded in achieving a rather strict order of conformity, which made cohabitation possible and often rather fruitful for the different groups and individuals within the larger community.

The basic source of this success was a collection of rights and privileges, which the *civitas* could obtain from the feudal lord of the city (who could be the sovereign, a religious leader, or a local lord) in the form of a covenant between him and the community. This covenant defined the services the community owed to the master, as well as the specific entitlements they got in return. This covenant defined the freedom of the city, and therefore the freedom of its citizens and the privileges of its inhabitants, and it was often honored as the constitution of the city. Whenever a dispute arose about the exact substance of the covenant, this constitution was referred to and interpreted. The covenant often defined the *city* as a legal entity, as a body politic, and determined its governance and the pillars of its own internal regime. It often gave remarkable freedom to the *civitas* to determine its own internal order, only defining their yearly duties to the master.

The rules of the city created a rather specific type of social being, the burgher. While originally the city was a military unit, as we saw earlier, it soon acquired other functions. The most important of them, since the times of the ancient Greek polis, was the political or self-governing function. Due to the fact that members of the *civitas* were either governing or governed by other members of the community, Aristotle called the citizens of the polis *zoon politikon*, or political animals. Citizens of the city were engaged in political activity from the time they were accepted as grown-ups until the very end of their lives. For them, therefore, the most severe punishment was having to leave the city, which was the punishment for homicide and high treason. The city dweller, therefore, is a person who finds meaning in his life (citizenship in ancient Greece was the privilege of men) in cohabitation and cooperation with others.

Democracy was a specific form of government according to Aristotle, which he defined as the deviant rule of the many (i.e., in the interest of the poor), in opposition to the proper rule of the many (i.e., in the interest of the entire city-state), which he called *politeia*. Further suitable forms of governing the city included that of the one (monarchy), and of the few (aristocracy). European cities were not democratic in the modern sense of the word. Yet one can argue that the modern form of representative democracy learned a great deal from the form of self-governance that the European cities developed. This form of governance is usually called republican, according to the Roman tradition, where *res publica* originally meant the common concern, or the people's affairs. Later it came to refer to what is called today the *state*, the *governance*, or *administration of public affairs*. Although by modern standards the basic principle, equality before the law, of both the ancient Greek *politeia* and the ancient Roman *res publica* was unsatisfactory, the principle of governing together was born, and it had a major effect on the self-perception of European urban communities. It was from these ideas, as well as from the Christian teaching of fellowship, that the medieval doctrine was born, according to which every human group has "an aboriginal and active Right of the group taken as a Whole."[66] This concept, related both to the Canon and Roman laws, as interpreted in the Middle Ages, made it possible to achieve two things: to attribute entitlements, privileges, and freedoms to communities, and to establish the fact that members of the community had an obligation to serve the community before taking care of their own self-interest. Both of these ideas were crucial to achieving the type of community life which characterized European cities from the Middle Ages up until the full development of the centralized modern bureaucratic state. It was the first of these ideas that allowed Europeans to view cities as the basic unit of their political life, even if these cities were not sovereign in the sense attributed to the term by Bodin in the late sixteenth century. Cities were political and legal entities, endowed with certain privileges and freedoms, which belonged to the community as a whole, and which allowed them to run their affairs based on their own common decisions, independently of the will of the sovereign or the lord of the city—as long as they also fulfilled their obligations. Cities had the right to defend themselves, and therefore it was the duty of their citizens to take part in military operations in defense of their city. Cities had their own self-governing bodies, and therefore it was also the duty of the citizens partly to take part in those bodies (usually elected for short terms), and partly to accept the rule of those bodies over them. The dependence of the citizen on the community, as expressed in the form of fighting together in war and governing together in peace, created a close connection between the members of the community and among fellow citizens. "The distinctiveness of the Occidental city is based on its character as a confraternity, *Verbrüderung*, the constitution of an association with a common cult, equality before the law, *connubium*, common meals, and solidarity against non-members."[67]

There are further aspects of city life, beyond waging wars together and governing together, which played a major role in the formation of this close link between the members of the community, and in identifying the community. One is that the city was also a religious unit. This was also true of the ancient city, but it is even more characteristic of the Christian period of the history of the European city. Each city had its own church, or after the Reformation its churches, and the citizens were united into a religious community (after the Reformation possibly into more than one religious community). As St Augustine explained, the city was regarded as a *civitas terrena*, with all the failures and sins of its inhabitants, but it also had its ideal aspect, called the *civitas dei*, and as members of the religious community, citizens were believers united in a common religion, potentially subject to God's grace, and as a result, receivers of redemption and eternal life.

Beyond the military, governance, and religious functions, cities had further common enterprises. Importantly, they had a well-organized economic life, based on two major types of occupation of their inhabitants: artisanship and trade. Professions of these kinds were gathered into guilds, which not only organized the daily lives of their members, but were responsible for defending the interests of their respective professions. Guilds could have important public functions, taking part both in the governance of the city and in the religious and cultural activities of the *civitas*. To be a partisan and a tradesperson also taught burghers certain manners and modes of behavior, as well as authorizing them in certain ways. Freedom of enterprise was crucial for them, so long as it did not result in unwanted, aggressive forms of competition and rivalry among themselves, which they took great pains to eliminate. One should not forget, however, that this ideology could not exclude those forms of business transactions in which the burghers made use of their armed forces, such as when establishing colonies, where they oppressed the local inhabitants by military means, or conducted the slave trade and kept slaves, which permitted a shamefully inhuman way of treating human beings for the profit of their owners, who were the masters over their slaves' lives. The distance of these practices from the ideology just outlined is an inexplicable internal contradiction of the political thought of the European burghers, which has had political effects up to the present day. While the ideology of the European city provided the means to criticize these practices, in fact theorists also developed detailed argumentations to support these activities, like Aristotle's teachings of natural slavery or the theory of white supremacy by European settlers. Keeping foreign colonies, where the indigenous people were treated unequally and inhumanly, and the slave trade and an economy based on slave-keeping were practiced as part of the custom of the European cities, and remains an unresolved dark shadow of the political legacy of the external policies of the European cities. This topic deserves a more detailed analysis than we have opportunity to provide here, as it leads to the bad conscience which is so characteristic of the European burgher-identity, determining the post–Second World War realities of Western culture, including the present moment. The present book looks at the European city from the perspective of Central Europe, where cities did not usually have the means to take part in these brutal practices, as these territories were themselves for a long time under the control of foreign powers, the victims of invading powers.

Internal and external peace was a crucial part of this ideology, anyway, as running a business required a settled state of affairs. Burghers learned how to communicate with each other or with foreigners, as their business success depended on their interaction with potential business partners. They also learned to cooperate, as their job required it—for example, the birth of the financial market, the banking and insurance sectors, required a high level of trust, and sophisticated ways of sharing both risks and profits. They learned the art of compromise, as once again their respective jobs required this skill, without which the prisoner's dilemma would have hindered their common and joint success.

The freedom-loving, peaceful, cooperative, communicative, and trustworthy manners of the burgher were brought together in an urban ideology, which developed from the ancient Roman urbanity, and the medieval ethos of the Christian knight. This ideology can be regarded as a civil version of the ideology of the ideal courtier, as developed by Castiglione's famous *Il Cortegiano* (1528). An important aspect of it was the ideology of the British gentleman, derived from the idealization of the feudal lord, when it became separated from the feudal conditions of birth, rank, and landed property. The ideals of the salon, of the club and of the coffee house were born in the context of the eighteenth century, in the witty essays of the 3rd Earl of Shaftesbury, and in Addison's and Steele's fashionable journal, the *Spectator*. Although the anti-clerical French Enlightenment and the blood-thirsty French Revolution led to the birth of a more martially spirited version of the *citoyen*, the progressive, Enlightened, and secularized modern Republican, by the time of the nineteenth century, Victorian manners of civil society and classical national liberalism were able to genuinely influence the life of European citizens. It also led to the creation of a modern art world, which allowed the birth of the artist, who can perhaps be regarded as a more refined version of these urbane and humane ways of thinking and feeling. As one can witness in the developments leading from the age of Goethe to that of Thomas Mann, the modern artist succeeded in liberating himself from the demands of the art market and its clients, and in the movements of the Romantic and Modernist periods the artist acquired a subversive, revolutionary potential in high culture. By the twentieth century, an age of totalitarianism and disillusionment, the ideal of the humane burgher was still a topic for literature, as represented by such Central European authors as Sándor Márai, the ideologist of the Central European burgher. He raised the manners, behavior, and way of thinking of the burgher to the level of a *Weltanschauung*. This was certainly an idealization: the figure of the urban burgher, as represented in Márai's works was based on his memory of his father. This figure was circumscribed by his community-building potential, his civilized way of behavior, which was based on understanding, and not only on toleration, and by tact (*tapintat*), equity, courtesy, and empathy in his human relationships. All of these—civic as well as civil—virtues were represented by the generation of his father, Géza Grosschmid, who was a lawyer, professor of the law academy of his hometown, and a local and national politician. As he saw it, his father's generation was perhaps the last generation of the European burgher.

Márai did not remain silent about the failures of this burgher society, however. At the beginning of his life he rebelled against the oppressive regimes of the middle classes, and he kept referring to their political responsibility for the country's political failures, and for the establishment of authoritarian regimes. One has to be aware, then, besides his virtues, of the dark side of the ethos and culture of the burgher. At the time of writing this summary, a political movement is trying to confront the offspring of the Western burghers with the sins of their forefathers. Statues of slave owners or supporters of slavery are being removed or demolished around the Western world, as an expression of dissatisfaction with the existing narrative of European history. Indeed, the idealized stories of the European burgher usually pass over in silence the unequal treatment by him of what was regarded as non-civilized or barbaric by this culture. It is well known that colonization and imperialism played a major role in the birth of Western culture, from the age of the Roman Empire, through the Crusades of the Middle Ages, to the discoveries of Columbus, Magellan, and the rest, and to the World Wars of the twentieth century. Western nations established a slave trade for their own benefit, slaughtering natives in the Americas, Africa, Asia, and Australasia. Unimaginable suffering was also caused in the name of spreading Christianity. Although free trade is a longstanding slogan of the Western invaders, the trade organizations of the European nations, responsible for supporting foreign trade on a global scale have always relied in the final analysis on the use or threat of arms, and made use of unfair ideologies to legally suppress the natives.

If a present-day heir of the legacy of the European city looks at his own portrait in this mirror of his history, he has to confess not only a brutality against the non-European, the alien, but also the false-hearted and double-tongued nature of his own way of thinking and behavior in that regard. The burgher needs to confess his sins against the non-Europeans, as the leader of the Catholic Church Pope Saint John Paul II did about the sins committed in the name of Christianity by the leaders and members of the Church around the world. Furthermore, the ideology of the city has to admit its history of brutality against its acclaimed enemies inside and outside the city walls, as well as the often unjust nature of the ideology and/or the practice of the middle classes against the poor and the alien. Sin is at the heart of European high culture, based on the ideology of the burgher, and Europe needs to admit as much to regain its self-confidence. Yet, as pointed out in this book, European culture has the potential for self-reflection, and the capacity to reform its way of thinking to resolve these internal tensions.

A further point that cannot be passed over is the burgher's support of tyrannical and totalitarian regimes, be they Fascist, Communist, or Nazi, in the last century. We know that these regimes could not have arisen or survived without the support of the middle classes. A special aspect of the political responsibility of the European burgher is his racism and antisemitism. The historical sins and tragedies caused by the prejudices of the burgher's mentality, including his tendency to become a fellow traveler in totalitarian regimes also left their mark on the self-perception of the European burgher, and an updated version of the ideology of the European city can only be viable in the context of the twenty-first century if deep and genuine soul-searching can take place in this respect as well, to get rid of the shadows of the past. It is necessary to admit the sins committed with the explicit or implicit support of the burghers of Europe against non-Europeans and certain minorities within Europe, against the Jews under Nazi rule, and for example, against believers, and the middle classes in the name of Communist ideology behind the Iron Curtain. This soul-searching is made possible by the healthy alertness of the burghers in the European tradition, but only when it is done on a case sensitive basis—the claim of collective guilt is, of course, unacceptable. It is important not to exaggerate our claims on the past in an anachronistic manner. History should not repeat itself with the birth of yet another movement of purification, a new regime of censure, taboo-creation and thought-police. The rightly proportioned aim is that the European burghers should attain more of the ideals of Christian modesty and should avoid in their economic and political transactions the earlier forms of outsourcing the costs of these very transactions. This is demanded by a right understanding of internal and external justice. The European tradition of self-governance is a tradition always ready for self-criticism and reform - its trial-and-error conservatism preserves what is valuable in the past and rejects the guilts of the past. If the present-day descendants of burghers are ready to confess and repent the sins of their forefathers (and I intentionally use religious language) on which the material wealth and cultural superiority of Europe is based, and are ready to reformulate the ideology of the burgher to exclude this possibility in the future, this can lead to the rebirth and further elaboration of the European burgher's ideology of local self-governance and of a virtuous life lived for the common good. This is possible, as the rich cultural and political tradition of the burgher enables its descendants and adherents to do so. The oeuvres of twentieth-century writers such as the German Thomas Mann, or the Hungarians Sándor Márai and Géza Ottlik prove that this ideology is still alive in Central Europe, and its self-critical edge remains sharp, which can help to reformulate the ideology so that it may contribute to creating a more livable world of humane manners and civil virtues in the twenty-first century as well.

NOTES

1. Rainer Maria Rilke, *Auguste Rodin*, Kindle Locations, 548–9.
2. Joan Vita Miller and Gary Marotta, *Rodin: The B. Gerald Cantor Collection*, (New York: The Metropolitan Museum of Art, 1986).
3. Ibid., 43.
4. Ibid.
5. Ibid. It is interesting to push the theological language one step further and compare the six of them to a small group of Apostles left alone after Christ's death. This comparison might be the more interesting if we recall that Rodin did not have religious belief in the orthodox sense of the word.
6. Ibid., 56.
7. Quoted from Froissart by *Rodin. The B. Gerald Cantor Collection*, 58.
8. Rilke, *Rodin*, 538–9.
9. Ibid., 542–3.
10. This is the interpetation of Paul Gsell, *Entretiens sur l'art réunis par Paul Gsell* (Paris, 1911, 1984), 37–38, quoted by Albert E. Elsen with Rosalyn Frankel Jamison, *Rodin's Art. The Rodin Collection of the Iris and B. Gerald Cantor Center for Visual Arts at Stanford University*, ed. Bernard Barryte (The Iris and B. Gerald Cantor Center for Visual Arts at Stanford University in association with Oxford University Press, 2003), 127.
11. The last two names are not given by Froissart. They were discovered in the Vatican Library in 1865. *Rodin. The B. Gerald Cantor Collection*, 65.
12. Ibid.
13. *Auguste Rodin* by Rainer Maria Rilke. I used the project Gutenberg version of this text, available online, without page numbers: http://www.gutenberg.org/ebooks/45605, 545.

14. The unity of the group, which, although it consisted of single figures, held closely together as a whole. Rilke, *Rodin*, 552–3.
15. Ibid., 553–4.
16. Ibid., 556.
17. Ibid., 558.
18. Ibid., 562–3.
19. Ibid., 564.
20. Ibid., 567–9.
21. Ibid., 570–71.
22. József Havasréti, *Szerb Antal*, 2nd ed. (Budapest: Magvető, 2019), 433.
23. Ibid., 366.
24. Ibid., 368.
25. Christopher Bollas, "Architecture and the Unconscious," *International Forum of Psychoanalysis* 9, no. 1–2 (2000): 28–42, DOI: 10.1080/080370600300055850, 28.
26. Ibid., 28.
27. Ibid.
28. Antal Szerb, *Journey by Moonlight*, trans. Len Rix (London: Pushkin Press, 2002), 82.
29. Ibid., 118.
30. Ibid., 122.
31. Ibid.
32. Ibid., 123.
33. Ibid.
34. Ibid.
35. Rainer Marie Rilke, "Archaïscher Torso Apollos." (Torso of an Archaic Apollo.), trans. C. F. MacIntyre: ". . . until there is no place / that does not see you. You must change your life." in Rilke, *Selected Poems* (Berkeley: University of California Press, 1957).
36. One can of course think about the novel by E. M. Forster with the title *A Room with a View*, which the writer started during a trip to Italy in the winter of 1901–02, finally published in 1908.
37. Szerb, *Journey*, 122.
38. Ibid., 122–23.
39. Mario Ascheri, "Beyond the *Comune*. The Italian City-State and the Problem of Definition," in *The Medieval World*, Second edition, ed. Peter Linehan, Janet L. Nelson, and Marios Costambeys (London and New York: Routledge, 2018), 530–48, 532.
40. Ibid., 532.
41. Ibid., 536.
42. Ibid., 537.
43. Ibid.
44. Ibid., 539.
45. Ibid., 540.
46. Ibid., 541.
47. Ibid., 542.

48. Ibid.
49. Ibid., 543.
50. Ibid., 544.
51. See the entry "Art of War in the Renaissance" by Ferenc Hörcher, in *Encyclopedia of Renaissance Philosophy*, ed. Marco Sgarbi (Berlin: Springer International Publishing AG, 2018), 1–3, available at: https://link.springer.com/content/pdf/10.1007%2F978-3-319-02848-4_895-1.pdf
52. Ascheri, *Beyond*, 544.
53. Ibid., 546.
54. Mario Ascheri, "Siena: A Long-Standing Republic," in *Republicanism: A Theoretical and Historical Perspective*, ed. Fabrizio Ricciardelli, and Marcello Fantoni (Roma: Viella, 2020), 129–45, 130.
55. Ibid., 130.
56. Ibid., 132.
57. Ibid., 131.
58. Ibid.
59. Ibid.
60. Ibid.
61. Ibid.
62. Ibid., 136, earlier quoted in Mario Ascheri, *Siena nel Rinascimento: istituzioni e sistema politico* (Siena: Il Leccio, 1985), 71–4.
63. Ascheri, *Siena*, 139.
64. Ibid., 144.
65. I use the term ideal type largely in the sense attributed to it by Max Weber.
66. Otto Gierke, *Political Theories of the Middle Age*, trans. with an intr. Frederic William Maitland (Cambridge: Cambridge University Press, 1900), 37.
67. Nippel, *Introductory Remarks*, 26.

Bibliography

Acton, John Emerich Edward Dalberg. *Selected Writings of Lord Acton*, 3 vols, edited by J. Rufus Fears. Indianapolis: Liberty Fund, 1985.
Allen, Grace. "Vernacular Encounters with Aristotle's *Politics* in Italy, 1260–1600." D. Phil. thesis, Warburg Institute and University of London, 2015.
Alpers, Svetlana. *The Art of Describing. Dutch Art in the Seventeenth Century.* Chicago: The University of Chicago Press, 1983.
Althusius, Johannis. *Civilis conversationis libri duo: methodié digesti & exemplis sacris & profanis passim illustrati*, edited by Philippo Althusio. Hanover, 1601.
——— *Politica. An Abridged Translation of Politics Methodically Set Forth and Illustrated with Sacred and Profane Examples*, edited and translated by Frederick S. Carney. Foreword by Daniel J. Elazar. Indianapolis: Liberty Fund, 1995.
Amelang, James. "The Europa delle città of Marino Berengo." *Rivista Storica Italiana* 113, no. 3 (2001): 754–63.
Angyal, Endre. "Lackner Kristóf és a barokk humanizmus kezdetei." *Soproni Szemle* VIII, no. 1 (1944): 1–14. 3.
Aquinas, Thomas. *Summa Theologica*, Part I-II. Translated by Fathers of the English Dominican Province, Project Gutenberg. Accessed: 14 October, 2014.
Aquinas, Thomas, and Peter of Auvergne. *In octos libros Politicorum Aristotelis expositio, I.i.12.* Translated from *Medieval Political Theory: A Reader: The Quest for the Body Politic 1100–1400*, edited by Cary Joseph Nederman and Kate Langdon Forhan. London and New York: Routledge, 1993.
Aquinas, Thomas, and Ptolemy of Lucca. "De regno ad regem Cypri," I.3.17. Translated by James M. Blythe. In Ptolemy of Lucca, *On the Government of Rulers: De Reminie Principum*. Philadelphia: University of Pennsylvania Press, 1997.
Aristotle. *In hoc libro contenta. Politicorum libri octo...*, Translated by Leonardo Bruni, comment by Jacques Lefèvre d'Étaples. Paris, 1526.
——— *Politics*, Translated by C.D.C. Reeve. Indianapolis/Cambridge: Hackett Publishing, 1998.

―――― *Politics and The Constitution of Athens*, edited by Stephen Everson. Cambridge Texts in the History of Political Thought. Cambridge: Cambridge University Press, 1996/2004.

―――― *Nicomachean Ethics*. Translated, with introduction and notes by C. D. C. Reeve. Indianapolis/Cambridge: Hackett Publishing, 2014.

Armani, Giuseppe. *Carlo Cattaneo. Il padre del federalismo italiano*. Milan: Garzanti, 1997.

Arribas, Sonia. "Bourgeois and Citoyen. Struggle as the Mediation of their Tragic Conflict in Hegel's Jena Manuscripts," *Hegel-Jahrbuch* 1 (1999): 213–9.

Ascheri, Mario. *Siena nel Rinascimento: istituzioni e sistema politico*. Siena: Il Leccio, 1985.

―――― "Beyond the Comune. The Italian city-state and the problem of definition." In *The Medieval World*, second edition, edited by Peter Linehan, Janet L. Nelson and Marios Costambeys. London and New York: Routledge, 2018.

―――― *Siena: A Long-Standing Republic, in: Republicanism. A Theoretical and Historical Perspective*, edited by Fabrizio Ricciardelli and Marcello Fantoni. Roma: Viella, 2020.

Atkins, Jed W. *Cicero on Politics and the Limits of Reason. The Republic and Laws*. Cambridge: Cambridge University Press, 2013.

Bachelard, Gaston. *The Poetics of Space*. Paris: Presses Universitaires de France, 1957.

Baron, Hans. "Cicero and the Roman Civic Spirit in the Middle Ages and Early Renaissance." *The Bulletin of the John Rylands Library* (Manchester: University Press) 22, no. 1 (1938): 72–97.

―――― "The Social Background of Political Liberty in the Early Italian Renaissance." *Comparative Studies in Society and History* 2 (July 1960): 446.

―――― *In Search of Florentine Civic Humanism*, I. Princeton: Princeton University Press, 1988.

Baudelaire, Charles. "The Swan." In *The Flowers of Evil*. Translated by William Aggeler. Fresno: Academy Library Guild, 1954.

―――― "Crowds." In *Paris Spleen*. Translated by Louise Varèse, 20–21. New York: New Direction Books, 1970.

―――― *Selected Writings on Art and Artists*. Translated and edited by P.E. Charwet. Harmondsworth: Penguin, 1972.

Bácskai, Vera. "A régi polgárságról." In *Zsombékok. Középosztályok és iskoláztatás Magyarországon*, edited by György Kövér, 15–37. Budapest: Századvég Politikai Iskola Alapítvány, 2006.

Becker, Marvin. "Some Aspects of Oligarchical, Dictatorial and Popular Signorie in Florence 1282–1382." *Comparative Studies in Society and History* 2 (July 1960): 421–39.

Behnen, Michael. "Herrscherbild und Herrschaftstechnik in der 'Politica' des Johannes Althusius." *Zeitschrift für historische Forschung* 11 (1984): 417–72., 422.

Bene, Sándor. "Eszmetörténet és irodalomtörténet, A magyar politikai hagyomány kutatása." *Budapesti Könyvszemle-BUKSZ* 19 (1/2007): 50–64.

Benjamin, Walter. "On Some Motifs in Baudelaire." In *Illuminations: Essays and Reflections*. Translated by Harry Zohn, edited by Hannah Arendt, 155–200. New York: Schocken, 1968.

——— *Das Passagen-Werk. Gesammelte Schriften*, Vol. 5, edited by R. Tiedemann. Franfurt am Main: Suhrkamp Verlag, 1982. Translated into French as Paris Capital du XIXe Siècle: *Le Livre des passages*. Translated by R. Lacoste, edited by R. Tiedemann. Paris: Ed. du CERF, 1989.

——— "On Some Motifs in Baudelaire." In *Selected Writings Volume IV, 1938–40*. Translated by Harry Zohn, 313–55. Cambridge, Mass.: Belknap, 2003.

——— *Some Motifs*. Commentary by John Phillips. Available at: https://courses.nus.edu.sg/course/elljwp/benmotifs.htm#_edn2 (approached May, 2020).

Berengo, Marino. *L'Europa delle città. Il volto della società urbana tra medioevo ed età moderna*. Turin: Einaudi, 1999.

Berman, Harold J., and Charles J. Reid, Jr., "Max Weber as Legal Historian." In *Cambridge Companion to Weber*, edited by Stephen Turner. Cambridge: Cambridge University Press, 2000.

Berti, Enrico. "Politica." In *Enciclopedia Dantesca*, 6 vols. Rome: Istituto della Enciclopedia Italiana fondata da Giovanni Treccani, 1970–1978.

Bianchi, Luca. "Continuity and Change in the Aristotelian Tradition." In *The Cambridge Companion to Renaissance Philosophy*, edited by James Hankins, 49–71. Cambridge: Cambridge University Press, 2007.

Bobbio, Norberto. *Una filosofia militante. Studi su Carlo Cattaneo*. Turin: Einaudi, 1971.

Bowlby, John. *Loss*. London: Pimlico, 1998.

——— *Attachment*, 2nd ed. New York: Basic Books, 1999.

——— *Separation*. New York: Basic Books, 2000.

Bracton, Henry de. *De Legibus et Consuetudinibus Angliae* of c.1260.

Brague, Rémi. *Europe, la voie romaine*. Paris: Criterion, 1992.

Braham, Randolph L., and Scott Miller, eds. *The Nazis' Last Victims: The Holocaust in Hungary*. Detroit: Wayne State University Press, 1998.

——— *The Politics of Genocide: The Holocaust in Hungary*, 1. New York: Columbia University Press, 2016.

Braudel, Fernand. *Civilization and Capitalism 15th–18th Centuries*. 3 volumes. Translated by Siân Reynold. London: Collins, 1982.

Brehaut, Ernest. *An Encyclopedist of the Dark Ages: Isidore of Seville*. New York: Columbia University, 1912.

Bridgeman, Jane. "Ambrogio Lorenzetti's Dancing 'Maidens': Case of Mistaken Identity." *Apollo* CXXXIII, no. 351 (1991): 245–51.

Bollas, Christopher. "Architecture and the Unconscious." *International Forum of Psychoanalysis* 9, no. 1–2 (2000): 28–42, DOI: 10.1080/080370600300055850, 28.

Brown, Alison. "Introduction" to *Dialogue on the Government of Florence*, by Francesco Guicciardini. Edited and translated by Alison Brown, vii–xxviii., x. Cambridge: Cambridge University Press, 2002.

Burke, Edmund. *Reflections on the Revolution in France*, edited by Iain Hampsher-Monk. Cambridge: Cambridge University Press, 2014.

Burke, Peter. *The Historical Anthropology of Early Modern Italy*. Cambridge: Cambridge University Press, 1987.
Buti, Francesco da. *Commento... sopra La Divina Commedia di Dante Alighieri*, edited by Crescentino Giannini. 3 volumes. Pisa: Fratelli Nistri, 1858–1862.
Buza, János. "Szepsi Csombor Márton Nürnbergjének forrásai," *Gerundium, Egyetemtörténeti közlemények* 8, no. 1 (2017): 127–35.
Calvin, Jean. *Commentary on Seneca's De Clementia*, Books For the Ages, Ages Software (Albany, OR: Version 1.0 © 1998), available at: http://media.sabda.org/alkitab-7/LIBRARY/CALVIN/CAL_SENE.PDF, downloaded in April, 2020.
Carmody, Francis J. ed., *Li livres dou trésor de Brunetto Latini*. Berkely and Los Angeles: University of California Publications in Modern Philology, 1948, 211.
Carney, Frederick S. "Translator's Introduction" to *An Abridged Translation of Politics Methodically Set Forth and Illustrated with Sacred and Profance Examples*, by Johannes Althusius. Edited and translated by Frederick S. Carney, foreword by Daniel J. Elazar, Indianapolis: Liberty Fund, 1964/1995), ix–xxxiii.
Cathecism of the Catholic Church, online source: https://www.vatican.va/archive/ENG0015/_INDEX.HTM#fonte
Cattaneo, Carlo. *Opere scelte*, ed. Delia Castelnuovo Frigessi, 4 vols. Turin: Einaudi, 1972.
——— *Scritti letterari*, edited by Piero Treves. 2 vols. Florence: Le Monnier, 1981.
Certeau, Michel de. "Walking in the City." In *The Certeau Reader*, edited by Graham Ward. Oxford: Blackwell, 2000.
Chittolini, Giorgio. "L'Europa delle città secondo Marino Berengo." *Storica* 14 (1999), 105–27.
Cicero. *On Duties*. Translated by Walter Miller. Loeb Classical Library. Cambridge: Harvard University Press, 1913.
——— *On the Republic, On the Laws*. Translated by Clinton Walker Keyes. Loeb Classical Librarty. Cambridge: Harvard University Press, 1928/2000.
——— *Pro Sestio*. http://perseus.uchicago.edu/perseus-cgi/citequery3.pl?dbname=LatinAugust2012&query=Cic.%20Sest.&getid=1
Collingwood, R. G. "The Historical Logic of Question and Answer." *In The History of Ideas. An Introduction to Method*, edited by Preston King. London and Canberra: Croom Helm; Totowa, NJ Barnes and Noble Books, 1983.
——— "An Autobiography." In *An Autobiography and Other Writings: With Essays on Collingwood's life and Work*, by R. G. Collingwood. Edited by Teresa Smith. Oxford: Oxford University Press, 2013.
Constant, Benjamin. *The Liberty of the Ancients Compared with that of the Moderns*. Translated by Jonathan Bennett. 2010. Online version: https://www.earlymoderntexts.com/assets/pdfs/constant1819.pdf, 2017.
Contareno, Gaspar Cardinal. *The Commonwealth and Government of Venice*. Translated out of Italian into English by Lewes Lewkenor. London, 1599.
"Creating Space for Beauty." The Interim Report of the Building Better, Building Beautiful Commission, July 2019, https://assets.publishing.service.gov.uk/government/uploads/system/uploads/attachment_data/file/815495/BBBB_Commission_Interim_Report_Appendices.pdf.

Crook, Malcolm, ed. *Revolutionary France 1788–1880*. Oxford: Oxford University Press, 2002.
Csánki, Dezső, and Albert Gárdonyi, eds. *Monumenta diplomatica civitatis Budapest*. (Budapest történetének okleveles emlékei) I. (1148–1301). Budapest, 1936.
Csonka, Ferenc. "Afterword." In János Bocatius. *Öt év börtönben (Five Years in Prison) (1606–1610)*. Translated by Ferenc Csonka. Budapest: Európa Publisher, 1985.
Dahrendorf, Ralf. *Society and Democracy in Germany*. London, 1968.
Dante Alighieri. *Divine Commedy*. Italian Text and Translation. Translated by Charles S. Singleton. Princeton: Princeton University Press, 1975.
——— *Convivio*. Translated by Christopher Ryan, The Banquet. Anma Libri, 1988.
——— *De monarchia*. The Online Library of Liberty. A Project Of Liberty Fund, Inc. 2011.
Diderot, Denis. "Cité." In *Diderot: Political Writings*. Translated and edited by John Hope Mason and Robert Wokler. Cambridge: Cambridge University Press, 1992.
Dominkovits, Péter. *"Egy nemzetek lévén..." A Nyugat-Dunántúl Bocskai István 1605. évi hadjárata idején*. Budapest: Martin Opitz Kiadó, 2006.
Dunn, John. *Democracy: The Unfinished Journey, 508 BC to AD 1993*. Oxford: Oxford University Press, 1992.
Eley, Geoff, Jürgen Kocka, and Allen Mitchell, eds. *Bourgeois Society in Nineteenth-Century Europe*. Oxford/Providence: Berg, 1993. and *Central European History* 27, no. 4 (1994): 518–23.
——— "Introduction 1: Is There a History of the Kaiserreich." In *Society, Culture, and their State in Germany, 1870–1930*, edited by Geoff Eley. Ann Arbor: The University of Michigan Press, 1997.
Elsen, Albert E. with Frankel Jamison. Rosalyn. *Rodin's Art. The Rodin Collection of the Iris and B. Gerald Cantor Center for Visual Arts at Stanford University*, edited by Bernard Barryte. The Iris and B. Gerald Cantor Center for Visual Arts at Stanford University in association with Oxford University Press, 2003.
Eötvös, József. *Magyarország 1514-ben*. Pest: Hartleben, 1847.
Espe, Hartmut. "Differences in the Perception of National Socialist and Classicist Architecture." *Journal of Environmental Psychology* 1, no. 1 (1981): 33–42.
Everson, Stephen. "Introduction." In Aristotle. *The Politics and The Constitution of Athens*. Cambridge: Cambridge University Press, 1996, 2017.
Fenzi, Enrico. "Brunetto Latini, ovvero il fondamento politico dell'arte della parola e il potere dell'intellettuale." In *A scuola con Ser Brunetto. Indagini sull ricezione di Brunetto Latini dal Medievo al Rinascimento*, edited by Irene Maffia Scariati. *Atti del Convegno internazionale di studi Università do Basilea*, 8–10 giugno 2006 (Florence, 2008): 323–372.
Figgis, John Neville. *The Political Aspects of St. Augustine's City of God*. Altenmünster: Jazzybee Verlag Jürgen Beck, 2017.
Forster, E. M. *A Room with a View*. Edward Arnold, London, 1908.
Friedeburg, Robert von. "Persona and Office: Althusius on the Formation of Magistrates and Councillors." In *The Philosopher in Early Modern Europe*, edited

by C. Condren, S. Gaukroger, and I. Hunter. Cambridge: Cambridge University Press, 2006.

Froissart, Jean. *Chronicles*. Translated by Geoffrey Brereton. Harmondsworth: Penguin Books, 1968.

Frugoni, Chiara, ed. *A Distant City: Images of Urban Experience in the Medieval World*. Translated by William McCuaig. New Jersey: Princeton, 1991.

Fubini, Riccardo. "Renaissance Historian," *Journal of Modern History* 64 (September, 1992): 542–44.

Furet, François. *La Révolution: de Turgot à Jules Ferry, 1770–1880*. Paris: Hachette, 1989.

Fustel de Coulanges, Numa Denis. *The Ancient City. A Study on the Religion, Laws, and Institutions of Greece and Rome*, with a new foreword by Arnaldo Momigliano and S. C. Humphreys. Baltimore and London: The Johns Hopkins University Press, 1980.

Geddes, Patrick. *Cities in Evolution. An Introduction to the Town Planning Movement and to the Study of Civics*. London: Williams and Norgate, 1915.

Giel, Robert. *Politische Öffentlichkeit im spätmittelalterlich-frühneuzeitlichen Köln (1450–1550)*. Berlin: Duncker & Humblot GmbH, 1998.

Gierke, Otto. *Political Theories of the Middle Age*. Translated, with an introduction by Frederic William Maitland. Cambridge: Cambridge University Press, 1900.

Gilbert, Allen. "Had Dante Read the *Politics* of Aristotle?" *PMLA* 43, no. 3 (1928): 602–13.

Gilbert, Felix. "The Venetian Constitution in Florentine Political Thought." In Nicolai Rubinstein. *Florentine Studies: Politics and Society in Renaissance Florence*. London: Faber and Faber, 1968.

Gilbert, William. *Renaissance and Reformation*. Lawrence, KS: Carrie, 1998, downloaded in April, 2020 from http://vlib.iue.it/carrie/texts/carrie_books/gilbert/14.html

Giles of Rome. *Del Reggimento de' principi*.

Goffman, Erving. *The Presentation of Self in Everyday Life*. Edinburgh: Edinburgh University Press, 1956.

Goldberger, Paul. "Mumford and the Master." *New York Times*, November 19, 1995, Section 7, 28.

Gordon, Daniel. *Citizens without Sovereignty. Equality and Sociability in French Thought, 1670–1789*. Princeton: Princeton University Press, 1994.

Granasztói, György. *A városi élet keretei a feudális kori Magyarországon. Kassa társadalma a 16. század derekán*. Budapest: Korall, 2012.

Greenaway, Peter. *Nightwatching: A View of Rembrandt's The Night Watch*. Amsterdam: Veenman Publishers, 2006.

Grüll, Tibor. "Lackner Kristóf beszéde Sopron város dícséretéről (1612)." *Lymbus Művelődéstörténeti Tár* 3 (1991): 45–97.

Guicciardini, Francesco. *Dialogo e discorsi del reggimento di Firenze*, edited by R. Palmarocchi. Bari: Laterza, 1932.

—— *Ricordi*, edited by R. Spongano. Florence: Sansoni, 1951.

—— "Considerations on the 'Discourses' of Machiavelli." In Francesco Guicciardini. *Selected Writings*, edited by C. and M. Grayson. Oxford: Oxford University Press, 1965.

────── *Dialogue on the Government of Florence*, edited and translated by Alison Brown. Cambridge: Cambridge University Press, 1994/2002.
Gyáni, Gábor, György Kövér, and Tibor Valuch, eds. *Social History of Hungary from the Reform Era to the End of the Twentieth Century*. New York: East European Monographs, 2004.
Haid, Josef. *Lebensrichtig – Ein neuer Weg für unser Denken und Handeln*. Chur: Asama Verlag, 1983.
Hale, J. R., ed. *The travel journal of Antonio de Beatis. Germany, Switzerland, the Low Countries, France and Italy 1517–1518*. London: The Hakluyt Society, 1979.
Hankins, James. *Virtue Politics. Soulcraft and Statecraft in Renaissance Italy*. Cambridge, MA: Belknap Press of Harvard University, 2019.
Hart, H. L. A. *The Concept of the Law*, 3., edited and introduction by Leslie Green. Oxford: Oxford University Press, 2012.
Havasréti, József. *Szerb Antal*, 2nd edition. Budapest: Magvető, 2019.
Hegedűs, Géza. *A magyar irodalom arcképcsarnoka*, available at: https://mek.oszk.hu/01100/01149/html/index.htm.
Herodotus, *The Histories*, with an English translation by A. D. Godley. Cambridge: Harvard University Press, 1920.
Hobbes, Thomas. *De Cive, Ch 5, §5, On the Citizen*, edited by Richard Tuck and Michael Silverthorne. Cambridge: Cambridge University Press, 1998.
Hoffmann-Rehnitz, Philip R. "Soziale Differenzierung und politische Integration. Zum Strukturwandel der politischen Ordnung in Lübeck (15–17. Jahrhundert)." In *Stadtgemeinde und Ständegesellschaft. Formen der Integration und Distinktion in der frühneuzeitlichen Stadt*, edited by Patrick Schmidt and Horst Carl. Berlin and Münster: LIT Verlag, 2007.
────── "Discontinuities. Political Transformation, Media Change, and the City in the Holy Roman Empire from the Fifteenth to Seventeenth Centuries." In *The Holy Roman Empire, Reconsidered*, edited by Jason Philip Coy, Benjamin Marschke and David Warren Sabean. New York, Oxford: Berghahn Books, 2010.
Holmberg, John, ed. Moralium Dogma Philosophorum, (in Arbeten utgivna med understöd av Vilhelm Ekmans Universitetsfond, Uppsala, vol. 37.
Horkay Hörcher, Ferenc (on other titles Hörcher, Ferenc). "Prudencia, kairosz, decorum. A konzervativizmus időszemléletéről." *Információs társadalom* 6, no. 4 (2006): 61–80.
Horváth, Robert A. "La France en 1618 vue par un statisticien hongrois, Marton Szepsi Csombor." *Population* 2 (1985): 335–46.
Hörcher, Ferenc. (on other titles Horkay Hörcher, Ferenc) "Culture, Self-Formation and Community-Building." *Ethos: Kwartalnik Instytutu Jana Pawla II KUL* 28, no. 109 (2015): 64–83.
────── "Art of War in the Renaissance." In *Encyclopedia of Renaissance Philosophy*, edited by Marco Sgarbi. Berlin: Springer International Publishing AG, 2018, available at: https://link.springer.com/content/pdf/10.1007%2F978-3-319-02848-4_895-1.pdf.

———— "The Dark Night of the City. Solar Construction and Urban Destruction in Communist Minsk." In *Conservative Critics of Political Utopia*, edited by Máté Botos. Budapest: L'Harmattan, 2019.

———— "A léptékhelyes város dicsérete. A herceg, az építész és a filozófus beszélgetése." In *A Kisváros dicsérete*, edited by Ferenc Hörcher et al. Balatonfüred: Tempevölgy Könyvek 37, 2019.

———— *A Political Philosophy of Conservatism. Prudence, Moderation and Tradition*. London – New York: Bloomsbury Academic, 2020.

———— "Overcoming Crisis in an Early Modern Urban Context. Althusius on Concord and Prudence" to be published in a volume by the European Society for the History of Political Thought.

Huizinga, Johan. *Dutch Civilisation in the Seventeenth Century*. 1941.

———— *The Autumn of the Middle Ages*. Translated by Rodney J. Payton and Ulrich Mammitzsch. Chicago: University of Chicago Press, 1996.

Inglese, Giorgio. "Brunetto Latini." In *Dizionario biografico degli italiani*. Roma: Istituto dell'Enciclopedia Italiana, 2005.

Israel, Jonathan I. *The Dutch Republic: Its Rise, Greatness, and Fall 1477–1806*. Oxford: Oxford University Press, 1995.

Jacobs, Jane. *The Death and Life of Great American Cities*. New York: Random House, 1961.

Jones, Philip. *The Italian City-State: From Commune to Signoria*. Oxford: Oxford University Press, 1997.

Joost-Gaugier, Christiane L. "Dante and the History of Art: The Case of a Tuscan Commune. Part II: The Sala del Consiglio at Lucignano." *Artibus et Historiae* 11, no. 22 (1990): 23–46.

Klaniczay, Tibor. "A magyar későreneszánsz problémái (Stoicizmus és manierizmus)." *Irodalomtörténet* 48, no. 1 (1960): 41–61.

Klinau, Artur. *Minsk, the Sun City of Dreams*. Berlin: Suhrkamp, 2006.

Kocka, Jürgen. "German History before Hitler: The Debate about the German Sonderweg." *Journal of Contemporary History* 23, no. 1 (January, 1988): 3–16.

———— ed. *Bürgertum im 19. Jahrhundert: Deutschland im europäischen Vergleich*, 3 volumes. Munich, 1988.

———— "Civil Society from a Historical Perspective." *European Review* 12, no. 1 (2004): 65–79.

Kocka, Jürgen. Conversation with Jürgen Kocka. 12-14-2017, Politika.

Kocka, Jürgen, and Allen Mitchell, ed. *Bourgeois Society in Nineteenth-Century Europe*. Oxford/Providence: Berg, 1993.

Kohr, Leopold. *Tribute to E. F. Schumacher, The Schumacher Lectures*, edited by Satish Kumar. New York: Harper and Row, 1980.

Kohr, Leopold. Acceptance speech, the eve of 1984, https://www.rightlivelihoodaward.org/speech/acceptance-speech-leopold-kohr/

Kovács, Sándor Iván. "Szepsi Csombor Márton." In *Szepsi Csombor Márton összes művei*, edited by Sándor Iván Kovács and Péter Kulcsár. Budapest: Akadémiai Kiadó, 1968.

Körösényi, András. "The Theory and Practice of Plebiscitary Leadership: Weber and the Orban Regime." *East European Politics and Societies*, 33, no. 2 (2019): 280–301.
Krier, Léon. *The City Within the City*. http://zeta.math.utsa.edu/~yxk833/KRIER/city.html, 2.
——— *The Architecture of Community*, edited by Dhiru A. Thadani and Peter J. Hetzel. Washington, London: Island Press, Covelo, 2009.
Kubinyi, András, ed. *Elenchus fontium historiae urbanae* III/2. Budapest: Balassi Kiadó, 1997.
——— "Buda, Pest, Óbuda és környékük 1686-ig." In *Budapest története a kezdetektől 1945-ig* by Vera Báeskai, Gábor Gyáni, and András Kubinyi. Budapest: Budapest Főváros Levéltára, 2000.
——— "Buda, Medieval Capital of Hungary." In *Medieval Buda in Context*, edited by Balázs Nagy, Martyn Rady, Katalin Szende and András Vadas. Leiden, Boston: Brill's Companions to European History, Brill, 2016.
Kulcsár, Péter, ed. *Szepsi Csombor, Europica varietas*. The text was edited by Péter, and the foreword was written by Sándor Iván Kovács. Budapest: Szépirodalmi Könyvkiadó, 1979.
Lana, Jacopo della. *Commento alla "Commedia,"* edited by Mirko Volpi and Arianna Terzi. 4 volumes. Rome, 2009).
Latini, Brunetto. *Tresor*, edited by Pietro Beltrami, Paolo Squillacioti, Plinio Torri and Sergio Vatteroni. Torino: Einaudi, 2007.
Lenihan, Thomas B. *Rembrandt's The Nightwatch: Epitome of the Dutch Golden Age, National Endowment for the Humanities Seminar: "The Dutch Republic and Britain: The Making of Modern Society and a European World Economy."* Dr. Gerard M. Koot, The University of Massachusetts-Dartsmouth. Available at: https://www.academia.edu/7384530/Rembrandts_The_Nightwatch_Epitome_of_the_Dutch_Golden_Age, 3.
Lewis, John D. *The Genossenschaft - Theory of Otto von Gierke; A Study in Political Thought*. Madison: University of Wisconsin, 1935.
Lieshout, H. van. *La Théorie Plotinienne de la vertu. Essau sur la génèse d'un article de lasomme Théologique de saint Thomas*. Freiburg i. Switzerland, 1926.
Lockwood, Louise dir., "Why Beauty Matters," television production, 28 November 2009, United Kingdom: British Broadcasting Corporation.
Lucia, Felici. "Theodor Zwinger's Methodus Apodemica: An Observatory of the City as Political Space in the Late Sixteenth Century." *Cromohs* 14 (2009): abstract.
Lukacs, John. *Budapest 1900. A Historical Portrait of a City and Its Culture*. New York: Grove Press, 1988.
Lyttelton, Adrian. "Shifting Identities: Nation, Region and City." In *Italian Regionalism: History, Identity and Politics*, ed. Carl Levy. Oxford: Berg, 1996.
MacCulloch, Diarmaid. *The Reformation*. New York: Penguin Books, 2005.
MacKenney, Richard. *The City-State, 1500–1700. Republican Liberty in an Age of Princely Power*. London: MacMillan, 1989.
Maes, Hans. "Sharing a Home in the World. A Conversation with Roger Scruton." In *Hans Maes, Conversation on Art and Aesthetics*. Oxford: Oxford University Press, 2017.

Mann, Thomas. *Buddwenbrooks Together with Lubeck as a Way of Life and Thought*. Translated by H. T. Lowe-Porter. New York: Alfred A. Knopf, 1983.
Martines, Lauro. *Power and Imagination: City-States in Renaissance Italy*. Baltimore: The Johns Hopkins University Press, 1988.
Mályusz, Elemér. "A mezővárosi fejlődés." In *Tanulmányok a parasztság történetéhez Magyarországon a 14. században*, edited by György Székely. Budapest: Akadémiai Kiadó, 1953.
Magraw, Roger. *France 1815–1914: The Bourgeois Century*. London: MacMillan, 1983.
Manent, Pierre. *Metamorphoses of the City. On the Western Dynamic*. Translated by Marc Lepain. Cambridge: Harvard University Press, 2013.
Marsilius of Padua. *The Defender of Peace*, edited by Alan Gewirth. New York: Columbia Hard Cover, 1951.
McPhee, Peter. "The Revolutionary Century? Revolts in Nineteenth-Century France." In *Crowd Actions in Britain and France from the Middle Ages to the Modern World*, edited by Michael T. Davis. London: Palgrave Macmillan, 2015.
Márai, Sándor. *A kassai polgárok* (The Burghers of Kassa). Budapest: Helikon, 1942/2003.
—— *Budán lakni világnézet* (To live in Buda is a worldview), edited by Tibor Mészáros and Noémi Saly. Budapest: Helikon, 2011.
Marx, Karl, and Engels, Frederick. Manifesto of the Communist Party, 1848.
Miller, Jaroslav. *Urban Societies in East-Central Europe, 1500–1700*. Farnham: Ashgate Publishing, 2008/London: Routledge, 2016.
Mitchell, Thomas N. *Cicero, the Senior Statesman*. New Haven: Yale University Press, 1991.
Molho, Antony. "Historians and Friends: Reflections on Some Contemporary Historians." *History of European Ideas* 45, no. 8 (2019): 1156–70.
Mommsen, Wolfgang J. *The Return to the Western Tradition: German Historiography since 1945*. Washington: German Historical Institute, 1991.
Moretti, Franco. *The Bourgeois. Between History and Literature*. London and New York: Verso, 2014.
Mumford, Lewis. *The City in History: Its Origins, Its Transformations, and Its Prospects*. Boston: Mariner Books, 1968.
Najemy, John M. "Brunetto Latini's Politics." *Dante Studies* 112 (1994): 33–52.
Nederman, Cary J. "The Meaning of 'Aristotelianism' in Medieval Moral and Political Thought." *Journal of the History of Ideas* 57, no. 4 (Oct. 1996): 563–85.
Németh, István H. "Állam és városok – A szakszerűsödés felé vezető első lépések a városi igazgatásban, 1670–1733" (State and Cities – The first Steps toward Professionalization in Urban Administration, 1670–1733). *Századok* 152, no. 4 (2018): 771–808.
—— "A Many Sided Intellectual on the Stage of Poetry and Politics: Joannes Bocatius," published in the blog of the *Hungarian National Archive*, https://mnl.gov.hu/mnl/ol/hirek/egy_sokoldalu_ertelmisegi_a_kolteszet_es_a_politika_szinpadan
Nippel, Wilfried. "Introductory Remarks: Max Weber's 'The City' Revisited." In *City States in Classical Antiquity and Medieval Italy*, edited by Anthony Molho,

Kurt Raaflaub and Julia Emlen, 19–30. Ann Arbor: The University of Michigan Press, 1991.

—— *Ancient and Modern Democracy. Two Concepts of Liberty.* Translated by Keith Tribe. Cambridge: Cambridge University Press, 2015.

Nolhac, Pierre de. *Pétrarque et l'humanisme*, 2nd edition, 2 volumes. Paris: Champion, 1907.

Novak, Frank G. Jr. ed. *Lewis Mumford and Patrick Geddes, The Correspondence.* Illustrated. New York: Routledge, 2014.

Oakeshott, Michael. *Lectures in the History of Political Thought*, edited by Terry Nardin and Luke O'Sullivan. Exeter: imprint-academic.com, 2006.

Oelze, Patrick. "Politische Kultur und soziale Ordnung in der frühneuzeitlichen Stadt. Das Projekt B4 im Kulturwissenschaftlichen Forschungskolleg/SFB 485 an der Universität Konstanz." *Jahrbuch der historischen Forschung* 2004 (Munich, 2005): 77–87.

Ortega y Gasset, Jose. *The Revolt of the Masses.* Ney York: WW Norton & Co, 1994.

Ottlik, Géza. *School at the Frontier.* Translated by Kathleen Szász. New York: A Helen and Kurt Wolff Book, Harcourt, Brace and World, inc., 1966.

—— "A másik Magyarország." In *A Valencia-rejtély. Hajónapló. Pályákon*, 72–92. Budapest: Magvető, 1989.

—— *Buda.* Translated by John Bátki. Budapest. Corvina, 2004.

—— "A régi Városi Színház lejtős folyosója." In *Próza*, 62–65. Budapest: Magvető, 2005.

Palmieri, Matteo. *Della vita Civile.* Milan, 1830.

Parkhurst Ferguson, Priscilla. *Paris as Revolution: Writing the 19th-Century City.* Berkeley: University of California Press, 1994.

—— "The flaneur on and off the streets of Paris." In *The Flaneur*, edited by Keith Tester, 22–42. London: Routledge, 1994.

Patten, Alan. "The Republican Critique of Liberalism." *British Journal of Political Science* 26, (1996): 25–44.

Paul, Joanne. *Counsel and Command in Early Modern English Thought.* Cambridge: Cambridge University Press, 2020.

Pálffy, Géza. "Egy elfelejtett kiegyezés a 17. századi magyar történelemben." In *Egy új együttműködés kezdete*, 17–59. Annales Archivi Soproniensis (1) Sopron: Magyar Nemzeti Levéltár Győr-Moson-Sopron megyei Soproni Levéltára; Budapest: MTA BTK, Történettudományi Intézet, 2014.

Pilinszky, János. "Egy város ürügyén" (On the pretext of a city). *Új Ember*, 12 June, 1966.

Pitz, Ernst. *Bürgereinung und Städteeinung: Studien zur Verfassungsgeschichte der Hanse-städte und der deutschen Hanse.* Cologne, Weimar, Vienna: Böhlau Verlag, 2001.

Plato. *Laws.* Translated by Benjamin Jowett. Online: https://www.gutenberg.org/files/1750/1750-h/1750-h.htm

Pope Pius XI. Quadragesimo anno, 1931.

Pocock, J. G. A. *The Machiavellian Moment.* Princeton: Princeton University Press, 1975.

Prak, Maarten. *The Dutch Republic in the Seventeenth Century*. Cambridge: Cambridge University Press, 2005.

——— "The Dutch Republic as a Bourgeois Society." *BMGN – Low Countries Historical Review* 125, no. 2–3 (2010): 107–39.

Prince of Wales, HRH. *A Vision of Britain. A Personal View of Architecture*. London, etc.: Doubleday, 1989.

Pullan, Brian. "The Roles of the State and of the Town in the European Crisis of the 1590s." In *The European Crisis of the 1590s: Essays in Comparative History*, edited by Peter Clark. London: George Allen & Unwin, 1985.

Rady, Martyn. *Medieval Buda: A Study of Municipal Government and Jurisdiction in the Kingdom of Hungary*. Boulder: East European Monographs, 1985.

——— "The Government of Medieval Buda." In *Medieval Buda in Context*, edited by Balázs Nagy et al., 303–21. Leiden: Brill, 2016.

Rand, E. K. *Cicero in the Courtroom of St. Thomas*. Milwaukee: The Bruce Publishing Co., 1946.

Read Foster, Elizabeth ed. *Proceedings in Parliament, 1610*. 2 volumes. New Haven: Yale University Press, 1966).

Right Livelyhood Award, https://www.rightlivelihoodaward.org/laureates/leopold-kohr/

Rilke, Rainer Maria. "Archaïscher Torso Apollos." (Torso of an Archaic Apollo). Translated by C. F. MacIntyre. In Rilke. *Selected Poems*. Berkeley: University of California Press, 1957.

——— *Auguste Rodin*. Kindle Locations, 548–9.

——— *Auguste Rodin*. http://www.gutenberg.org/ebooks/45605, 545.

Rodin, August. *Entretiens sur l'art réunis par Paul Gsell*. Paris, 1911, 1984.

Rosenblatt, Helena. *Rousseau and Geneva*. Cambridge: Cambridge University Press, 1997.

Ross, Sir David. *Aristotle*. London: Routledge, 1995.

Rousseau, Jean-Jacques. "A Discourse on Political Economy." In Rousseau. *The Social Contract and Discourses*, 127–168. Translated with introduction by G. D. H. Cole. London: Everyman, 1993.

——— "The Social Contract." In Rousseau. *The Social Contract and Discourses*. Translated with introduction by G.D.H. Cole, 180–341. London: Everyman, 1993.

——— "Dedication to the Republic of Geneva." In Rousseau. *A Discourse on a Subject Proposed by the Academy of Dijon: What is the Origin of Inequality among Men, And Is It Authorized by Natural Law*. In *The Social Contract and Discourses*. Translated by G.D.H. Cole. Revised and augmented by J. H. Brumfitt and John C. Hall, updated by P.D. Jimack, 31–42. London: Everyman, 1993.

Rubiés, Joan-Pau. "Instructions for Travellers: Teaching the Eye to See." *History and Anthropology* 9, no. 2–3 (1996): 139–90.

——— "Travel Writing as a Genre: Facts, Fictions and the Invention of a Scientific Discourse in Early Modern Europe." *International Journal of Travel and Travel Writing* 5, no. 33 (2000): 5–33.

Rubinstein, Nicolai. "Political Ideas in Sienese Art: The Frescoes by Ambrogio Lorenzetti and Taddeo di Bartolo in the Palazzo Pubblico." *Journal of the Warburg and Courtauld Institutes* 21 (1958): 179–207.

——— "Florence and Venice: Guicciardini." In *The Cambridge History of Political Thought, 1450–1700*, 58–65. Cambridge: Cambridge University Press, 1991.

Sale, Kirckpatrick. "Foreword." In Leopold Kohr. *The Breakdown of Nations* (1957, 1978). Available at: http://www.ditext.com/kohr/foreword.html.

Ságvári, Ágnes. *Budapest: the History of a Capital*. Budapest: Corvina, 1973.

Sánchez de Juan, Joan-Anton. "Civitas et Urbs. The Idea of the City and the Historical Imagination of Urban Governance in Spain, 19th–20th Centuries." PhD diss., Department of History and Civilization, European University Institute, Florence, 2001.

Schlögl, Rudolf. "Kommunikation und Vergesellschaftung unter Anwesenden. Formen des Sozialen und ihre Transformation in der Frühen Neuzeit." *Geschichte und Gesellschaft* 34 (2008): 155–224.

Schumacher, Diana. "Who Was Fritz Schumacher?" *The Gandhi Foundation*, November 25, 2011, https://gandhifoundation.org/2011/11/25/who-was-fritz-schumacher-by-diana-schumacher/.

Schumacher, E.F. *Small Is Beautiful*. London: Abacu, 1974, 1987.

Schütrumpf, Eckart. *The Earliest Translations of Aristotle's Politics and the Creation of Political Terminology*. Morphomata Lectures. Cologne: Wilhelm Fink, 2014.

Schwerhoff, Gerd. "Apud populum potestas? Ratherrschaft und korporative Partizipation im spätmittelalterlichen und frühneuzeitlichen Köln." In *Stadtregiment und Bürgerfreiheit. Handlungsspielräume in deutschen und italienischen Städten des Späten Mittelalters und der Frühen Neuzeit*, edited by Klaus Schreiner and Ulrich Meier, 188–243. Bürgertum, 7. Göttingen: Vandenhoeck & Ruprecht, 1994.

Scruton, Roger. *Gentle Regrets. Thoughts from a Life*. London: Continuum, 2005.

——— "Cities for Living. Antimodernist Léon Krier designs urban environments to human scale." *City Journal* (Spring, 2008), https://www.city-journal.org/html/cities-living-13088.html.

——— "Settling Down and Marking Time," CUSP Essay Series on the Morality of Sustainable Prosperity, no. 2, published February 2017, at: https://www.cusp.ac.uk/themes/m/rs_m1-2/.

——— "The Fabric of the City." The Colin Amery Memorial Lecture by Sir Roger Scruton for Policy Exchange, 14 November 2018, https://policyexchange.org.uk/wp-content/uploads/2018/11/The-Fabric-of-the-City.pdf.

Shakespeare, William. *The Tragedy of Romeo and Juliet*, edited by Barbara A. Mowat and Paul Werstine. *Folger Shakespeare Library*, http://www.folgerdigitaltexts.org, 7–243, 243. https://www.folgerdigitaltexts.org/download/pdf/Rom.pdf.

Sheldrake, Philip F. "A Spiritual City? Place, Memory, and City Making." In *Architecture, Ethics, and the Personhood of Place*, edited by Gregory Caicco. Hanover and London: University Press of New England, 2007.

Shields, Rob. "Fancy Footwork. Walter Benjamin's Notes on Flanerie." In *The Flaneur*, edited edited by Keith Tester, 61–80. London: Routledge, 1994.

Skinner, Quentin. "Ambrogio Lorenzetti's Buon Governo Frescoes: Two Old Questions, Two New Answers." *Journal of the Warburg and Courtould Institutes* 62 (1999): 1–28.

—— A Third Concept of Liberty. Inaugural Isaiah Berlin Lecture, The British Academy, 21 November 2001. https://www.thebritishacademy.ac.uk/documents/754/11-skinner.pdf.

—— "A Third Concept of Liberty, Isaiah Berlin Lecture." *Proceedings of the British Academy* 117, The British Academy (2002): 237–68.

—— "Ambrogio Lorenzetti and the Portrayal of Virtuous Government" and "Ambrogio Lorenzetti on the Power and Glory of Republics." In Skinner, *Visions of Politics*, vol. 2. Cambridge: Cambridge University Press, 2002.

—— "Ambrogio Lorenzetti and the portrayal of virtuous government." In Skinner. *Visions of Politics*, I–III, 39–92. Cambridge: Cambridge University Press, 2017.

Smith, Adam. *The Theory of Moral Sentiments*, edited by D. D. Raphael and A. L. Macfie. Oxford: Oxford University Press, 1976.

Smith, Leonardo, ed. Epistolario di Pier Paolo Vergerio. Roma, 1934.

Smith, W. Reed. "Megalopolis versus Social Retardation: The Continuing Relevance of the Views of Spengler and Toynbee on the Variability of the Rate of Cultural Change," *Comparative Civilizations Review* 61, no. 61 (2009): Article 8., 119–46.

Spengler, Oswald. *The Decline of the West*, One-Volume edition. New York: Knopf, 1932.

Spruyt, Hendrik. *The Sovereign State and Its Competitors: An Analysis of Systems Change*. Princeton: Princeton University Press, 1994.

Stagl, Justin. *A History of Curiosity. The Theory of Travel, 1550–1800*. Amsterdam: Harwood Academic Publishers, 1995, 1997.

Swift, Adam. *Political Philosophy: A Beginners' Guide for Students and Politicians*. Cambridge, Polity Press, 2001.

Szegedy-Maszák, Mihály. "The Bourgeois as Artist. Sándor Márai (1900–1989)." *The New Hungarian Quarterly* 33, no. 125 (1992): 12–19.

Szelényi, Balázs A. *The Failure of the Central European Bourgeoisie. New Perspectives on Hungarian History*. New York: Palgrave-MacMillan, 2006.

Szende, Katalin. "Dominkovits Péter: 'Egy nemzetek lévén...' A Nyugat-Dunántúl Bocskai István 1605. évi hadjárata idején, Budapest, 2006." *Soproni Szemle* 1 (2009): 152–55. http://epa.oszk.hu/01900/01977/00242/pdf/EPA01977_soproni_szemle_2009_1_152-155.pdf.

Szepsi Csombor, Márton. "Europica varietas." In *Szepsi Csombor Márton összes művei*, edited by Sándor Iván Kovács and Péter Kulcsár. Budapest: Akadémiai Kiadó, 1968.

—— *Europica Varietas, or A Brief Account of the Various Things Seen and Heard By in His Journeying in Poland, Mazovia, Prussia, Denmark, Frizia, Holland, Zealand, Britannia, Gaul, Germany and the Czech Lands, and on the Seas of Prussia, Pomerania, Sweden, Norway, Frisia, Zealand and Britannia, which may serve not only to the delight of all Readers but also to their great benefit* (Kassa:

printed by János Festus, 1620). Translated and introduction by Bernard Adams. Budapest: Corvina, 2014.

Szerb, Antal. *Journey by Moonlight.* Translated by Len Rix. London: Pushkin Press, 2002.

Tester, Keith. "Introduction." In The Flaneur, edited by Keith Tester, 1–21. London and New York: Routledge, 1994.

Thom, Martin. "City, Region and Nation: Carlo Cattaneo and the Making of Italy." *Citizenship Studies* 2, no. 2 (1999): 187–200.

——— "City and Language in the Thought of Carlo Cattaneo." *Journal of Modern Italian Studies* 5, no. 1 (2000): 1–21.

Tilly, Charles. "Entanglements of European cities and states." In *Cities and the Rise of States in Europe AD 1000–1800*, edited by C. Tilly and W. P. Blockmans. Boulder: Westreview Press, 1994.

——— "What Good Is Urban History?" *Journal of Urban History* 22 (1996), 702–19.

Thucydides. *The Peloponnesian War.* London, J. M. Dent; New York, E. P. Dutton, 1910.

Tocqueville, Alexis de. *Democracy in America*, 2 volumes. New York: Schocken, 1961.

Tormay, Cécile. *The Old House.* A régi ház, 1914.

Tóth, Gergely. *Lackner Kristófnak, mindkét jog doktorának rövid önéletrajza.* Sopron, 2008.

Viroli, Maurizio. *From Politics to Reason of State.* Cambridge: Cambridge University Press, 1992.

——— "The City as a Political Order and Urban Space." In *City, Civility and Capitalism.* 9-19. Stockholm: Bokförlaget Stolpe, 2020.

Vita Miller, Joan, and Marotta, Gary. *Rodin. The B. Gerald Cantor Collection.* The Metropolitan Museum of Art, New York, 1986.

Weber, Max. *The City* Translated and edited by Don Martindale and Gertrud Neuwirth. New York: The Free Press, etc., 1958/1966.

——— *Protestant Ethic and the Spirit of Capitalism* (1920). Present day edition translated by Stephen Kalberg. New York: Oxford University Press, 2010.

Weinacht, Paul Ludwig. "Althusius – ein Aristoteliker? Über die Funktion praktischer Philosophie in politischen Calvinismus." In Karl-Wilhelm Dahm, Werner Krawietz, and Dieter Wyduckel, eds. "Politische Theorie des Johannes Althusius." *Rechtstheorie*, Supplementary vol. 7 (Berlin, 1987): 443–64.

Weinstein, David, and Avihu Zakai. *Jewish Exiles and European Thought in the Shadow of the Third Reich.* Cambridge: Cambridge University Press, 2017.

Westermann, Mariët. *A Worldly Art: The Dutch Republic, 1585–1718.* New Haven: Yale University Press, 1996.

Whetstone Johnston, Harold. *Selected Orations and Letters of Cicero; To Which Is Added the Catiline of Sallust, rev. Hugh MacMaster Kingery.* Chicago and New York: Scott, Foresman and Company, 1910.

Yates, Steven. "Who Was Leopold Kohr?" *American Daily Herald*, Saturday, January 21, 2012, web.archive.org/web/20120124010516/http://www.americandailyherald.com/steven-yates/who-was-leopold-kohr.

Zolnai, Béla. *A magyar biedermeier.* Budapest: Franklin Társulat, 1940.

Name Index

Aczél, György, 34, 38
Addison, Joseph, 193, 250
Adorno, Theodore, 16
Alain-Fournier, Henri-Alban Fournier, 236
Albertano da Brescia, 159
Albert the Great, 156
Albertus Magnus, 41
Alderotti, Florenzo Taddeo, 155
Alemannus, Hermanus, 155
Alexander the Great, 131, 132, 140
Allen, Grace, 156, 172nn125, 128, 172–73nn132, 136, 138, 141, 173nn144–45, 174n158
Alpers, Svetlana, 45, 67nn78, 80
Althusius, Johannes, 47, 98–103, 106, 122nn110, 116, 122, 125, 123nn127, 129, 134
Amelang, James, 90, 91, 120n84
Andrieu d'Andres, 232
Andromache, 179
Aquinas, Saint Thomas of, 149, 150, 152–54, 156, 159, 166, 167, 171n110, 172nn129, 130, 132
Archduke Maximilian, 112
Arendt, Hannah, 2, 164, 196, 221n9
Aristotle, 2, 4–6, 8, 11n11, 76, 81, 84, 99, 100, 102, 118n34, 126, 127, 129, 131–35, 137, 143, 144, 147–57, 159, 161, 163, 167, 169nn22, 23, 25, 170n53, 171n81, 172nn113, 125, 126, 128, 173nn138, 141, 150, 174n152, 176n206, 201, 205, 209, 210, 214, 225n117, 226n123, 247, 250
Ascheri, Mario, vii, 242–45, 254n39, 255nn52, 54, 62

Babits, Mihály, 195, 234
Bachofen, Johann Jakob, 237
Bacon, Francis, 44, 170n63
Bacon, Roger, 152
Balzac, Honore de, 31, 182
Barbaro, Francesco, 85, 119n61, 161
Baron Haussmann, Georges Eugène, 16, 181, 182
Baron, Hans, 75, 118n20, 158–64, 171n111, 174nn159, 161, 166
Bartók, Béla, 192
Bartolo, Taddeo di, 147, 173n142
Bartolomeo I della Scala, 72
Bataille, Georges, 17
Báthory, Zsigmond, 112
Baudelaire, Charles, 2, 14–16, 63n7, 179–82, 221nn7, 9, 222nn11, 14, 231
Baxandall, Michael, 167
Becket, Thomas, 40
Béla IV, Hungarian King, 24–26

273

Belgioioso, Barbiano di, 113
Belsius, Elisabeth, 112, 114
Benjamin, Walter, 15–17, 19, 63nn11–12, 180, 181, 221n9, 222nn10, 11, 236
Berengo, Marino, 86, 89–91, 120nn79, 82, 84, 87, 121n88
Berlin, Isaiah, Sir, 164–65, 170n72
Bethlen, Gábor, 116
Bevilaqua-Borsodi, Béla, 193
Blickle, Peter, 93
Bobbio, Norberto, 87, 120n69
Bocatius, Johannes, 111–16, 124n167
Bocskai, István (Stephen), 110, 113–16, 124nn164–65
Bodin, Jean, 87, 107, 248
Boethius, 150
Bollas, Christopher, 237, 238, 254n25
Bonaventura, Federico, 105
Bowlby, John, 217, 227n152
Boys Smith, Nicholas, 219
Brague, Rémi, 125, 140, 168n1, 170n73
Braudel, Fernand, 82, 88, 119n48
Braun (Georg)-Hogenberg, Hans, 45
Brown, Alison, 75, 118nn23, 36
Bruni, Leonardo, 76, 106, 152–54, 160–62, 172n126, 173n138
Brutus, Lucius Junius, 147–49, 172n112
Bucer, Martin, 97
Budai, György, 28
Burckhardt, Jacob, 45, 118n21
Buti, Francesco da, 157, 174n157
Butterfield, Herbert, 164

Calvin, Jean, 7, 95–100, 121n105, 122n106, 163
Canoniero, Pietro Andrea, 105
Cantimori, Delio, 89, 120n82
Captain Banning Cocq, Frans, 51
Carney, Frederick S., 99, 122n110
Casa, Giovanni della, 101
Castellio, Sebastian, 97
Castiglione, Baldassare, 33, 250
Catherine the Great, 198
Cattaneo, Carlo, 86–91, 120nn68–71, 78

Certeau, Michel de, 2, 14, 18, 19, 64n18, 236
Chittolini, Giorgio, 91, 121n88
Cicero, 23, 62, 73, 86, 100–102, 107, 122n118, 123nn129–30, 147, 140, 143–49, 152, 154, 155, 157–62, 160–68, 171nn79, 90, 92–94, 171nn110–11, 174nn159, 171, 176nn208, 212, 243
Cimon, 136
Cleisthenes, 128
Cocteau, Jean, 236
Collingwood, R.G., 1, 3, 11nn1, 4
Columbus, Christopher, 251
Constant, Benjamin, 128, 137–39, 164, 170n64
Contarini, Gasparo, 83–85, 119n55
Conze, Werner, 185

Daedalus, 18
Dahrendorf, Ralf, 185, 187, 222n23
D'Alembert, Jean le Rond, 7
Dante, Alighieri, 42, 147–50, 155–57, 161–62, 171nn103, 109, 111, 112, 116, 174nn152–55, 157
Delamare, Nicolas, 6
Descartes, René, 5, 44, 170n63
Dickens, Charles, 182
Diderot, Denis, 6, 11n15
Dostoyevsky, F.M., 31, 182
Dunn, John, 127, 168n4
Durkheim, Émile, 60

Edward III, 230
Eliot, T.S., 40
Engels, Frederick, 182, 222n19
Eötvös, József, 27, 64n37
Ephialtes, 135, 136
Eustache de Saint-Pierre, 230, 232
Everson, Stephen, 133, 168n23

Fabritius, Georg, 115
Ferdinando de Medici, 241
Figgis, John Neville, 205, 225n105
Fliess, Wilhelm, 237

Foucault, Michel, 50, 81
Frachetta, Girolamo, 105
Franz Joseph, 194
Frazer, James George, 237
Freud, Sigmund, 198, 237, 238
Froissart, Jean, 230, 232, 253nn7, 11
Furet, Francois, 182, 222n15
Fustel de Coulanges, Numa Denis, 4, 5, 11n5, 60, 87, 219, 227n161

Gall, Lothar, 185
Geddes, Patrick, 177, 178, 199, 202, 221nn1, 6
George of Trebizond, 85
Geremek, Bronislaw, 186
Gide, André, 206
Giel, Robert, 93, 121n103
Gierke, Otto, 2, 9, 12n27, 58, 60, 205, 255n66
Gilbert, Allen, 174n152
Gilbert, Felix, 85, 119nn61–62, 162
Gilbert, William, 121n105, 122n107
Giles of Rome, 156, 157, 173n148
Giustiniani, Leonardo, 161
Goethe, Johann Wolfgang von, 32, 33, 190, 193, 236, 239, 251
Goetz, Walter, 163
Gordon, Daniel, 6, 11n14
Gropius, Walter, 215, 216
Grosschmid, Géza, 251
Grosseteste, 152
Guicciardini, Francesco, 75–79, 83, 85, 118nn21, 23, 25, 27, 30, 34, 36
Guido, the Pisan cleric, 159

Habermas, Jürgen, 93, 186
Haid, Josef, 206, 225n106
Hankins, James, vii, 84, 119n54, 122n117, 162, 172nn123, 124, 173n139
Harrison, Jane, 237
Hart, H.L.A., 14, 63n3
Haussmann, Baron, 16, 181, 182
Havel, Václav, 186
Hayek, Friedrich, 218

Hedley, Sir Thomas, 165
Hegel, Georg Wilhelm Freidrich, 32, 184, 185, 222n18
Hemingway, Ernest, 203
Henri III, 48
Henricus IV, 48
Henry IV, 181
Hesiod, 217
Hitler, Adolf, 34, 53, 57, 187–89, 195, 197, 204, 222n22
Hobbes, Thomas, 3, 13, 85, 87, 131, 169nn19–20, 233, 234, 243
Hoffmann-Rehnitz, Philip R., 93, 121nn89, 101
Holofernes, 149
Honter, 45
Horace, 46
Horthy, Miklós, 187
Howard, Ebenezer, 199
Hugo, Victor, 179
Huizinga, Johan, 52–55, 57, 58, 66n64, 68n118
Hume, David, 193

Icarus, 18
Illich, Ivan, 204
Isidore of Seville, 5, 11n8

Jacob, burgher, 42
Jacobs, Jane, 215, 226n142
Jean d'Aire, 232
Jean de Fiennes, 232
John of Salisbury, 159
John, the Goldsmith—János ötvös, 28
Jókai, Mór, 115
Judith, 149, 150, 172n113

Kant, Immanuel, 186
Keane, John, 186
Keckermann, Bartholomäus, 46
Kertész, André, 192
Keynes, John Maynard, 203, 206, 207
King Albert the Magnanimous, 28
King Louis II, 30
King Louis XIII, 48

Name Index

King Sigismund, 28
King Solomon, 149, 172n113
Kissinger, Henry, 207
Klaniczay, Tibor, 104, 123n137
Klinau, Artur, 198, 224n82
Kocka, Jürgen, 183, 185–88, 222nn22, 25, 26, 223nn27, 28, 32, 33
Kohr, Leopold, 202–7, 225nn99, 100, 103, 104, 107, 108
Konrád, György, 186
Kosselleck, Reinhart, 185
Körmendi, Ferenc, 189, 190
Krier, Léon, 212–16, 220, 221, 226nn126, 139, 143, 227n165
Kropotkin, Pyotr, 199

Lackner, Kristóf, 103–11, 114, 123nn142, 145–47, 124n163
Ladislas IV, 26
Landino, Ristoforo, 162
Latini, Brunetto, 149, 152, 155–57, 165, 166, 173nn143–45, 176n201
Le Corbusier, Charles-Edouard Jeanneret, 215, 216
Leonardo da Vinci, 241
Lipsius, Justus, 101, 102, 104, 106
Livy, 165
Locke, John, 135, 186
Lord Acton, John Emerich Dalberg, 164, 175n190, 205
Lorenzetti, Ambrogio, 155, 165–67, 173n142, 175nn197, 198, 201, 204, 243
Lucas de Penna, 150
Lucretia, 149
Luhmann, Niklas, 93
Lukacs, John, 183, 188–96, 223nn45, 48, 224n69
Luther, Martin, 21, 22, 95, 99, 111, 112, 114
Luzi, Mario, 244
Luzzato, Gino, 89

Machiavelli, Niccolo, 13, 75–77, 84, 85, 88, 105, 108, 118nn25, 36, 119n52

MacKenney, Richard, 80, 82, 119n37
Macrobius, 158
Maes, Hans, 216, 226n144
Magellan, Fernão de, 251
Maitland, Frederic William, 58, 255n66
Malraux, André, 203
Mályusz, Elemér, 25, 64n30
Manent, Pierre, 127, 168n5
Manetti, Gianozzo, 162
Mann, Thomas, 23, 39, 40, 55–58, 69n124, 163, 189, 190, 251, 253
Márai, Sándor, 23, 30, 32, 38–43, 65n47, 66nn60–62, 65, 111, 225n101, 251, 253
Marie de Medici, 48, 51
Marsilius of Padua, 150, 172n118
Martel, Charles/Carlo Martello, 157
Marx, Karl, 2, 15–17, 90, 182, 184, 185, 199, 207, 222n19
Master John, 41, 43
Max-Neef, Artur Manfred, 206, 225n107
Mazzini, Giuseppe, 87
Medici, Cosimo I., 77, 241
Medici, Duke Alessandro de', 77
Meinecke, Friedrich, 162
Melanchton, Philipp, 101
Mercator, Gerardus, 45
Moerbeke, William of, 152, 154, 156
Moholy-Nagy, László, 192
Molho, Antony, 69n131, 90, 120n80
Molière, Jean-Baptiste Poquelin, 33
Mommsen, Theodor, 87, 175n188
Montaigne, Michel de, 44
Montalembert, Charles de, 5
Montesquieu, Charles-Louis de Secondat, Baron de, 135
More, Thomas, 83, 84
Mucius Scaevola, Gaius, 147, 148
Mumford, Lewis, 2, 178, 179, 196–202, 221n6, 224n79, 236
Mussolini, Benito, 197
Münster, Sebastian, 45

Napoleon, I, Bonaparte, 197

Name Index 277

Napoleon III, 16, 179, 187
Németh, István, vii, 109, 123n136, 124nn162, 167, 169
Nero, 197, 238
Nicias, 136
Nietzsche, Friedrich, 43, 198
Nippel, Wilfried, 69n131, 70n147, 126–28, 131, 168nn3, 6, 255n67

Oakeshott, Michael, 141, 142, 170nn74, 75, 218
Octavian (Augustus), 141, 142
Ortega y Gasset, 170n61, 182
Orwell, George, 199, 203, 204, 206
Ottlik, Géza, 23, 30–32, 34–38, 65nn41, 49, 66nn51, 54, 253
Ovid, 179
Owen, Robert, 205

Palatine Amade, 40
Palmieri, Matteo, 161, 175n178
Peisistratos, 128
Pericles, 129–31, 134–37
Peter the Great, 198
Petrarch, Francesco, 148, 149, 154, 159–61, 174n171
Philip, king of Macedon, 131–32
Philip II of Spain, 206
Philip IV, 156
Philip VI, 230
Piacentini, Marcello, 197
Pierre and Jacques de Wiessant, 232
Pilinszky, János, 220, 227n164
Pilsudski, József, 187
Pius XI., 208, 225n110
Plato, 3, 84, 85, 100, 107, 119n61, 126, 127, 131, 137, 143–46, 158, 171n80, 220
Plotinus, 158
Pocock, J.G.A., 83–86, 119nn52, 55, 61
Polybius, 143, 144, 146
Prak, Maartin, 52, 53, 55, 68n115, 122
Prince Charles, Prince of Wales, 212–14, 226n130
Pritz, Ernst, 93

Proust, Marcel, 31, 38, 217
Pyrckmair, Hilarius, 44, 46

Rady, Martyn, 27, 65nn27, 29–31
Ranke, Leopold von, 89
Raphael, Raffaello Sanzio, 126
Rathenau, Walter, 163
Read, Herbert, 204
Reitz, Edgar, 217
Rembrandt, Harmenszoon van Rijn, 51, 52, 54, 55, 68nn108, 110
Richelieu, Armand Jean du Plessis de, 181
Rodin, Auguste, 40, 229–35, 241, 253nn1, 2, 5, 7, 10, 13, 254n14
Rokkan, Stein, 87
Romagnosi, Gian Dominico, 89
Romulus, 220
Rousseau, Jean-Jacques, 2, 6–12, 12nn17, 18, 25, 28, 30, 88, 96, 184, 201
Rubinstein, Nicolai, 75, 77, 118nn21, 28–32, 119n61, 155, 165, 167, 173n142, 176nn200, 206
Rudolph II., king of Hungary, 112, 114

Sale, Kirkpatrick, 203, 225n99
Sallust, 73, 165, 176n212
Salutati, Coluccio, 160
Savonarola, Girolamo, 78
Scala, Cangrande della, 42, 148
Schiller, Friedrich, 32, 33, 184
Schlögl, Rudolf, 93, 121n98
Schumacher, E.F., 202–4, 206–11, 225nn108, 109, 111, 226n124
Scipio, 144–46, 158, 160, 161
Scruton, Sir Roger, vii, 211, 212, 214–21, 226nn139, 140, 143, 144, 227nn145, 149, 165
Seneca, 23, 50, 96, 101, 112, 122n106, 161, 166
Servetus, Michael, 97
Shaftesbury, 3rd Earl of, 193, 250
Shakespeare, William, 72, 73, 83, 117n1, 167

Shaw, George Bernard, 234
Simmel, Georg, 2, 236
Sismondi, Charles Léonard de, 90, 138
Skinner, Quentin, 139, 155, 164–68, 170n72, 173n142, 175nn194, 197, 198
Smart, Peter Alistair Marshall, 167
Smith, Adam, 63n9, 88, 90
Socrates, 23, 127, 132, 220, 221
Solon, 127, 128, 135, 136
Speer, Albert, 197
Spengler, Oswald, 66n64, 178, 179, 221nn2, 3
Spontone, Ciro, 105
St Ambrose, 158
St Augustine, 5, 158, 205, 225n105, 249
St Jerome, 159
Steele, Richard, 250
Stendhal, Marie-Henri Beyle, 31, 236
Sterne, Laurence, 236
Strauss, Leo, 164
Sun King, Louis XIV, 197
Szende, Katalin, vii, 64n27, 110, 124n165
Szepsi, Csombor Márton, 43, 45–52, 67nn79, 83, 68nn94, 111
Szerb, Antal, 195, 229, 235–41, 254nn22, 28

Tacitus, 77, 78, 165
Taylor, Charles, 186
Theocritus, 217
Thom, Martin, 88, 120n68, 70, 77
Thucydides, 130, 131, 136, 169n17

Tilly, Charles, 87, 90, 120nn73, 85
Tocqueville, Alexis de, 198, 205, 224n84
Tönnies, Ferdinand, 2, 60, 61
Troeltsch, Ernst, 163
Turler, Hieronymus, 44, 46
Tylek, Iwona, vii, 2

Vellutello, Alessandro, 162
Verancsics, Antal, 112
Vergerio, Pier Paolo, 160, 175n174
Vermeer, Johannes, 44, 45, 67nn77, 78
Virgil, 23, 88
Virgin Mary, 149
Viroli, Maurizio, vii, 13, 63n1, 2, 120n67
Viterbo, Giovanni da, 166

Waldheim, Rudi, 236
Weber, Max, 43, 52–61, 69nn131, 132, 69nn133, 142, 145, 147, 70n150, 108, 130, 163, 169n16, 188, 199, 209, 229, 255n65
Wehler, Hans-Ulrich, 185
Weinstein, David, 162, 175n183
Wenders, Wim, 19
William of Orange, 51
Wittgenstein, Ludwig, 215, 216

Zakai, Avihu, 162, 175n183
Zeno, Carlo, 161
Zweig, Stefan, 190
Zwinger, Theodor, 44, 46, 67n74

Subject Index

Aberdeen, 193
absolutism, 79, 83, 218
absolutist state, 3, 48
academy, 12n18, 20–22, 98, 99, 111, 131, 164, 170n72, 175n192, 221n6, 244, 251
administration of justice, 133
Æneas, 5
aesthetic interest, 18
Alcoy, 203
alien, 27, 52, 59, 120n82, 131, 191, 197, 206, 252
Amsterdam, 48–51, 68n111, 82
ancestors, 85, 220, 231
ancien régime, 40, 189
ancient city, 4, 11n5, 60, 87, 198, 219, 227n161, 249
ancient Greek, 3, 122n117, 125, 126, 131, 137, 149, 150, 152, 163, 179, 214, 220, 247, 248
Anguilla, 204
Antipatros, 132
anti-semitic subculture, 34
anti-Semitism, 195
Anverpia, 50
Arabic culture, 150
archons, 129
Areopagus, 129, 137
aristocracy, 23, 33, 53, 54, 78, 79, 84, 104, 114, 136, 137, 146, 153, 161, 191, 195, 248
Aristotelian, 3, 6, 57, 62, 76, 78, 84–86, 101, 102, 106, 126, 134, 136, 143, 144, 150–57, 165–68, 172n124, 173n139, 186, 197, 201, 205, 209, 210, 243
ars apodemica, 43, 46
artes liberales, 106
artisan/s, 23, 28, 38, 41, 94, 155, 190, 195, 247
assembly, 1, 4, 8, 12n28, 28, 29, 61, 94, 95, 108, 128, 129, 141, 143, 150
assimilate, 192, 194, 236
Athens, 13, 88, 125–32, 134–40, 163, 165, 169n23, 170n53, 177, 220
attachment, 19, 20, 22, 24, 37, 42, 88, 107, 132, 149, 217–19, 227n152
Augustinian, 101, 156
authority, 73, 94, 95, 97, 99, 103, 129, 130, 134, 136–38, 142, 144–46, 153, 208, 242
autobiography, 3, 11n4
autocephaly, 59
autocratic, 74, 78, 93–95
autonomy, 27, 30, 43, 54, 55, 58–60, 79, 82, 92, 98, 103, 104, 109, 110, 112, 116, 191, 204, 210, 242, 245

autopsy, 43, 46

bad conscience, 250
balance, 18, 62, 77, 78, 80, 86, 88, 94, 95, 103, 118n34, 127, 131, 135, 141–44, 146, 178, 190–92, 200, 210–12, 239
balanced constitution, 78, 82, 86, 137
balance of power, 77, 80, 103, 143, 178, 212
Baroque, 55, 81, 170n63, 194
barracks, 38, 247
Bártfa, 113
Basel, 44, 99
Battle of Lepanto, 83
bel esprit, 212
belonging, 21, 37, 39, 128, 129, 133, 180, 218, 232
Berlin, 16, 18, 22, 42, 162–63, 186, 189, 194, 196, 206
Berlin Wall, 22, 186, 189
Bern(e), 12n17, 96
Biedermeier, 187, 194, 223n38
Big Brother, 199
Bildung, 33
Bildungsbürger, 33, 42, 194
Bildungsbürgertum, 24, 162, 186
Bloomsbury, 215
body politic, 5, 7–9, 91, 100, 131, 172n129, 247
Bologna, 239
Bonn, 206, 209, 210
boule, 129, 136
bourgeois, 2, 6, 10, 15–17, 21, 31–35, 38, 39, 42, 53–58, 65n40, 66n61, 68n115, 78, 98, 111, 113, 179, 183–86, 189, 190, 193, 194, 222nn15, 17–19, 25, 223n28, 229, 242; bourgeois literature, 32; bourgeois spirit, 57, 58
bourgeois-citoyen distinction, 6, 32, 184, 222n18
bourgeoisie, 7, 33, 34, 38–40, 52, 53, 55–57, 65nn40, 45, 65nn46, 47, 81, 177, 183–91, 194
Brassó, 41

Buda, 20–32, 34–36, 39, 41, 48, 64nn27, 29, 31, 39, 65n41, 65n47, 114, 190, 192, 237; Buda Law Code, 27
Budapest, 14, 19, 20, 22, 35–36, 39, 64n26, 64nn28, 33, 65n39, 186, 188–96, 223n45, 224n69, 235–37
Buon governo frescoes, 165, 173n142
Bürgerlichkeit, 56, 57, 185, 186, 188
Bürgertum, 121n104, 163, 185, 187, 223n27
burgher(s), 1, 10, 18, 20, 21, 24–29, 32–34, 36, 42, 53, 55–59, 61–62, 66n65, 112, 155, 168, 186, 229–31, 233–35, 249–53; community (-ies), 13, 24, 34, 38, 58, 61, 62, 233, 235
Burghers of Calais, The, 40, 229, 235
Burgstadt, 38
Burke/an, 9, 217, 218, 227n159

Caesarism, 130
Calais, 40, 229–31, 233–35
Calvinist church, 7
Cambridge, 1, 69n145, 75, 118n21, 141, 162, 172n124, 206; school, 1
Campaign for the Preservation (subsequently Protection) of Rural England, 219
campanilismo, 244
Campo, 241
captain of the Quarter, 41
Carbonari movement, 87
cardinal virtues, 150, 167
casati, 245
Caspe, 203
Castle Hill (in Buda), 20, 22, 24, 25
cathedral, 21, 22, 40, 42, 234, 240
Catholic, 21, 22, 48, 49, 82, 99, 101, 105, 112–14, 116, 188, 190, 195, 201, 207, 208, 210, 225n10, 252
Central and Eastern Europe, 20, 194
central government, 25, 55
centralized state(s), 13, 56, 80, 82, 86, 95, 98, 113, 117, 181
Chalcis, 131, 132

character(s), 1, 15, 29, 41, 43, 49, 52, 53, 55, 58, 59, 101, 106, 122n118, 125, 132, 140, 143, 149, 179, 189, 190, 217, 241, 249
checks and balances, 62, 144, 146, 153, 243
Chelsea, 215
chief judge, 40
chief justice (*főbíró, judex*), 111, 112
Christian culture, 37, 158, 220
Christian Europe, 125, 140, 147, 151, 163
Christian humanist, 154
Christian middle class(es), 34, 38, 65n47, 191
church(es), 7, 21, 22, 26, 29, 42, 46, 47, 50, 54, 59, 60, 61, 73, 90, 95–99, 113, 114, 120n82, 125, 149, 158, 207, 210, 216, 218–20, 225n110, 246, 247, 249, 252; and state, 59, 98
citadel, 240, 247
cité, 6, 11n15
citizen(s), 1, 2, 5, 6, 8–11, 11n14, 14, 25, 26, 33, 34, 36–38, 41, 52, 58, 59, 61–63n2, 77–79, 84, 88, 89, 91–97, 100, 106–10, 114–16, 127, 128, 130, 132–36, 138–41, 146, 151, 152, 154, 155, 157, 159–62, 164, 166, 168, 169n20, 183–88, 194, 216, 217, 219, 226n123, 230–32, 242, 243, 245, 247–50
citizen body/citizenry, 1, 2, 8–10, 42, 43, 52, 56, 62, 63n2, 84, 88, 96–98, 129, 134, 137, 151, 157, 166, 168, 188, 230, 231, 236, 243
citizen of a state, 133, 184
citizenship, 7, 39, 53, 89, 98, 112, 120n68, 127, 130, 131, 133, 134, 136, 139, 140, 160, 182, 248
citizen's participation, 243
citoyen, 6, 10, 32, 98, 184, 187, 222n18, 250
città, 88, 89, 120nn79, 84, 121n88, 161
city alliance(s), 32, 98, 113, 140

city council, 28, 42, 97, 99, 102, 109, 112, 116, 231, 245
city gate, 21, 114
city government, 27, 51
city law, 59, 62
city magistracy, 59, 96
city notary, 112
city republic, 76, 137, 165, 229
cityscape, 18
city-state(s), 30, 71, 73, 74, 79, 80, 82, 86, 87, 89–93, 95, 107, 113, 117nn8, 10, 119n37, 132, 134, 135, 137, 140–42, 151–55, 157, 160, 163, 165, 168, 172n123, 173n138, 173n144, 203, 205, 206, 242–44, 248, 254n39
city wall(s), 59, 98, 108, 181, 230, 246, 252
civic, 2, 26, 29, 38, 44, 51, 55, 58, 61, 67n82, 68n111, 74, 91, 94, 95, 143, 159–62, 166, 194, 219, 221n1, 244, 245, 251
civic assembly(ies), 93–95
civic autonomy, 242
civic consensus/agreement, 93
civic corporation(s), 94
civic guard, civil militia, 51–53, 58
civic harmony, 143
civic humanism, 159–61, 171n111
civic life, 161, 162
civic participation, 93
civic peace, 166
civic responsibility, 32
civic rituals, 27
civic sentiment, 244
civic spirit, 159, 160, 162, 174n159
civic tradition, 162
civil, 7, 33, 35, 38, 47, 53, 55, 66n56, 77, 96, 99, 102, 106, 109, 131, 158, 218, 250, 251, 253
civil activism, 148, 158
civility, 37, 55, 63n2, 74, 193, 216
civilization, 11n12, 35, 68n118, 108, 119n48, 138, 163, 178, 179, 192, 197, 201, 216, 221n2, 237
civilizing process, 88

civil liberty, 8, 9
civil narrative, 62
civil society, 53, 74, 184, 186–88, 218, 223n33, 250
civil war, 96, 110, 117, 203
civitas, 4, 5, 8, 11n12, 23, 29–32, 36, 40, 41, 46, 49, 51, 62, 73, 104, 132, 140, 141, 190, 199–201, 212, 216, 233–35, 244–47, 249
civitas libera, 165, 167, 176n212
clan loyalty, 242
classical republican virtues, 149
cleric, 157–60, 187
cloister, 26, 59, 247
coffee house, 192, 193, 250
collective absolutism, 83
Collegio, 86
Cologne, 60, 70n150, 93, 95, 99, 153
colonization, 251
commercial society, 7
common good, 1, 30, 48, 61, 62, 78, 85, 86, 104, 107, 109, 139, 155–57, 163, 165, 184, 207, 216, 253
commonwealth, 83, 84, 100, 102, 119n55, 127, 146, 148
communal government, 154–56, 243
communality/*Gemeinde*, 70n147, 92, 93–95
communal memory, 35
commune(s), 60, 69–70n147, 71, 73, 74, 81, 117n10, 147, 152–54, 165, 166, 171n103, 173n138, 201, 203, 206, 242, 243, 246
community, 2, 5–7, 9, 10, 13, 14, 24, 26, 29–33, 36, 38, 40, 41, 43, 49–52, 58, 60–63n2, 65n43, 78, 81, 82, 86, 88, 89, 91, 93, 95, 100–106, 109, 110, 115, 116, 127–29, 133, 134, 138–41, 150–51, 153–55, 157–61, 165, 173n139, 200, 205, 207, 213, 216, 218, 220, 226n143, 230–33, 235, 238, 242, 244–49, 251
compromise, 28, 74, 104, 105, 111, 191, 192, 250
conceptual history, 185, 186

concordia/concord, 49, 73, 77, 78, 86, 101, 108, 122n110, 117n3, 146, 147, 165, 166, 195
confined territory, 214
conformity, 247
confraternity, 60, 70n147, 249
congregation(s), 21, 109, 113
conjuration, 60
connubium, 249
conservatism, 83, 85, 188, 212, 252
conservative, 8–10, 40, 49, 53, 54, 57, 66n62, 80, 83, 85, 92, 94, 102, 141, 145, 168, 185, 188–90, 201, 211, 212, 214, 216, 218, 224n82
Consiglio de' Pregati, 86
Consiglio Grande, 86
consilium/judgement, 146
constitutionalism, 243
constitutional traditions, 191
contado, 88
conurbation, 177, 199, 201
corporate body, 6, 9, 10, 41, 43, 56, 59, 61, 94, 108
corporation(s), 60, 93–95
council(s), 8, 9, 20, 21, 23, 26, 28, 40–42, 50, 62, 64n26, 78, 82, 84, 93–99, 102, 103, 108, 109, 111–14, 116, 129, 135, 144, 147, 148, 167, 231, 243, 245; council hall, 42, 147–49, 167; council house, 47, 50, 52; council member, 26, 41, 106, 112, 147
court(s), 23, 25–29, 32, 48, 59, 80–83, 92, 95, 102–5, 109–11, 113, 114, 116, 127, 131, 132, 135, 153, 177, 208, 209, 230
courtesy, 41, 251
covenant, 247
cultura civica e repubblicana, 91
cultural refinement, 193

dandy, 17, 180
Danube, 20, 22, 24, 25, 31, 34
Danzig, 43, 48–50
decorum, 63n2, 101, 168n2

Subject Index

Delft, 44, 67nn77, 78
democracy, 78, 79, 100, 118n34, 126–31, 134–37, 143, 146, 153–54, 168n3, 168n4, 173n139, 182, 199, 200, 205, 222n23, 224n84, 248; "guided," 131
demos, 128–30
dialogue, 2, 3, 75, 76, 79, 85, 118nn23, 28, 34, 158, 238
Diet, 20–22, 29, 102, 105, 110, 111, 113–15
dikasteria, 136
discord, 72, 73, 76, 166–67, 192
Dorchester, 212–15, 220
Dover, 231
Dresden, 111
duty, 9, 43, 52, 58, 102, 109, 142, 149, 220, 248
dwelling, 4, 15, 17–19, 177

early modern, 3, 7, 8, 10, 12n17, 13, 19, 32, 42–45, 48–55, 66n75, 71, 73, 79, 80, 82, 86, 87, 89, 91–95, 98, 102–4, 109–11, 116, 117, 119n45, 122nn110, 116, 123n135, 135, 151, 163, 165, 167, 170n63, 177, 183, 188, 197, 201, 208, 210, 211, 244
Eastern Europe, 90, 190
Ecole Normale, 192
Edinburgh, 193
Emden, 47, 98–100, 103
emperor(s), 99, 112, 113, 141, 197, 213
empire(s), 17, 32, 56, 57, 60, 63n4, 71, 73, 81, 88, 90–93, 98–102, 106, 112–14, 116, 121n89, 132, 140, 157, 158, 164, 178, 180, 190, 197, 198, 203, 205, 210, 211, 251
Eperjes, 112, 113
equality before the law, 248, 249
eudaimonia, 133, 134, 167, 218

face-to-face society, 8, 17, 93, 201
faction(s), 72, 73, 84, 96, 120n82, 134, 135, 143, 166
Fascist(s), 86, 197, 239, 244, 252

fatherland, 10, 37, 104
flaneur, 14–19, 63nn5, 10, 12, 180, 222n11
Florence, 11n12, 62, 71, 72, 74–79, 81–83, 89, 118nn19, 21, 23, 34, 119n61, 147, 154, 155, 160, 161, 239, 242, 244, 245
forefathers, 8, 168, 238, 251, 253
fortress, 38, 58, 240, 247
free royal city, 104, 107
French Enlightenment, 6, 250
French Revolution, 128, 137, 138, 179, 181, 184, 217, 250
friendship/*philia*, 34, 132, 143, 146, 156–57, 195, 201
frontier city, 36, 37
Fürmender, 41, 42

Gemeinschaft, 60, 61
general will, 9, 12n28
Geneva, 6–10, 12nn17, 18, 25, 31, 88, 95–99, 121n105
Geneva of the North, 98, 99
Genossenschaft, 9, 12n27, 60, 61, 70n147
gentleness, 144
gentry, 33, 34, 187, 191, 192, 194, 195
German city, 25, 47, 71, 92, 137
Germania, 197
Gesellschaft, 60, 121n98, 186
giantism, 199, 200, 210
Glasgow, 193
glory, 8, 48, 52, 106, 166, 179, 181, 183
golden mean, 153
good government, 165
good manners, 216
grand tour, 54, 71, 239
Greek polis, 3, 163, 214, 247
guild(s), 1, 27, 28, 51, 81, 94, 195, 249

Hanseatic League, Hansa, 32, 41, 88, 93, 95, 98
harmony, 9, 63n2, 78, 80, 86, 100, 118, 143, 146, 161, 200, 211, 213, 244
Heidelberg, 99

Herborn, 99, 101
Holy Roman Empire, 32, 56, 57, 71, 81, 91–93, 98–102, 106, 114, 121n89, 205
homeland, 35, 110, 245
hometown, 8, 20, 30, 39, 40, 42, 47, 48, 56, 115, 164, 189, 197, 198, 203, 204, 251
homo economicus, 184
homo politicus, 184
honor civitatis, 243
human flourishing, 131, 133, 134, 168, 218. See also eudaimonia
humanist(s), 33, 46, 100–102, 107, 111, 113, 122n117, 148, 150–52, 154, 159–62, 167–68
humanity, 144, 215, 240
human nature, 9, 18, 101, 143, 144, 146, 166
humility, 213
Hungarian Kingdom, 24, 25, 49, 104, 106, 107, 109, 111–13, 189
Hunsrück, 217

ideal city, 8, 108, 178
ideology, 7, 13, 33–35, 49, 52, 62, 73, 78, 83, 84, 94, 99, 108, 110, 154, 155, 167, 168, 198, 211, 243–45, 249–50, 252, 253
Iglau, 111
impartial spectator, 15
imperial city/cities, 92, 93, 153
imperialism, 251
independence, 27, 38, 41, 54, 55, 73, 80, 82, 92, 96, 139, 147, 191, 204
individual responsibility, 139, 190
inner city, 20
Innsbruck, 203
insurrection, 87, 88
internal struggle(s), 73, 75, 78, 90, 99, 160
Iron Curtain, 63n4, 252
Italian commune(s), 71, 73, 147, 154, 201, 242
Italian federalism, 87

Jewish bourgeoisie, 186, 191
Jewish identity, 16
Jews, 30, 34, 38, 59, 188, 194–96, 252
judge(s), 23, 26–28, 40, 42, 102, 136, 153, 159, 165–66, 209
jus gladii, 107
justice, 55, 76, 77, 83, 111, 112, 133, 144, 146–50, 153, 165, 167, 188, 245

Kassa, 32, 39–43, 48, 66n59, 66n65, 111–17, 225n101
Kensington, 215
Kingdom of Sicily, 153
Kisszeben, 113
koinonia, 6
Kolozsvár/Cluj, 29
Körmöcbánya, 111
Korpona, 114
Kőszeg, 36, 38
Kraków, 2, 48, 49

landscape, 9, 39, 45
Lauschitz, 111, 112
Lawbook of Buda, 28, 29
lebensrichtig, 205, 225n106
Leiden, 52, 54
Leviathan, 3, 13, 85, 233, 234, 243
liberalism, 165, 175n193, 252
liberty, 1, 6, 8, 10, 33, 63n2, 74, 76, 77, 85, 87, 107, 118n20, 119n37, 128, 137–39, 145, 146, 149, 164–67, 168n3, 170n64, 170n72, 175n190, 218
Lisibona, 50
little platoon, 218
local attachment, 24, 42, 218
local autonomy, 30, 103
local community, 10, 128, 242
local governance, 52, 54
Lőcse, 41, 113
Lombardy, 87, 88
London, 72, 210, 215, 222n11
Louvre, 48
lower nobility, 33

loyalty, 32, 37, 38, 107–10, 114, 115, 148, 191, 208, 242
Lübeck, 41, 56, 57, 69n124, 93–95, 121n107
Lubló, 41
Lucca, 82, 89
Lucignano, 147, 150, 171n103
Lugano, 88
Lutheran, 21, 22, 95, 99, 111, 114
Lyceion/Lyceum, 131, 132

Macedon, 131, 132
Machiavelli(an), 13, 75–77, 84, 85, 88, 105, 108, 118n25, 118n36, 119n52
magistrate, 9, 10, 26, 54, 96, 100–106, 111, 122n116, 127, 140–42, 145, 154–57
market, 1, 22, 25, 45, 47, 49, 59, 81, 184, 218, 219, 230, 246, 247, 250, 251
market settlement, 58
mayor, 26, 104, 109, 110, 114, 116
medieval city, 27, 43, 60, 92, 163, 177, 219
medieval university, 159
megalopolis/world-city, 2, 177–79, 196–202, 210, 216, 219, 220nn3–4
mental landscape, 39
mental map, 18, 182, 183
meritocracy, 77, 79
metropolis, 2, 16, 49, 180, 181, 189–91, 193
Middle Ages, 13, 26, 43, 51, 52, 54, 58, 60, 66n64, 74, 92, 93, 150, 158–60, 174n159, 183, 205, 222n15, 248, 251
middle class, 31–40, 52–57, 65n45, 65nn46–47, 66n62, 77, 78, 111, 134, 135, 179, 183, 185–88, 190–91, 194, 237, 251, 252
middle way/via media, 57, 118n34, 187
middling rank, 77, 78
Milan, 71, 87–89
military revolution, 80
Minsk, 198, 224n82
Mittelstand, 184

mixed constitution, 62, 77, 82, 84–86, 135, 143, 146, 153–54, 167, 171n79
moderation, 9, 134, 150, 167, 172n112, 200
modernized city/modernist city, 177
Mohács, 30, 36
Mona Lisa, 241
monastery, 205
monastic seclusion, 159, 160

Naples, 153
National Gallery (Budapest), 22
nationalism, 39, 42, 190, 192
nation-state, 13, 87, 88, 245
native city, 8, 154
Nazi, 17, 34, 35, 40, 65n48, 160, 162, 163, 184, 185, 187, 196, 197, 206, 252
Neoplatonic, 158
New York, 14, 18, 206, 210
Nikolsburg, 116
nomos, 140
non-European, 252
nostalgia, 2, 16, 212, 236
notary, 26, 106, 112, 155
Nuremberg, 28

Oberndorf, 203
Obrigkeit, 94, 109
oikophilia, 217
oligarchy, 75, 77–79, 82, 135, 143
optimates, 79, 145
Oriental city, 69n132
ostracism, 128
otium, negotium, 154, 158–62
overgrowth, 178, 197, 204
Oxford, 20, 206, 207

Padua, 44
Palazzo del Comune, 147
Palazzo Publico, 147
Palio, 244
Paris, 7, 14–16, 21, 31, 38, 39, 47, 48, 63nn10–12, 17, 96, 153, 170n62,

178–83, 189, 192, 194–95, 221n7, 222nn11, 14, 15, 235, 241
participatory democracy, 78
partnership, 132
passion, 14, 28, 41, 47, 100, 101, 103, 181, 192, 202, 221n6, 234
peace and unity, 245
periphery, 16, 214
Pest, 20, 24–26, 64n39, 114, 190, 192
petty bourgeoisie, 38, 186
phronesis/practical wisdom, 4, 13, 101, 103, 146, 149
phyle, 128. *See also* friendship
Platonist, 84
podesta, 74
policentric city, 215
politeia, 78, 108, 126, 248
political consensus, 95
political crisis, 24, 162
political culture, 4, 146
political loyalty, 37
Polybian, 76, 84, 144
popolo, 62, 245
popular assembly/*ekklesia*, 128–30, 136, 141, 143
populares, 145
port city, 229
Poundbury, 212–16, 219
Pozsony/Bratislava, 113
practical knowledge, 2, 152–54
practical philosophy, 2, 134, 150–51, 154, 159
Prague, 113–15, 186
Principality of Transylvania, 32, 105, 110, 114
privilege, 25, 26, 48, 58, 59, 78, 91, 98, 103, 104, 107–10, 133, 191, 244, 247, 248
proletariat, 38, 182, 184
Protestant, 43, 48–50, 57, 59–61, 69nn142, 145, 97, 100, 105, 108–10, 113, 114, 162, 163, 188
province, 55, 83, 98, 152–54, 178
provincial city, 9, 195

prudence, 13, 55, 100–103, 122n110, 146, 149–50, 172n112
prudentia, 13, 105, 159
public administration, 108, 110, 128, 182, 191, 202, 219
public affairs, 102, 108, 128–30, 137, 166, 243, 248
public building, 22, 26, 47, 49, 50, 52, 219, 247
public realm, 34, 100
Puerto Rico, 204

quarter, 20, 21, 41, 181, 189–91, 213–16, 219–20
Quinzai, 50

racism, 252
ratio civilis, 105
reason of state/*ragion di stato*, 13, 63n1, 80, 102–5
Rechtsstaat, 243
rector, 26, 97–99, 112, 116
Reformation, 43, 54, 60, 92–96, 98, 99, 102, 103, 106, 109, 111, 121n105, 122nn107–8, 125, 249
refugee, 66n52, 96, 97
regionalism, 88, 120n77
Regnum Italicum, 165
religious community, 247
republic, 3, 6–10, 12n18, 13, 55, 68nn108–9, 71, 73–85, 88, 90, 91, 104, 105, 118n24, 126, 129, 137–41, 144, 145, 148–49, 154, 156–60, 162–63, 165, 168, 171nn79, 90, 176n193, 182, 201, 229, 244, 248, 250, 255n54
republican liberty, 119n37, 162, 165
republican Rome, 73, 77, 139
republican tradition, 10, 76, 77, 83
republican values, 148
res publica/common affairs, 62, 92, 100, 115, 128, 137, 139, 141, 156, 248
revolution, 10, 20, 36, 44, 60–61, 64n10, 74, 78, 80, 87, 88, 100, 128, 137, 138, 144, 145, 164, 179–83,

187, 188, 196, 211, 216–18, 222n15, 225n159, 250, 251
Riga, 164
right livelihood, 204, 206
Risorgimento, 87, 89, 120n68
Roman Empire, 60, 88, 157–58, 251. *See also* Holy Roman Empire
Roman republic, 129, 137, 139–41, 147, 157, 165
Rome, 5, 11n5, 71, 87, 107, 125, 126, 130, 137–42, 144, 148, 156, 159, 163–64, 167, 172n112, 177, 178, 197, 201, 205, 236–38
Romeo and Juliet, 72, 117n1
royal architecture, 25
Royal Palace, 22
royal patronage, 26
royal seat, 7, 24, 29, 48
rule of law, 76, 84–86, 169, 243

sacred city, 238
Saint-Pierre, 231
Salzburg, 203
Saxony, 111
scale, 1, 38, 48, 57, 74, 83, 88, 98, 100, 102, 104, 109, 122n121, 132, 133, 148, 153, 177, 188, 198, 201, 203–13, 218, 226n139, 240, 252
school, 2, 16, 36, 38, 47, 49, 50, 54, 65n46, 66n54, 66n57, 85, 88, 98, 106, 109, 111, 112, 120n82, 126, 131, 132, 135, 150–52, 183, 185, 187, 192, 194, 201, 203, 215, 218, 247
Schulphilosophie, 100, 101
secular authority, 97
self-government, 26, 30, 73, 91, 107, 165, 242
self-rule, 75, 86, 92, 96, 98, 154
self-sacrifice, 148
self-sufficiency, 167–68
senate, 77, 79, 82, 109, 115, 141–46
senator/consul, 61, 62, 74, 112, 116, 141–44, 148, 171n108, 172n112

shooting company, 53, 68n107
Siena, 82, 147, 155, 165–67, 229, 235, 236, 239–46, 255nn54, 62, 63
signoria, 74, 117n10
size, 8, 13, 18, 52, 81, 102, 132, 153, 177, 198, 203–12, 214, 230, 240, 246
slave trade, 249–51
Small is beautiful, 202–4, 207, 225nn111–12, 114, 118, 226n124
small-scale, 211
small town, 17, 37, 53, 89, 147, 203, 206
sobriety, 200
sociability, 11n14, 52, 60, 101–2, 157, 167, 193–94
social cohesion, 101
solidarity, 245, 249
Sonderweg, 184, 185, 222n22
Sopron, 103–11, 114, 123n146
sovereignty, 8, 92, 98, 106
Sparta, 87, 88, 126, 138, 144
spatial aspects, 32
sprawling, 179, 200
Stadtluft macht frei, 9, 139
Stadtrechtsbuchs, 27
statesmanship, 110
statism, 11
Stoic, 2, 104, 123nn137, 147
Strasbourg, 97
strategoi, 129
stroller, 18, 19, 91
subsidiarity, 201, 207, 208, 210
suburb, 28, 179, 195, 198, 219
supreme ruler, 166
symbiosis, 101, 195
symphonia, 101
Szatmár, 48
Szeben, 41
Szeged, 20
Székesfehérvár, 29
Szerencs, 114

tact, 251
tavernical bench, 28
temperance, 148

territorial state, 80, 83, 86, 91, 92, 103, 110, 111
the right size of the city, 209
Ticino, 88
totalitarian, 34, 35, 38, 40, 57, 86, 89, 164, 179, 196–98, 200–201, 204, 211, 215, 251, 252
Town and Country Association, 219
town chronicle, 56
town hall, 22, 40, 147, 150, 216, 219, 230
townsman, 6, 38, 56
traditional, 56, 60, 69n145, 76, 80, 81, 87, 88, 91, 92, 96, 108, 113, 126, 133, 140–42, 186, 190–91, 205, 212, 215, 216, 219, 220, 231
travel account, 50
travelog, 43, 46, 47, 50, 51, 236, 239
treaty of Westphalia, 30, 92
Troy, 4
trust, 95, 105, 135, 195, 210, 219, 250
tyranny of the majority, 9

universitas, 92, 100
unum corpus, 244
urban cooperation, 98
urban democracy, 153
urban disorder, 199
urban elite, 1, 29, 94
urban humanism, 147, 151
urban ideology, 49, 62, 154, 250
urbanism, 177, 178, 180, 203, 215, 220
urbanization, 30, 74, 177, 180–82, 199
urban landscape, 9
urban mass, 183, 199
urban politics, 8, 80, 86, 90, 93, 105, 108, 117, 125, 154

urban poor, 28, 30, 81, 183
urban republicanism, 55, 56, 75, 91, 104, 105, 168
urban values, 35
urbs, 4, 5, 8, 11n12, 17, 18, 23, 29–32, 36, 40, 46, 49, 132, 190, 199, 200, 212, 216, 233, 234, 244–46
utopian, 2, 48, 205

Venice, 50, 62, 71, 72, 74–79, 82–86, 89–91, 118n21, 119n55, 161, 234, 236, 239; myth of, 82, 84, 85, 91
Verona, 42, 72, 160
Versailles, 197
Vetschau, 111
Vicenza, 42
Vienna, 20–23, 37, 104, 112–14, 189, 195, 203, 224n69
ville, 6, 221n7
Vinnheim, 46
virtue, 9, 10, 50, 55, 57, 68n105, 84–85, 101–3, 119n54, 122n117, 134, 148–50, 155, 159, 165, 167, 172nn112, 123, 173n139, 175n198, 190, 201, 210, 213, 216, 230, 245, 251, 253
voyeur, 14, 18

Warsaw, 186, 196
Washington, 52, 197
Weimar, 32, 163
Westminster, 215
Whitechapel, 215
white supremacy, 250
Wittenberg, 111, 112

zoon politikon, 201, 248

About the Author

Ferenc Hörcher (1964) is a historian of political thought and political philosopher. He is research professor and head of the Research Institute of Politics of the University of Public Service in Budapest and senior research fellow in the Institute of Philosophy of Eötvös Loránd Research Network. His research focuses on early modern history of, and contemporary political and aesthetic thought, including the conceptual framework of conservatism and liberalism. His last published book was *A Political Philosophy of Conservatism: Prudence, Moderation and Tradition* (2020, Bloomsbury Academic). He is the author of the article "Philosophers and the City in Early Modern Europe" in *The Routledge Handbook of the Philosophy of the City* (2020, Routledge).

www.ingramcontent.com/pod-product-compliance
Lightning Source LLC
Chambersburg PA
CBHW020111010526
44115CB00008B/783